1C

The Liturgical Sermons of Lancelot Andrewes

Volume I
Nativity, Lenten and Passion

The Liturgical Sermons
of
Lancelot Andrewes

Volume I
Nativity, Lenten and Passion

Introduced & Edited

by

Marianne Dorman

THE PENTLAND PRESS LTD.
EDINBURGH · CAMBRIDGE · DURHAM

First published in 1992 by
The Pentland Press Ltd.
1 Hutton Close
South Church
Durham

ISBN 1 872795 77 3

Typeset by Spire Origination, Norwich
Printed and bound by Antony Rowe Ltd., Chippenham

To the Glory of God
and in Thanksgiving
for His many Blessings
and especially in the life of
Wilfred John Hudson, K.B.E. Bishop
(Bishop of Carpentaria 1950–1960
Co-Adjutor Bishop of Brisbane, 1961–1973)
and
my Spiritual Father
and
loving friend
in his last years

All that we can desire is for us to be with Him, with God, and He to be with us; and we from Him, or He from us, never to be parted.

Andrewes, Vol. 1, p. 145

ACKNOWLEDGEMENTS

To Jesus College, for its College portrait of Lancelot Andrewes. Reproduced by kind permission of the Principal, Fellows and Scholars of Jesus College, Oxford.

To Basia Sokolowska, a young Polish artist, who now resides in Sydney, Australia, and who works for the Art Gallery of New South Wales, arranging exhibitions and lecturing. The colour plates used to introduce each collection of sermons in this volume are part of a collection, titled *Sentimental Journey*, taken by Ms. Sokolowska when visiting her homeland in 1988 and 1989.

To Oxford University Press for permission to quote from N. Lossky, *Lancelot Andrewes, The Preacher (1555–1626)*, (1991).

To SPCK for permission to quote from P. A. Wellesby *Lancelot Andrewes*, (1958).

To Faber and Faber Limited, Publishers, for permission to quote from T. S. Eliot *For Lancelot Andrewes: Essays on Style and Order*, (1928).

CONTENTS

FOREWORD

Lancelot Andrewes has "a place second to none in the history of the formation of the English Church". The verdict was that of Mr. T. S. Eliot in his essay of sixty years ago in which he re-introduced Andrewes to twentieth century readers as the first great preacher of the English Catholic Church. For Eliot, Bishop Andrewes' sermons rank with the finest English prose of their time, any time.

Yet the modern reader has to work at them, and get inside them, in order to appreciate their richness and profundity. Andrewes was a scholar of distinction. He read widely, was deeply versed in the scriptures and the writings of the Fathers. He had a great knowledge of Church history, as well as the mastery of many languages — Aramaic, Syriac and Arabic, in addition, later, to Greek and Hebrew. And it was said that he was also familiar with fifteen modern languages. Canon Brightman described his mind as "scholarly, historical and inductive rather than speculative and creative. His imagination was collective and organising . . . rather than originative. . . . He took up what he found and fused it into a new whole, and that often was something of real poetic distinction".

His sermons recall not only the depth of his scholarship but also of his own personal piety. Andrewes' *Preces Privatae* are the first classic expression of Christian devotion by an Anglican divine. His life and spirituality were anchored in the liturgical tradition of the Church. Those who worshipped with him in his chapel found the experience elevating; "some were so taken with it that they desired to end their days in the Bishop's chapel". The sermons that Andrewes delivered were solidly rooted in the teaching of the scriptures, the Fathers, and the continuing life and faith of the people of God through the centuries. And they arose out of his own personal prayer and reflection, formed and deepened in the liturgical life of the Church.

Andrewes preached what he did his utmost to live: "union with God in prayer, fasting, repentance and continued communion, the hearing of the Word and participation in the Sacrament". His theology and spirituality were fully integrated, embedded in the communal experience of the Church, and were alive both to the doctrinal and to the political issues of his day. The liturgical sermons were preached in the royal court. The more educated and cultured of his hearers appreciated their style, and were charmed by the way they were delivered as well as by the bishop's scholarship and holiness of life.

The heart of Andrewes' preaching lies in the Incarnation: God made man. The Word became flesh. Andrewes' aim is to draw his listeners into union and fellowship with Christ, the God-man. The purpose of the Christian dispensation, the goal of our human life, is that we should become partakers of the divine nature. This is the vision and the possibility that Andrewes holds out before us. The message is as timely now as it was when he expounded it in all its richness and profundity five centuries ago.

Marianne Dorman's edition of Bishop Andrewes' liturgical sermons in two volumes distils the essence of his teaching, and makes them accessible to our generation. We are in her debt for this labour of love.

+ Colin Winton
Wolvesey
July 1992

PREFACE

Very few people seem to know of Lancelot Andrewes today, let alone read his sermons. As one of the great exponents of Anglicanism, he is sadly neglected. Nicholas Lossky in his very recent fine and most welcome work on Andrewes, (the translation of which I read after editing the Liturgical Sermons), also mourns his neglect. He writes:

Andrewes, it has to be recognized, is poorly known. Not only is that so for the general public, but even among students of Anglican theology there are very few for whom he represents more than an illustrious name.[1]

One of the reasons for this may be because of the style of the sermons. Although, in Eliot's words, "they rank with the finest English prose of their time, of any time"[2] they are not the easiest to undertake. This is due mainly to Andrewes' insistence on wanting to cram in so much detail into his sermons as he develops his theological and spiritual thoughts. As a result his theme is often blurred or even temporarily lost. However his sermons have a spirituality and sensitivity hardly reached by any other preacher of his time, or since. The chief reason for this is that his sermons were the product of Andrewes' own living out of the Christian faith: his love of God, faith, prayer, repentence, confession, fasting and above all his devotion to our Lord in the blessed Sacrament.

The aim of editing these sermons is to make them accessible once again for reading and studying. With this in mind I have endeavoured to focus on the predominent theme in each sermon. Hence I have arranged each sermon in sections, preceded by a short introduction to pin-point the main thought. Hopefully in doing so I have not destroyed the force and flavour of Andrewes' language, teaching and spirituality.

To facilitate reading I have used modern spelling, punctuation and ellipsis.

In editing these sermons there are three people I particularly would like to thank. The first is the Rev'd Dr. Rowan Williams, Lady Margaret Professor of Oxford (and recently appointed Bishop of Monmouth), who gave me so much support and encouragement to undertake such a challenging job; the second is Mr. Michael Rowett who gave so generously of his time in reading my editing of many of these sermons initially; and the third is Herr Bruno Schwander without whose support I could not have had these sermons published.

To give this book a bonus, as it were, I am extremely grateful to the talent of the young Polish artist, Basia Sokolowska for allowing me to incorporate three colour plates from her series *Sentimental Journey* in this volume of Andrewes' sermons. As the reader will quickly realize, Andrewes uses nature, especially its cyclical expression, to teach us so much about the truths of the Christian faith. I am sure these three plates, all reflecting appropriate aspects of nature to introduce each liturgical season, will in themselves be a source of reflection as well as leading us into deeper thoughts inspired by Lancelot Andrewes' sermons.

Oxford.
The Feast of St. Mary
Magdalen, 1991

1. N. Lossky, *Lancelot Andrewes, The Preacher, (1555–1626)*, translated by Andrew Louth, (Clarendon Press, 1991), p.1.
2. T. S. Eliot, *Lancelot Andrewes and Other Essays,* (London, 1928), p. 14.

AN INTRODUCTION
TO
LANCELOT ANDREWES

His life [was] most innocent, . . .
his knowledge and learning most
flourishing and eminent, and . . .
his purpose and life most holy
and devout.

Andrewes, Vol. 5, p. 288.

So preached his friend Bishop John Buckeridge at his funeral in 1625. Undoubtedly the teaching of Lancelot Andrewes through his sermons and lectures, beginning in the latter part of Elizabeth's reign, contributed greatly to what today we describe as *Anglicanism*. Indeed, his sermons reflect very much the Renaissance spirit; Eliot described him as having "that breath of culture, an ease with humanism and Renaissance learning."[1] For well over a quarter of a century, he was the most popular preacher at court. Festival after festival, year after year, he delivered his sermons before Queen Elizabeth I and James I. In all he preached seventeen Nativity, fourteen Lenten, three Passion, eighteen Paschal and fifteen Pentecostal sermons. As well as preaching before court, he also preached in his parish of St. Giles', Cripplegate and within the university of Cambridge. Thus his sermons touched the lives of monarchs, courtiers, aristocrats, academics and students, as well as the ordinary parishioners. Except for the odd exception, here and there, his sermons do not refer to any of the political or religious events of the day,[2] but are simply the vehicle to preach the doctrines of the Church as they arose in the Christian year. In this context they reveal the joy of being a Christian which radiates from believing in a God who is above all loving, good, beautiful, compassionate and merciful to all of His creation which is continually sanctified by the Spirit. For Andrewes God cannot act contrary to His own nature. Thus God is always Love, and it is this Love which bore our human flesh.

Born in 1555 in the parish of All Hallows, Barking, Andrewes began to make his impact in the early 1580s after his appointment as Catechist at Pembroke College, Cambridge, some eleven years after first coming to this university town as an undergraduate in 1571. After gaining his first degree, he devoted his life to theological studies. Much of this was undertaken in the shadows of the spires and towers of Cambridge. It was not until his appointment to the see of Chichester by James I in 1605 that Andrewes resigned as Master of Pembroke, an office he had held since 1589. However his links with his old college and Cambridge were soon renewed in 1609 when as bishop of Ely he was the official Visitor to the university. For another ten years he was a Cambridgeshire man until his appointment to the ancient see of Winchester. Before accepting Chichester, Andrewes had been offered the sees of Salisbury and Ely by Elizabeth I. Both he had refused as he could not agree with the Queen's demand for him to alienate Church revenue from either diocese.[3]

During his Cambridge days, Andrewes also held other appointments such as chaplain to the Archbishop, John Whitgift, Dean of Westminster Abbey and the Chapel Royal respectively, and Vicar of the London parish of St. Giles', Cripplegate.

His time at Cambridge is also noted for his generous giving and help to students. These included many whose names are very much part of seventeenth century Church life such as John Cosin, later Bishop of Durham, William Laud, sometime Archbishop of Canterbury, George Herbert, poet and priest, and Matthew Wren who also became a Bishop of Ely, some eighteen years after Andrewes, in 1637. Wren in defending himself after his impeachment by Parliament in 1640, publicly acknowledged his indebtedness to Andrewes. He informed the House of Lords that he had learnt all his religious practices from the teaching and example of that learned and holy prelate Bishop Andrewes, a man "of holy account for his piety, knowledge and great learning, and one who had conversed with most of these holy Fathers who lived in the Church at the beginning of the Reformation under Elizabeth, it could not be but that he had received the same from their usage and practice."[4] Another student who also publicly acknowledged Andrewes was John Hacket. In his *Scrinia Reserata*, he wrote: "for he was the first who planted me in my tender studies and watered them continually with his bounty."[5] Not only students but theologians experienced Andrewes' friendship. One of these was Isaac Casaubon, the French theologian, who adopted England as his home in his last years. Of these years he described his friendship with Andrewes as one of those real treasures in life.

As mentioned in the Preface, Andrewes practised what he preached. His daily living was rooted in prayer. Five hours he set aside each day for prayer on his knees and meditation. His day began with a prayer like this:

> Glory be to You, O Lord; glory be to You.

> Glory be to You who has granted me sleep
>   for the repose of weakness,
> and for the relief of the toils
>   of this travailing flesh.[6]

Richard Drake who was the first to translate his *Preces* and to have it published in 1648, reveals the extent of Andrewes' piety when in his preface he describes the condition in which he found the manuscript:

> *Had you see the original manuscript, happy in the glorious deformity thereof, being slubbered with his pious hands, and watered with his penitential tears, you would have been forced to confess that book belonged to no other than pure and primitive devotion.*[7]

For Andrewes there was never a time when there could not be prayer, "Always, without ceasing: at all times," he writes in his preparation of the *Preces*; and in his points of meditations before prayers, he insists:

You are careful about many things: but one thing is needful.
But we will give ourselves continually to pray and to the ministry of the Word.[8]

It is hardly surprising then to discover that in his last months when his health deteriorated "he gave himself wholly up to converse with God." Such was his communion with God "that when sickness had deprived him of his voice, yet his eyes and hands prayed and when both these failed, his heart still prayed till it pleased God to accept it as his last sacrifice."[9] Thus at his funeral Buckeridge could rightly say: "What he taught in his life and works, he taught and expressed in his death."[10]

The structure of the *Preces* follows that of the Church's Daily Offices in the Prayer Book: confession, thanksgiving, praise, intercession and petition. Thus even in his own private prayers Andrewes prayed very much in tune with the whole Catholic Church. Much of its contents therefore were derived not only from Holy Scripture and the Prayer Book, but also from the Western and Eastern Fathers and, to a lesser extent, from the Jewish Church. The great Orthodox liturgists SS. Basil, James and Chrysostom are quoted *ad verbantum*, as are SS. Augustine, Ambrose, Bernard, Aquinas, Bede and many other outstanding Western theologians.

As we would expect, his intercessory prayers were catholic, covering every possible aspect of life, including the plea for Christian unity, something which we tend to see as a late twentieth century development. Yet four hundred years ago Andrewes was praying in this vein:

For the Catholic Church:
* for the churches throughout the world:*
*   their truth, unity and stability to wit:*
*   in all let charity thrive, truth live:*
* for our own church:*
*   that the things that are wanting therein be supplied,*
*   that are not right be set in order.*[11]

A modern biographer, P. A. Welsby, commenting on Andrewes' *Preces* stated that:

Nothing can be more comprehensive, more complete in their proportions than his devotions for each day; nothing more tender and solemn; nothing more compressed and nervous than their language. The full order of prayer and all its parts is always there: the introductory contemplation, to sober, to elevate, to kindle; the confession, the profession of faith, the intercession, the praise and thanksgiving.

The confessional and penitential prayers, in a "restrained and precise language" offer "the infinite hope in God's mercy and love." Such hope can only come from "one who searched and judged himself with keen and unflinching truth . . . [and has] surrendered himself to the impulses of exulting wonder and rejoicing at the greatness" of being a Christian. Furthermore his prayers conjuring up various images of nature and God's kingdom exhibit the poetical and imaginative side of Andrewes' character.[12]

Hence his own prayer life sets the pattern for his family as they worshipped together in the various beautiful chapels. He certainly inspired others to a deeper reverence and piety. His first biographer, Henry Isaacson, stated that his "principal virtue was his singular zeal and piety, which showed itself, not only in his private and secret devotion between God and Himself . . . but also in his exemplary public prayers with his family in chapel", while in church "he behaved himself so humbly, devoutly, and reverently, that it could not but move others to follow his example."[13]

Beside his *Preces* his devotional writings included prayer manuals for use in time of sickness, and at Holy Communion.

Andrewes' private prayers reflected his love for God and his fellow man. As he preached so often in his sermons, love had to put into practice as God had. Each Christian festival is thus a manifestation of God's love. For example, Andrewes describes Pentecost as "the feast of love"; it is indeed the feast of "the Holy Spirit, love itself, the essential love and love-knot of the two persons of the Godhead, Father and Son." This "love-knot" is the same which exists between God and man, and even more so "between Christ and His Church". Christmas day is also a day of *love*, the day Christ became our brother. He "became flesh" that we might love Him, and to love each other as our brothers and sisters.[14] As God gave because He loves, so must we. Love therefore is the essence of our faith, and without it, everything we do is worthless. Thus it is not surprising that Buckeridge in his funeral oration emphasized Andrewes' charity towards those less fortunate than himself. He regularly invited his poor parishioners and prisoners to share his dining table. Although he himself ate very frugally, he always made sure there was plenty for his *guests*.[15] He acknowledged so freely that everything he had was given to him from God, and had to be used as Christ would. Thus Buckeridge could preach at his funeral:

He wholly spent himself and his studies and estates in these sacrifices, in prayer and the praise of God, and compassion and works of charity, as if he had minded nothing else all his life long but this, to offer himself, his soul and body, a contrite and a broken heart, 'a living sacrifice, holy and acceptable to God by Jesus Christ which is our reasonable service'.[16]

Turning now to his sermons. These sermons from the famous Ninety-six were all delivered at court over a period of a quarter of century. Preaching therefore to a regular congregation, Andrewes could give a continuity of teaching and pastoral care. This continuity is illustrated for instance in his 1620 Nativity sermon when he announces, "We pass now this year from the shepherds and the angels, to the wise men and their star."[17] As we would expect his sermons are basically doctrinal, rooted in the Catholic faith as taught from Christ's time. Yet each sermon brings a freshness to one of the main Christian doctrines, and the encouragement to live out the Faith. Through his sermons we are also able to perceive his concern for saving souls. Thus at Christmastide Andrewes emphasizes salvation, for the man who has been rescued from everlasting perdition, "there is no joy in the world to the joy of a man saved; no joy so great, no news so welcome, as to one ready to perish, in case of a lost man, to hear of one [who] will save him." Moreover the very "name of a saviour" brings joy, and thus we all have "cause to be glad for the birth of this Saviour celebrated on *diem Meum.*'' On ''His day'' there is ''joy in Heaven, joy in earth'' when Love became Man, so that every man could be saved.[18]

In his Lenten sermons he insists we are given time to ponder on the urgency of repenting and returning to God. Now is the time to do it. ''It may be the last Spring, the last swallow-time, the last Wednesday of this name or nature, we shall ever live, to hear this point preached.'' Hence we should not ''let this time slip.''[19]

Good Friday is the day to be spent with our Redeemer, and so Andrewes encourages his congregation to gaze and gaze on the crucified Lord because:

It was the sin of our polluted hands that pierced His hands, the swiftness of our feet to do evil that nailed His feet, the wicked devices of our heads that gored His head, and the wretched desires of our hearts that pierced His heart.

As we meditate on our Saviour's sufferings, Andrewes suggests:

Pierce that in you, that was the cause of Christ's piercing; that is sin and the lusts thereof. . . . Look and be pierced with love of Him, who so loved you, that He gave Himself in this sort to be pierced for you. . . . Look upon Him, and His heart opened, and from that gate of hope promise yourself, and look for all manner of things that good are: . . . the deliverance from the evil of our present misery . . . [and] the restoring to the good of our primitive felicity. . . . Look back upon it with some pain; for one way or other, look upon it we must.[20]

By keeping Good Friday aright we can then hasten to the Paschal garden as Easter ushers in a new era, the Christian era: ''Easter-day [is] the day of Christ's rising'', that act ''made an end of all Sabbaths'' and made ''the Lord's day . . . the Christian's day.'' In His Resurrection, Christ has become ''the first fruits''. This is our hope.[21] On this Queen of all Christian festivals, Andrewes filled his Easter sermons with so much tenderness. This is no better illustrated than when he speaks of the women, and especially of Mary Magdalene, who came to the tomb on that ''*very first day of the week*, . . . to anoint Him'', not with some cheap ointment, but costly, sweet-smelling spices.[22] Of Mary Magdalene, our Saviour only had to utter the two syllables of her name, and all her tears vanished, and her heart overflowed with joy of finding her Lord.[23]

However wonderful Easter is, it is not complete without the events of Pentecost. Thus his Pentecostal sermons manifest that not only is this feast the celebration of the outpouring of the Holy Spirit upon the Church but also is the *festum charitatis*, when love itself is especially honoured. The Spirit is also ''sent to be the union, love and love-knot of the natures united in Christ; even of God with man.'' Whitsunday was also His ''*dies donorum*'', a day on which, Andrewes assures us, He will bestow some gift upon His people; ''Some gift He will give, either from the wind, inward, or from the tongue, outward.''[24]

As well as these sixty-seven Liturgical Sermons there are also his nineteen sermons preached on prayer and the Lord's Prayer, the seven on the Temptation of Christ, and those preached at St. Giles' Cripplegate and on various anniversaries of the Gunpowder plot. His Catechetical lectures given in Cambridge were printed as *The Moral Law Expounded*, whilst his response in Latin to Cardinals Perron and Bellarmine in defending the position of the Anglican Church also reveal his outstanding scholarly ability, and his undaunting belief in the catholicity of the Church of England.

His series of sermons on the Lord's Prayer, preached while Master at Pembroke Hall, are worth looking at briefly because not only are they good examples of how methodically and meticulously Andrewes approaches his sermons as he takes the various sections of this prayer, but they are also rich in his teaching of the meaning of prayer in the Christian life.

The first two sermons deal with the invocation, *Our Father who art in heaven*, in which Andrewes reminds us that when we call "God, *our Father* and not *my Father*", we are reminded of "our love to our neighbour, whom we are to love no less than ourselves", and of our charity towards others. It also acts as a reminder that "God created man according to His own image." Furthermore "*Father* does promise unto us forgiveness of sins, and the blessings not of this life only, but especially of [what] is to come." Hence *heaven* is our place of citizenship where "He will at . . . length bring us to . . . where He is." Yet this heaven, Andrewes reminds us, is not something remote but begins "here on earth".25

The next eleven sermons cover the seven petitions made in the Prayer, the first of which concerns God, when we pray *hallowed be Thy name*. This petition teaches us "not [to] use the name of God, which is wonderful and holy, either contemptuously to magic or cursing, or negligently abuse it upon any slight occasion;" or "in vain", but rather "to praise and bless His name for the benefits [and means] of sanctification", and to commence all our actions in His name.26

The next six petitions concern "ourselves", of which "the first three are spent in praying for [what] is good, . . . [and] the other three" praying to be emancipated from evil. The first *good* petition seeks *the kingdom of God*, rather than "the kingdom of this earth" which provides "many stumbling-blocks for the hindrance of God's Kingdom." Thus "we must entreat God by the power of His Spirit to plant in our hearts [what] is good, and to root out and remove out of them . . . the bad." The second *good* petition asks for "grace and righteousness" in order to do "His will here". Andrewes stresses that as "our will is wholly inclined to . . . evil", we should pray not so much that God's will may be done, but rather what God wills may be our will, so that His will may be accomplished on earth as it is in heaven. The "spiritual and eternal" needs are followed by the temporal ones. Thus the third *good* petition pleads that God will "give us all things that are necessary for us" in our daily life, remembering "that we have bread and other things" only through "God's free bounty and liberality". Our prayers, Andrewes emphasizes, should be for daily necessities, and never for "dainty meat, but such as is fit to relieve our hunger." However it is senseless to seek for earthly sustenance, unless at the same time we beg to be given that "sanctified bread which is the heavenly manna."27

The remaining petitions are concerned with "the removing of all evil", that is, "of sins past, and to come, and of the evil of punishment." Just as it is essential to pray for the good things in life, so Andrewes informs us it is necessary "to pray that God will forgive us our sins, which otherwise" are hindrances to "God's graces" and to His "Kingdom". God "bids us" to pray daily "for pardon of our sins", irrespective of "whether they be penny debts or talents; whether fifty or a thousand." When we ask for forgiveness, we can be assured "He is ready daily to remit them." Yet after seeking forgiveness for our sins Andrewes warns us to take "care that hereafter we fall not into sin." Although "God's *grace is sufficient*", when we commit "sins of infirmity, *there is no more sacrifice for sin*, when "we willingly sin after remission." There is no point in asking for forgiveness unless we possess charity and are prepared to forgive others, and forget. "If your heart tells you that you forgave your brother, doubt not but God does likewise forgive you".[28]

In the petition *and lead us not into temptation*, Andrewes leads us to pray to be spared those "sins to come . . . for sin consists not only of an offence or guilt, but of an issue or inclination to sin." Thus we must "not think ourselves secure, when we have forgiveness of our sins." It is then that the devil "is most malicious", but as Andrewes stresses there is comfort here, as "Satan is chained by God so that he cannot go further than God will give him leave." Therefore our prayer should be that God's grace is sufficient "to withstand the least temptation . . . but particularly from the temptation of any several sin whereunto we are inclined".[29]

The last petition requests to "be delivered from evil, [and] . . . suffer no evil." In fact this petition is very similar to the preceding one. The same principles apply as the devil desires "to carry us away into sin and transgression, to the end he may endanger our souls." Nevertheless God's grace is always available to direct us away from his claws as we cannot "trust to ourselves". However Andrewes insists it is not always as simple as this, nor had it been for any of the saints. "There is none upon whom the devil has not at least laid his nails, and as it were scratched with his claws by outward affliction." All Christians suffer some "tribulation", "the cross in this life", yet God "does mix some comfort with our affliction." Consequently this petition pleads for "patience to endure our affliction", realizing that in time God "turns the evils that are come upon us to our greater good."[30]

Just as there is a proper introduction to the Lord's Prayer, so Andrewes reminds us there is also a fitting conclusion with its doxology. "The beginning and end of it are an acknowledgement of God's riches, power and goodness", as well as revealing His inclination" to supply "our wants, for that He is not only willing as a Father but able as a King." While the beginning acknowledges God's "goodness", the end reveals His "power". In these we do "give" to God while in the petitions we "take" from him. The doxology is a further reminder that "all the world is His Kingdom by right of inheritance, but we who are His Church are His Kingdom by right of purchase", and that "Kingdom is everlasting as His power endures for ever." Hence "we are taught to pray for glory everlasting." The prayer concludes with the "*Amen* [which] must come from the heart", by which we ratify all the petitions asked for. It further manifests "our faith, in as much as we acknowledge those things to be true, and . . . our love, whereby we testify our desire for the accomplishment of these petitions."[31] Moreover our *Amen* joins us with "the saints in heaven who continually cry, *Amen, blessing, and glory, and wisdom, and honour, and power, be to God.*" Therefore "if we will come where they are, we must sound out the praises of God as they do" with our "*Yes and Amen.*"[32]

As already mentioned the doctrine preached by Andrewes was the faith of the universal church, the Catholic faith, handed down by the Apostles, enshrined in the teachings of the patristics and laid down in the early Councils of the Church. "For one Canon given of God, two testaments, three symbols, the four first councils, five centuries and the series of Fathers therein, fix the rule of religion."[33] Eliot refers to him as "the first great preacher of the English Catholic Church" who always speaks as "a man who had a formed visible Church behind him."[34] In his 1607 Nativity sermon Andrewes defends this Catholic faith against the "false conceit" that has crept "into the minds of men, to think points of religion that be manifest to be certain petty points scarce worth the hearing." For Andrewes those aspects which were vital to Christian belief had been made "plain" enough, and those not "plain" were "not necessary". Yet many disputed the Faith; "We see . . . how men languish about some points, which they would have thought to be great; and great controversies there be, and great books of controversies about them." Andrewes pleads for the end of controversy over essential Christian doctrine. "I hope there will be no more question or controversy . . . than there is of the mystery itself and the greatness of it."[35] For Andrewes the Faith is a great "mystery", and therefore above the cavilling and contention of men. The "great mystery" is God Himself who chose to manifest Himself in the flesh, not only in the "cratch" but "on the cross".[36] This certainly was not the ground for controversy!

In his sermons, as he had in his *Preces*, Andrewes utilizes a vast selection sources. Hardly a book in the Bible is not quoted at some stage, while the Eastern and Western Fathers such as Irenaeus, Tertullian, Augustine, Jerome, John Chrysostom, Gregory of Nyssa, Bernard and Aquinas are referred to constantly. In a Pentecostal sermon he pays tribute to them when he describes their works as "lights of the Church, in whom the scent of this ointment was fresh, and the temper true."[37] He even quoted from the Classical writers of ancient Greece and Rome such as Euripides, Cicero and Seneca, in order to contrast the pagan philosophical interpretation of life to that as taught by Christ. Hence these pagan writers "provoke Christian men to emulation, by showing them their own blindness in matter of knowledge, that see not so much as the heathen did by light of nature; or their slackness in matter of conversation, that cannot be got so far forward by God's law as the poor pagan can by his philosophy."[38]

When he uses the Holy Scriptures, Andrewes frequently intwines the Old with the New with a very analytical approach. For example in his sermon for Christmas Day in 1613, he takes as his text, St. John's reference of Abraham rejoicing in seeing "My day". (viii:56) To illustrate how we "have Abraham for our example", Andrewes takes us back to Genesis to the valley of Mamre, and relates how here Abraham saw the birth of Christ, just as clearly as the shepherds did:

But this day he saw at Mamre. Then was Christ in Person there, one of the Three; then made Abraham the confession we before spake of. Then is twice mention made of the time of life, which is this time, if ever any. . . .

And so certainly he then saw it there, as after we see he sware his servant on his thigh. His thigh became ad sancta Die evangelia.

This is then explained by using one of the patristics, St. Augustine who had posed the question, "*What has the God of heaven to do with Abraham's thigh?*" And the answer? "*Nisi, quia, but only because he saw certainly the Son of God was from thence to take flesh* — semen Abrahae de femore Abrahae, *and so to make us this blessed day.*"[39]

The joy that Abraham experienced for Christmas is compared with "the joy of Job's Easter", another Old Testament reference. This leads to further probing into Genesis, where Abraham acknowledged his need of a Redeemer when he "complains" that "I am but dust and ashes", and refers to God as "*Judge of the world*". Thus this is the reason, explains Andrewes, why Abraham "should desire this *ut*, to see this day; [and] why, but for this day Abraham had been but ashes of the furnace."[40]

In explaining how Abraham could see this day, Andrewes returns to the New Testament by using St. Paul's interpretation of man. As he is both a physical and a spiritual being, he is able to behold the visible and invisible aspects of life. For the latter he needs "*the light of faith*". It was by this means that Abraham was able to see Christ as clearly as Simeon saw the baby Jesus through his physical eyes.[41]

As well as his sermons teaching the main Christian doctrines: creation, redemption, resurrection, and sanctification, they also conveyed other aspects of our Faith. For instance Andrewes had much to say about worship. Important as the sermon was in the context of the Liturgy, Andrewes emphasizes that his sermons, any sermon, are not worship by itself, but merely part of it. For him all worship focused on the altar where the Eucharist is celebrated and offered. He himself had a profound love for our Lord in His Sacrament, and so into most of his sermons he has woven some teaching. and devotion towards the blessed Sacrament. He could never stress enough how essential it is to receive this heavenly Food on our earthly pilgrimage. It is "the means to re-establish our hearts with *grace*, and to repair the decays of our spiritual strength; even *His own flesh, the Bread of life*, and *His own blood, the Cup of salvation.*" This "Bread made of Himself, [is] the true *Granum frumenti*, . . . [and the] "Wine . . . *the true Vine.*"[42] His Nativity sermons especially focused on the blessed Sacrament because on Christmas day Bethlehem and the altar are one:

> *Now the bread which we break, is it not the partaking of the body, of the flesh, of Jesus Christ? It is surely, and by it and by nothing more are we made partakers of this blessed union . . . because He has so done, taken ours of us, we also ensuing His steps will participate with Him and with His flesh which He has taken of us. It is most kindly to take part with Him in that which He took part in with us, and that, to no other end, but that He might make the receiving of it by us a means whereby He might dwell in us, and we in Him. He taking our flesh, and we receiving His Spirit; by His flesh which He took of us receiving His Spirit which He imparts to us; that, as He by ours became* consors humanae naturae, *so we by His might become* consortes Divinae naturae, *partakers of His divine nature.*[43]

Thus the focal point of the Holy Eucharist, is at that most precious moment of our union with Him in the act of Communion itself. "Never can we more truly . . . say, in *Christo Jesu Domino nostro*, as when we come new from that holy action, for then He is in us, and we in Him." This Sacrament also had another significance for Andrewes, it was the *locus* of unity, or "the Sacrament of *accord*", manifested first by the Apostles as they broke bread with one accord. This "perfect unity" is also represented "in the many grains kneaded into *one loaf*, and the many grapes pressed into one cup; and what it represents lively, it works as effectually."[44]

With his profound love for the blessed Sacrament, Andrewes deplores the attitude of those who showed no reverence towards it, and who refused to kneel to receive their Lord, or for that matter during the celebration of the Liturgy. He deeply lamented the neglect of adoration. "Most come and go without it, no they scarce know what it is. And with how little reverence, how evil beseeming us, we use ourselves in the church." He also deplored the neglect of the altar where "the highest and most solemn service of God" fares worse than any other. Regrettably people attended Divine Service not for worship but to hear a sermon. Unfortunately "all our *holiness* is in hearing, all our service, ear-service."[45]

As we can see his sermons also express the need for reverence, dignity and sincerity in worship. This should be no less than that of "the glorious saints in heaven" who cast "their crown . . . before the throne and fall down." Indeed worship "is [what] Cornelius did to Peter; he *met him, fell down at his feet, and worshipped him.* And [what] John did to the Angel; that is, he *fell down before his feet to worship him.*" Having in mind those who showed little outward reverence in the Church's worship, Andrewes argues that as man is a composite of body and soul, both parts must be expressed in worship to Him. Indeed "the inward affection" can only be expressed by the outward action. It is never possible, Andrewes asserts for "a man . . . [to] be too reverent to God." However "we think it a great disgrace, and debasing of ourselves, if we use any bodily worship to God." Sadly we would not be as irreverent to "come before a mean prince as we do before the King of kings, and Lord of lords, even the God of heaven and earth." Our attitude should be like "*The four-and-twenty elders [who] fell down before Him Who sat on the throne, and worshipped Him Who lives for ever, and cast their crowns before His throne.*" Thus at worship, he insists we should make the *knees to bow*, and *kneel before the Lord their Maker.* Our feet are [also] to *come before His face; for the Lord is a great God, and a great King above all gods.*" Furthermore "the wandering eye must learn to be *fastened on Him*, and *the work of justice* and *peace.*" In other words every part of the body is involved in worship.[46]

For those who scorn bodily acts of reverence, Andrewes warns, are in danger of losing their souls. Therefore it is imperative we follow the example of those "in heaven" and "under the earth". For "they in heaven *cast down their crowns, and fall down* themselves of their own accord; and confess Him singing, as at His birth." Even those "under the earth do it too, but not *ultro.*" Instead they "are thrown down, and even made His *footstool*, . . . though sore against their wills; and confess Him too, though roaring. . . . as it were upon the rack." We who live on earth, as in between, "partake of both." Hence the alternative was "either fall on our knees now, or be cast flat on our faces" later; it is a matter of "either confess Him *cantando*, with Saints and Angels, or *ululando*, with devils and damned spirits."[47]

Andrewes also enunciates the other reverent acts of worship such as acknowledging the holy name of Jesus. Yet when bowing the knee, it is not only "at the name of Jesus but also "at the holy mysteries" too; "where His name is, I am sure, and more than His name, even the body and blood of our Lord Jesus Christ". He laments that though we receive His "inestimable high benefits of grace . . . so high, so heavenly a gift" many lacked the "humility to receive upon their knees." Despite the fact that many spurn this reverent act, he insists, "it has ever been the manner in Christ's Church, whether we offer to Him, or receive aught offered from Him, in this wise to do it."[48]

Andrewes admits there had been "superstition" in the past towards his name, but warned that in driving away the superstition we should be careful not to drive away "all reverent regard and decency". He also examines the issue between worshipping God with the *knee* and the *tongue*; as both confess. He explains, "why the knee first?" By "having bowed the knee" it shows that we come to "Him in fear and reverence", and therefore are "fitter to speak to Him"; and "not be so homely with Him as" some are "in their gesture and speech . . . as if they were *Hail fellow* even familiar with God." Andrewes maintains if "a heart [is] possessed with the humble fear of God, from such a heart, confession is ever most kindly."[49]

One of the few religious controversies Andrewes felt compelled to defend during his life was over *grace*. Just as grace penetrates every aspect of creation and worked in harmony with nature, it is also available to every man who seeks it. Thus within the context of the Cambridge debates of the 1590's he challenged the Calvinists who taught that grace and redemption were not given nor available to all as most men were predestined to a life of reprobation. Responding to the Lambeth Articles of 1595, which made such restraints on grace, Andrewes insists:

> That the reprobate are such, not by the absolute decree of God, as the Articles affirm, but on account of sin; that some previous dispositions are offered to do, and indeed conferred upon all men, and that saving grace itself would be conferred upon ALL men were they not obstinate; that all men are not drawn to the Father is due not to the absolute will of God but to the depraved will of man.[50]

Linked with the issue of grace was *certitudo* of salvation and *securitas*. Andrewes reiterates St. Paul's warning against false assurance. Those who feel anchored in *securitas* should be aware of sudden destruction. Like Lot's wife, we can reach the entry to the gates, "so near her safety", but still perish. "Remember, that near to [the] Zoar gates there stands a salt-stone." Therefore we can never be secure of our salvation. From "youth . . . until . . . old age" we must not grow weary on the plain but continue faithfully to the end, "for if we stand still, . . . we are [likely] . . . to be made a pillar." Furthermore we must "remember the judgment that is upon them after their relapse." Thus it is imperative to "remember that we shall justify Sodom by so doing, and her frozen sin shall condemn our melting virtue." We must remember also "they in the wilfulness of their wickedness persisted till fire from Heaven consumed them." Andrewes warns how important it was for the "obdurate in sin, . . . to be constant in virtue, and to practise "the Queen of virtues", "perseverance".[51]

In other words it was possible for us, even after we have sought grace to fall from it. We are responsible for our every action, and if and when we sin, unless repented, severs our relationship with God. Nothing could be more forceful than Andrewes' preaching on the consequence of sin. "Sin . . . will destroy us all". There is "nothing so dangerous, so deadly unto us, as is the sin in our bosom".[52] Sin when first committed may seem "sweet", . . . but after it is committed, the sinner finds . . . that it turns to a bitter and choleric matter''. Perhaps sin at first may seem ''a matter of liberty'', yet it really is like ''a worm which never leaves gnawing''.[53] We must realize as Andrewes points out that Christ died not only for our sins, but for us to cease from sin, so that it does not reign within us.[54] He quotes St. Augustine who had insisted it was harder ''to raise a soul from the death of sin . . . than to raise a dead body out of the dust of death.'' Thus ''Mary Magdalene's resurrection in soul, from her long lying dead in sin was a greater miracle than her brother Lazarus' resurrection'' after being in the grave for four days.[55]

What Christians needed to practise to assure themselves of living in a state of grace was regular repentance and confession. In regards to the latter Andrewes defends the need for auricular confession by indicating how much it has been neglected by people, and thus denying the parish priest of one aspect of his pastoral care:

I take it to be an error . . . to think the fruits of repentence, and the worth of them, to be a matter any common man can skill of well enough; needs never ask St. John or St. Paul what he should do, knows what he should do as well as St. Paul or St. John either; and that it is not rather a matter wherein we need the counsel and direction of such as are professed that way. Truly it is neither the least nor the last part of our learning to be able to give answer and direction in this point. But therefore laid aside and neglected by us, because not sought after by you. Therefore not studied but by very few, quia nemo nos interrogat, *because it is grown out of request quite.''*[56]

In our understanding of God and man Andrewes acknowledges the place of nature and reason as well as the Scriptures. He had especially focused on this approach in his catechistical lectures which were given every Saturday and Sunday afternoon at 3 p.m. at Cambridge in the 1580s and which were collected and eventually published as *The Moral Law Expounded*. In them he argues that ''true reason [is] a help to faith and faith to it. . . . When we have yielded ourselves to belief and have strengthened it by reason.'' Yet it must always be remembered that faith, although imperfect, is a higher teacher than reason.

. . though faith be an imperfect way, and we imperfect, yet may we walk in it. We are therefore to pray to God, that by the inspiration of His Spirit, He would keep us in this way.

Although the natural world teaches us much about God, we nevertheless must also seek for knowledge greater than own ''natural knowledge'', otherwise ''[we] will come to more grossness and absurdities, than the very beasts.'' That ''higher knowledge'' is given to us by God through grace, whereby we also obtain ''faith . . . [and] eternal life.''[57] Thus to know God and ourselves, and the relationship between the two, it was essential for us to use every gift God has given. Andrewes' sermons indeed teach us that all of life is hallowed and sacramental.

As stated in the Preface, his sermons in the words of Eliot, ''rank with the finest English prose of their time.'' To conclude this introduction to Andrewes and especially to his sermons, I would like to comment briefly on them from a literary approach. As previously mentioned there is in his sermons a spiritual and sensitive depth which was hardly reached by any other preacher of his time or after. This is achieved firstly by his presentation. In each of his sermons there are distinctly three parts: the working and manifestation of the Divine, the benefits received from the Divine, and the application of these benefits by the receiver. And secondly in his language skills. This is achieved through his dextrous use of words, and how he manipulated and played on them to extract every meaning possible in relation to his subject matter in which he himself was totally engrossed, spiritually, intellectually and emotionally, and I dare say he expected his auditors to be so too. Therefore as we read them and persevere with his style, we become aware of this deep penetrating spirituality as well as a subtlety and a sense of urgency as Andrewes unfolds the mysteries of the great teachings of the Church.

He is very much a metaphysical preacher. For example in his 1615 Nativity sermon, he wants to convey that it is in the little and lowly things that greatness comes. To achieve this he uses repetition and juxtapositioning quite often. So we find this sermon dispersed with all kinds of references to *littleness*. Bethlehem is described as "sorry poor village, scarce worth an Apostrophe"; it is "diminutively little"; it is "the very least of all". It is "*least* for the small number of the inhabitants, *least* for the thinness and meanness of the buildings, as was seen at Christ's Birth." This *littleness* is simultaneously juxtapositioned with "so great a State"; "That birth is sure too big for this place"; and "so great a birth." To contrast further the smallness of Bethlehem with the greatness of the event which happened there, Andrewes compares these with the oak tree and mustard plant both of which grow to an enormous size from a minute beginning. "How huge an oak from how small an acorn! From how little a grain of mustard seed, the very *Bethlehem minima, the least of all seeds*, how large a plant! of how fair a spread!"[58]

Another reason for stressing *little* is that despite the greatness of the event, it shows that God in becoming man, unveils His humility — a great humility in being born in such "a sorry poor village". Though *little*, Bethlehem becomes to represent the virtue of humility, "where He in great humility was found this day". To come to such a *little* place, only the humble will come such as the shepherds; and those such as "the Pharisees" are "too big for Bethlehem."[59] His message is clear; only those Christians who are humble will want to venture to such a little and insignificant place, but if they do, they will discover something big!

In this same sermon he cleverly plays on the word *bread*, to stress its importance as the staff of life in both the natural and spiritual. Bethlehem itself means "the *house of Bread*"; *lehem* means *bread* and *beth, house*. This was the Bethlehem of *Ephratah*, and so this particular town means the *house of plenty Bread*. This day, Christmas day, this *Bread* is here, in His House on the altar. He who is born in Bethlehem is "the true *Bread of life who came down from heaven*, . . . called by Him so, the true Bread, the Bread of Heaven, the Bread of life — and where that Bread is, there is Bethlehem ever." And so when we come to His house there is always Bread and therefore "never take Him without bread, His house is the house of bread, inasmuch as He Himself is Bread; that in the house or out of it — wheresoever He is, there is Bethlehem. There can no bread want."[60]

In the opening of his 1611 Pentecostal sermon, Andrewes by his use of parallelism again displays his command of using words to the maximum effect. Much of this sermon revolves around the significance of *go* and *send*. To stress the fact that Christ must *go* in order to *send* the Holy Spirit which he promised, we read: *"But if I go, I will send Him to you. And He did go, and He sent Him, and this day He did send Him."* This *going* is the fulfilment of *"the promise of the sending,* and *the sending of the promise*; the promise of the sending, the substance of the text, and the sending of the promise, the substance of the solemnity; it being the solemnity of *mittam* and *veniet*, both in the text, the sending and coming of the Holy Spirit."[61] So often Andrewes circles his thoughts and so here he links the *coming* with the *going*. "This coming, or not coming, depends upon Christ's going, or His staying. *If Christ go not He comes not; if Christ goes, He comes."*[62] Indeed parallelism features all through this Pentecostal sermon.

His Good Friday sermon for 1597 is a good example of how Andrewes in a sermon achieves what Eliot refers to as "squeezing and squeezing the word until it yields a full juice of meaning which we should never have supposed any word to possess."[63] The words that Andrewes concentrates on are *die, pierce* and *heart/ hart* as he wants us not only to view the Crucifixion but to feel its very pain through "piercing". Beginning with a basic quotation from Isaiah, *"Die he will . . ."*, he takes the word *die* as a command for the following sentences, each one building in its intensity in order to describe the kind of death. Thus we read:

Die — but what death? a natural or violent? Daniel tells us He shall die, not a natural, but a violent death. But many are slain after many sorts, and [many] kinds there be of violent deaths. The psalmist . . . describes it thus: 'they pierced My hands and My feet', which is only proper to the death of the cross. Die, and be slain, and be crucified.

This dying by crucifixion by Christ was no normal one as it was especially violent as not only were Christ's hands and feet pierced with nails in the normal way but His heart was also, which made it extraordinary. Thus everything climaxes in this extraordinary crucifixion.[64]

In his application of *pierce* and *heart/hart* Andrewes intensifies their meaning by using them over and over again in a slightly different context. Thus he weaves throughout his sermon that Christ's "piercing of the heart" is the fulfilment of the prophecy, *"And they will look upon Me Whom they have pierced"*. Christ is compared *"to the morning hart"*. Just as the *hart* is hounded "all his life long" until his end, and so Christ "this day brought to His end, . . . and stricken and pierced through side, heart, and all."[65] This "piercing" comes from the "spear-point which pierced, and went through, His very heart itself; for of that wound, of the wound in His heart, is this spoken. . . . So that we extend this piercing of Christ farther than to the visible gash in His side, even to a piercing of another nature, whereby not His heart only was stabbed, but His very spirit wounded too."[66]

The *hart* having being slain by the *spear-point*, Andrewes continues his theme of piercing the heart by redirecting *heart* and *hart*, *pierce* and *piercing* to his listeners.

Yes, Christ Himself, is pierced as He is, invites us to it. . . . 'Look and be pierced', yet that it might be 'that with looking on Him we might be pricked in our hearts', and have it enter past the skin, . . . and pierce that in you that was the

cause of Christ's piercing upon Him and pierce. . . . 'look and be pierced with
love of Him' who so loved you, that He gave Himself in this sort to be pierced for
you.[67]

Andrewes also uses images to great effect. In his 1623 Paschal sermon he
wishes to convey the Unity of Good Friday and Easter Day, that Christ in sacrific-
ing His life for us on the Cross conquers death through His resurrection. To
achieve this he uses winery imagery: Christ is the winepress but "a double
winepress". Firstly He is "Himself trodden and pressed; He was the grapes and
clusters Himself", and secondly, "He who was trodden on before, gets up again
and does tread upon and tread down." In the former the winepress represents
"His cross and passion", and for the latter, His release from it, "in His descent
and resurrection." In the first example when grapes are trodden, a liquid, a red
liquid flows, wine, but now the precious Blood of Christ. To heighten the intent of
Christ pouring out His blood for mankind, he takes Him as representing that man
who came from Bozrah wearing "red garments". Thus Andrewes speaks of the
man "*from Bozrah* imbrued with blood, the blood of his enemies", and Isaiah's
Suffering Servant "was led as a *sheep to be slain*, and so was slain there".
Furthermore this bloody man from Bozrah was going to Edom, the place "upon
earth [which] comes nearest to the kingdom of darkness in hell", symbolising
Christ as the second imagery descending into hell![68]

The other intention for using winery images is to teach on the sacraments.
Christ "is the *true Vine*, and . . . to make wine of Him, He and the clusters . . .
must be pressed." In His passion this blood ran forth three times. "One, in
Gethsemane that made Him sweat blood." Secondly in "Gabbatha which made
the blood run forth at His head with the thorns, [and] out of His whole body with
the scourges." Thirdly "at Golgotha where He was so pressed that they pressed
the very soul out of His body, and out ran blood and water both." This leads to the
point He wants to make. From His body flowed "the twin sacraments of the
Church", and for this particular sermon the emphasis is on the blood, the wine
from the Vine which becomes "the cup of salvation". *Red* now is identified with
the wine as expressed in psalm seventy-five, "the wine is red, it is full mixed, and
He pours out of it." This wine unlike the wine made from sour grapes which was
offered to Christ on the cross is pressed from good grapes and is poured into the
"cup of blessing" for our salvation.[69]

Andrewes also uses natural imagery with as much success. In desiring to
convey that eternal life made possible by the Resurrection is something glorious,
lovely, fresh and new, he takes spring imagery. In both his 1608 and 1616 Easter
sermons Andrewes describes the Resurrection as occurring at "the freshest time
of the year", with its annual miracle of new life, representing man's regeneration:

. . . there goes from His resurrection an influence, which shall have an oper-
ation like that of the dew of the spring; which when He will let fall, the earth shall
yield her dead, as at the falling of the dew, the herbs now rise and shoot forth
again. . . . For He rose in the dawning—then is the day regenerate: and in 'prima
sabbati' — that, the first begetting of the week; and in the spring, when all that
were winter-starved, withered and dead, are regenerated again and rise up
anew.[70]

It is God who makes "all our gardens green, sends us yearly the spring, and all the herbs and flowers we then gather". Yet in heaven, spring is eternal with its lushness and loveliness; there "nothing fades, but all springs fresh and green." Christ "made such a herb grow out of the ground this day as the like was never seen before, a dead body to shoot forth alive out of the grace." Thus at this time, here, but, at all times there, "a perpetual spring; no other season there but that." In his 1620 sermon he extends this spring imagery to include the gardener who makes it all possible. The true gardener is Christ Himself who in the garden of our souls "waters them with the dew" and thus brings forth flowers of grace. He "will garden our bodies too, turn all our graves into garden-plots", with the firm assurance that "one day [He will] turn land and sea and all into a great garden, and so husband them, as they shall in due time bring forth live bodies, even all our bodies alive again."[71]

Just as many of his Easter sermons were linked with the season of spring, so were most of his Lenten addresses for his teaching on repentance. Indeed "there cannot be a fitter time than the Church has set . . . forth" for teaching repentance as "now is the time of the year to plant . . . [when] you will see nothing but men grafting and setting trees: it is the husbandry and the business of the month". Hence how "wonderfully fitly chosen . . . that this [Lenten] tree may keep time with the rest." We must not defer repentance "but take the time while it is [the] season . . . [so] that the mortifying of sin might end in the rising of Christ in us."[72]

Nature is extended to included bird-life imagery. Accordingly in one of his Ash Wednesday sermon Andrewes compares this day as the time for repentance with the life cycle of those various birds (the stork, turtle, crane and swallow) described in Jeremiah viii:7, which know instinctively that "they have a time to return . . . [and] observe". "*The stork in the air knows her appointed times, while the turtle, the crane and the swallow observe the time of their coming; but my people know not the judgment of the Lord.*" Yet it is something we must know, and respond to, just as instinctively as these birds do for their "appointed times" for returning, leaving and nesting. That "appointed time" for them is "now"; but "who knows whether he shall live to see them return any more?" The urgency for this repentance is emphasised by the repetition of the word *last*. Thus "it may be the last Spring, the last swallow-time, the last Wednesday of this name or nature, we shall ever live, to hear this point preached." Hence we should not "let this time slip."[73] There are also other aspects of repentance and piety we can learn from these birds: From the turtle, "that *vox turturis*, which is gemebam [strikes] a mournful note" teaches us to bewail mournfully for "our life past". The stork by its "very name and nature . . . [is] full of mercy and compassion" and encourages us to "works of mercy"; the swallow makes his nest so "*near the altar of God*", that he sets the example for us to be ever near "the house and altar of God"; while the crane with a "painful watching, and abstinence . . . especially when they take flight", should inspire in us to abstain and watch in "time of our return".[74]

His sermons also convey much tenderness, warmth and joy. A good example of this is in his 1620 Paschal sermon revolving around Mary Magdalene's searching for her Lord in the Easter garden. Her urgent but tender desire to find her Master is highlighted by the repetition of *Him*: "If you have taken Him away, tell me where you have laid Him''. ''Him?'' ''Which Him?'' She repeats, ''if you have taken Him away, tell me where you have laid Him, and I will fetch Him.'' As dawn breaks the scene is climaxed with another word, *Mary*. The warmth and joy that Mary felt is conveyed by Andrewe's description of the rising sun penetrating the clouds and mist. ''A cloud may be so thick we shall not see the sun through it: this one word, these two syllables *Mary* from His mouth, scatters it all. No sooner had His voice sounded in her ears, but it drives away all the mist, dries up her tears, lightens her eyes, that she knew Him straight and answers Him with her wonted salutation *Rabboni*.''[75]

His sermons are rich, rich of detail and devotion, but reflecting that meticulousness that Andrewes had for all of life. For Andrewes only the best was ever good enough for God and as we read and meditate on these Liturgical sermons, we sense they were, like incense, offered up to the heavenly court as an act of worship. These are then the Liturgical sermons of Lancelot Andrewes, ''the ointment of whose name is *sweeter than all spices*.''[76]

References

[1] Eliot, p. 18.

[2] One exception was his 1599 Ash Wednesday sermon which was preached in direct relation to the Irish campaign under the Earl of Essex's command.

[3] It was often a practice of Elizabeth to keep sees vacant as long as possible in order to collect their revenue — a practice which Andrewes deplored!

[4] C. Wren, *Parentalia* (London 1750), p. 81.

[5] J. Hacket, *Scrinia Reserata* (London, 1693), p. 45.

[6] L. Andrewes, *The Private Devotions of Lancelot Andrewes (Preces Privatae)*, translated with an introduction and notes by F. E. Brightman, and including ''Lancelot Andrewes'', (1926) by T. S. Eliot, (Gloucester, Mass., 1978), p. 24. Hereafter referred to as Brightman.

[7] R. Drake, Ed. *A Manual of The Private Devotions and Meditations of . . . Lancelot Andrewes*, (London, 1648), Preface.

[8] Brightman, *op. cit.*, p. 7.

[9] L. Andrewes, *The Works of Lancelot Andrewes*, eds. J. Bliss and J. P. Wilson, 11 vols. (The Library of Anglo-Catholic Theology, Oxford, 1841–54), Vol. 11, pp. 225, 244. Hereafter referred to as Andrewes.

[10] *ibid.*, Vol. 5, p. 287.

[11] Brightman, p. 32.

[12] P. A. Welsby, *Lancelot Andrewes* (London 1958), pp. 87–8.

[13] Andrewes, Vol. 11, p. xiii.

[14] *ibid.*, Vol. 3, pp. 147–8.

[15] *ibid.*, Vol. 11, p. xiii.

[16] *ibid.*, Vol. 5, p. 288.

[17] *ibid.*, Vol. 1, p. 233.

[18] *ibid.*, Vol. 1, pp. 73–4, 118, 122, 132.

[19] *ibid.*, p. 355.

[20] *ibid.*, Vol. 2, pp. 131–135.

[21] *ibid.*, pp. 208–9, Vol. 3, p. 4.

[22] *ibid.*, p. 226.

[23] *ibid.*, Vol. 3, p. 20.

[24] *ibid.*, pp. 113, 129.

[25] *ibid.*, Vol. 5, pp. 363–4, 366, 368, 372, 376, 380.

[26] *ibid.*, pp. 385, 388.

27 *ibid.*, pp. 385, 388, 390, 392–4, 413–4, 417, 421, 423.

28 *ibid.*, pp. 424–5, 430–1, 432, 436.

29 *ibid.*, pp. 441–3, 445, 448.

30 *ibid.*, pp. 450, 453–6.

31 *ibid.*, pp. 458–60, 462, 466.

32 *ibid.*, pp. 467, 472, 475–6.

33 *ibid.*, Vol. 8, p. 90; Vol. 9, p. 26.

34 Eliot, *op. cit.*, p. 18.

35 Andrewes, Vol. 1, p. 35.

36 *ibid.*, p. 36.

37 *ibid.*, Vol. 3, p. 287.

38 *ibid.*, Vol. 5, p. 62.

39 *ibid.*, Vol. 1, pp. 118–9, 128–9.

40 *ibid.*, pp. 123–4.

41 *ibid.*, p. 128.

42 *ibid.*, p. 169.

43 *ibid.*, p. 16.

44 *ibid.*, Vol. 2 p. 205, Vol. 3, p. 128.

45 *ibid.*, Vol. 2, p. 335, Vol. 4, pp. 374–5, 379–80.

46 *ibid.*, Vol. 5, pp. 554–5.

47 *ibid.*, Vol. 2, pp. 338–9.

48 *ibid.*, pp. 335–6.

49 *ibid.*, p. 338.

50 Translation by Wellesby, In Wellesby, *op. cit.*, p. 44; Andrewes, Vol. 6, pp. 289–305.

51 *ibid.*, Vol. 2, pp. 73–6.

52 *ibid.*, Vol. 1, p. 74.

53 *ibid.*, Vol. 5, p. 86.

54 *ibid.*, Vol. 2, p. 200.

55 *ibid.*, p. 203.

56 *ibid.*, Vol. 1, pp. 450.

57 L. Andrewes, *The Moral Law Expounded*, (London, 1642) pp. 23–24, 124, 127–8.

58 Andrewes, Vol. 1, pp. 157–9.

59 *ibid.*, p. 171.

60 *ibid.*, pp. 168, 173.

61 *ibid.*, Vol. 3, p. 163.

62 *ibid.*, p. 165.

63 Eliot, *op. cit.*, pp. 24–5.

64 Andrewes, Vol. 2, p. 121.

65 *ibid.*, pp. 119–20.

66 *ibid.*, pp. 122–3.

67 *ibid.*, pp. 130–2.

68 *ibid.*, Vol. 3, pp. 61, 64, 66, 70.

69 *ibid.*, pp. 70–3.

70 *ibid.*, Vol. 2, pp. 231, 376.

71 *ibid.*, p. 379, Vol. 3, pp. 15–6.

72 *ibid.*, Vol. 1, p. 453.

73 *ibid.*, pp. 338, 350–1, 355.

74 *ibid.*, pp. 351–2.

75 *ibid.*, Vol. 3, p. 17.

76 Hacket, *op. cit.*, p. 45.

INTRODUCTION
TO
THE NATIVITY SERMONS

The tenor of it is all about a Child
to be born, a Child with an ecce; *in*
whom and in Whose birth, God should be
with us — so with us as never before.
On Whose so being with us depends all
our well or evil being here, and for ever.
For better not to be at all than be without
Him; and having Him we need nothing else.

Andrewes, Vol. 1, p. 135.

At the loveliest of all Christian festivals, Christmas, Andrewes expounds those eternal truths man needs to hear. Each one of us needs to hear that our Saviour was born to redeem, restore and renew mankind. It is now up to man to act, and so Andrewes within these sermons directs us to the Christ-Child in the cratch and upon the altar in order to respond to Love's gift.

There are seventeen recorded sermons preached by Andrewes at Christmas, covering a period of approximately twenty years, delivered before His Majesty King James I at Whitehall, from 1605 to 1624. As well as describing those joyful and glorious events of Christmas which we have all known since our cradle days, Andrewes teaches most extensively on the Incarnation which ranges from the rather *simple* doctrine that Christ was born to save us from our sins, and therefore there is joy in the heart of every sinner at this time, to the more complex one of *Filius Meus Tu, you are my Son,* as being the fulfilling of the law in the terms of St. Paul's *lex fidei* and *lex factorum.* Yet Andrewes achieves a sense of unity in all his themes as he presents and ponders on that "great mystery".

For this saintly man the feast of the Nativity is that glorious time when all the splendour and love of God is manifested. In Christ's birth the Father is glorified, the "choir of angels singing, and joying, and making melody, for this *good-will of God towards men."* [1]

The Christ-Child is Love incarnate; God loved us so much that He was begotten and took our flesh upon Him in order to restore us to our former dignity. In the simple shepherds and the magi, man is present with simplicity and style at His birth, respectively.

No wonder Andrewes' sermons ooze with joy, the sheer joy of the message of the Incarnation. For the man who has been rescued from self "there is no joy in the world to the joy of a man saved." On "His day" there is "joy in Heaven, joy in earth" when Love becomes Man, so that every man could be saved. [2]

1

Yet the most wonderful aspect of this love was "Love, not only condescending to take our nature upon Him, but to take it by the same way and after the same manner that we do, by being conceived." He is flesh of our flesh, and therefore every day He sees us "in Himself, as He cannot look upon His flesh but He must think upon us." Undoubtedly through God's love "He has made our flesh His tabernacle." Thus *our very body may rest in hope, to be restored again, and made like to His glorious Body.*"[3]

More wonderfully still, through the Incarnation we have the potential to perfection; indeed "at our very highest perfection . . . we come near" to the likeness of "an angel."[4]

The paradox of Christ's birth is that in the greatness of this event there is the lowliness of the place of birth. God was content to be born in "a sorry poor village" and "instead of a palace, a poor stable; . . . a beast's cratch; no pillow but a lock of hay; no hangings but dust and cobwebs; no attendants, but *in medio animalium.*" Thus today we see God "in the flesh of a poor babe crying" lying in his cradle, the first of many examples of God's humility.[5]

Just as the greatness and humility of God are clearly presented by Andrewes so are the two natures in Christ. He makes us very much aware that the birth of Christ reveals both His divinity and humanity. "At His birth, a cratch for the Child, a star for the Son; a company of shepherds viewing the Child, a choir of angels celebrating the Son."[6] Yet Andrewes takes pains to make clear that these two natures are never distinct but always fuse:

And now, if we will put together natus *and* Servator, Servator *and* Christus, Christus and Dominus, Dominus *and* natus; . . . *take them which way you will in combination, . . . then have we His two natures in one Person. In* Servator, *His Godhead; none but God is a Saviour. In* Christus, *His Manhood; God cannot be annointed, man may. In* Dominus, *His Divine again,* the Lord from Heaven. *In* Natus, *His human nature directly, born of a woman, both ever carefully joined, and to be joined together.*[7]

The Nativity is also the means of reconciliation. In the coming of the Christ Child heaven and earth are reconciled; "by the virtue of this birth, heaven is at peace with itself; and heaven with earth is now at peace. So is earth too with itself." *The partition wall* has also been broken down between Jews and Gentiles, while the Old and New Testament are "bound together now in one volume" as He who gave the Law is now the Gospel.[8] Reconciliation enables the angels' message of *peace on earth* to be implemented.

Another reason for so much joy at the Nativity is that it reminds us that Christmas is always with us. The Incarnation overflows into the sacramental life of the Church, and in turn more particularly into the lives of the regular communicants. The Christ-Child and we are united each time we kneel at the altar rails to receive the Sacrament. Many times Andrewes stresses this, but never was this meeting so poignant as it is on Christmas day itself: "On this day they both meet, and never but on this." To illustrate his meaning he made this comparison:

*For Christ in the Sacrament is not altogether unlike Christ in the cratch. To the cratch we may well like the husk or outward symbols of it. Outwardly it seems little worth but it is rich of contents, as was the crib this day with Christ in it.*⁹

The little town where He was born, Bethlehem, is also significant in relation to the blessed Sacrament. Andrewes even suggests that Christ chose to be born in Bethlehem, as its name means *"the house of bread, . . . the house of good bread. . . . He is . . . Bethlehem, our house of Bread, He Himself is Bread"*, and therefore no one can ever want from Bread. More importantly Christ leads and feeds us, and conducts *"us from Bethlehem where this day we come first acquainted with Him, to the state of eternity . . . there to live and reign with Him for ever."* Thus Bethlehem *"gives us our introduction to Paradise."*¹⁰

For those who have strayed from their faith Andrewes urges that if we make our Communion at Christmas we will be richly rewarded as it is:

The means to re-establish our hearts with grace, *and to repair the decays of our spiritual strength; even* His own flesh, the Bread of life, *and* His own blood, the Cup of salvation. *[This] Bread [is] made of Himself, the true Granum frumenti, . . . [and the] Wine . . .* the true Vine.¹¹

If we ever forget this we have a reminder: "Bethlehem, *the house of bread,* would serve to put us in remembrance of it. Even of the breaking of bread, which the Church as this day ever has, and still uses as the Child-house feast." Furthermore when we come hither to Bethlehem we come to our home, the church, from which we never have to leave for "here is to be had the *true Bread of life that came down from Heaven, which is His flesh* this day born, [and] which *He gave for the life of the world."* Wherever "that Bread is, there is Bethlehem ever." Thus "the Church in this sense is very Bethlehem no less than the town itself", where we shall always be able to go for Bread. Hence the star is always over it as our Saviour is there.¹²

When we finish reading the seventeen sermons we are firstly aware of Andrewes' achievement of developing his various themes so as to give an overall unison to them. Secondly, we cannot help but feel Andrewes is urging us to hasten our footsteps to the stable illuminated by the heavenly stars, to prostrate ourselves before the Christ-Child and to let His humility and love so penetrate through our selfishness, and self absorption that we gladly vow to live unto Christ.

3

References

[1] Andrewes, Vol. 1, p. 3.
[2] *ibid*., pp. 73–4, 118, 121, 132.
[3] *ibid*., pp. 97–8, 140.
[4] *ibid*., p. 4.
[5] *ibid*., pp. 38, 157, 204.
[6] *ibid*., p. 22.
[7] *ibid*., p.80.
[8] *ibid*., p. 189,
[9] *ibid*., pp. 213–4.
[10] *ibid*., pp. 160, 168, 155.
[11] *ibid*., p. 169.
[12] *ibid*., pp. 162, 173.

NATIVITY SERMON No. 1
CHRISTMAS DAY 1605

Text: Hebrews 2:16

For verily He took not on Him the nature
of angels; but He took on Him the seed
of Abraham.

*Nusquam enim angelos apprehendit; sed semen
Abrahae apprehendit.*

In this sermon Andrewes suggests how extraordinarily wonderful it is that
God chose to take our nature, as vile as it is, in preference to that of the angels
who were *glorious, heavenly* and *immortal.* In so doing He gave to man a
dignity not even the angels possessed. Yet it was the angels, these *glorious*
and *heavenly* spirits who so enthusiastically announced His birth to man and
so enabled him through the simple shepherds and the scholarly magi to be
part of the nativity scene as they knelt in adoration.

In order to reveal the tremendous love God has for mankind, Andrewes
compares the base vileness and corruption of man with the holiness of the
angels.

''And even because this day He took not the angels' nature upon Him, but took
our nature in *the seed of Abraham,* therefore hold we this day as a high feast;
therefore meet we thus every year in a holy assembly, upon us a dignity which
upon the angels He bestowed not. That He, . . . was made Man, was not made an
angel; that is, [He] did more for [man] . . . than He did for the angels of Heaven.
. . .

[Yet] even this day, the day it was done, an angel was the first that came to bring
news of it to the shepherds; and he no sooner had delivered his message, but
presently there was with him a whole choir of angels, singing, and joying and
making melody, for this *good-will of God towards men. . . .*

No long process will need to lay before you how far inferior our nature is to that
of angels; it is a comparison without comparison. . . . This one thing may suffice
to show the odds; that our nature, that we, when we are at our very highest
perfection . . . we come near, or are therein like to, or as an angel. . . .

And what is *the seed of Abraham*? Flesh. And what is the very harvest of this
seed of flesh? what, but corruption, and rottenness, and worms? This is the
substance of our bodies.

They, glorious Spirits; we vile bodies . . . *conceived of unclean seed. . . .*

They, heavenly spirits, angels of heaven; that is, their place of abode is in
Heaven above. Ours is here below in the dust. . . .

5

They, immortal spirits; that is their durance. Our time is proclaimed in the prophet: flesh; *all flesh is grass, and the glory of it as the flower of the field; . . . the wind but blows and we are gone, . . . fading* sooner than the *flower of the grass. . . .*

This we are to them, if you lay us together, . . . and if you value us, *man is but a thing of nought;* there is our worth. . . . [Truly], there is no comparison; they are, incomparably, far better than the best of us. . . .

Here then comes the matter of admiration: notwithstanding these things stand thus, between the angels and *Abraham seed;* they, spirits, glorious, heavenly, immortal; — yet *took He not* them, . . . *but the seed of Abraham . . .* with their . . . earthly bodies of clay, bodies of mortality, corruption and death. . . . Men, and not angels; so it is: and that granted to us that denied to them. Granted to us, so base, that denied them so glorious. . . . They, every way, in every thing else, above and before us; in this beneath and behind us. And we, unworthy, wretched men that we are, above and before the angels, the cherubim, the seraphim, and all the principalities, and thrones, in this dignity. This being beyond the rules and reach of all reason is surely matter of astonishment. St. Chrysostom [says], this . . . casts me into an ecstasy, and makes me to imagine of our nature some great matter, I cannot well express what.''[1]

***

Andrewes continues this thought of amazement, that God could so love us, that He would abandon heaven to take our flesh, and by His nativity make us His *brethren by natural union.*

''. . . this He did, . . . rose out of His place, and came after us, and with hand and foot made after us, followed us with His feet; and seized on us with His hands. . . . 7ll these if we lay together, and when we have done, weigh them well, it is able to work with us. Surely it must demonstrate to us the care, the love, the affection, He had to us, we know no cause why; being but, as Abraham was, *dust;* and as Abraham's seed Jacob said, *less,* and not worthy of any one of these; no, not of the *meanest of His mercies.* Especially, when the same thing so graciously granted us was denied to no less persons than the angels, far more worthy than we. Sure He would not have done it for us, and not for them, if He had not esteemed of us, made more account of us than of them.

And yet, behold a far greater than all these; . . . *He took the seed,* that is, the nature of man. . . . To take the flesh and blood, He must needs take the seed, for from the seed the flesh and blood does proceed; which is nothing else but the blessed *apprehension* of our nature by this day's nativity. Whereby He and we become not only *one flesh,* as man and wife do by conjugal union; . . . which is it . . . that does consummate, and knit up all this point, and is the head of all. . . . One we are, He and we, and so we must be; one, as this day, so for ever.''[2]

***

If man was to be delivered from the bondage of sin, it was imperative for our Lord to become man, in order as sinless Man to die for our sins, so that man could turn *from sin to grace.* Thus as man He became our *deliverer* from the jaws of death, and thus He is also our Guide in our emancipation.

". . . God lays hold on them, and brings them back from error to truth, and from sin to grace, who have been from the beginning, or shall be to the end of the world. . . . All those, and all these, whereby men daily are laid hold in spirit, and taken from the by-paths of sins and error, and reduced in the right way; and so their persons recovered to God, and seized to His use. . . . They all have their beginning and their being from this day's *taking*, . . . our receiving His Spirit, for *His taking our flesh*. . . .

And the end why He thus took upon Him *the seed of Abraham* was because He took upon Him to deliver *the seed of Abraham*. Deliver them He could not except He destroyed *death, and the lord of death, the devil*. . . . He became mortal, died, destroyed death, delivered us; was Himself *apprehended* that we might be let go. . . .

Our Deliverer to rid us from him who has *power of death*, our Guide to Him who has *power of life*, to lead us even by the way of truth to the path of life by the stations of well-doing to the *mansions in His Father's House*. Seeing He has signified it is His pleasure not to let go our hands, but to hold us still till He has brought us, *that where He is, we may also be*. . . .

Man's case was more to be pitied than theirs [i.e. the angels] because man was tempted by another; . . . the angels had none. . . . but themselves. . . .

Again, of the angels, when some fell, other some stood, and so they all did not perish. But in the first man all men fell, and so every mother's child had died, and no flesh been saved, for all were in Adam; and so, in and with Adam, all had come to nought."[3]

***

In becoming man, God was also made under, and subject to the Law. Thus His circumcision manifested His keeping of the law.

"For being circumcised, He *became a debtor to keep the whole Law of God*; which bond we had broken, and forfeited, and incurred the curse annexed, and were ready to be apprehended and committed for it. That so, He keeping the Law might recover back the *chirographum contra nos, the handwriting what was against us*, and so set us free of the debt. . . . Without fail, two distinct benefits [here] are: 1. *Factus homo*, and 2. *Factus sub lege*; and so does St. Paul recount them. *Made man*, that is, *the seed of the woman*; and *made under the Law*, that is, *the seed of Abraham*. To little purpose He should have taken the one, if He had not also undertaken the other, and as *the seed of Abraham* entered bond for us, and taken our death upon Him. . . .

For, *for his sake were all nations blessed*. And Christ, though He took *the seed of woman*, yet does not benefit any but *the seed of Abraham*, even those who follow the steps of his faith."[4]

If we are the seed of Abraham, redeemed by Christ, we must also imitate the works of Abraham.

"As Christ Himself . . . [said], *If you be Abraham's sons, then must you do the works of Abraham*, which the Apostle well calls, the *steps* or impressions of

7

Abraham's faith; or we may call them the fruits of this seed here. . . . It brought forth a *Benedictus* and a *Magnificat*, from the true seed of Abraham. . . .

[Moreover,] we are to understand this, *that to whom much is given, of them will much be required*; and as St. Gregory Wells says, *As the gifts grow, so grow the accounts too*; therefore, that by this new dignity befallen us, *there is a certain necessity laid upon us*, says St. Augustine to become in some measure suitable unto it; in that we are one — one flesh and one blood, with the Son of God. . . . For if we do indeed think our nature is ennobled by this so high a conjunction, we shall henceforth hold ourselves more dear, and at a higher rate, than to prostitute ourselves to sin, for every base, trifling, and transitory pleasure. . . .

St. Paul tells us further, that if we henceforth *walk like men*, like even carnal or natural men, it is a fault in us. Something must appear in us more than in ordinary men, who are vouchsafed so extraordinary a favour. Something more than common would come from us, if it but for this day's sake.''[5]

***

On the feast of the Nativity we can be united with Him in a very special way, through the blessed Sacrament. It is only on this feast that the cradle and altar are one. He took our flesh, so that we in receiving His, inherit His divinity.

''For *the Word* He is, and in the word He is received by us. But that is not the proper of this day, unless there be another joined unto it. This day *Verbum caro factum est*. But specially in His flesh as this day gives it, as this day would have us. Now *the bread which we break, is it not the partaking of the body, of the flesh, of Jesus Christ?* It is surely, and by it and by nothing more are we made partakers of this blessed union. . . . Because He has so done, taken ours of us, we also ensuing His steps will participate with Him and with His flesh which He has taken of us. It is most kindly to take part with Him in that which He took part in with us, and that, to no other end, but that He might make the receiving of it by us a means whereby He might *dwell in us, and we in Him*. He taking our flesh, and we receiving His Spirit; by His flesh which He took of us receiving His Spirit which He imparts to us; that, as He by ours became *consors humanae naturae*, so we by His might become *consortes Divinae naturae*, partakers of the Divine nature. [Truly], it is the most straight and perfect *taking hold* that is. No union so knits as it. Not consanguinity; brethren fall out. Not marriage; man and wife are severed. But that which is nourished, and the nourishment wherewith — they never are, never can be severed, but remain one for ever. With this act then of mutual *taking*, taking of His flesh as He has taken ours, let us seal our duty to Him this day, for taking not angels, but *the seed of Abraham*.''[6]

References

[1] Andrewes, Vol. I, pp. 1, 3–6.
[2] *ibid.*, pp. 8–9.
[3] *ibid.*, pp. 9–12.
[4] *ibid.*, pp. 12–3.
[5] *ibid.*, pp.14–6.
[6] *ibid.*, pp. 16–7.

NATIVITY SERMON No. 2
CHRISTMAS DAY 1606

Text: Isaiah 9:6

For unto us a Child is born, unto us a
Son is given, and the government shall
be upon His Shoulder; and His name shall
be called Wonderful, Counsellor, the Mighty
God, the Everlasting Father, the Prince of
Peace.

Parvulus enim natus est nobis, et Filius datus
est nobis, et factus est principatus super
Humerum ejus: et vocabitur nomen ejus,
Admirabilis, Consiliarius, Deus, fortis,
Pater futuri saeculi, Princeps Pacis.

Throughout this sermon Andrewes emphasizes our rescue from the slavery of sin. He rejoices that Christ's coming was foretold in the days of Ahaz when the Israelites were captives. Thus the promise of a Messiah became identified with release from captivity for the Jews, while for Christians, Isaiah's prophecy means a *far greater deliverance*, a deliverance from sin.

''There is no one thing so great to our faith, as that we find the things we believe so plainly foretold so many years before. . . . But for . . . six hundred years before He is born, to cause prophecies, plain direct prophecies to be written of Him, that passes all conceit; cannot be imagined, how possibly it may be, but by God alone. . . .

This prophecy is of a certain Child. And if we ask of this place, as the Eunuch did of another in this prophet, *Of whom speaks the Prophet this?* we must make the answer that there Philip does, *of Christ*; and *the testimony of Jesus is the spirit of this prophecy. . . .*

But how came Isaiah to speak of Christ to Ahaz? . . . Ahaz was then in very great distress; he had lost in one day eighty thousand of his people, and two hundred thousand of them more, carried away captives. . . .

But what is this to Ahaz's case? He looked for another message from him, how to escape his enemies. A cold comfort might he think it to be preached to of Emmanuel. Indeed, he so thought it; and therefore he gave over Isaiah, and betook him to Shebna, who wished him to seek to the King of Ashur for help, and let Emmanuel go. Yet for all that, even then to speak of Christ, being looked into, it is neither imperative, nor out of season. With all the prophets it is usual, in the calamities of this people, to have recourse still to the fundamental promise of the

Messiah. For that, till He were come, they might be sure they could not be rooted out; but must be preserved, if it were but for this Child's sake, till He was born. . . . The prophets [argued], He will not deny you this favour, for He will grant a far greater than this, even His own Son, and by Him a far greater deliverance; and if He can deliver you from the devouring fire of hell, much more from them; and if give you peace with God, much more with them. So teaching those who will learn, the only right way to compass their own safety is by making sure work of *Emmanuel, God with us.* To the true regard of Whom God has annexed the *promises as well of this, as of the other life.*"[1]

***

The name *Emmanuel* means that both *Child* and *Son* are duly emphasized; both have their part in the nativity scene, because both are needed in God's plan of redemption.

" We have two words, *Child* and *Son*; neither waste . . . Weigh the words: *Child* is not said but *in humanis, among men. Son* may be *in divinis, from heaven.* . . .

Isaiah promised the sign we should have, should be from . . . both *a Child* from *beneath*, and *a Son* from *above.* . . .

All along His life you will see these two. At His birth, a cratch for the Child, a star for the Son; a company of shepherds viewing the Child, a choir of angels celebrating the Son. In His life, hungry Himself, to show the nature of the Child; yet feeding five thousand to show the power of the Son. At His death, dying on the cross as the Son of Adam; at the same time disposing of Paradise, as the *Son of God.*"[2]

***

Why were both necessary? A Child He had to be because of our sins, and a *Son* to be the Sacrifice needed for them. It is impossible to have one without the other.

". . . why both these? . . . Our nature had sinned, that therefore ought to suffer; the reason, why a Child. But [what] our nature should, our nature could not bear; not the weight of God's wrath due to our sin: but the Son could. . . . Therefore, either alone would not serve; they must be joined, Child and Son. But that He was a Child, He could not have suffered. But that he was a Son, He had sunk in His suffering, and not gone through with it. God had no shoulders; man had, but too weak to sustain such a weight. Therefore, that He might be liable, He was a Child, that He might be able He was the Son; that He might be both, He was both.

This, why God. But why this Person, the Son? Behold, *Adam would* have *become one of us* — the fault; behold, one of Us will become Adam, is the satisfaction. . . . Flesh would have been the Word, as wise as the Word — the cause of our ruin; meet then the *Word become flesh*, that so our ruin repaired. . . .

The *Child* and the *Son*; these two make but one Person clearly; for both these have but one name, . . . and both these have one pair of shoulders. Therefore,

10

though two natures, yet but one Person in both. A meet person to make a Mediator of God and man, . . . A meet person to cease hostility, as having taken pledges of both heaven and earth, the chief nature in Heaven, and the chief on earth; to set forward commerce between heaven and earth by Jacob's ladder, *one end touching earth, the other reaching to heaven*; to incorporate either to other, Himself by His birth being become the *Son of Man*, by our new birth giving us a capacity to become the *sons of God.*''[3]

***

As well as a *Child* and a *Son,* He is also a *Prince* with His own principality which He bears on His strong shoulders for *the iniquities of us all,* thus making His government distinct from other rulers. It is also different in that His sovereignty is only recognized by those who acknowledge Christ as their ruler.

"Yet a Prince He is, and so He styled; *born* and *given* to establish a *government.* . . . He brings a government with Him, they who be His must live in subjection under a government; else neither in Child nor Son, in birth nor gift, have they any interest.

And this *government* is by name a principality, wherein neither the popular confusion of many, nor the factious ambition of a few, bear all the sway, but where One is sovereign. Such is the government of heaven, such is Christ's government. . . .

Upon His shoulders . . . He, and none but He, upon His own shoulders, and none but His own, bare He all. He will bear so great things; bear their weaknesses as the lost sheep, bear their sins as the scape-goat."[4]

***

His very name, *Jesus Christ*, being *half Hebrew, half Greek* manifests His sovereignty over all. However once again it is only effective for those who *believe* in Him as their Lord.

"[His sovereignty] is of . . . a larger extent. The angel so interpreted it this day to the shepherds, *joy that shall be to all people.* Not the people of the Jews, or the people of the Gentiles, but simply *to all people.* His name is Jesus Christ, half Hebrew, half Greek; Jesus, Hebrew, Christ, Greek; so sorted of purpose to show Jews and Greeks have equal interest in Him. . . .

But yet, it is inclusive of none but those who include themselves, *who believe*, and therefore say *to us He is born, to us He is given.*''[5]

***

We have gained many benefits from such a prophecy, notably Christ's birth, when He took our very nature. Consequently we can share in His *childhood* and *sonship.*

"By His very birth there grows to us an interest in Him, thereby partaker of our nature, our flesh and our blood. That which is *de nobis*, He took of us, is ours; flesh and blood is our own, and to that is our own we have good right.

His humanity is clearly ours; good right to that. But no right to His deity. . . . So that, what by participation of our nature, what by good conveyance, both are ours. Whether a Child, He is ours, or whether a Son, He is ours. We gave Him the one; His Father gave us the other. So both ours; and He ours, so far as both these can make Him. [Thus] . . . we might have strong consolation, and ride as it were a double anchor.

I want . . . to tell of the benefit which the Prophet calls the *harvest* . . . of His Nativity. . . . If the tree be ours, the fruit is; if He be ours, His birth is ours; His life is ours; His death is ours, His satisfaction, His merit, all He did, all He suffered, is ours. . . . All that the Father has is His, He is Heir of all; then, all that is ours too.''[6]

***

As God has given all to us, in great humility and with overflowing love, what we can give Him in return? Andrewes suggests that the first priority is to give Him thanks, followed by our confidence in, our reverence for, and our obedience to Him as the Child, Son and Prince respectively. In all of these we are to cherish Him.

"And now, shall we bring forth nothing for Him who was thus born? . . . Yes, *thanks to the Father for His great bounty in giving*. Sure, so good a giving, so perfect a gift, there never came down *from the Father of lights*. And to the Son, for being willing so to be born, and so to be burdened as He was. For Him to condescend to be born, as children are born, to become a child: great humility; great *that the Word not be able to speak a word, He who thunders in heaven cry in a cradle, He who is so great and so high should become so little a child*, and so low as a manger. Not to *abhor the Virgin's womb*, not to abhor the beasts' manger, not to disdain to be fed with *butter and honey*; all great humility. . . . He bare for us more than that He was born for; for greater is *mors crucis* than *nativitas praesepis*; worse to drink vinegar and gall, than to eat butter and honey; worse to endure an infamous death, than to be content with an inglorious birth.

Let us therefore sing to the Father, with Zacharias' *Benedictus*, and to the Son, with the Blessed Virgin's *Magnificat*, and with the angels, *Gloria in excelsis* to the Prince with His *government on His shoulders*.

Nothing but thanks? Yes, by way of duty too, to render unto the Child, confidence; to the Son reverence; to the Prince obedience; . . . and . . . then cherish Him.''[7]

***

By His Incarnation, our Lord particularly demonstrated four characteristics: humility, willingness to be a ransom, giving Himself in the Sacrament, and promising a final reward.

"He is given to us . . . . *for an example* to follow. . . . It is [what] the angel set up for a sign and sample, upon this very day. . . . As faith to His conception, . . . so humility to His birth. . . . *It has pleased Him to do greater things for us in this estate* than ever He did in the high degree of His majesty; as we know the work of redemption passes that of creation by much.

He is given to us *for a price*. A price either of ransom, to bring us out *de loco caliginoso*; or a price of purchase of that, where without it we have no interest [in] the kingdom of heaven. . . . He gave us as a thing of greatest price to offer for what needs a great price, our sins, so many in number, and so foul in quality. . . .

He is given to us as Himself says as *the living bread from heaven* which Bread is His *flesh* born this day, and after *given for the life of the world*. For look how we do give back that He gave us, even so does He give back to us that which we gave Him, that which He had of us. This He gave for us in Sacrifice, and this He gives us in the Sacrament that the Sacrifice may by the Sacrament be truly applied to us. And let me commend this to you; He never bade, *accipite*, plainly *take* but in this only; and that, because the effect of this day's union is no ways more lively represented, no way more effectually wrought, than by this use.

And lastly, He is given to us *in praemium*; not now to be seen, only in hope, but hereafter by His blessed fruition to be our final reward when *where He is we shall be*, and what He is we shall be; in the same place, and in the same state of glory, joy, and bliss, to endure for evermore."[8]

***

Andrewes concludes bidding us to follow St. Augustine's advice.

"*Let us follow Him for our pattern, offer Him for our price, receive Him for our sacramental food, and wait for Him as our endless and exceeding great reward.*"[9]

References

[1] Andrewes, Vol. I, pp. 18–20.
[2] *ibid*., pp. 21–2.
[3] *ibid*., pp. 22–3.
[4] *ibid*., pp. 24, 26.
[5] *ibid*., p. 27.
[6] *ibid*., p. 28.
[7] *ibid*., pp.28–9.
[8] *ibid*., pp. 30–1.
[9] *ibid*., p. 31.

NATIVITY SERMON No. 3
CHRISTMAS DAY 1607

Text: 1 Timothy 3:16.

And without controversy great is the
mystery of godliness: God was manifest
in the flesh, justified in the Spirit, seen
of angels, preached unto the Gentiles,
believed on in the world, received up
into glory.

Et manifeste magnum est pietatis sacramentum,
quod manifestatum est in carne, justificatum
est in Spiritu, apparuit angelis, praedicatum
est Gentibus, creditum est in mundo, assumptum
est in gloria.

Christmas is the feast of the *great mystery*. Andrewes develops the significance of *mystery* by comparing it and its various characteristics with the
worldly concept of knowledge. The world has always had its various mysteries, so why should we baulk at spiritual mysteries? Although many mysteries were shrouded in controversy, Andrewes pleads that there should be
none in this *great mystery*. If *we walk in the ways of peace* God will reveal all
to us.

"In that it is a great mystery, it makes the feast great. In that it is a mystery of
godliness, it should make it likewise a feast of godliness, . . . and no more
controversy. . . .

The manifestation of God in the flesh the Evangelists set down by way of a
history; the Apostle [i.e. Paul] goes further, and finds a deep mystery in it, and for a
mystery commends it unto us. . . .

A mystery it is, presented to us in that term by the Apostle to stir up our
attention. *All men even by nature love to be knowing. . . .*

And even to this day . . . does the *tree of knowledge* still work in the sons of
Eve; we still reckon the attaining of knowledge a thing to be desired, and be it good
or evil, we love to be knowing, all the sort of us. Knowing, but what? Not such
things as every one knows that goes by the way, vulgar and trivial; tush, those are
nothing. . . . Mysteries that are the secrets of divinity; such as few besides are
admitted to; [yet] those be the things we desire to know. We see it in the Beth-
shemites, they longed to be prying into the ark of God. . . . We see it in the people
of God too, they pressed too near the mount. . . . It is because it is held a point of a

14

deep wit to search out secrets, as in Joseph. . . . All desire to be in credit. The mention of mysteries will make us stand attentive. . . .

The world has her mysteries in all arts and trades . . . the . . . *mysterium iniquitatis,* and it were somewhat hard that there should not be *mysterium pietatis,* to encounter and to match it, that *Babylon* should be allowed the name of *mystery* and Sion not. . . .

It is not only a *mystery of godliness,* but a *great* one, . . . a *great one without controversy.* For even of those mysteries that are great, all are not great alike. Many great there are, yet is not the greatness of all generally acknowledged *in confesso.* Doubts are made, questions arise about them; all are not *manifesto magna.* We see in our days how men languish about some points, which they would have thought to be great; and great controversies there be, and great books of controversies about them. Well, howsover it is with other, it is not so with this. . . . The manifesting of God in the flesh is a mystery manifestly great. . . . Though questions grow about the greatness of others, . . . I hope there will be no more question, or controversy of our account, and our great account of it, than there is of the mystery itself, and the greatness of it. . . .

Now yet, blessed be God Who, among [several] other mysteries about which there are so many mists and clouds of controversies raised in all ages, and even in this of ours, has yet left us some clear and without controversy; manifest and yet great; and again, great and yet manifest. So great as no exception to be taken; so manifest as no question to be made about them. . . .

For a false conceit is crept into the minds of men, to think points of religion that be manifest to be certain petty points scarce worth the hearing. . . . Those that are necessary He has made plain: those that [are] not plain, not necessary. What better proof than this here hold?

This here a mystery, a great one — religion has no greater – yet manifest, and *in confesso,* with all Christians. Zacharias' prophecy and promise touching Christ, wherewith He concluded his *Benedictus,* . . . will not deceive us for this mystery; He came *to guide our feet into the way of peace.* A way of peace then will be whereof all parts will agree, even in the midst of a world of controversies. That there need not such ado in complaining, if men did not delight rather to be treading mazes than to walk in the ways of peace. For even still such a way there is, which lies fair enough and would lead us sure enough to salvation; if leaving those other rough labrinyths we would but *be shod with the preparation of the Gospel of peace.* . . .

Those things . . . would God reveal unto us. That is He makes no controversy but controversies would cease, if conscience were made of the practice of [what] is out of controversy. And I would to God it were so, . . . [just as] with [St. Paul] . . . it was so. He showed plainly what reckoning he made of this plain mystery, in that having been *ravished in spirit up to the third heavens, and there heard wonderful high mysteries, past man's utterance*; yet reckoned he all those nothing, in comparison of this plain mystery here.''[1]

***

15

The *great mystery* is God Himself and His character. Yet He chose to manifest Himself in the flesh, not only in the *cratch* but *on the cross*. In His choosing of *flesh*, it was not the beautiful, but the *disgraceful*, He embraced. Unlike our human instinct when we do something regarded as shameful we want to hide, Christ on the cross had to face the gaze of many an onlooker, and take the insults sneered at Him, not because he had done something shameful, but because something shameful was being done to him.

"*God is manifested in the flesh*. Being one of the mysteries of godliness, it cannot be but God must be a . . . chief part of it. And God being a part makes it great. . . . [Many] things, many *invisible things of God* had been formerly made manifest; His eternal power, wisdom, providence, in and since the creation. They be no mysteries, but this is; that not the things of God, but God's own self; not *the beams of His brightness*, but the very character of His substance, the very Nature and Person of God. This is a great mystery.

Of God, the prophet Isaiah says, God is of Himself a mystery, and hidden; and [what] is strange, hidden with light which will make any eyes past looking on Him. But a hidden God our nature did not endure. . . .

Not only manifest at all; that is great; but manifest in the flesh; that is greater . . . We cannot choose but hold this mystery for great, and say with St. Augustine, *God; what more glorious? flesh; what more base? Then, God in the flesh; what more marvellous?* . . . In what flesh? . . . in the pride and beauty of our nature? No; but in the most disgraceful estate of it that might be. And how manifested? *Ad gloriam*, for *His credit or glory* No; but *ad ignominiam, to His great contempt and shame*. . . .

To-day, in the flesh of a poor babe crying in the cratch, *in medio animalium* ; after, in the rent and torn flesh of a condemned person hanging on the cross, *in medio latronum* , in the midst of other manner persons than Moses and Elijah; that men even hid their faces at Him, not for the brightness of His glory, but for sorrow and shame. Call you this manifesting? . . . Well does the Apostle call it the *veil of flesh*, as whereby He was rather obscured than any way set forth; yes eclipsed in all the darkest points of it. [Truly] the condition of the flesh was more than the flesh itself, and the manner of the manifestation far more than the manifestation itself was. Both still make the mystery greater and greater. . . .

And yet to go further; I say that this word *manifested* . . . does greatly . . . enlarge the mystery yet still. . . . More for God to be manifested, than to be in the flesh. It is well known, when a great high person does fall into low estate, he cares not so much for being so, as for appearing such. . . . More it is for him to be made known, than to be what he is. . . . And why would Nicodemus come to Christ . . . but by candlelight, but that to be seen manifestly to come, was with him a far greater matter than to come. By all which it appears, that in the case of abasement to seem is more than to be. . . . [Yet] He abhorred not to become flesh. He abhorred not to have it manifestly known. It was not done, this, in a corner, in an out-corner of Galilee; but in the city of David. His poor clouts manifested by a star; His shameful death published by a great eclipse; yes that it might be manifest indeed . . . He would have it preached over all the world."[2]

Yet mystery is nothing without love, as St. Paul reminds us. God Himself showed this when this great mystery came to pass through His love for mankind.

"But when we have done and said all that ever we can, if we had all mysteries and no love, [St. Paul] tells us it is nothing. We can have no mystery except love be manifest. . . . Several times does the Apostle tell us, . . . At the opening of this mystery there appeared the grace of God, and the love of God towards mankind, *as manifest as God was in the flesh, so manifest was His love unto flesh*. And then, because great love a great mystery, *Dilexit* goes never alone, but with *sic*; so Christ: *ecce quantum charitatem*; so St. John. Sure, how great and apparent humility, so great and apparent love. And His humility was too apparent. So we have *God manifested in the flesh, Deus charitas*; for if ever He were love or showed it in this He was it, and showed it both. God who is *love* was *manifested in the flesh.*"[3]

In case there was confusion between *mystery* and *ceremony*, especially in *the fulfilling of all prophecies*, Andrewes shows there is a difference between the two.

"I know it were a thing very easy for a speculative Divine to lead you along, and let you see that this mystery is the substance of all the ceremonies. and the fullfilling of all prophecies; that all Moses' veils, and all the prophets' visions, are recapitulated in it. But it is a point of speculation . . ..

There is this difference between a ceremony and a mystery. A ceremony represents and signifies, but works nothing; a mystery does both. Besides that it signifies, it has his operation; and work it does, else mystery is it none. You may see it by the mystery of iniquity; that does *operari, was at work* in the Apostles' time; and it is no way to be admitted, but that *the mystery of godliness* should have like operative force."[4]

We have to respond to that manifestation in a way fitting for the common flesh we now share with God. In our daily living it is important for us to reveal the fruits of this *great mystery*. We are initiated into such mysteries and grow *into the fellowship of this and what mysteries soever*, including the Eucharist. This mystery will last until His second *appearing* when *the fullness of this mystery* will be manifested. Meanwhile *our godliness* must not only be *mystical* but also loving. St. John informs us *by this we know, ourselves*, while Our Lord says *by this shall all men know* that we belong to Him.

"First within, after the manner of a mystery, by entering into ourselves, and saying with St. Peter, *Seeing then God has dealt with us, what manner of person ought we to be, in all holy conversation and godliness?* How ought we to esteem

Him who so esteemed us? How to esteem ourselves whom He hath so esteemed? How without soil or spot to keep that flesh wherein God has *manifested* Himself, that nothing comes from it but such as may become that flesh which is now all one with the flesh of the Son of God.

Provided that it be not all within; for we deal not with a mystery alone, but with a manifestation too. That therefore our godliness be not only mystical but manifest, as God was. As the mystery, so the godliness of it; *great* and conspicious, both. For that is the complaint, that in our godliness, nowadays, we go very mystically to work indeed; we keep it under a veil, and nothing manifest but *opera carnis*, which makes St. James cry, *ostende mihi, show it me*, and St. Paul tells us, that the life of Jesus must not only be had in our spirit, but manifest in our flesh. For godliness is not only faith . . . but it is love too. . . . And if faith work by love, the mystery will be so manifest in us, as we shall need no prospective glasses, . . . to make it visible; all men shall take notice of it.

And yet remains there one point, . . . [what] the Apostle calls initiating; whereby we grow into the fellowship of this and what mysteries soever. For this we are to understand that mysteries go not all by hearing; no, they be dispensed also; and men are to esteem of us, says he; not only as of the unfolders, but as of *the stewards*, or dispensers *of the mysteries of God*.''5

***

The great *mystery of godliness* was the blessed Sacrament which on this day is bound with the Babe in the manger.

''I understand the mystery of godliness . . . [to be] the Sacrament; . . . whereby the Church offers to initiate us into the fellowship of this day's mystery. Nothing sorts better than these two mysteries one with the other; the dispensation of a mystery with the mystery of dispensation. . . . There is in it even by the very institution both a manifestation, and that visibly, to set before us this flesh; and a mystical communication to . . . make us partakers of it. For the elements; what can be more properly fit to represent unto us the union with our nature, than things that do unite themselves to our nature? And if we be to dispense the mysteries in due season, what season more due than that His flesh and Blood be set before us that time that He was *manifested in flesh and blood* for us? . . .

You look to hear of a consummation of it too; and consummate it will be, but not yet. . . . When He who was this day *manifested in the flesh*, will manifest to the flesh the fullness of this mystery, His eternity, glory, and bliss. . . . To the consummation of which great mystery, He . . . [brings] us all.''6

References

1 Andrewes, Vol. I, pp. 32–6.
2 *ibid*., pp. 36–40.
3 *ibid*., p. 40.
4 *ibid*., p. 41.
5 *ibid*, pp. 42–3.
6 *ibid*., pp. 43–4.

NATIVITY SERMON No. 4
CHRISTMAS DAY 1609

Text: Galatians 4:4-5.

But when the fullness of time was come,
God sent forth His Son, made of a woman,
made under the Law,
To redeem them who were under the Law,
that we might receive the adoption of sons.

At ubi venit plenitudo temporis, misit
Deus Filium suum factum ex muliere, factum sub Lege,
Ut eos, qui sub lege erant, redimeret, ut
adoptionem filiorum reciperemus.

Andrewes describes Christmas as the time when we are honoured by the *yearly representation of the fullness of time with its Christa missa,* the sending of Christ. In this sermon the predominating theme is thus *fullness*: in time; from Christ's benefits and blessings; from receiving the blessed Sacrament; and in our overall receiving. All of these should be recognized in our heartfelt thankfulness.

"When the *fullness of time* came, *God sent His Son.* . . . This day therefore, . . . [is] a yearly representation of *the fullness of time.* . . .

So that *Christa missa*, is the sending of Christ. . . . What time so seasonable to entreat of it as this? . . . on the yearly return and memorial of it? . . .

We shall see as it is of fullness so a kind of fullness there is in it, every word more full than the other; every word a step in it whereby it rises still higher, till by seven several degrees it comes to the top and so the measure is full. 1. *God sent*; 2. *sent His Son;* 3. *His Son made;* 4. And that twice made; *made of a woman*; 5. *Made under the Law*; . . . 6. Redemption, . . . from the state of persons cast and condemned under the Law; . . . [and] 7. Translation into the state of adopted children of God.

And all this, for some persons, and some purpose; the persons . . . *we;* the purpose, that *we might receive.* He might redeem, and we might receive; that is, He pays for it, and we reap the benefit. A double benefit of Redemption first, from the state of persons cast and condemned under the Law, . . . and then, translation into the state of adopted children of God. . . .

And our fullness in [these]. . . . That when we were strangers from the adoption, and not that only, but lay under the Law, as men whom sentence has passed on; from this latter we are redeemed, *He under the Law*, that we from under the Law, that being so redeemed we might further *receive the adoption of children*, and as

He the *Son of man*, so we might be made the *sons of God*, which two are as much as we can wish. And this is our fullness.

And to these I shall crave leave to add another fullness. . . . That as it is the time when we from God receive the fullness of His bounty, so it might be the time also when He from us may likewise receive the fullness . . . of our thankfulness, that it may be *downward and upward, from Him to us and from us to Him again;* and so both ways *the fullness of time.*"[1]

***

Andrewes asked, when was *the fullness of time*? The answer: when the world was of age to receive Him, that is, after Moses and the prophets had helped to prepare for His coming.

"He filled up certain times of the year under Moses and the prophets; . . . but for all them, the measure was not yet full; filled perhaps to a certain degree, but not full to the brim; . . . till God sent [Him of whom] a more full could not be sent. . . .

And well might that be called *the fullness of time*. For when He was sent into the world, *in Whom the fullness of the Godhead dwelt bodily*; in Whom *the Spirit was not by measure*; in Whom was *the fullness of grace and truth; of Whose fullness we all receive*; . . .

And well also might it be called *the fullness of time* in another regard. For till then all was but in promise, in shadows and figures and prophecies only, . . . but when the performance of those promises, . . . the fulfilling . . . of all those prophecies came, then came *the fullness of time*, truly so called. . . .

And well might it be called *the fullness of time* in a third respect. For then the heir, that is, the world, was come to his full age; and so that the fittest time for Him to be sent. For to that compares the Apostle their estate then; that the former times under Moses and the prophets were as the non-age of the world. . . . Their estate then, as of children in their minority, little differing from servants. For all this while, *the fullness of time* was not yet come. But a time there was, as for man, so for mankind to come to his full years; that time came with Christ's coming, and Christ's coming with it, and never till then was *the fullness of time.*"[2]

***

God in sending His Son to be born of a woman and subject to the Law was done for sheer love of us. There was no other motive. In doing so it was *the fullest thing He had*. Being born of a woman meant he took our nature upon Him, and identified Himself with it, while under the Law He was circumcised, condemned to His death for the sins of the world.

"*Misit Deus, God sent*. That stands first, . . . and so we would reckon of it, if we knew the Sender, and Who He is; the Majesty of His presence how great it is, and how glorious, how far surpassing all we can see on earth. . . .

God . . . sent His Son. . . . Now greater there is not than *His Son*, . . . *in Whom the fullness of the Godhead dwelt*; in sending Him He sent the greatest, the best, the fullest thing He had. . . .

He sent Him not for need; but for mere love to us, and nothing else. There was no absolute necessity that He should have sent Him. He might have done what He intended by the means and ministry of some besides. God could have enabled a creature; a creature enabled by God, and the power of His might, could soon have trod down Satan under our feet. But if it had been any other He had sent, His love and regard to us had not showed so full. . . . That therefore it might be full, and so appear to us for full, . . . *Misit Deus Filium suum*. . . .

God . . . sent Him and sent Him *made*. . . . To make Him anything is to mar Him, be it what it will be . . . . To have made Him a body and taken it upon Him for a time till He had performed His embassage, and then laid it off again, that had been much; but so to be made as once made and ever made; so to take it as never lay it off more, but continue so still, *it is to become His very nature*; so to be made is to make the union full. And to make the union with us full, He was content not to be sent alone but to be made. . . . Our manhood becoming His nature, no less than the Godhead itself. This is *Filium factum* indeed.

Made . . . of a woman. . . . For . . . if the Son of God must be made a creature, it were meet He should be made the best creature of all. . . .

And this He was *made*, . . . *made of a woman, did not abhor the Virgin's womb*, as we sing daily to the high praise of the fullness of His humility, to which His love brought Him for our sakes. For whatsoever else He had been *made*, it would have done us no good. In this then was *the fullness* of His love, as before of His Father's — that He would be made, and was made, not what was fittest for Him, but what was best for us; not what was most for His glory, but what was most for our benefit. . . .

And so have we here now in one both . . . His natures. *God sent His Son*, there His divine; *made of a woman*, here His human nature. . . . This now is full for the union with our nature to be *made of a woman*. . . .

He be also *made under the Law* . . . For if one be in debt and danger of the law, to have a brother of the same blood, made of the same woman, both as we say lying in one belly, will little avail him, except he will also come *under the law*, that is, become his surety and undertake for him. . . .

His second making *made under the law*; under which if He had not been made, we had been marred; even quite undone for ever, if this had not been done for us too. Therefore He became bound for us also, entered bond anew, took on Him not only our nature but our debt, . . .

And when did He this? When He [was] made under the Law. . . . At His circumcision then He entered bond anew with us; and in sign that so He did, He shed then a few drops of His blood, . . . *as a pledge or earnest* that *when the fullness of time came, He would be ready to shed all the rest*; as He did; . . . *made under the Law* . . . [and] the debt of a capital law is death. And under that, under death He went, and that the worst death law had to inflict, *even the death of the cross*, the most bitter, reproachful, cursed death of the cross. . . . Well, this He did undertake for us at His circumcision, and therefore then and not till then He had His name given Him, the name of Jesus, a Saviour. For then took He on Him the obligation to save us. And look, what then at His circumcision He undertook, at His Passion He paid even to the full; and having paid it, *cancelled the sentence of the Law*, that till then was of record and stood in full force against us.

However, all this was but one part of the Law; but He was *under the whole law*; and that not by His death only, but by His life too. The one half of the law . . . satisfied it by the innocency of His life, without breaking so much as one jot or tittle of the Law. . . . The other half of the Law which is the penalty, He . . . satisfied it by suffering a wrongful death, no way deserved, or due by Him. . . .

These two then, . . . *made of a woman* . . . [and] *made under the Law*, . . . [are] both very requisite. Therefore [both] . . . have . . . a . . . feast, . . . six days [apart]."3

***

The purpose of His sending, and His Sonship, was simply for us, in order that we may reach the last steps in *fullness* of life through redemption and adoption. This is all we could ever wish for.

"For if we come now to ask, for whom is all this ado, this sending, this making, over and over again? It is for us, . . . that we might from this fullness receive the full of our wish. For in these two . . . redemption and adoption; to be redeemed and to be adopted are the full of all we can wish ourselves. . . .

Our desire can extend itself no further than to be rid of all evil, and to attain all that good is. By these two, being redeemed and being adopted, we are made partakers of them both. *To be redeemed from under the Law*, is to be quit of all evil. *To receive the adoption of children*, is to be stated in all that is good. For all evil is in being *under the Law* from whence we are redeemed, and all good in being invested in the heavenly inheritance whereunto we are adopted. Thus stood the case with us, *aliens we were from God, His covenant, and His kingdom*. More than that, prisoners we were, fast laid up under the Law. From this latter we are freed; of the former we are seized; and what would we more?

Only this . . . *that we by adoption might be made the sons of God*." 4

***

Andrewes then explains what is meant by *redemption* and *adoption*.

"Redeeming . . . is a second buying, or buying back of a thing before aliened or sold. . . . Our nature aliened in Adam, . . . [and] daily we ourselves alien them for some trifling pleasure or profit, matters not much more worth. And when we have thus passed ourselves away, by this *selling ourselves under sin*, the Law seized on us, . . . the sentence passed on us, and we waiting but for execution. . . . Sold we were, and bought we must be; a price must be laid down for us. . . . But with a high price He purchased us; it cost Him dear to bring it about. . . . *His precious Blood was the price we stood Him in*. Which He paid, when *He gave His life a ransom for many*. . . . For till now, we were not our own, we were not ourselves; but now we are. Till this it was the old year still with us, but with the new year comes our new estate.

. . . He leaves . . . us not here; but to make the measure complete, yes even to flow over, He gives us not over when He had rid us out of this wretched estate, till He has brought us to an estate as good as Himself is in . . . . He now goes one step further, which is the highest and farthest step of all. . . . From the estate of prisoners condemned [to] be translated into the estate of children adopted. . . . We made the sons of God, as He the Son of man; we made partakers of His divine, as He of our human nature. . . . For who has ever heard of a condemned man adopted afterward . . .? For this adoption is the fullness of our option; we cannot extend — we our wish, or He — His love and goodness any farther. For what can we ask, or He give more, seeing in giving this He gives all He is worth?''[5]

***

Christmas is a time of the *fullness* of joy and thanksgiving because we celebrate what God has done for us by His many benefits in us through the coming of the Christ-Child.

''And a time of fullness it will be, . . . *with the joy*, says Isaiah a verse or two before *Puer natus est nobis, unto us a Child is born, that men rejoice in the harvest;* . . . that this outward joy eat not up, evacuate not our spiritual joy proper to the feast; that we have in mind in the midst of our mirth the cause of it, Christ's sending, and the benefits that come thereby. And it still be a good sign unto us if we can this rejoice, if this our joy can be full, if we can make a spiritual blessing the object of our mirth. . . .

And after our . . . fullness of joy, our fullness of thanks . . is to ensue. . . . Our minds first, and then our mouths, to be filled with blessing, and praise, and thanks to Him, Who has made our times not to fall into those empty ages of the world, but to fall within this *fullness of time.* . . .

To render our thanks then, and to remember to do it fully, to forget none; to Him who was sent, and to Him who *sent*; *sent His Son* in this, *the Spirit of His Son.*''[6]

***

Andrewes concludes his sermon on *fullness* by his declaration that this *fullness* is completed on this day with the celebrating of the Eucharist, and by us receiving His very Body and Blood.

''. . . to consecrate this first day of this fullness of time even with our service to Him at the full; which is then at the full when no part is missing, when all our duties of preaching, and praying, of hymns, of offering, of Sacrament and all, meet together. No fullness there is of our Liturgy or public solemn service, without the Sacrament. Some part, yes the chief part is wanting, if that be wanting. But our thanks are surely not full without the Holy Eucharist, which is by interpretation, thanksgiving itself. Fully we cannot say *Quid retribuam Domino?* but we must answer, *Calicem salutaris accipiam, we will take the Cup of Salvation,* and with it in our hands give thanks to Him, render Him our true Eucharist, or real thanksgiving indeed. In which the Cup is the Blood not only of our redemption, of the covenant that frees us from the Law and makes the destroyer pass over us; but of our adoption, of the New Testament also which entitles us and conveys unto us, testament-wise or by the way of legacy, the estate we have in the joy and bliss of His heavenly kingdom whereto we are adopted. We are then made partakers of Him, and with Him of both these His benefits. . . . So that our freeing from under the Law, our investiture into our new adopted state, are not fully consummate without it.''[7]

***

After our growing in grace from this sacrament we finally partake in *the fullness of eternity.*

''And so, growing from grace to grace, finally from this *fullness* we shall come to be partakers of another, . . . the fullness of eternity, when time will run out and his glass empty, *et tempus non erit amplius*, which is at His next sending. For yet once more will God send Him, and He come again. At which time we shall then indeed receive the fullness of our redemption, not from the Law – that we have already — but from corruption to which our bodies are yet subject, and receive the full fruition of the inheritance whereto we are but adopted. And then it will be perfect, complete, absolute fullness indeed, when we shall all be filled with *the fullness of Him who fills all in all*. For so will all be, when nothing will be wanting in any; for *God will be all in all*. Not as here He is, something and by something in every one; but then, *omnia in omnibus*. And then, the measure will be so full as it cannot enter into us, we cannot hold it. We must enter into it; *intra in gaudium Domini tui*.

To this we aspire, and to this in the fullness appointed of every one of our times Almighty God bring us by Him, and for His sake, Who in this *fullness of time* was sent to work it for us in His Person; and work it in us by the operation of His blessed Spirit.[8]

References

[1] Andrews, Vol. I, pp. 45–7.
[2] *ibid.*, pp. 49–50.
[3] *ibid.*, pp. 50–6.
[4] *ibid.*, pp. 56–7.
[5] *ibid.*, pp. 57–60
[6] *ibid.*, p. 61.
[7] *ibid.*, pp. 62–3.
[8] *ibid.*, p. 63.

NATIVITY SERMON No. 5
CHRISTMAS DAY 1610

Text: St. Luke 2:10-11.

And the angel said unto them, Fear not:
for, behold, I bring you good tidings
of great joy, which shall be to all
people.
For unto you is born this day in the
city of David a Saviour, Who is Christ
the Lord.

Et dixit illis angelus: Nolite timere:
ecce enim evangelizo vobis gaudium magnum,
quod erit omni populo.

The main theme is joy because a Saviour is born to us, and the key-word in the text is *Hodie*, as on this day, and on no other day, not only was Christ born but the news of it was proclaimed by the angelic choir to men. Therefore Christmas day has that speciality which belongs to no other day.

". . . this day Christ was born, never but to-day only. For of no day in the year can it be said *hodie natus* but of this. By which word the Holy Spirit may seem to have marked it out, and made it the peculiar text of the day. . . .

To-morrow, the word *hodie* will be lost; this day and not any day else it is in season. . . .

The very first news that came . . . this day . . . by an angel . . . [which] was glad to find any to tell it to, . . . [yet] none were then awake, ... but . . . poor shepherds, and to them he told it."[1]

***

Once the angel had delivered his message, the whole choir of heaven broke out in joyful praise. The angels' message to the shepherds is joyful as it dispels fear before announcing the birth of the Saviour of the world. So, *hodie* is filled with *gaudium, joy*, and so joy abounds.

". . . *gaudium magnum, great joy,* for the great benefit and great honour vouchsafed our nature and us this day. *Joy* is in the text. . . . We keep the text, if we hold the time with joy, for so the angel does warrant us to hold it. . . .

They were afraid, and that *sore afraid*, . . . [so] this fear must be removed. . . .
To settle them then . . . no other way, . . . to begin with but *fear not*. . . .

25

But fear will not be cast out . . . till they see some reason to quiet them. . . . [Thus] *I bring you good news*, [which means] . . . *fear not* but be of good cheer. . . . Fear no ill, there is none to fear; there is no ill, no there is good towards. For good news is good, in that it represents the good itself to us before it [comes]. . . .

This it is then, *quod natus est*. The birth of a Child, *that there is One born this day* the cause of all this joy.

There is joy at every birth. . . . . But the greater he is who is born, and the more beneficial his birth, the greater ado is made. . . .

Now of Him who is born here it may truly be said, *Ecce major hîc, Behold a greater is born here*. One, whose birth is good news even from the poorest shepherd to the richest prince upon the earth. . . .

But we are not so much to regard the *ecce* how great it is, as *gaudium* what joy is in it. . . . And for that, men may talk what they will, but sure there is no joy in the world to the joy of a man saved; no joy so great, no news so welcome, as to one ready to perish, in case of a lost man, to hear of one who will save him. . . . It is the best news he ever heard in his life. There is joy in the name of a Saviour. . . . We have therefore all cause to be glad for the birth of this Saviour.''[2]

***

Andrewes explains what is savoured in the word *Saviour*.

''. . . when we hear of saving or mention of a Saviour, . . . our mind is carried to the saving of our skin, of our temporal state, of our bodily life, and farther saving we think not of. But there is another life not to be forgotten, and greater the dangers, and the destruction there more to be feared than of this here, and it would be well sometimes we were remembered of it. Besides our skin and flesh, a soul we have . . . that also has need of a Saviour. . . . Indeed our chief thought and care [should] be for that; how to escape the wrath, how to be saved from the destruction to come, whither our sins will certainly bring us.''[3]

***

We need a Saviour because of our sins, without which we would perish.

''Sin . . . will destroy us all. . . . Nothing so dangerous, so deadly unto us, as is the sin in our bosom; nothing from which we have so much need to be saved. . . . We need a Saviour for our souls, and from our sins; and from the everlasting destruction which sin will bring upon us in the other life. . . . We have not that sense of our souls and the dangers of them, that we have of our bodies; nor that fear of our ghostly enemies, nor that lively apprehension of the eternal torments of that place. . . . Our carnal part is quick and sensible, our spiritual is dead and dull. We have not the feeling of our sins that we have of our sickness; [otherwise] . . . we would hear this news . . . of the birth of such a Saviour with joy indeed, . . . and find there is no joy in the earth to the joy of a Saviour.''[4]

***

26

The angels further greeted the shepherds with the joyful news that this *Saviour* is also *Christ,* the fulfilment of all the prophecies. As such He is Priest, Prophet and King.

"And what is meant by this term Christ? A Saviour anointed; or . . . a Saviour *sealed* — a Saviour under God's Great Seal. That is, not as those other were, saviours raised up of a sudden upon some occasion, to serve the turn for the present, and never heard of till they came; but a Saviour in God's fore-counsel resolved on, and given forth from the beginning; promised and foretold, and now signed and sent with absolute commission and fullness of power to be the perfect and complete Saviour of all. . . .

His anointing appointed, set forth, and sent into the world to exercise this function of a Saviour; not for a time, but for ever; not to the Jews, as did the rest, but even to all the ends of the earth. . . .

And there is yet more particularity in this word Christ: three offices did God from the beginning erect to save His people by. . . . 1. Priests, to purge or expiate; 2. Prophets, to illuminate or direct them; 3. Kings, to set all right, and to keep all right in that perfection which this world admits. And all these three had their several anointings. Aaron the Priest, Elisha the Prophet, Saul the King. In the Saviour Who is Christ, His will was all should meet, that nothing in Him might want to the perfecting of this work. That He might be a perfect Saviour of all, He was all."[5]

***

Just as there is joy in a Saviour, there is also much joy in Christ who anoints us with the oil of gladness.

"If we would be saved, we would be saved *unctione, by oil.* . . . And the oil which He uses . . . . is the oil of gladness . . . [He] bestows . . . upon us [and] upon them especially that through a wounded conscience were troubled with the spirit of heaviness, to turn their heaviness into joy."[6]

***

The angels also announced the Child as *Lord,* and so Andrewes explained why being *Lord* is essential for our salvation.

"And yet to make our joy more full the Angel adds the third. *A Saviour Who is Christ, Christ the Lord,* . . . Lord of men and angels, Lord of heaven and earth, and all the hosts of them. . . .

But why the Lord? . . . As He is Christ, that is, anointed, He is man only. It is His name as Man, for God cannot be anointed. But He who should save us would be more than Man; and so, more than Christ. Indeed, Christ cannot save us. He who must save us must be the Lord . . . which the former saviours could not do. . . . But this Saviour, this Christ, because He is the Lord, *endures for ever, has an everlasting Priesthood*, Kingdom and Prophecy and so *is able perfectly to save them who come to God by Him. . . .*

He [is] for ever . . . [the] *Author of eternal salvation* to all who depend on Him. . . . To begin and to end; to save soul and body from bodily and ghostly enemies; from sin the root, and misery the branches; for a time and for ever; to be a Saviour and to be salvation itself; Christ the Lord is all this, and can do all this. Now then we are right, and never till now. . . .

But the name *Lord* goes yet further, not only to save us and set us free from danger, to deliver us from evil; but to state us in as good and better condition than we forfeited by our fall, or else though we were saved we should not save by the match. To make us then savers, and not savers only, but gainers. . . . He does further impart also the estate annexed of this last title, even whatsoever He is Lord of Himself. And He is *Lord of life*, says St. Paul, life then He imparts. And He is *Lord of glory*, says St. Peter, glory then He imparts. And He is Lord of joy, . . . joy then He imparts. Life and glory and joy; and makes us lords of them, and of whatsoever is within the name and title of Lord. . . . He is well pleased to . . . admit us with Himself into His estate of joint-purchase of heaven, . . . that in right of it we may enter into the life, glory, and joy of our Lord, and so be saved and be savers, and more than savers every way."[7]

***

The Child as *Saviour, Christ* and *Lord* is our gift at Christmas because *Puer natus est vobis*, or as Andrewes suggested *nobis* rather than *vobis*. *For us* is more meaningful as it signifies our share with the Child in everything He came to give.

"And if given us, bestowed upon us, then He is ours. Ours His benefit, His office, His power. His benefit to save us, His office to undertake us, His power to assure us. Ours, His salvation as Jesus, His anointing as Christ, His dominion as the Lord. And if He be ours, then all His are ours; His birth ours, and if His birth, all that follow His birth, ours too."[8]

***

What then can we give in return? Andrewes suggests the best gift is to offer up the Child on this day to God.

". . . And how can we do that better than as God has offered Him to us this day who He was born for us, so we reciprocally this day that He is born offer Him again to God as the best pleasing oblation that we can offer Him. To-day, as in the Temple alive for our morning oblation; and when the time comes of His death, offer Him as on the Cross slain for our evening sacrifice."[9]

***

And should we not on this day perform some duty as well? The most fitting duty commended by Andrewes is to receive Him at the altar.

"If *born for us, and given us*, it is our part then, we can do no less than receive Him. . . .

How shall we receive Him? . . . *Accipite, Take, this is my Body, by the offering whereof you are sanctified. Take, this is my Blood*, by the shedding whereof you are saved. Both in the holy mysteries ordained by God as pledges to assure us, and as conduit pipes to convey into us this and all other the benefits that come by this our Saviour.

Verily upon His memorable days, of which this is the first, we are bound to do something in memory, or remembrance of Him."[10]

***

It is also fitting for us to render Him thanks for His birth, and a most appropriate time for this is while receiving the *Cup of Salvation.*

"Something would be thought on *to return Him for all His benefits*, and this day for this first, the fountain of all the rest, His birth. Some thanks would be rendered [to] him for it. And how can we do that better than . . . [to] *take the Cup of salvation*. And so do it: so, with it taken into our hands, *give thanks to the name of the Lord*. And what better than to-day, *hodie*, as we are here directed? What better day than on this day, the very day He was bestowed on us. To defer Him no longer than He did us. He deferred not us at all, but as soon as He was born sent us word the same instant; and shall we defer Him to hear of us another time, and not be as ready on our part to receive Him instantly as He was on His to bestow Himself; even presently, as soon as He was born? Sure, somewhat would be done more than ordinary this day of His birth; the day itself is more than ordinary."[11]

***

If ever there was an *accepted time* for us, it is on this *day of salvation*. Therefore, Andrewes concludes, let us accept this day with its life-giving gift and embrace our *Saviour, Christ* and *Lord* whole-heartedly.

"If ever an accepted time, *ecce tempus acceptum*, behold, now it is, this is that time. . . .

Let us honour this day with our receiving, which He has honoured by His first giving; yielding Him evermore . . . our unfeigned hearty thanksgiving for this so good news, for this so great a gift, both of them this day [given to] us; in Him and for Him, Who was Himself the gift, our *Saviour, Christ the Lord*."[12]

References

[1] Andrewes, Vol. I, pp. 64–5.
[2] *ibid.*, pp. 66–8, 73–4.
[3] *ibid.*, p. 74.
[4] *ibid.*, pp. 74–5.
[5] *ibid.*, pp. 76–7.
[6] *ibid.*, pp.77–8.
[7] *ibid.*, pp. 78–80.
[8] *ibid.*, p. 82.
[9] *ibid.*
[10] *ibid.*, p. 83.
[11] *ibid.*, pp. 83–4.
[12] *ibid.*, p. 84.

NATIVITY SERMON No. 6

CHRISTMAS DAY 1611

Text: St. John 1:14

And the Word was made flesh, and dwelt
among us, (and we beheld His glory,
the glory as of the only-begotten of
the Father,) full of grace and truth.

Et Verbum caro factum est, et habitavit
in nobis: et vidimus gloriam ejus, gloriam
quasi unigeniti a Patre plenum gratiae,
et veritatis.

St. John unveiled the mystery of the Word, and hence the main theme in this sermon is mystery, the great mystery of the Incarnation. *Verbu caro, the word became flesh,* in order to dwell amongst us, and to share His two natures with us. As He came not empty but *full of grace and truth,* it meant we can share in these too.

"This feast is held . . . for no other end but to celebrate the contents of the text, that the Word being made flesh this day came to dwell among us. . . .
There is not anything that concerns this mystery, but is within the text. His two natures, *the Word,* and *flesh*: 1. *Word,* divine; 2. *flesh,* human. The union of them in *factum est*; union into a Person, in *habitavit.* . . . 3. His office. . . . [He] not only took a house, but *pitched a pavilion in us*; not only *made our neighbour,* but made a champion for us to understand our quarrel and to fight a combat. 4. And last, the benefit, *made* that he might *dwell*; and *dwell* that He might impart to us, and we derive from Him, that whereof He was full, and we were empty; we had need, and He had store; *grace and truth.*"[1]

***

Andrewes takes the three key-words, *Verbum, caro, and factum est* and outlines the essence of each. Firstly *Verbum.* It could mean words written about Jesus, or the written Word about God, or Jesus teaching us. Yet it is more than all these. *It is the Only-begotten of the Father.*

"This Word . . . is *the Only-begotten of the Father.* These two are one and the same, but need to be set in two terms, that what is wanting in the one may be supplied by the other. . . . In this they agree; as the Son is to the Father, so is the word to the mind. . . .

The Son refers to a living nature, the Word adds further an intellectual nature; that there is in Him not only the nature and life, but the wisdom of the Father. . . .

For there is not in all the world a more pure, simple, inconcrete procreation than that whereby the mind conceives the word within it, by *dixit in corde*. For in itself and of itself does the mind produce it without help of any mixture of ought, without any passion stirring or agitation at all. Such was the issue of the Word eternal. But then, lest we might imagine God's Word to be Him no other than ours is to us, not of our substance; He makes amends for that and tells us *He is the Only-begotten*, and so of the substance of his Father, . . . as all begotten sons be. The Word, to show His proceeding pure and merely spiritual; the Son, to show that for all that it is true and substantial. Truly consubstantial with the Father, as the Son; but in all clean and pure manner conceived, as the Word.''[2]

***

Secondly, *Caro*. Christ has taken our human flesh. Significantly the Hebrew word for *flesh* is also the Hebrew word for *good tidings*. The *good tidings* is of course that the *Word was made flesh*.

''As the Word and the Only-begotten refer to One, so does *caro* and *in nobis*, flesh and in us; that is such flesh as in us, human flesh. . . . He [condescended] to become man, nothing so much as to become flesh, the very lowest, and basest part of man.

Besides, from the flesh, as from Eve, came the beginning of trangression, longing after the forbidden fruit, refused the Word quite; so, of all other, least likely to be taken. The Word not refusing it, the rest have good hope. . . .

Yet one more. It will not be amiss to tell you; the word that is Hebrew for flesh the same is also Hebrew for good tidings, as we call it, the Gospel; sure, not without the Holy Spirit so dispensing it. There could be no other meaning but that some incarnation, or making flesh, should be generally good news for the whole world. To let us know this good tidings is come to pass He tells us, the Word is now become flesh.''[3]

***

Thirdly *factum est*. Unlike the Manichees' teaching that God did not have a true body, Andrewes emphasizes that God was truly made man, and as man was content to live humbly and to end His life in shameful humiliation. From His humility and ceaseless love there are many benefits we receive from the Word becoming flesh.

''Why then, *factum est caro, the Word is made flesh*; this makes up all. . . . *Made* it was; against Manicheus holding that He had no true body; as if *factum* had been *fictum*. . . .

But *made* He was . . . *by taking the seed of Abraham*. . . . So, into the Godhead was the manhood taken; the natures preserved without confusion, the person entire without division. . . .

What flesh? The flesh of an infant. What the Word an infant? . . . How born, how entertained? In a stately palace, cradle of ivory, robes of estate? No; but a stable for His palace, a manger for His cradle, poor clouts for His array. This was His beginning. Follow Him further, if no better afterwards; what flesh afterwards? *Sudans et algens, in cold and heat, hungry and thirsty, faint and weary. Is His end any better? that makes up all: what flesh then? black and blue, bloody and swollen, rent and torn, the thorns and nails sticking in His flesh; and such flesh He was made. A great factum* certainly, and much to be made of. To have been made *caput Angelorum* had been an abasement; to be *minoratus Angelis* is more; but to be *novissimus virorum, in worst case of all men*, no, *a worm and no man;* so to be born, so arrayed, and so housed, and so handled — there is not the meanest flesh but is better. So to be made, and so unmade; to take it on, and lay it off, with so great indignity: weigh it and wonder at it that ever He would endure to be made flesh, and to be made on this manner. What was it made the Word thus to be made flesh? . . . It was God and in God nothing but love; . . . Love only did it.''[4]

***

Habitavit. The extension of *factum est* was to dwell amongst us. This meant for a time He was prepared to live amongst us, not *solitary* but as a *neighbour.* Hence the shepherds and magi could come and worship Him, while later on, the inner apostles could witness His internal glory on the holy mount, and later still many of His disciples saw His going up into heaven.

''And *habitavit* is a word of continuance. . . . Not only made, but made stay, made His abode with us; not appeared and was gone again straight, but for a time took up His dwelling. . . .

He dwelt; and not invisibly or obscurely, but so as He might be and was seen. Even this very day, *vidimus*, might the shepherds say, *we saw* His angels and heard them sing, and then went to Bethlehem and saw Himself. *Vidimus*, might the wise man say; *we saw His star in the East*, and we are come to see [Him]. . . .

Peter, James and [John] were in the holy Mount together, and saw Him transfigured. . . . [Later], one hundred and twenty saw Him taken up into heaven, out of their sight, in the Mount of Olives. . . .

What saw they? . . . His glory . . . Which glory was an infallible demontration of His presence there. *Through the veil of His flesh* such beams He cast, as behind those clouds they might know there was a sun; as that way only could He be made visible to the eyes of flesh, which otherwise could not behold Him.''[5]

***

He also came *full, full of grace and truth*, both of which are needed by us to live in Christ, and to live out Christ in our daily lives.

''[With] grace and truth . . . He comes, with the fullness of them; not of one of them, but of both. Grace referred to the Son, truth to the Word, grace is to adopt us, truth to beget us anew. . . .

And these do very fitly follow after glory. Glory of itself terrifies and makes stand aloof, grace invites; and His glory is such as is full of grace. . . . but though there be grace, unless there be truth too, all is nothing. . . . His truth is, as it were, the flesh of His grace. . . .

Out of grace we were and without grace, as sinners and in errors wandering up and down; as even the best of our nature did at His coming into the flesh. This is the state He found us in when He came among us. . . .

He brought us in grace again, through His beloved Son. . . . He brought us truth to set us in the right way. . . . We cannot be without either. . . .

The bringing of these two together is a great matter; and together they must be. Grace, take it from truth, and it is *fallax,* . . . but a mere illusion. Truth sever if from grace, and it is *ingrata, but an unpleasant thing.* Grace and truth kept in sunder, and never met before; but when the Word and flesh met, then *did they meet and kiss each other* says the [psalmist]. . . .

They must meet, and grace be first, as here. We shall never endure the severity of His truth, unless grace come before and allay it. But when grace has brought us to Him, truth will hold us with Him. By grace we shall accomplish what truth requires at our hands; that so, receiving grace, and walking in truth, we may come to the . . . reward of both, glory. . . . We shall not need to go to any other storehouse, or help to supply or fill up Christ with any other . . . He is full. . . . Our care is to be make ourselves fit vessels and there is all."[6]

***

There are other benefits we gain from *Verbum caro,* such as our acceptance. Being made man, it means that God can never hate our flesh, that is, his brethren, us. Our nature is therefore held in high esteem, and therefore this is our hope. As He dwelt amongst us, every sinner can resort to Him for our inheritance. By taking our flesh, it means that flesh will inherit the kingdom of heaven, and we as a result are inheritors of this kingdom.

"He sees us daily in Himself, He cannot look upon His flesh but He must think upon us. And God the Father cannot now hate the flesh which the Word is made; which is now taken into one person with His only Son, and united to the Deity itself. If He [loves] the Word, He must love it too, for the Word is become it; either love both, or hate both. But love it certainly; for, as this day, *when He brought His Son* clothed with it *into the world, He gave express commandment all His angels should worship Him,* so clothed, and our flesh in Him; a new dignity which is this day accrued to our nature, to be adored of the blessed angels. Our nature questionless is set in high favour with God. . . .

Besides, good hope we now have that He being now flesh, all flesh may come to Him to present Him with their requests. . . . For since He dwelt amongst us, all may resort to Him, yes, even sinners. . . .

A second hope, that seeing He has made our flesh His Tabernacle, He will not suffer this of ours — the same with that of His — to fall down quite and come to nothing; the same He dwells in Himself not to perish utterly; but repair it again and raise it out of the dust. . . .

34

A third [hope], that where it was *flesh and blood will not inherit the Kingdom of God*, it is reversed; flesh and blood will, for flesh and blood already has. . . . *Since sure it is that the Son of God is made the Son of man, it is not incredible but that the sons of men may be made the sons of God*. Not incredible, no, *securitas nobis data est*.''[7]

***

What can we do to in return to show our gratitude for *Verbum caro*, the Word becoming flesh?

''. . . what we for Him, . . . If the Word become flesh. . . . That flesh is then so to be preserved; . . . kept with such care, and in such cleanness, as it might beseem His flesh to be kept. . . .

We have a word . . . the very Word, or wisdom of God; and that is the word which is preached unto us. That word we may, and are to incarnate according to this day's pattern. That we so do.''[8]

***

Caro and the Sacrament of the altar are one. Andrewes concludes that at Christmas we have the privilege not only to celebrate this feast day of their union but also to be partakers thereof. The Nativity further means Grace and Truth are always available to us.

''To go to the word and flesh together. . . . But at this now, we are not to content ourselves with one alone; but since He offers to communicate Himself both ways, never restrain Him to one. The word we hear is the abstract of *Verbum*; the Sacrament is the antetype of *caro*, His flesh. What better way than where these are actually joined, actually to partake them both? Not either alone, the word or flesh; but the word and flesh both, for there they are both. . . . If it be grace and truth we respect, how may we better establish our hearts with grace, or settle our minds in the truth of His promise, than by partaking these the conduit-pipes of His grace, and seals of His truth unto us? Grace and truth now proceeding not from the Word alone, but even from the flesh thereto united; the fountain of the Word flowing into the cistern of His flesh, and from thence deriving down to us this grace and truth, to them who partake Him aright. . . .

On the feast of their union, they would be united; the day they were joined by Him, they would not be sundered by any; but we to celebrate both, in honour of both, . . . that we may hold this feast aright, and do the duty that properly belongs to it, let us by both do honour to both, that from both we may receive the fruit of both — grace, to enable us; truth, to guide us to the hope of glory, . . . [and thus] to see Him as He is, and by seeing to be transformed into the same image of glory.''[9]

References

[1] Andrewes, Vol. I, pp. 86–7.
[2] *ibid.*, pp. 87–8.
[3] *ibid.*, p. 89.
[4] *ibid.*, pp. 90–2.
[5] *ibid.*, pp. 93–5.
[6] *ibid.*, pp. 95–7.
[7] *ibid.*, pp. 97–8.
[8] *ibid.*, p.99.
[9] *ibid.*, pp. 100–1.

NATIVITY SERMON No. 7
CHRISTMAS DAY 1612

Text: Hebrews 1:1–3

God, Who at sundry times and in divers
manners spoke in time past unto the
Fathers by the prophets,
Has in these last days spoken unto us
by His Son, Whom He has appointed Heir
of all things, by whom also He made the
worlds;
Who being the brightness of His glory,
and the express image of His person,
and upholding all things by the word of
His power, when He had by Himself purged
our sins, sat down on the right hand of
the Majesty on high.

Multifariam, multisque modis olim Deus
loquens patribus in prophetis,
Novissime diebus istis locutus est nobis
in Filio, Quem constituit Heredem
universorum, per Quem fecit et saecula;
Qui cum sit Splendor gloriae, et Figura
substantiae Ejus, portansque omnia verba
virtutis Suae, purgationem peccatorum
faciens, sedet ad dexteram majestatis
in excelsis.

From his text Andrewes explains that as God was manifested in the flesh on
Christmas day, that day has become the first of the last days, and as such is a
high feast. He illustrates its importance by comparing *now* with the *times
past*. In both times God has been revealed, but in different ways. The essential difference is that *in times past* His revelation was like *candlelight* as
compared with the *daylight* of *now* in Christ. As God has spoken *now* through
His Son, we do not have to look any further afield. He is the *Truth*. Therefore
God will not speak again. This is the last time.

‘‘And this text tells us of a great prerogative of these last days above the first. Of
which last days, this is the first day; the day of Christ's birth. For, make a partition
of the two times, *olim*, and *dies novisssimi*: and this day will be found to end *olim*,
and to begin *dies novissimi*; to be the first day of these last days; . . . from whence
we begin our [Christian] era. . . .

The dignity of this day, and ours in it, is here set out two ways. First, by a case of comparison — of comparison between the times past and these now; between the Fathers and us. . . .

God in times past spoke by the prophets . . . from Moses to John Baptist who was the horizon of the Law and Gospel. . . .

The prophets were *holy men* but men. And there is a nature more perfect than that of man, even the nature of God, And in the House of God they were faithful servants, but yet, servants; and that we know, is but an imperfect condition in comparison of a son. To us in the last days is given, what we have not from any prophet, though never so excellent from the Lord of the prophets; not from any servant, though in never so great place, but from the Son; and, not from any of the sons of men, but from His own Son, the Son of God. . . .

And all prophecy hangs in suspense as imperfect, till the fulfilling of it; which was done by Christ, to Whom they all gave witness. Now *when that is perfect is come, that that is imperfect must away.* Not to rest in them then, but to Christ; and never rest till we come to Him.

And, as never to rest till we come to Him, so there to rest, when we are come to Him. As soon as His voice has sounded in our ears, that they itch no more after any new revelations. For, *in Him are all the treasures of wisdom, and knowledge. God spoke once and twice,* a third time He will not speak. This is the last time; He will speak no more. Look for no more pieces, nor fancy no more fashions; *consummatum est,* there are no more to look for. He is *the Truth,* and he who has found the truth . . . seeks no further. . . . To get us therefore to Christ, and never be got from Him, but there hold us.''[1]

***

Andrewes then proceeds to point out that for rest of his text the writer to the Hebrews deliberates on the Sonship. Firstly, His nature; secondly, His person; thirdly, His office; and lastly His agency.

"His nature . . . not only man . . . but God also. . . . that He is, *His Son, the splendour of His glory, the Character of His substance, the Maker and Upholder of the world and all in it.*

His person, in this word *semet ipso.* He did it Himself, that is, in His own person. . . .

[In] His offices, . . . He unfolds the mysteries of God. In His purging our sins is His priesthood; and His Kingdom, in the throne of Majesty wherein He sits.

His agency, *to us He speaks; our sins He purges.* To us, and for us, He is who He is. All His speaking and doing, *propter nos homines, et propter salutem nostram, for us men and for our salvation,* and our part in Him and His.''[2]

***

Andrewes concentrates on three aspects of His divinity: *Son, brightness* and *character.*

38

"In *Son* there is true identity of nature; upon it is grounded *being of one substance*, even as the Son is with the Father. But the Son comes after the Father in time, and that a good time; amends is made for that in the next term, *brightness*. For, it is not to be imagined that there ever was or could be a light body, but in the very same instant there must stream from it a brightness. So upon this is grounded co-eternal.

But then, there is some inequality between the light body itself and the beam of brightness of it; the beam not full out so clear. This is the imperfection in the term *brightness*. But that is supplied by the next, *character*; for that is ever just equal, neither bigger nor lesser than the type or stamp that made it. . . .

Agreeable to these threes, we believe of Him who is consubstantial, as the *Son*; co-eternal as *the brightness*; co-equal as *the character*. . . .

He was such a Son, as did no way eclipse His Father's glory, but as a beam made it shine more bright. *The character,* the true stamp of His substance."[3]

***

From the Son we are given the benefit of *inheritance*. However our *inheritance* was bought at a price, a high price by our Saviour because of our sins.

"Heirs are either born or made; so by nature, or so made by purchase. He was His Son, and His only Son, and so born His heir. He was born, and yet He would be made. . . . Heir born He was, and so claims all as His inheritance, by due of birthright. . . . To what end? Not for Himself? . . . He was born heir for Himself, but *made heir* for us. . . . He now is but on our behalf . . . *at the right hand of His Father.* . . .

For He could not bring us to sit with Him in His throne thus purchased, being so spotted and foul as we were, by means of the pollution of our sins. He was then to purge and make clean our nature first, that He might exalt it to partake His purchase, being so cleansed. Where first our case is set down wherein He found us, and wherein we are without Him. A sinner's case, how gloriously soever he or she glister in the eyes of men, being in God's eyes as the case of a foul diseased person; and we thereby taught so to conceive of sins as of foul spots without, or of such humours within as go from us by purging. . . . Unless they be purged, there is no entering into the heavenly Jerusalem where the throne is. . . .

Exalt us He could not, being in that plight; for love or pity therefore purge us He would. And here now is . . . the highest point of elevation in this text, *Who being the brightness,* . . . that is, a party so excellent in nature, glory, Person and power; nature as *Son*, glory as *Brightness*, Person as *Character*, power as *Maker and Supporter of all*, who though He were all this, did not abhor to come and visit us being in that foul and wretched case. . . .

And not only visit him, but not refuse the base office to look to his *purging* from that his uncleanness. . . . Not cause it to be done by another, but . . . *by His own self in person.* . . . In doing, not to stand by and prescribe, but Himself to minister and make the medicine, . . . to make it Himself, and make it of Himself."[4]

***

This high price involved sacrifice, the spilling of precious Blood, for our sins, by our dear Lord.

"And how, or of what? Spots will out with water; some will not with anything but with blood; *without shedding of blood, there is no taking away sin.* And not every blood will serve, but it must be lamb's blood, and *a Lamb without spot.* And not every lamb neither, but *the Lamb of God,* or, to speak plainly, a Lamb that is God. His blood, and nothing else will serve to do this. . . .

His best, most precious, His heart-blood, . . . brings certain death with it. With that blood He was to make the medicine. Die He must, and His side be opened, that there might issue both the Water and the Blood that was to be the ingredients of it. By Himself, His Ownself, and by Himself slain; by His death, and by His Blood-shedding,and by no other means. . . . The Physician slain, and of His Flesh and Blood a receipt made, that the patient might recover!"[5]

***

Not only is the purging of our sins through Calvary but also in the Eucharist.

"And now, we may be at our choice whether we will conceive of sin as of some outward soil in the soul; and then, the purging of it . . . [through] a bath of the water that came out of His side . . . that from thence might flow *a fountain for sin and for uncleanness.* Water, and mixed with His Blood; as forcible to take out the stains of the soul, . . . or, . . . as of some inward pestilent humour in the soul and conscience, casting us into peril of mortal, or rather immortal death; then, the purging of us to be by way of electuary[6] or potion; and so He purges our sins too. To that end He has made an electuary of His own Body, *Take, eat it,* and tempered a Cup with His own Blood, *Drink you all of it,* which by the operation of His eternal Spirit in it is able effectually *to purge the conscience from dead works* or actual sins, and from the deadly effect of them; no balsam or medicine in the world like it. . . . By both He purged us from both."[7]

***

His work for us was not completed on the Cross, that could only be accomplished after His return to Heaven where He continues his work by interceding for us as our High Priest.

". . . we are not to conceive . . . that His labour being done, He took His rest, and there is all; but that His sitting down is a taking possession of that His dear-made purchase; and that, not in His own name, He had it before; He was in glory, and in the self-same glory with His Father, before ever the world was. . . .

And these two, *purging* and *sitting down in the throne,* as the *alpha* and *omega,* the first and last of what He does for us. . . . To purge our sins He began this day,

40

the first day, the day of His birth; wherein He purified and sanctified, by His holy Nativity. . . . And *sit in the throne* was His last work, on the last day of His ascension.''[8]

***

In responding, our duty is *to honour, fear, love* and *serve* Him. Above all we must listen for Him and to Him because He is ever ready to speak to us, especially of love and humility.

''Our duty then is, for His excellency to honour Him; for His power to fear Him; for His love showed, reciprocally to love Him again; for His hope promised, truly to serve Him. . . .
And even so He speaks to us, if we can understand. . . . He sends forth such a voice; it speaks humility, . . . and great love.''[9]

***

Our purging is also accomplished in the Eucharist. Here both Son and Sacrament meet.

''And this day they first came together, the Word and flesh; therefore, of all days, this day they would not be parted. For, will you sever the flesh from the Word that day on which God joined them? God forbid! There is a correspondency between the word and His brightness, and between the Sacrament and His character. . . . The parts of the Sacrament they are permanent, and stick by us; they are a remembrance of the characters made in His skin and flesh. And if you seek to be rid of your sins, *this was broken for you*, and *this was shed for you*, for that very end, *for the remission of sins*.''[10]

***

Our hope on earth is ever for the heavenly kingdom.

''His kingdom . . . *the last day indeed*, . . . is yet in hope only. That same flesh that cleansed our sins, the same now sits on the throne, and so has both virtues; for the present a power to purge, for the future a power likewise to exalt. The same blood is the blood of Sacrifice for remission of sins, and the blood of the New Testament for the passing to us the bequest, which is the right of His purchase for which He was made Heir. And the very angels which this day adored Him in our flesh and it in Him, thereby showed plainly not the purging only but the exalting of it also by this day's work. And that to-day, wherein they sang aloud in the sky, we have cause to make much of, and to rejoice in it, the day of the greatest *glory to God, peace to the earth, and good-will towards men* that ever rose upon the world.''[11]

41

References

[1] Andrewes, Vol. I, pp. 102–3, 105–7.
[2] *ibid.*, pp. 107–8.
[3] *ibid.*, pp. 108–9.
[4] *ibid.*, pp. 111–2.
[5] *ibid.*, pp. 112–3.
[6] A medicinal powder, mixed with honey or another sweet substance.
[7] Andrewes, Vol. I, p 113.
[8] *ibid.*, p. 114.
[9] *ibid.*, pp. 115–6.
[10] *ibid.*, p. 116.
[11] *ibid.*, pp. 116–7.

NATIVITY SERMON No. 8

CHRISTMAS DAY 1613

Text: St. John 8:56

Your father Abraham rejoiced to see My
day: and he saw it, and was glad.

*Abraham pater vester exultavit ut videret
diem Meum: vidit, et gavisus est.*

The dominant theme of this sermon is *joy*. Christmas day is *diem Meum, My
day*, and therefore a day of joy. It was for this day that Abraham had rejoiced
in, knowing that His Saviour would come. Thus we have Abraham as an
example for our rejoicing.

"Here is joy, joy at a sight, at the sight of a day, and that day Christ's. It is Christ
who calls it here, *diem Meum*, and no day so properly His, as His birth-day. So the
text comes full upon the day.

But to deduce it point by point. First, Christ has a day proper to Him, which in
express terms He calls here *diem Meum, My day*.

Secondly, this day to be seen as a day of joy. Double joy: 1. *Exultavit,* and 2.
Gavisus est, both in the text.

And thirdly, which is somewhat strange, it was so to the patriarch Abraham.
Him we find here doing [what] we now are about; seeing and rejoicing at the sight
of Christ's day; taking notice of it, and taking joy in it. . . .

And what are we now disposing ourselves to do, but even the very same that is
in the text here to rejoice to see Christ's day. . . . We have Abraham for our
example; we do but as He did. In his time, Christ's day was a day of joy; and a day
of joy is a feast, and so holden by him we see . . . Christ Himself, Abraham's joy;
. . . His day Abraham's joy too. . . .

He makes His day the object of all this exultation and joy. His day, I say, and not
Himself, commends Him, that He rejoiced at the sight not of Himself, but of it. . . .
This speech of His is much to the honour of His day; and the very solemnity of the
feast, and all the joy and gladness thereon. . . .

My day he so highly esteemed, as glad he was that he might see it; . . . we
Abraham's children, [also]. There is joy with us at the sight of His day; we renew
our joy so often as by the revolution of the year it comes about. And for this very
point we find ourselves the nearer to Abraham, even for the joy of His day. . . . and
so, a time of joy God makes it to us!"[1]

***

43

Andrewes illustrates why it is His nativity rather than His passion that makes it *Diem Meum*. Christmas is a day of rejoicing while Good Friday is a day of sorrows.

". . . it is *diem Meum, Christ's day;* Christ is God and Man, Son to both. His day as the Son of God, or as the Son of Man, Son to both. . . . Not as the Son of God, as the Son of God He has no day. . . . But as the Son of man He has more days than one. . . .

Now, there be but two such eminent days to stand for this: the first, and the last. First, of His Genesis; or last, of His exodus, . . . that is the first of His Nativity, or of the last of His Passion. Which of these?

Not of His Passion. . . . that was none of His. . . . It was not His day, . . . but *tenebrarum*, . . . night rather than day, . . . without all question, no day of joy. The heavens are darkened, the earth quaking, the stones renting, every one going their ways, *beating their breasts* for sorrow. That was no sight to rejoice at, that no day to rejoice in.

Then is it of necessity to be His birth-day; that was a day, the angel calls it to-day; *To-day is born*. And His day it was, for every man claims a kind of property in His birthday. Men, in the day of the beginning of their life. As kings, in the days of the beginning of their reigns; . . . as churches, their *encaenia* when they are first [dedicated]. . . . His day then; and sure, a day of joy. . . . Joy in heaven, joy in earth. In heaven for a day of *glory to God on high*; in earth, for a day of *peace here below, and for good-will towards men* — as ever, no more than ever was any. The angel so proclaimed it a day of *joy to all people*. . . . He was first seen, first showed to the world, as the Son of man; as the very day whereon the first-fruits of all the joy then, and ever since.''[2]

***

This day has ever been desired. As far back as Abraham there has been the desire to see this day. His desire sprang from his sensitivity of knowing he was in need of a Redeemer. We too can take similar comfort from this day.

"This day . . . is *dies desiderii* . . . To be desired, even of Abraham; and if of him, of all. . . .

Why should Abraham so desire to see this day, two thousand years and more after his days were at an end, and he in his grave? What was it to him? How was he concerned in it? . . . What need had he of it that he should so desire it? Yes, Christ's birth he needed. . . .

[Like] the joy of Job's Easter, the same is the joy of Abraham's Christmas; even that a day should come, wherein his Redeemer should come into the world. For Abraham's case was not such, but that a Redeemer he stood in need of. . . . Him, he needed; and Him he desired. And desired His day for His sake; *diem* for *Meum*; the day, for Him Who was born on the day. . . .

That very time when he had . . . the first glimpse of it; thus complains he there of his need, and complaining implies his desire; *And lo, I am but dust ashes*. . . . Inasmuch then as dust he was, and ashes he was to be; dust by creation, ashes by

44

condemnation, and both these he confessed himself liable unto; he needed One, as to restore the ruins of the first, so to prevent the danger of the second. Being in need, he desired; desiring, he was glad to hear of; but more glad would be to see that day that should bring Him into the world. And O, when will that day be? And sure, the sun must go down with us too; and what fear we shall then be in, or whether we shall see the furnace, I know not; but sure I am, that joyful it will be then to have a comfortable sight and apprehension of the benefit and beginning of this day.''3

***

St. John the Baptist while still in the womb also desired to see this day when he leapt in Elizabeth's womb. Thus old and young, both rejoiced in the news of their Saviour.

"For the same word you will observe is used of the Baptist, while he was yet but an embyro.... That at the interview and voice of the blessed Virgin Mary, he then a babe *gave a spring in the womb of Elizabeth his mother.* So that we see both old and young, Abraham and John Baptist, from the eldest in years to the child unborn, it concerns all. All need it, all are bound to be glad of it, all is for the joy and honour of this day.''4

***

If we are to experience the joy of this day, firstly we must desire Him upon His day with great fervency, even to the degree that Zaccheus desired to see Him. Then we shall be able to experience *Diem Meum* as Abraham did, that is, in the light of faith, with his vision at Mamre.

"And with this we must begin, even with desire, and seek to possess our souls of it.... For where the desire is, there will the eye be also; and where it is not, no prospect . . . no window open that way.... For the truth is, therefore we joy not because we desire not. True it is, and pity it is; millions there be never have true sight of Him. Why? they have no desire to Him. We must then begin there with desire, with *ut videret,* or we shall never come to *et vidit....* For there is vigour and vehemency in *exultarem ut.* It is a fervent desire, a kind of hunger and thirst, a *desiderio desideravi,* this *exultarem ut,* I would do anything, I would give anything to have a sight of it....

Take Zaccheus, . . . he, out of a desire to see Christ at His coming to Jericho, *and could not for the [crowd], . . . got him up into a tree,* so as to have a sight of Him. It was so well taken, this very desire, as he not only saw Him, but received Him to his house....

The patriarchs . . . did not only desire to see this day, but see it they did. . . . They knew and saw *in genere* such a day there should come; and then come when it would, . . . all joy they wished to that day for the joy it was to bring them. . . .

But then . . . you ask how he saw it? . . . as if Abraham could not see His day, unless Christ had been in the flesh in the days of Abraham. That is one kind of seeing indeed. For so Simeon saw, *for mine eyes have seen*. . . . what Simeon saw, the same saw Abraham. . . . The same Christ both, and the same day, though not both in the same manner. But let me tell you, this of Abraham's was the better. . . .

If not with his eyes, how? Yes; with his eyes too, though not of the body, . . . [but of] an inward man . . . He saw it *in lumine fidei*, . . . By faith . . . Christ was as verily present unto [him] as if [he] had seen Him this day in the manger with the shepherds; or with Simeon had . . . beheld Him. . . .

But where was this, and when? . . . He saw His birth at the valley of Mamre; . . . then was Christ in Person there.''[5]

***

Once Abraham had beheld Christ's birth at the valley of Mamre, there was nothing else for the object of his joy, even the promises made to him and his descendants, from whose *seed* the Saviour of the world came. Andrewes urges us to have a similar intensity of joy, especially as we have a greater need of a Redeemer.

''For that it was no earthly thing which was the object of his joy, nothing but heaven, thence it may appear, that when God promised him, *his seed should be as the dust of the earth*, it never moved him; it was no object that of his faith or desire, not so much as a *credibit* follows upon it. But after, . . . when God bade him look up, and told him, *they should be as the stars of heaven*; then presently follows, *Credidit Abraham Deo*, he caught hold of that; *believed*, . . . and *it was counted to him for righteousness*. . . . that his seed should be his Saviour, and out of his root should rise his Redeemer. . . .

Now to ourselves. And the first point is, whether we shall be . . . with Abraham, in the fellowship of this day's joy. If all be well weighed, we have greater cause to desire the day than he; we have more need of it I am sure. Dust as he, but more in danger to be made ashes than he. . . . The benefit of His day and the like, they . . . do nothing so much concern the just such as Abraham, as they do sinful Manasses . . . and such are we; and ever the more sinner, the more it imports him to love the dawning of this day. Greater cause we have than he.''[6]

***

Recognizing that we are sinners our joy therefore begins with *exultavit*, and ends with *gavisus est*. It is the inward joy and gladness of the spirit which are more important than any bodily rejoicing. Thus our joy for this day begins in His House at His feast at the altar, that joy that one day will be perfect when we behold Him on the last day.

''Our joy . . . [is twofold]: Exultation, a motion of the body [and] the other joy, a fruit of the spirit: . . . let the body have his part. Reason would the body and the flesh should be allowed their parts, since all the joy is for *corpus aptasi Mihi*, and that *Verbum caro factum est* . . . .But let not *exultavit* be all, whole and sole. Then we joy but by halves; we lose half our joy, and the better half; for the joy of the

46

spirit is the better part, when all is done. The flesh fades daily; so do the joys of it: *the spirit is the better part that shall not be taken from us*. That of the spirit should exceed the joy of the outward man. . . . Time will come, that one lesson in this kind, learned this day and laid up well, will do us more pleasure than all the sports we shall see the whole twelve days after. . . .

[Next] our joy be for *diem Meum*, and that our joy in *diem* be for *Meum*. . . . That is, that we joy in it, as it is His — Christ's. . . . this is to desire Him for the day, not the day for Him. . . .

The beginning of the joy of His day would be in His House. . . . He invites us to His feast. His Church so does in His name; even this day prepares and sets Christ's feast before us, wherein He offers Himself to us. . . .

For we are come hither for this cause; here then show your joy in His feast-day by partaking His feast on His day, the only feast of all the rest for which the soul is the better. Thus shall we with joy keep this day aright. . . .

All will be, how to make that a day of joy to us when we see it; to have that day rise clear and cheerful to us, will be the joy of all joys. For here first as *we see but in part* so we can joy but in part. . . . But there *we shall see as we are seen* ; our sight being perfect, so shall our joy be. . . . And it shall not endure for twelve days, or be a feast of a fortnight; but shall be from month to month, from jubilee to jubilee, for ever and ever.''[7]

References

[1] Andrewes, Vol. I, pp. 118–120.
[2] *ibid.*, pp. 121–2.
[3] *ibid.*, pp. 123–4.
[4] *ibid.*, pp. 125–6.
[5] *ibid.*, pp. 126–8.
[6] *ibid.*, pp. 130–1.
[7] *ibid.*, pp. 131–4.

NATIVITY SERMON No. 9
CHRISTMAS DAY 1614

Text: Isaiah 8:14

Behold, a virgin shall conceive, and
bear a Son, and shall call His name Emmanuel.

Ecce virgo concipiet, et pariet Filium, et
vocabitur nomen Ejus Immanuel.

Isaiah foretells the coming of the Christ-Child, with its proclamation of God being with us. Thus his prophecy pre-empts the same message that the angel Gabriel declares on that first Christmas night as recorded by St. Luke. Both Isaiah and Luke draw attention to the command, *behold*. To *behold* what? The birth of a son by a virgin. Thus this *ecce* echoes the mystery of the Incarnation, the Nativity and Circumcision directing us to both the Mother and the Child.

Firstly *concipiet*. Unlike the Manichees who held that Christ had a ghostly body, Christians believe that Christ's very nature and substance was His Mother's flesh, who although a virgin conceived through the power of the Holy Spirit. *With God all things are possible.*

"Of all the writers of the Old Testament, the prophet Isaiah has the honour to be the first that is vouched in the New. And of all the places this place the honour to be the first of all, even in the first evangelist, St. Matthew, and in the very first chapter of him. . . .

But the angel Gabriel does it more, who takes this verse as it stands, word for word, and makes it serve for his annunciation or message to the Blessed Virgin without any alteration; not so much as the *ecce* left out.

The tenor of it is all about a Child to be born, a Child with an *ecce;* in Whom and in Whose birth, God should be with us — so with us as never before. On Whose so being with us depends all our well or evil being here, and for ever. For better not to be at all than be without Him; and having Him we need nothing else.

Ecce has in it two powers. One for the ear, to awake it to something matter more than ordinary. Two another for the eye, to direct it by pointing to some certainty; as here to two certain persons, mother and child. And shows us two strange sights in them *mater virgo*, and *Deus homo; a virgin to become a mother, God to become man.* A virgin to bear; God to be born. In both, and in either of them, three points are offered to us. . . . 1. The mystery of His holy Incarnation, in *concipiet*; 2. His holy Nativity, in *pariet*; 3. His Circumcision, *vocabit nomen*. . . .

Firstly, Christ as embryo, in His conception. . . . and it first points to *ecce Virgo*.
. . .

For he calls us to see a sign, and that with an *ecce*; and what is that? if it be but a young woman to conceive, and no virgin, where is the sign, what is become of the *ecce?* It is no sign or wonder, unless it be beside the course of nature. . . .

To conceive this conceiving, to join these two, a virgin, and yet conceive or bear; or conceive and bear, and yet be a virgin. For before the birth, yes, before the conceiving come, the virginity is gone. True — in nature; but this is a sign, and so above nature. . . . For what God can do faith can believe, reason cannot comprehend. . . .

The blessed Virgin herself asked, *How it might be?* . . .

Why should it be thought a thing incredible? . . . As the angel concluded, so do I, *With God nothing is impossible* . . . And where they meet, they make no less a miracle than *Mater* and *Virgo,* or *Deus* and *Homo* . . . . And this, for *Virgo concipiet.* . . .

First, *concipiet* . . . by way of conception there comes of man nothing but man; nothing but of the same nature and substance with that he was conceived of. . . . The blessed Virgin . . . [gave] of her own substance whereof His body was framed; and take or receive power from the Holy Spirit, whereby was supplied the office and efficacy of the masculine seed. This is *concipiet.*''[1]

***

Christ's conception reveals the extent of God's love for us and the many benefits we receive from Him. Even while an embryo, He was working towards our cleansing and restoration from the stain of sin.

''From which His conceiving we may conceive His great love to us-ward. Love, not only condescending to take our nature upon Him, but to take it by the same way and after the same manner that we do, by being conceived. . . . The womb of the Virgin . . . He might well have abhorred . . . [but] He stayed . . . nine months. . . .

This sure is matter of love; but came there any good to us by it? There did. For our conception being the root as it were, the very groundsill of our nature; that He might go to the root and repair of our nature from the very foundation, thither He went; that what had been there defiled and decayed by the first Adam, might by the Second be cleansed and set right again. That had our conception been stained, by Him therefore, *primum ante omnia,* to be restored again. He was not idle all the time He was an embyro — all the nine months He was in the womb; but then and there He even ate out the core of corruption that cleft to our nature and us, and made both us and it an unpleasing object in the sight of God.

And what came of this? We who were abhorred by God, *filii irae* was our title, were by this means made beloved in Him. He cannot, we may be sure, account evil of that nature, that is now become the nature of His own Son — His now no less than ours. . . . This honour is to us by the dishonour of Him; this the good by Christ an embyro.''[2]

***

Secondly, the Nativity — *pariet*. With His appearing we are assured of His being with us, now and ever. Thirdly, His *et vocabit nomen*. His naming is important. We need to be assured that God is with us, and in that name *Emmanuel*, He will save us from our sins.

"And *pariet* makes all appear. We could not tell it was *Filium* . . . till He came into the world. . . . But when He was born, when come into the world, we see Him and handle Him; then He was *with us* indeed. *With us,* not as conceived of the same nature with us, but as born and now a Person among us. [What] was potential in *concipiet*, made actual by *pariet*. . . .

And now He is born, might we not leave here, and go no further. What care we for the name? Yes, we must; for *Christus anonymus* will not serve. Therefore Isaiah, therefore the angel are careful to bear Him to His baptism, to add His name; the prophet to intimate it, St. Matthew to interpret it. . . . But His name, St. Matthew tells us the prophet but brought, it was God who sent it. . . .

Now there were [several] names given him at [many] times. . . . There was Jacob's name, Shiloh, that was in respect of His Father, by Whom and from Whom He was sent. There was Paul's name, Messiah, Christ; that was regard had to the Holy Spirit, by or wherewith He was annointed. But what were these? . . . We have no part in them. . . . But in this Emmanuel, here come we in first. . . .

It will be said, this was not His name in the end for all this, but Jesus. True; and St. Matthew knew that well enough, for he sets it down so. Yet even in that place he sets it down, . . . as if Emmanuel and Jesus both came to one, as indeed they do; one infers the other. Emmanuel, *God with us.* Why? To what end? To save us from our sins, and from perishing by them."[3]

***

Andrewes dissects Emmanuel into its syllables to give each its meaning: *Em, with; anu, we;* and *el, God. God with us.* Through Christ, as the *cum*, God and man are now joined for ever, sealed by His blood at His naming. Thus He is in every part of our humanity, except our sinning. There is nothing more we could desire.

"And now, to look into the name. It is compounded, and to be taken in pieces. . . .*El* is God . . . By the name we take our first notice that this Child is God. . . .*El* is God; and not God every way, but as the force of the word is, God in His full strength and virtue; God *with all that ever He can do*; and that is enough I am sure.

For the other, *Emmanu* . . . [does] more concern us; . . . *anu,* we, poor we, poor indeed if we have all the world beside if we have not Him to be with us; . . . *Em,* which is *cum,* and that *cum* in the midst between *nobis* and *Deus,* God and us — to couple God and us. . . .

This *cum* we shall never conceive to purpose, but *carendo*; the value of *with* no way so well as by without, by stripping of *cum* from *nobis.* And so let *nobis,* us, stand by ourselves without Him, to see what our case is but for this Emmanuel; . . . for if this Child be *Emmanuel, God with us,* then without this Child, this Emmanuel, we be without God. . . . What with Him? Why, if we have Him, and God

50

by Him, we need no more; *Emmanu-el* and *Emmanu-all*. All that we can desire is for us to be with Him, with God, and He to be with us; and we from Him, or He from us, never to be parted. We were with Him once before, and we were well; and when we left Him, and He no longer *with us*, then began all our misery. Whensoever we go from Him, so shall we be in evil case, and never be well till we back with Him again.

Then, if this be our case that we cannot be without Him, no remedy then but to get a *cum* by whose means *nobis* and *Deus* may come together again. And Christ is that *cum* to bring it to pass. The parties are God and we; and now this day He is both. God before eternally, and now to-day Man; and so both, and takes hold of both, and brings both together again. For two natures here are in Him. If conceived and born of a woman, then a man; if God with us, then God. . . . And both these natures in the unity of one Person, called by one name, even this name Emmanuel. . . .

To be *cum*, to come between, that is, to be a Mediator, to make Him who was *contra nos, nobiscum* again. . . .

So a second kind of Trinity — God, we, and Christ. *El* is God, *anu* we; for Christ is nothing left but *Em*, that is *cum* or *with*. For it is He who makes the unity in this Trinity; makes God with us, and us with God; and both, in and by Him, to our eternal comfort and joy.

He . . . is . . . *with us* in His nature, that is *with us* as man . . . in all things, *sin only except. . . .* [But] unity of nature is not enough, He is to be *with us* in unity of Person likewise. So He was. The debtor and surety make but one person in law. That He was, and then He was *Cum, with us*, thoroughly, as deep in as we.

And this is the proper *Emmanu* of His name. . . . And till He was thus *with us*, no name He had; He was *Christus anonymus, Christ unchristened*, as it were. For His name came not till He become One *with us* in person; not till His circumcision; not till for us and in our names, He became debtor of the whole Law, principal, forfeiture, and all. To the *hand-writing*, He then signed with the first-fruits, of His blood. And then, name the Child, and gave Him this name, *Emmanuel*. For this He was a right *Emmanuel*, truly *with us*. *With us* as men; *with us* as sinful men; *with us* in all things, sin itself not excepted.''[4]

***

To be *with us* always demanded great sacrifice by the Mediator, the shedding of His blood on behalf of us. Since that sacrifice He is *with us* in every imaginable way, at the altar, in His Resurrection and Ascension, and indeed to the end of the world.

''. . . His mother [gave] Him the name . . . when He dropped a little blood as the sealing of the bond. But He was fain not to drop blood, but to sweat blood, and to shed His blood, every drop of it, [before] this *with us* were full answered. . . . He had proved Himself fully, *with us per omnia*, when neither womb nor birth, cratch nor cross, cross nor curse, could pluck him away from us, or make Him not to be *with us.* . . .

This is the great *with us*; for of this follow all the rest. *With us* once thus, and then *with us* in His oblation on the altar of the Temple; *with us* in His sacrifice on the altar of the cross; *with us* in all the virtues and merits of His life; . . . *with us* in the satisfaction and satis-passion of His death; *with us* in His Resurrection, to raise us up from the earth; *with us* in His Ascension, to exalt us to heaven; *with us* even then, when He seemed to be taken from us — that day by His Spirit, as this day by His flesh. . . . And lo, I am true *Emmanuel with you* by the love of My manhood; *with you* by the power of My Godhead, still *to the end of the world.*"[5]

***

The fact that *emmanu* comes before *El* reveals that we were more precious to God than Himself. We would have thought that God would always come before us, but no, such is the extent of His love. It also manifests that He wants us *to be made the sons of God.* This we can inherit through our Baptism.

"*Emmanuel, nobiscum* before *Deus.* . . . He the priority of the place in all reason. . . . But He giving it Himself would have it stand thus; us set before Him. There is a meaning in it. . . . That in the very name we might read that we are dearer to Him than Himself; that He so preferred us, and that His own name does no less, but give out to all the world the *ecce* of St. John's Gospel . . . [and] his Epistle. . . . *See how He loved them! Behold, how great love He bare to them!* . . . Whether was greater, humility or charity in Him! Hard to say whether, but both unspeakable.

Is this all? No; there is another in the very body of the word itself. *With us* — to make us that to God that He was this day made to man. And this indeed was the chief end of His being *with us*; to give us . . . *a power to be made the sons of God,* by being born again of water and of the Spirit; the same original that Himself took in the womb of the Virgin to us-ward, the same has He placed for us in the fountain of Baptism to God-ward. Well therefore call the womb of the Church to the Virgin's womb, with a power given it of *concipiet et pariet filius* to God. So His being conceived and born the Son of man does conceive and bring forth our being born, our being born, our being the sons of God. His participation of our human, our participation of His Divine nature."[6]

***

We can also be with Him, especially on this day, when the Sacrament and Nativity are one, as they meet at the altar. This we always have until finally we meet Him in heaven.

"We are with Him; our prayers, our praises are with Him; but that is in our spirits whence they come.

These are well, but these are not all we can; and none of these, the proper *with Him* of the day. That has a special *Cum* of itself, peculiar to it. Namely, that we be so with Him, as He this day was with us; that was in flesh, not in spirit only. That

52

flesh that was conceived and this day born, that body that was this day fitted to Him. And if we be not with Him thus, if this His flesh be not *with us*, if we partake it not, which way soever else we be with Him, we come short of the *Em* of this day. . . . Sure no being with Him so kindly, so pleasing to Him, so fitting, as to grow into one with Him; as upon the same day, so the very same way He did with us. . . .

This then I commend to you, even the being with Him in the Sacrament of His Body, that Body that was conceived and born, as for the other ends so for this specially, to be *with you*; and this day, as for other intents, so even for this, for the Holy Eucharist. Thus, as the kindliest for the time, as the surest for the manner of being with [you]. . . .

This is all we can come to here . . . upon earth. But this is not all; there is [more] to come still. For we are not together; we are parted. . . . He in heaven, and we in earth. But it shall not always so be. Beside this day *Emmanuel* has another day,. and that day will come; and when it does come, He will come and take us to Himself. That as He has been our *Emmanuel* up on earth, so He may be our *Emmanuel* in heaven; He with us, and we with Him, there for ever.

This of the Sacrament is a preparation to that; will conceive and bring forth the other. For immediately after He had given them the Holy Eucharist, He prayed . . . that they had so been with in the blessed Sacrament; *Father, My will is*, My prayer, My last prayer, *that where I am they may be also.*

And He is in heaven, in the joy and glory there; and there He would have us. . . . Thither may it bring us, and thither may we come and there be — He *with us*, and we with Him for ever. *Emmanuel* is the end of the verse; the same be our end, that so we may be happy and blessed without end!'' [7]

References

[1] Andrewes, Vol. I, pp. 135–140.
[2] *ibid.*, pp. 140–1.
[3] *ibid.*, pp. 141–3.
[4] *ibid.*, pp. 144–7.
[5] *ibid.*, p. 147.
[6] *ibid.*, pp. 148, 150–1.
[7] *ibid.*, pp. 151–2.

NATIVITY SERMON No. 10
CHRISTMAS DAY 1615

Text: Micah 5:2

But you, Bethlehem, Ephratah, though there
be little among the thousands of Judah,
yet out of you shall He come forth unto me
Who is to be ruler in Israel; Whose goings
forth have been from of old, from everlasting.

*Et tu Bethlehem Ephrata, parvulus es in
millibus Juda: ex te mihi egreditur Qui sit
Dominator in Israel; et egressus Ejus ab
initio a diebus aeternitatis.*

Bethlehem, the place where Christ was born, and foretold by Micah, is the focal point in this sermon. Thus not only Isaiah but Micah also had his share in prophesying about the Nativity. His was the place, where the Child would be born. *Et tu Bethlehem.*

"The prophet Isaiah had the honour to be the first, . . . [while] the prophet Micah . . . the second. . . .
Isaiah, His birth, . . . Micah, the place of His birth. *Behold a Virgin shall bear*, said Isaiah, and Bethlehem will be the place where she will do it, says Micah. His name, says, Isaiah, *will be God with us*; with us, says Micah, *to be our Guide* and conduct us. He with us in Bethlehem in the beginning of the verse, that we with Him in eternity in the end of it."[1]

***

Within the Christmas narrative, it is the Star which enables the birthplace, Bethlehem, to be known and thus for the Child to be visited and manifested.

"The star does lead us to Bethlehem. . . . Never stood still till it came thither, and there it stood directly over the place, as much to say as, *Lo, there He is born.*
. . .
The place of the birth [leads] to the birth itself, and the birth to the [Person] born, Who . . . comes forth . . . to lead us and feed us, and so to conduct us from Bethlehem where this day we come first acquainted with Him, to the state of eternity [from] whence He came out to bring us in; there to live and reign with Him for ever."[2]

Andrewes dwells on the place of Christ's birth. Although Bethlehem is a tiny town, born in it is something great, God Himself, who is the ruler of the universe. From now onwards Bethlehem will be great. Choosing such a little town, was in character with God who always delighted in bringing *maxima de minimis*, the great from something small. Such a feat was common in nature; we see it in the oak from the acorn and the large mustard plant from a grain.

"Bethlehem . . . is a sorry, poor village, . . . and as little likelihood, that so great a State as the Guide of the whole world should come creeping out such a corner. . . . That birth is sure too big for this place. . . . As little as it is, no little Person shall come out of it. . . .

One, Whose only coming forth of it was able to make it not the least, [but] the greatest and most famous of all the dwellings of Jacob, of the whole land, no, of the whole world. . . .

What shall we make of this? . . . Nothing but . . . that with God it is no new thing . . . to bring *maxima de minimis*, Christ out of Bethlehem. Which is plain even in nature. How huge an oak from how small an acorn! . . . From how little a grain of mustard-seed, the very *Bethlehem minima, the least of all seeds,* how large a plant! of how fair a spread! and that in a little time."3

***

The smallness of Bethlehem is congruous with the lowly nature of the Christ-Child. We can learn from Him to temper pride with lowliness.

". . . that it was *minima* . . . For in so being, it was a place well suiting with His estate . . . which was the state of humility, eminent in His . . . birth. Bethlehem was not so *little*, but He as *little* as it. . . .

And O you little Bethlehem, and O you little Bethlemite, how do you both, both place and person, confound the haughtiness of many that yet would be called Christians, and even near Christ Himself. There is in both of you, if it were well taken to heart, enough to prick the swelling, and let out . . . pride from . . . many of us, whose look, gesture . . . and . . . vanity are too big for Bethlehem."4

***

For the sake of what Bethlehem signifies, Andrewes pleads that we give due honour to it as He Who comes out of it will bring us to eternity.

"For little Bethlehem's sake . . . love the virtue that is like it, and for the virtue's sake to honour it. Honour it. There is a star over it, there is a Saviour in it. Honour it for Who comes out of it, for the fruit it yields. More good comes forth out of that poor town, says the prophet, . . . than from all the great and glorious cities in the world. . . . Bethlehem . . . *gives us our introduction to paradise.*"5

***

From the place, Andrewes turns to the Person who comes from it. As His birth place is a temporal thing, unlike His permanent heavenly home, He must leave it, and so the emphasis must be on the Person. Just as the Son of God left heaven, so the Son of Man must leave Bethlehem.

"Now for the Person who comes from this place. . . . The Child who . . . comes . . . *once out of Bethlehem*, . . . another *from everlasting*. . . . These two set out to us His two comings forth, that is, His two nativities. . . .
Out of [Bethlehem] He came. . . . For as eternal, no place contains Him, He is everywhere; [He] fills both heaven and earth. . . .
His *outgoings* [were] . . . as the Son of God before all times, and as Son of man *in the fullness of time*. . . . Even that *out of Bethlehem* He should come; be *the Son of man, the Saviour of mankind*, and their *Guide* to eternity."[6]

***

Once Christ came forth from Bethlehem, He became our Guide to lead us along the path to eternity. Having a Guide means we cannot get lost unless we choose to; it also enables us to be provided for along the way, but it also implies a duty from the guided to follow in obedience.

"He came to be our Guide to a place. . . . For a guide serves properly to bring one to a place. There is in that word both the office He to perform to us, and the benefit we to receive by Him guiding. And it implies also our duty to Him. . . . For if He to lead, we to be led by Him. . . .
None can bring to a place so well as He who has been there. . . . He who knows not whither he goes, wanders. . . . And sure, the way is not ready to hit; not so easy a fool may find it. . . .
[Many] by-ways there be, . . . many cross paths and turnings in and out; and we like enough to miss it, if we venture on it without a guide."[7]

***

Before setting out on any journey, one has to be convinced it will be easier with help. The road to heaven is no exception. We have to believe *He is the way*. Once *our feet* set out along the path, we can go *in the way of peace*.

"The first point then is to find our own want, to think we are in case to need a guide. For if we need none, this text is superfluous; and you Bethlehem, and You Christ, . . . may both well be spared. . . .
Well, he was a wise man and a great counsellor who said . . . *How can I without a guide?* . . . Let us follow [Him] . . .
One then who is skilful. And where shall we have any so skilful as . . . this of ours? [who] . . . is the Way and the End both. . . .

56

Nothing remains but that we now set forward in this way, . . . as we daily sing in the *Benedictus* He came . . . *to guide our feet . . . into the way of peace.*"8

***

A good guide always provides nourishment for a journey, and the Son of man is no exception. As the journey is heaven-bound He provides heavenly Bread which is sufficient sustenance. Indeed Bethlehem Ephratah itself reminds us of this, as the names mean *house of bread* and *plenty* respectively. Thus His House always has Bread when we come because He is the Bread of life.

"He is not a good guide who . . . cannot lead us where we may [have] . . . necessary food for our relief. . . . [Our] Guide . . . will lead *as a shepherd does his flock . . .* to *good green pasture, besides the waters of comfort*; [and] see they want nothing. . . .
The name of the place [where] He was born in seems to favour this most. . . . *Beth* is a house, *lehem* bread, and *Ephratah* is plenty. . . . Bethlehem then sure a fit place for . . . [Him] to be born in. . . . He can never say that Bethlehem is his house, and that is *donus panis*, and *in domo panis semper est panis*. Never take Him without bread, His house is the house of bread, inasmuch as He Himself is Bread; that in the house or out of it — wheresoever He is, there is Bethlehem. There can no bread want."9

***

Andrewes in further elaborating on Christ as the Bread of Life and Bethlehem as the House of Bread, compares Christ's nourishing of His people with that of Moses' provision for the Israelites in their wanderings in the desert.

"You may see all this represented in the shadows of the Old Testament. . . .
Moses, when he came to lead the people, found them . . . *scattered over all the land of Egypt, to seek stubble for brick.* . . . Our case right the very pattern of it; when our Guide finds us wandering in vanity, picking up straws, things that will not profit us; . . . till we be so happy as to light into His guiding.
Secondly, Moses was to them not only *dux viae, a guide for the way*; but when enemies came forth against them, *dux militiae, a captain for the war.* Christ was so too, and far beyond Moses. For He made us [a] way with laying down of His life.
. . .
Thirdly, Moses when they fainted by the way obtained in their hunger manna *from Heaven*, and in their thirst *water out of the rock for them.* Christ is Himself the *true Manna* ; Christ, the spiritual Rock. Whom He leads He feeds; carries Bethlehem about Him."10

***

As always with Andrewes nourishment for the journey comes mainly from the Sacrament. By receiving Him regularly under the guise of Bread and Wine, we are strengthened on our pilgrimage.

"The ordaining of His last sacrament, [was] . . . the means to re-establish *our hearts with grace*, and to repair the decays of our spiritual strength; even *His own flesh, the Bread of life*, and *His own blood, the Cup of salvation*. Bread made of Himself, the true *Granum frumenti. Wine made of Himself, the true Vine*. Went under the sickle, flail, millstone, and oven, even to be made this Bread; *trod, or was trodden, in the wine-press alone*, to prepare this Cup for us.

And in this respect it may well be said, Bethlehem was never Bethlehem right, had never the name truly till this day this birth, this Bread was born and brought forth there. Before it was the house of bread, but of the bread that perishes; but [now] of the *Bread that endures to everlasting life.*"11

***

Although Christ is now in heaven, He has left His footprints for us to trace His steps. The most important thing to-day is for us to go to Bethlehem as the *unlettered* shepherds and wise men did.

"There is the rendezvous to-day, there He will be first seen and saluted, there He began with us, then we to begin with Him; where He set forth, there our setting forth to be also. Indeed, there is no finding Him but there, this feast. There the shepherds found Him this day the first; there the wise men on [the] twelfth day. But thither they came both; both the shepherds directed by the angel, and the wise men guided by the stars. . . . Be what we will be, at Bethlehem to begin all. Thither to go to Him, thence to set out after Him."12

***

As we journey, we must take with us the lesson learnt from this little town of Bethlehem, *humility*. Significantly too, this Bethlehem being in Ephratah signfies *fruitfulness* as compared to the Bethlehem in Zebulon, denoting barrenness. Our lives must follow the first of these Bethlehems, bearing forth the fruit of good works.

"Bethlehem is *little*. And look, what little and low is in quantity, that is little in our own eyes and lowly in quality. Get that first, humility, it is the Bethlehem of virtues where He in great humility was found this day. If we begin not there, we lose our way at the first setting out. For this is sure; where eternity is the *terminus ad quem*, there humility is the *terminus a quo*. . . .

The next station is to the next virtue, and that is Ephratah, *fruitfulness* . . . for He has brought forth . . . *a lasting seed*; the fruit whereof to this day *shakes like Libanus, and as the green grass covers all the earth.* . . . [Thus] to humility to add

58

fruitfulness, I mean plenteousness in all good works. Else it is not Ephratah; . . . not right repentance unless it be Ephratah, *bring forth fruits of repentance*; nor faith, *without the work of faith*; nor love, *without the labour of love*; nor any other virtue without her Ephratah. . . .

Fruitful then, . . . not the fruit of the lips, a few good words *but the precious fruit of the earth*, as St James calls it — *lehem, good bread*, that fruit. Such fruit as St. Paul carried to the poor saints at Jerusalem, *alms and offerings* . . .

Now if we could bring these together, . . . straight we cease to be little; we begin to talk of merit and worth, and I [know] not what."[13]

***

Andrewes concludes that if we follow Him He will lead us to the Tree of Life, even the Bread of life. By eating thereof we shall have life yes, even life immortal. That is His food He leads us to. And if we would forget this, Bethlehem where the star perpetually shines above, will remind us. *There we receive the breaking of bread, which the Church as this day ever has, and still uses at the Child-house feast.* Our perseverance along the way will bring us to paradise.

"*Going thither* [to Bethlehem]. That may we even locally do and never go out of this room, . . . as here is to be had the *true Bread of life that came down from Heaven.* Which is His *flesh* this day born, which *He gave for the life of the world*, called by Him so, the true Bread, the Bread of heaven, the Bread of life — and where that Bread is, there is Bethlehem for ever. . . . There shall ever be this day a Bethlehem to go to — a house wherein there is bread, and this bread. And will there be Bethlehem, and so near us, and shall we not go to it? Or, shall we go to it, to the House of Bread, this Bread, and come away without it? Shall we forsake our Guide leading us to a place so much for our benefit? . . .

Thither He will bring us . . . to that whereunto, even from paradise, we should have been translated, to the state of eternity, to the joys and joyful days there; even to glory, joy and bliss eternal."[14]

References

[1] Andrewes, Vol. I, p. 153.
[2] *ibid.*, pp. 154–5.
[3] *ibid.*, pp. 157–9.
[4] *ibid.*, pp. 160–1.
[5] *ibid.*, p. 162.
[6] *ibid.*, pp. 162–4.
[7] *ibid.*, pp. 164–6.
[8] *ibid.*, pp. 166–7.
[9] *ibid.*, pp. 167–8.
[10] *ibid.*, pp. 168–9.
[11] *ibid.*, pp. 169–70.
[12] *ibid.*, pp. 170–1.
[13] *ibid.*, pp. 171–3.
[14] *ibid.*, pp. 173–4.

NATIVITY SERMON No. 11
CHRISTMAS DAY 1617

Text: Psalm 85: 10–11

Mercy and Truth are met together;
Righteousness and Peace will kiss each other.
Truth shall spring out of the earth;
and Righteousness shall look down
from heaven.

Misericordia et Veritas obviaverunt sibi;
Justitia et Pax osculatae sunt
Veritas de terra orta est; et Justitia de
Caelo prospexit.

Truth and *Righteousness* are the key words in this text which comes from one of the psalms selected by the primitive Church for Christmas day, and is still retained as part of the office for that great feast. In this psalm, its author, in foretelling release from the Jewish captivity, anticipates another deliverer who will free those under a greater bondage, the captivity of sin.

". . . it cannot be denied but the psalm was first set according to the letter upon the turning back of the captivity of Babel. But the [psalmist] knew well that was not their worst captivity, nor should be their best delivery. . . . [This] was reserved to the Messiah to free them from [captivity]."[1]

***

After a long estrangement, at Christ's birth, both *Truth* and *Righteousness* met and kissed each other when from heaven *Righteousness* witnessed and smiled upon the manifestation of *Truth* on earth in the manger at Bethlehem. At last there is a reconciliation between them.

"There is a meeting here. A meeting at a birth. A birth that did them in heaven, Righteousness by name, good to behold. The meeting in *obviaverunt*, the birth in *orta*, the pleasure to behold it in *prospexit de Caelo*. *Prospexit* is to see with delight, as when we look into some pleasant prospect.

A meeting qualified, for the manner. For they do not meet and pass by, but meet and salute as friends with an *osculate sunt*, a sign of love begun or renewed. . . .

At a birth, at *orta est*, these four meet here; at *orta est Veritas, the birth of truth de terra, from the earth.* For two *ortus* there were; and this, not His *antesaecularis ortus de Caelo, His birth before all worlds from heaven,* but His *ortus de terra, His temporal birth from the earth.*

60

Lastly, the birth, . . . such a spectacle it was as it drew Righteousness itself from Heaven to look at it. Time was when Righteousness would not have done so much. . . . That then and ever since she has beheld the earth and the dwellers in it with a far more favourable regard than before. And all for this birth's sake.

And when was all this? When He said of Himself *I am the Truth*, when He was born upon earth; for *orta est Veritas*, and *natus est Christus* will fall out to be one birth. . . . And that was this day, of all the days of the year. The meeting and the day of this meeting here all one, and the birth of Christ the cause of both.

. . . Not every set meeting is memorable; this is . . . Righteousness, who is to be our Judge and to give the last sentence upon us, beholds us with an aspect that promises favour.''[2]

***

Andrewes directs us to the other two attributes of God as expressed in the psalm: *mercy* and *peace*. Just as *truth* and *righteousness* compliment one another, so do *mercy* and *peace*. These two are in fact more favourably disposed towards man than ever *Righteousness* was. *Mercy* finds herself instinctively seeking *Peace*, and being attracted to *Truth,* while *Peace* and *Righteousness* seek each other. That they were divided at all resulted from our wrongs. Before Adam's fall, these four attributes were undivided in the bosom of God. Once Adam lied, *Truth* perished until Christ's birth; then it became the bridge for all to meet.

"Mercy and Peace, they two pair well; . . . so the other two, Truth and Righteousness, seem to be of one complexion and disposition, and commonly take part together. Of these Mercy seems to favour us; and Peace no enemy to us nor to any . . . mild and gentle persons both. For Righteousness I know not well what to say: *gestat gladium*, and I fear *non frustra*. Nor of Truth, which is *vera* and *severa*. . . . . These I doubt are not like affected. . . . So then two for us, two against us.

For their order. Mercy is first, and Peace last. . . . On the one side, Mercy before; on the other, Peace behind.

Another, that in this double meeting Mercy sorts not herself, goes not to Righteousness; nor Righteousness to her, but to Peace. A kind of cross meeting, as it were, there is — the better hope of accord. Mercy and Righteousness have no symbolizing quality at all, no hope of them; but Truth with Mercy has. There is Truth as well in the promise of Mercy as in the threat of Justice.

And it stands yet better between the other two, Righteousness and Peace. Melchhizedek, which is by interpretation *King of Righteousness*, the same is *King of Salem*, that is *of peace*. He who *is after the order of Melchizedek*, King of both, like enough to set accord between them two, both of them His lieges. . . .

Since naturally they are not strangers, all four in the bosom of God from all eternity — attributes all four of His undivided Essence, So, not divided of themselves. . . . That they were divided, it was about us; . . . [we] made them

61

part company. . . . If at Christ's birth they met, at Adam's fall they parted; if when Truth was born on earth they came together, when Truth perished from the earth they fell in sunder. That was when the first lie was told . . . by Adam, and thereby God much wronged. . . .

Out of Christ and before His birth, they met in opposition; in Christ and at His birth, did these four lights come to meet and to be in conjunction now."3

***

Before Christ's birth the only attribute to look with any favour on man had been *Mercy* which ever offers *Pity* and help to fallen man. Yet *Mercy* must always be tempered with *Truth* and *Righteousness*. God can never falsify Himself, and He must always judge justly. *Peace* acts as a buffer between them both.

"While Mercy and Peace would have Adam's and our case relieved, Righteousness and Truth would by no means endure it. . . . Mercy began, for out of her readiness to do good she is here, she is ever foremost. Her inclination is . . . to pity such as are in misery, and if she can to relieve them, yes, though they deserve it not. For . . . she looks not to . . . what he is or what he has done or deserved, but what he suffers, in how woeful and wretched case he is. And her plea is, *nunquid in vanum? What has God made all men for nought?* . . . It will make God's enemies rejoice, ... if . . . He [will] cast them off for ever. . . . [Rather] she [enters] into God's [heart], and makes [it] yearn and melt into compassion. . . .

But Truth must be heard too . . . . What is God but His Word? . . . God may not falsify His word; His word is the truth. Falsify the truth? That may not be.

God . . . is [also] *righteous in all His works.* . . . God forbid, the Judge of the world should judge unjustly! That were, as before to make truth false, so here to do right wrong. . . .

As for Peace, she went between both, to see if she could make them meet again on better terms."4

***

Yet even *Peace* could not reconcile *Righteousness* and *Truth* with *Mercy* until the four attributes could meet once again. This wonderful meeting occurred in the silent hours of the night in Bethlehem upon this very day for that Babe was the Word from heaven, but now also of the earth. From this moment *Truth* will now meet *Mercy*.

"To us they meet this day at the Child-house. . . .
Veritas will fit Christ well Who of Himself said, *I am the Truth* . . . He [is also] the *Veritas prima, the first Truth* within. . . .
For now by His coming He is the adequation of the Word and the Work, the Promise and the Performance. That way He is Truth too, the truth of all types. . . . the truth of all prophecies; for *in Him are all the promises yes and Amen* . . .
And as truth fits His nature, so does earth man. . . . *Let this earth bring forth a Saviour.* . . . *What the truth? Christ. What the earth? our flesh.* In those words they find this feast all. . . .

And Truth being now born of our nature, it will never we may be sure be against our nature; being come of the earth, it will be true to his own country; being made man, will be for man now all he can."[5]

***

Mercy, Peace and *Truth* have all agreed; only *Righteousness* remains. As *Righteousness* looked down from Heaven upon the Christ Child she was moved. Nevertheless she demanded to see a sinless life. Once this was achieved, they all embraced.

"It is three to one now. Righteousness is left all alone and there is good hope she will not stand out long. . . . When she beheld *Verbum caro factum*, the truth freshly sprung there where it had been a strange plant long time before, she looked and looked again at it. For a sight it was to move, to draw the eye; yes a sight for Heaven to be a spectator of, for the Angels to come down and look at, for Righteousness itself to do so too. . . .

For what could Righteousness desire to see and satisfy herself with, that in Him was not to be seen? A clean birth, a holy life, an innocent death; a Spirit and a mouth without guile, a soul and a body without sin. In Him she beheld them all. Them, and whatsoever else might yield her full satisfaction. . . .

Upon this sight she is not only content . . . to do it but she breaks a window through to do it. And then she looks upon the earth with a good aspect.

For upon the view of this birth they all ran first and *kissed the Son*. And that done, Truth ran to Mercy and embraced her; and Righteousness to Peace, and kissed her. They that had so long been parted and stood out in difference, now meet and are made friends. . . .

All meet in Him, for indeed all He is; that no marvel they all four meet where He is that is all four. . . .

Thus you see Christ by His coming *has pacified the things in heaven.* A peace of Hosannah is *pax in Caelis*; there cannot be *pax in terris* till there it be first. But no sooner there it is, but it is peace in earth straight, which accordingly was this day proclaimed by the angels. So by the virtue of this birth, heaven is at peace with itself; and heaven with earth is now at peace. So is earth with itself."[6]

***

How do we relate to these four in regards to our Christian living? For instance, *Mercy* and *Truth* meet in confession of sins. After a true confession, *Righteousness* will approve from her heavenly throne, which in turn reaches out to *Peace*. From hence all are bound together; they no longer function separately.

"Mercy and Truth first to meet. Truth of confession; confession of our sins; which if with fig-leaves we seek to cover and confess not, *there is no truth in us.* . . . But when this truth comes forth, Mercy meets it straight . . .

63

For where a true confession is by man made, Truth is budded *out of the earth.* And so it must [before] *Righteousness will give us a good look from Heaven. . . .* and show herself from Heaven to our justification. . . .

Truth is but the light to guide us, Righteousness is the way to bring us thither. . . .

And then, turn Righteousness to Peace, and they will not meet barely but more than meet, *kiss* in sign there is between them more than ordinary affection. . . . Peace . . . will come forth herself to meet Righteousness and kiss her. . . .

Now mark the order how they stand. Mercy leads to Truth and the knowledge of it; and Truth to Righteousness, and the practice of it; and Righteousness to Peace, and the ways of it. . . .

Err not . . . to single any out . . . Each of these is a quarter of Christianity. . . . Sever them, and farewell all. . . . For how loose a thing is mercy, if it be quite devoid of justice? . . . And how harsh a thing justice, if it be utterly without all temper of mercy! . . . Mercy, take Truth away, what hold is there of it? Who will trust it? Truth, take Mercy from it, it is severity rather than verity. Then Righteousness without Peace, certainly wrong is much better, better than perpetual brabbling. And Peace without Righteousness, better a sword far. . . . But temper these together, and how blessed a mixture![7]

***

On this feast day there is a renewal of the meeting of these four as we celebrate the Nativity, and especially when we receive Him at the altar. The blessings we receive at this meeting will prepare us for the final meeting.

"But Christ this day born, this day to meet of course. One special end that He was born was that at His birth this meeting might be. . . .

What is then the proper work of this day, but still to renew this meeting on it? . . . At His birth Christ bethought Himself of all the virtues which He would have to attend on Him then; and these He made choice of then, and for ever, to be the virtues of this feast.

The sooner and the better to procure this meeting, the Church meets us, as Melchizedek did Abraham, *with bread and wine,* but of a higher nature than his far; prepares ever this day, a love-feast, whereat they may the rather meet. Where Truth from the earth may look up to heaven and confess, and Righteousness from Heaven may look down to earth and pardon; where we may show Mercy in giving where need is; and offer Peace in forgiving where cause is; that so there may be a *meeting* of all hands. . . .

So may all the blessings that came to mankind by this meeting, or by the birth of Christ the cause of it, meet in us and remain upon us, till as we now meet together at the birth, so we may then meet in a *perfect man in the measure of the fullness of the age of Christ.*"[8]

References

[1] Andrewes, Vol. I, pp. 175–6.
[2] *ibid.*, pp. 176–7.
[3] *ibid.*, pp. 178–80.
[4] *ibid.*, pp. 180–1.
[5] *ibid.*, pp. 185–6.
[6] *ibid.*, pp. 186–9.
[7] *ibid.*, pp. 189–192, 194.
[8] *ibid.*, pp. 194–5.

NATIVITY SERMON No. 12

CHRISTMAS DAY 1618

Text: St. Luke 2:12–14
And this shall be a sign unto you; you
will find the Babe wrapped in swaddling
clothes, lying in a manger.

And suddenly there was with the angel a
multitude of heavenly host, praising God
and saying,
Glory to God in the highest, and on earth
peace, good-will towards men.

*Et hoc erit vobis signum: invenietis
Infantem pannis involutum, et positum
    in praesepio.
Et subito facta est cum angelo multitudo
militiae caelestis laudantium Deum, et
dicentiam:
Gloria in altissimis Deo, et in terra
pax hominibus bonae voluntatis.*

Although Christ's birth provided the gateway for salvation, we must open the gate for it. Thus the main theme of this sermon is to find Christ. This becomes our main work for Christ's day. Thus the initiative of the shepherds in proceeding to Bethlehem after the angel's announcement, sets the example for us, and like them we shall be rewarded in finding Christ in the stable.

"For this is a double feast; not only the feast of His Nativity, but the feast of His Invention also. Therefore the angel makes not an end with *unto you is born*, but tells them further; it is not enough Christ is born, but to take benefit by His birth we are to find Him. *Natus est* His part, *Invenietis* ours. . . .
Invenietis leads us to *Hoc erit signum* for how will they find Him without a sign? So come we from *Christus natus* to *Christus signatus*. . . . Born He is, that they know; and when, they know — *hodie*. And where, they know — in Bethlehem. To Bethlehem they will; but when they come there, how then? . . . The town so full of strangers, *as no room in the inns*, whither should they turn? . . .
The angel will not suffer that, [and] before he ends his speech he takes order for their sign, and this it is. When you come to Bethlehem, never search in any house or chamber; [but] in a stable there you will find a *Babe swaddled and laid in a manger*."[1]

***

66

In their *Gloria in excelsis* which balances the sign given, the angelic choir emphasised three points, *glory to God, . . . peace to the earth . . . . [and] to men a good-will.* At the same time they serenaded Him who lay in the cratch. From the angels' song, we too can learn firstly, how to find Christ, and then to praise Him.

"The song . . . consists of three strains. . . . 1. glory to God; 2. peace to the earth; 3. to men a good-will.

So have you the sign and the song, the one to balance or counterpoise the other; the song to sing away the sign, to make amends for the manger. The sign very poor and mean, the song exceeding high and heavenly. . . . That well might Leo ask, *What Child is this so little, and so great withal? so little as He lies in a cratch, so great though as He has angels to sing to Him;* the whole choir of heaven to make Him melody. . . .

Out of these we shall learn, First, what our duty is, to find Christ. The angel presupposes this, that being born we shall not leave till we have found Him; . . . [secondly] then how to find Him, at what sign. And last, when we have found Him how to salute Him, with what words to praise God for Him."[2]

***

To find Him we need to look for the correct sign, and the clue to that is in the collect; he came *in great humility.* Thus His birth is of lowly nature, but such a birth enabled the poor as well as the rich to welcome His birth. And *though the cratch be not worth the going to, Christ is worth the going for.* Indeed if we are not prepared to find Him, then we are not worthy of Christ. Finding that right sign, to recognize Him at Christmas, will help us to know Him at Calvary.

"Find Him we cannot, if first we find not a sign to find Him by. *A sign you shall have* and *this will be it,* said the angel, *you will find Him swaddled and laid in a manger.* . . .

His coming now was, as we say in the collect, *to visit us in great humility;* and so, His sign to be according. . . . If Christ had come in His excellency, that had been no sign, no more than the sun in the firmament shining in his full strength. . . .

For if He had been so gloriously born, such as these should never have been suffered to come near Him. But this is a sign for you, you who keep sheep, and such other poor people; you have a Saviour too. He is not the Saviour of great states only, but even of poor shepherds. The poorest of the earth may repair to Him, being no other place but this, and by this sign to find Him, and so *hoc erit signum vobis* . . .

We may well begin with Christ in the cratch; we must end with Christ on the cross. The cratch is a sign of the cross. . . . The scandal of the cratch is a good preparation to the scandal of the cross. To be swaddled thus as a child, does that offend? What then, when you will see Him pinioned and bound as a malefactor? To lie in a manger, is that so much? How then, when you will see Him hang on the cross? . . .

But . . . the less glorious His sign, the more glorious He, . . . that He is of Himself all sufficient. . . . [Thus] we are sent . . . not to an empty crib; Christ is in it. Be the sign never so simple. . . .

If then Christ be a treasure,as in Him are *all the treasures of the wisdom and bounty of God* what skills it what be His sign? . . . Though the cratch be not worth the going to, Christ is worth the going for. He is not worthy of Christ who will not go any whither to find Christ. . . .

And so I hope we shall not let the shepherds go alone, but go along with them too for company, to find Christ *by this sign.*"3

***

Andrewes pursues this sign of *humility*, and in elaborating, introduces his next theme, *Learn of Me*. Humility vaporizes pride. By pride we perish but by humility we are revigorated. So we should be grateful to the sign the angel has given to us. It was man's pride which brought God to lie in the cratch, and if the proud ever reach it, let them from then onwards loathe this vice.

"There lies He, the Lord of glory without glory. Instead of a palace, a poor stable; of a cradle of state, a beast's cratch; no pillow but a lock of hay; no hangings but dust and cobwebs; no attendants, but *in medio animalium.* . . .

But if we stand but gazing and wondering at this sign, the angel will blame us at the Nativity, as they did the Apostles for the like at His Ascension. What learn we by it? . . .

Christ, though as yet He cannot speak as a new born babe, yet by it He speaks, and out of His crib, as a pulpit, this day preaches to us; and his theme is *Discite a Me*, *Learn of Me*, *for I a humble*, humble in My birth you all see. . . .

For the word of God has two edges; and if it go one way thus for humility, it cuts as deep the contrary against pride. And withal, under one leads us to the cause straight, and shows us the malignity of the disease of pride, for the cure whereof this so profound humility was requisite in Christ. . . . Our first parents . . . [made] themselves equal with God. . . . For their puffing up, *He was made empty*; for their lifting up, *was He brought thus low*; for their comparing with God, came He to be *compared to the beasts that perish.* . . .

Never blame the angel for giving this sign; he had no other to give. . . . Ask Christ why He would be so born. . . . His *coming* was to recover man. Man was to be recovered by the contrary of that by which he perished. By pride he perished, . . . then, by humility to be recovered. . . . So He to come in humility. The pride was high, the contrary as low, *as low as they,* lie in their cratch.

It is strange this point of Christ in the cratch, how tedious, how harsh it is to be stood on. Harsh, but to none more . . . as to the proud; and they of all other have least cause to be offended with it, it is they who were the cause of it. . . . If there they find Him, it is they and none but they who laid Him. If He be otherwise than He should, their pride is to blame for it. But for it we had found Him in a better place. And fie upon pride, say I, if it were but for this only; enough to make us loathe this vice that laid this so great a disgrace as we count it upon the Son of God. . . .

68

For if humility be the sign of finding Christ, pride must needs be the sign of losing Him; and whoso loses Him, is himself even the child of perdition; and therefore look to this sign well.''4

***

It is not only *humility* shining out from this sign but also *love*. His love for us was such that He *did not abhor the Virgin's womb*, or the poverty into which He came.

But what of us? When we have been showered with so much love from Him, we still thrust Him aside. Shall we allow only the beasts to continue to adore Him?

''But humility is not all we find in this sign. . . . Indicant it is of humility; co-indicant of [what] in Him and on His part, as pride on ours, was the cause that made Him stoop to this humility, and that was His love. . . . It was a sign of love too this. . . . Signal love indeed, that for our sakes refused not first our nature, our mortality — that alone had been love enough — but not the basest estate of our nature, not poverty; poverty, and such poverty as the like was never heard of, to be found where He was found, there to lie. . . .

Us who even at that time when He showed so great love to us showed so little to Him, that if the beasts had not been better to Him than we, He had found no place to be born in? *For us* He came, and we thrust Him out from us and from all place with us, into the place of beasts. And if He had not borrowed their stable, *He had no roof to cover Him;* if He had not borrowed their crib, *He had lain on the cold ground* at this time of the year. . . .

For all this was not so much to show the love in Himself, as to work . . . to regain His Father's love, to make Him well-pleased towards men by His humility with whom for their pride He was justly displeased. Thus unlovely He became to make us beloved, thus poor to make us rich in the grace and favour of God, more worth when the time comes than all the riches of the world. . . .

The cratch is the cradle of His love, no less than of His humility, and able to provoke our love again. . . .

Will you now to this inglorious sign hear a glorious song? to this cratch of humility a hymn of celestial harmony? If the sign mislike you, you cannot but like the song, and the choir that sings it. The song I shall not be able to reach to; will you but see the choir?''5

***

Andrewes highlights the part of the angelic choir in bridging the hostility which had existed between heaven and earth. It is up to us to build on this angelic theme of *peace, good-will*, and *glory*.

''*What has heaven or heavenly personages to do here with the cratch?* . . .
There had been no peace with heaven, but plain hostility between earth and it, . . . ever since the cherubim first drew upon Adam, and with a shaken sword kept

69

the entry of paradise, ever since in arms till this very day. . . . By virtue of Christ's Nativity, *peace to earth* from heaven, *good-will to men* from God. So now upon His birth they were to disarm; but before they put their armour off, . . . sing of the new world that was now to ensue. . . .

For angels to praise God is no new thing. . . . But to praise Him for a Child in a cratch, that lo, is new, a new thing, a new song, and if you will a new sign too. . . . To Him sitting in the throne sing they their *Sanctus*. For to Christ was the *Sanctus* sung. . . .

For Him this glory, by Him this peace, through Him this good-will . . . And mark that the word *cratch* is the last word in the sermon and the word *glory* the first in the song; and nothing comes between to part these two. Nothing to part humility below from glory on high. . . .

Shall we be . . . at the news, at the birth, and at the sign, and be out at this of *laudatium Deum*? No, I trust. The choir of heaven did it, but to set us in; we to bear a part, and it should be a chief part, since the best part of it is ours. They but took it up; we to keep it up, and never to let it go down or die on our hands, but from year to year as we have occasion still to renew it. The angels began here; the shepherds they follow and praise God, *for that they had heard and seen.* We to come in at our turn, and to do the like.''[6]

***

Andrewes concludes with the other sign linked with the cratch, the Sacrament; we must find Him at the altar as well as in the manger. The thanksgiving prayer at the end of the Eucharist, with its emphasis on this as *a sacrifice of praise and thanksgiving* harmonizes with the angelic song. But before saying the thanksgiving prayer, when we receive the Sacrament is the time we come closest to being like the angels. It is a taste of heavenly bliss. On this day when the cratch and altar are one, let us *praise Him with the angels' hymn* as part of our preparation towards our heavenly home.

"The Sacrament we shall have besides, and of the Sacrament we may well say, *Hoc erit signum.* For a sign it is, and by it *you will find this Child.* For finding His flesh and blood, you cannot miss but find Him too. . . . For Christ in the Sacrament is not altogether unlike Christ in the cratch. To the cratch we may well like the husk or outward symbols of it. Outwardly it seems little worth but it is rich of contents, as was the crib this day with Christ in it. For what are they, but *weak and poor elements* of themselves? yet in them find we Christ. Even as they did this day in the beasts' crib the food of angels; which very food our signs both represent, and present unto us.

Let me say this farther; it is the last word in the Sacrament, *this is a sacrifice of praise and thanksgiving*, and the whole text resolves into *laudatium Deum*, and not to praise Him alone, but to praise Him with this hymn of angels. Now being to praise Him with the angels' hymn, it behoves to be in or as near the state of angels as we can; . . . And when are we so? If at any time, at that time when we have newly taken the holy Sacrament of His blessed Body and most precious Blood — when we come fresh from it. And as if there were some near alliance between this song of the angels and these signs, to show that the signs or Sacrament have a special interest in this hymn; therefore is it, that even then upon the administration of it has the Church ordered this very hymn ever to be sung or said, whatever day it fall in the whole year. For then sure of all other times are we on earth most near to angelic perfection, then meet to give glory unto God, then at peace with the whole earth, then a good-will and purpose in us if ever.

But as the time falls out we have more inducements than one. The day itself is one most proper, for it is the very day this hymn was first sung on. And the celebration of the Sacrament, that is another; but the Sacrament now falling on the day, a double. . . . For the Sacrament, that comes at other times; the day, but once a year. On this day they both meet, and never but on this; not to slip it then, but then when it is most proper, most kindly, then to do it. I would to God we were as meet to do it as the Sacrament is to do it at, and as the time is to do it on. But as we may, let us endeavour to do it. So inuring ourselves to record it as often as we may, especially when most meetly we may, here *on earth* among men, that in His good time we may be counted worthy to do it *on high* with the angels in the bliss of heaven.'' [7]

References

[1] Andrewes, Vol. I, pp. 196–7.
[2] *ibid*., p. 198.
[3] *ibid*., pp. 199–203.
[4] *ibid*., pp. 204–7.
[5] *ibid*., pp. 207–9.
[6] *ibid*., pp. 210–3.
[7] *ibid*., pp. 213–4.

NATIVITY SERMON No. 13

CHRISTMAS DAY 1619

Text: St. Luke 2:14

Glory to God in the highest, and on
earth peace, good-will towards men.

*Gloria in altissimis Deo, et in terra
pax, hominibus bonae voluntatis (vel
in homines bona voluntas).*

The angels' anthem of praise at Christ's birth is echoed each time the *Gloria*
is sung by us, and in so doing earth and heaven are joined in one concert, and
in unity with Him Who is the Reconciler between heaven and earth. Hence
laudantium, praise to God is the continuous theme of this sermon.

"The anthem of the choir of heaven for this day; . . . we praise God with the
tongue of angels, whensoever we praise Him with this, with *Gloria in excelsis*.
    The sum of it is, that though all days of the year and for all benefits, yet this day
and for this now above all God is highly to be glorified. . . .
    That Heaven and earth and men are to join in one concert; Heaven and earth
first; Heaven on high, earth beneath to take up one hymn; both in honour of His
birth — both are better by it. Heaven has glory, earth peace, by means of it. . . .
Warranted by this song, at Your nativity, O Lord, let the heavens rejoice for the
glory, let the earth be glad for the peace that come to them by it.
    And men, though they rest and come in last after both, yet they to do it as much,
. . . for God's good-will toward them which brought all this to pass in heaven and
earth both; restoring men to God's favour and grace, and all by means of this
Child, their Reconciler to God who has been, their Pacifier on earth that is, their
Glorifier in Heaven that shall be. . . . And now if ever, no more than ever, to bear
their part in this glorious hymn at the cratchside."[1]

***

The anthem sung on that first Christmas night proclaiming *glory, peace* and
good-will foreshadows the benefits from the Nativity with its renewing the
relationship between God and man. Christ Himself as God and Man en-
genders this *good-will*.

"*Thus sing they at His Nativity of those things that came by His Nativity*. Came
to heaven, to earth, to men. Glory to heaven, peace to earth, grace and favour to
men. . . . [This] good-will to men [is] in the midst between both, compound of
both.

You will mark, the Child here is God and Man. God from on high, Man from the earth. To heaven whence He is God, thither goes glory; to earth whence Man, thither peace. Then as God and Man is one Christ, and as the reasonable soul and flesh is one man; so Christ consisting of these two brings *the fullness of God's favour,* the true and real cause of both; yielding them peace while here on earth, and assuring them of glory when there on high; as thither on high we trust to be delivered after our time here spent in procuring Heaven glory and earth peace.''2

***

For man, the most important of the three announcements is *good-will*, as it signifies the *good pleasure* God showed towards His son, and in turn to us.

''Glory from us to Him, peace from Him to us. From men on earth to God on high, glory; from God on high to men on earth, peace. Men I say, towards whom He is now appeased, and with whom now He well-pleased; and both, for this Child's sake here in the cratch, in Whom He is so absolutely well-pleased, as of the fullness of His favour we all receive. God spoke it once, and twice, once at His Baptism; and again in the Holy Mount.

And *hoc erit signum*, this may be a sure sign that He is well-pleased with our nature, that He has in this Child taken it and united it to His own; which, if He had not been highly well-pleased, He would never have done. What greater good-will can there be than this? It passes the greatest, even that of marriage, union of nature, unity of person. . . . Now has God glory, now earth peace. Men are now received to favour and grace. . . .

Glory now is, or shall be to God for this birth. . . . Before it was *gloria in excelsis*, but *Deo* was left out. All nations in a manner worshipping the Host of Heaven. . . . But by this birth now, down should all idolatry go, as down it went wheresoever Christian religion took place. From the creature there, all to the Creator. To none on high, but God on high. The point of glory much mended; God more glory than before. And the earth more at peace if you take peace in things spiritual, matters concerning the soul. . . .

As for the point of God's good-will and favour, that was never in kind till this day. Many favours, much good-will before, never so as when God and man, the Godhead and manhood meet both in one. God never so pleased, as when He was pleased to assume it into one Person with Himself, uniting both with the straightest union that can be. Never that till this day when for *good-will towards men,* He forsook *gloriam in excelsis* to come into the cratch for them.''3

***

Andrewes proceeds to discuss the three parts of the angelic hymn. Firstly, *in excelsis Deo*. As God has bestowed good-will upon men, it is therefore more imperative that we glorify God in our churches and homes on this wonderful festival.

"Now the more He is glorified, the higher His glory. Higher if by Heaven and earth, on high and below, by men and Angels, than by either alone.

This then they wish, when they say *glory be in the highest*; that high and low, heaven and earth, men and angels would do their parts, to make His praise glorious, glorious at the highest. On earth, sound it out far and wide all the world over, to the ends of the earth; and lift up our voices, and help them with instruments of all kinds, and make them to be heard up to the very heavens, that so it may be in *altissimis* indeed. Yes, that all creatures in both, ravished with the consideration of the great favour and good-will of God in this day's birth testified, would take occasion to fill their mouths with the praise of His goodness in resolving, His wisdom in contriving, His mercy in promising, His truth in performing the work of this day, the blessed birth of His Son.

For the work of the day, to make the day of the work a glorious day, causing it to be attended with a number of days according to the number of months of the year, as no feast else. Glorious in all places, as well at home with carols, as in the Church with anthems. Glorious in all ages; even this day, this year, as on the very day on which He was born. Glorious in habit, in fare; but specially, as we see the angels here do, with the service of God, the most solemn service, the highest, the most melodious hymns we have; and namely, with this here of the choir of heaven. In a word, all the ways we can; all the ways God can have any glory from us, to let Him have it; and have it even at the height, *in altissimis*.

And good reason we should so wish; Christ lost his glory by being thus in the cratch. We took some from Him; to wish Him some for it again. That was *ignominia in infinis*, to wish Him *gloria in altissimis* in lieu of it.''[4]

***

Secondly, *peace*. Andrewes outlines three kinds of peace on earth: an earthly peace, similar to what Augustus gave the Roman world; a spiritual peace when there is harmony with heaven; and a personal peace within the depth of our being, especially important at our departing this world.

"The next is *votum pacis*; they wish peace may be upon earth. Even Augustus' peace first, that is the first comes to our minds when we hear that word, the shutting of Janus, for that also was a blessed fruit of his birth. . . .

The taking down also of the *partition wall* which formerly Moses had set up between the Jew and Gentile, the making of them both one in the body of His flesh; St. Paul's peace.

And yet further. For both these are *peace upon earth*, of earth with earth. Augustus can, the world can give that peace, though many times they will not. But He speaks in a place of the *peace which the world cannot*, that is peace with heaven. . . . There should . . . be . . . Jacob's ladder set up from Bethel to heaven, a peaceable intercourse with that place by the angels *descending and ascending* between us and them.

And further yet, peace at home with ourselves, and with our own consciences. *Turn again to your rest, O my soul*; for in finding Him we will find rest to our souls.

And last, . . . peace at the parting, which is worth all; Simeon's peace, a good *nunc dimittis in pace*."[5]

***

Thirdly, *good-will towards men*. This, Andrewes explains, is a kind of peace, peculiar to men and not to other parts of creation, as a consequence of the Son of God being also the Son of Man.

"The third is, there may be in God a *good-will towards men*. And good-will is a kind of peace, . . . a kind of peace peculiar to men which the other parts of the earth are not capable of. So a farther matter to men than bare peace; even to *think well*, to bear good-will, to be well-pleased with men. . . . It is high glory, that for His and this His birth's sake, which we now celebrate, [what] is verified of His Person is verified of both His natures; of Him not only as Son of God, but even as Son of Man too. And what is verified of Him as Son of Man, may be verified also of the sons of men, of all mankind."[6]

***

In this hymn *glory* and *peace* go together. They are inseparable, and must always remain so. However the order is important. *Glory* must always supersede *peace*.

"If we sing Glory without Peace, we sing but two halves. No Glory on high will be admitted without peace upon earth. No gift on His altar, which is a special part of His glory, but *lay down your gift and there leave it, and first go your way and make peace on earth*; and that done come again, and you will then be accepted to give glory to Heaven, and not before. And O that we would go and do the like, have like regard of His glory that He has of our peace. But this knot of *Gloria et Pax* is against those who are still wrangling with one thing or other, and all for the glory of God forsooth, as if these two could not join. God could not have His glory if the Church were at peace, as if no remedy the angels' *et* must out.

Glory and Peace; but Glory first, and then Peace. There is much in the order. Glory to be first, else you change the clef, the clef is in Glory, that the key of the song. That is to be first and before all, Peace to give place to her; Glory is the elder sister. . . . To set Peace before Glory is to set earth above heaven. Keep the order then, each in her place. So goes the song; the Child born is God and Man — God from on high, Man from the earth."[7]

***

Yet after giving God His worth in our praises, there is nothing more precious than *peace*. Yet we on earth do not pursue *peace* as a precious jewel; instead we so often persecute her. Earth must be content with *peace*, as no *glory* is due to man. This is reserved for God alone in heaven. However by pursuing *peace* we can have a taste of heaven while on earth.

"But then next after His glory nothing more dear, more precious, . . . to us than . . . peace. If she hide herself, seek her out *and pursue her*; if she fly away, follow her hard. Peace is not sought, no man follows her to make any pursuit; they know not the value of Peace that lose her so easily, that follow her so faintly. . . . Instead of pursuit, [they] persecute her and drive her away, and make the chasing her away the seeking of God's glory. . . .

Earth is not the place of glory, it is *in excelsis*, on high; earth is not on high. And as earth is not the place, so man is not the person. . . . No glory to man then, especially none this day of all days. . . . If we sing to any but Him we sing a false note. Men do so now and then, but the angels are never out; and thus sing they, and set out glory for God's part.

Let *earth* be content with *peace*; peace is her portion, and a blessed portion if she may well hold it; a fair portion, a rich wish. . . .

And a kind of heaven there is upon earth, when there is peace upon earth; and justly are they blessed, and rightly are they *called the children of God*, the most blessed that are, or shall be at any time, who are the procurers of it."[8]

***

We must never lose sight of the devil's desires which labours against *glory* and *peace*. He entices us to believe that we too must have *glory*, and to usurp God's place. Following the devil's temptations results only in disharmony and discord. It is against such sins that the angels are still on guard, in order to protect heaven from them.

"The devil does all he can to mar the angels' music, . . . to procure contempt to God's *glory on high,* to bring God's glory as low as he can, to make [tumult] upon earth, to work men all evil-will, mischief, and malice that he can.

And first, to make a confusion in this division, persuades earth not to stand content with the angels' partition, but earth . . . must have glory, must be dealing with heaven's part. It is well said *to God on high*; there be certain gods here below aspire to glory. . . . And we beneath are too ready to sing it otherwhile, to deify those who are on high, and give that belongs to *God on high* to gods below. Now that earth is thus willing to entitle herself to heaven's part, this brings all out of tune. . . .

By seeking glory peace is lost clear. Yielding glory to God does bring with it *pacem in terris*; diverting it from Him does take *pacem de terris*. . . . It is [what] makes the angels here keep on their armour still. Upon glory detained from God, or transferred whither it should not, they are up in arms straight, have power to take peace from the earth, till the point of glory be set right again."[9]

***

There is no reason for men to listen to the devil's luring, as this angelic message gives them a prerogative they have never had under the old Covenant. The coming of the Christ-Child has ensured this through the *good-will* of God.

76

"To men a good-will. For besides earth's peace wherein they enter common, men have a part by themselves which is their prerogative. And first, I would have you to note that here it is entered first into the music of heaven. In the angels' hymn in Isaiah . . . [there is] no mention at all, not a word of them in that. . . . In the angels' hymn here in the New Testament, here men are in; that all may know that for this Child's sake now made Man, men are now come into the angels' song, to be a part and a principal part there who before were left out. . . .

For Him this glory, for Christ; through Him this peace, through Christ. But Christ Himself, whence? Whence, but from the *good-will* of God towards men? . . . His will was men should be restored, therefore His will was Christ should be incarnate and born." [10]

***

We have gained many prerogatives: *pardon* for our grievous sins, the *acceptance* of our imperfect works and nature and the receiving of *free grace and favour.*

"To or towards men . . . for this Child's sake, . . . He is pleased first to receive men to pardon, though grievous sinners, and so utterly unworthy of it.

Secondly, He is pleased to reward their works also, . . . to take them well in worth, though they want worth, and to [make] them a reward, and that a high reward, for *it is your heavenly Father's good pleasures to give you a kingdom.*

Thirdly, . . . to accept . . . according to [what] he has, not according to [what] he has not. . . . That He places not acceptance, neither in . . . wit, nor in . . . power, but in *readiness of good-will,* an honest true meaning, an unfeigned hearty desire; *though there be weakness in the act, yet if there be soundness in the will,* out of His *good-will towards men* He will accept this good-will in men. . . .

And this, if it were well weighed and digested aright, if Christ, if all that comes by Christ, and that is *all in all,* be by His free grace and favour; if men were but rightly conceited in this point, it would soon bring them out of conceit . . . [and] make them truly humble. And it is the humble man who gives God the true glory, that sings this song right." [11]

***

After learning what this song is all about, Andrewes advocates for us to imitate the angels and *sing* it too. The most appropriate time is when we are nearest to heaven and the angelic host, that is, just after receiving the blessed Sacrament.

"And now you have heard all the parts, what will we do with this song? Sing it. . . . But if by men, of very congruity, and angels' song would be by men when is some degree they drew something near to the angels' estate. . . .

And when is that? . . . If ever men do rise above themselves and approach in any sort near to those blessed spirits; if ever they be in state with angels and archangels to laud and magnify His glorious name; if in all their lives they be in peace and

77

charity, the bond of perfection, the *bona voluntas* we speak of; if at any time it be in men, and they *homines bonae voluntatis*, upon the taking of the Sacrament it is; at that time, then or never, they lift up their hearts in true devotion. So then in best case that in all our lives to sing it, if Christ *dwell in our hearts* by faith, if we be *temples of the Holy Spirit*."[12]

***

The receiving of the blessed Sacrament on this great feast day also enables us to be partakers of His very flesh in which we duly honour and praise the Christ-Child.

"... there is another congruity for the Sacrament, that the *great mystery of godliness* which is *God manifested in the flesh*, might not be celebrated without the mystery of His flesh; that the day He came among us to be partaker of flesh and blood, we also might be partakers of the flesh and blood which He took from us to give them us again."[13]

***

There is nothing more appropriate, Andrewes concludes, than for us to sing the angels' anthem on Christ's day. Our hearts' desire and fervent prayer should be to glorify God for His *good-will to men*, and thus to entice peace on earth.

"And if we will keep time with the angels, . . . what fitter time to sing it than the day it was first sung. . . . When should the *hymn of Christ's birth be better sung, than on Christ's birthday?* . . .

And what should we wish from our hearts but that the angels may have their wish? . . . And for . . . *what we wish for we should not stand wishing only but endeavour withal it may come to pass, that it be our labour too,* with all our endeavours to procure the glory of heaven, and the peace of the earth; to find peace in the good-will of God, and to give Him all glory for it, Who has appointed peace our portion here, and glory our hope laid up there."[14]

References

[1] Andrewes, Vol. I, pp. 215–6.
[2] *ibid.*, pp. 216–7.
[3] *ibid.*, pp. 218–20.
[4] *ibid.*, pp. 220–221.
[5] *ibid.*, pp. 221–2.
[6] *ibid.*, p. 222.
[7] *ibid.*, p. 223.
[8] *ibid.*, pp. 223–5.
[9] *ibid.*, pp. 226 -7.
[10] *ibid.*, pp. 227–8.
[11] *ibid.*, pp. 228–9.
[12] *ibid.*, p. 231.
[13] *ibid.*
[14] *ibid.*, pp. 231–2.

NATIVITY SERMON No. 14

CHRISTMAS DAY 1620

Text: St. Matthew 2:1–2

Now when Jesus was born in Bethlehem of
Judaea, in the days of Herod the King,
behold there came wise men from the East
to Jerusalem,
Saying, Where is He Who is born King of
the Jews? For we have seen His star in
the East, and are come to worship Him.

Cum ergo natus esset Jesus in Bethlehem
Judae, in diebus Herodis Regis, ecce magi
ab Oriente venerunt Jerosolymam, dicentes,
Ubi est Qui natus est Rex Judaeorum? Vidimus
enim stellam Ejus in Orientes, et venimus
adorare Eum.

Coming to Christ by coming to Bethlehem is the theme in this sermon. Just as
the shepherds came to the stable in the name of the poor and lowly, so do the
Magi on behalf of the learned and stately.

"We pass now this year from the shepherds and the angels to the wise men and
their star. . . . They set forth this very day. For they came when *Jesus was born*,
and this day was He born. Howsoever the star brought them not to their journey's
end till twelve days hence. This star, and their coming, no less proper to this day
than those others were. One begins, the other ends the feast.
We pass from one of them to the other, but from the less to the greater. . . . The
other of the shepherds, a poor one, poor and mean. This of the wise men a sign of
some state, highly and heavenly."[1]

***

The searching for Christ by these wise men brought forth a new manifestation in the heavens, a new star. This star would lead them to Bethlehem, and
reveal Christ to the Gentiles, and therefore to all mankind.

"A new light kindles in heaven, a star never seen before. The world could not
but look up at it, and ask what it meant, . . . *and [so] the news of it [went] to the*
utmost parts of the earth. . . .
This made another manner *venerunt*. Upon this came there to Jerusalem not a
rout of shepherds, but a troop of great persons. And not from a heath or sheep-
common hard by, but from afar, *from the east*, twelve days journey off. All

Jerusalem rang of it. . . . These here who *came from the East*, first they were Gentiles. Gentiles, who concern us, for so are we. We may then look out, if we can see this star. It is ours, it is the Gentiles' star. We may set our course by it, to seek and find, and worship Him as well as they. . . .

But there is yet more grace offered to some in particular. The shepherds were a sort of poor simple men altogether unlearned. But here come a troop of men of great place, high account in their country; and withal of great learned men, their name gives them for no less. . . . [Hence] wealth, worth, or wisdom shall hinder none, but they may have their part in Christ's birth as well as those of low degree."2

***

When the magi arrived in Jerusalem they asked *where* rather than *whether* He is born. Knowing He had been born, kindled another star, a star of faith in their hearts. Faith led them to the stable. Since then the door of faith has been opened to all Gentiles.

"So they ask *ubi est*? Not whether He be born, but *where He is born*. For born He is they are sure, by the same token they have seen His star. . . .

So the star in heaven kindled another star in earth. St. Peter calls it the *Day-star which rises in the heart*, that is faith, which shined and manifested itself by their labour in coming, diligence in enquiring, dutying in worshipping.

Christ's birth made manifest to them by the star in heaven. Their faith *the star in Heaven* made manifest to Christ and to all by the travel of it, which showed it manifestly.

That upon the matter there falls a threefold manifestation, you may call them three stars if you please. 1. The star in heaven, 2. The day-star in their hearts. 3. And Christ Himself, *the bright morning star,* whom both the other guide us to; the Star of this morning which makes the day the greatest day in the year.

The sum of all rises to this, that God has *opened a door of faith to the Gentiles*; and among them to wise men and great men, as well as to the simpler sort. But with this condition, that they say with them, *venite adoremus*; and so come and seek, and find and worship Him, that is do as these did."3

***

Andrewes has us linger here at this place, Bethlehem. In this town which means *house of bread*, Christ *the Living Bread* was born in great humility.

"*Ubi* [is] Bethlehem, . . . the place where David himself was born. And what place more meet for the Son of David to be born in than . . . the *house of Bread,* . . . [and] more proper for Him Who is *the living Bread that came down from heaven*, to give life to the world? It was the least and lowest of all *the thousands of Judah*. What little and low is in things natural, that lowliness and humility is in [the] spiritual. This natural birth place of His shows His spirituality. Humility is His place . . . the Bethlehem of virtues: where you find it. *Lo there is He born*. So born in us, as born for us."4

Just as humility marks the place, so affliction does the time when Christ was born. The evil days under Herod were symbolized in the season of His birth, the very depth of winter with its very long dark days. However the consoling note is that in darkness the stars shine brighter.

"Of the time. The days of Herod the King. And those were evil days, days of great affliction to that land. Judahs's *sceptre* clean broken; not *a lawgiver left between his feet*. Edom, that is Herod the Edomite, cried, *Down with them, down to the ground*. Not so much as a sort of silly babes but barbarously slain in their mothers' arms, enough to make Rachael mourn as she lay in her grave. Dismal days certainly. . . . When it is dark, then rises the star. . . .

For all the world like the time of the year His birth fell in, [is] in the sharpest season, in the deep of winter. As humility His place, so affliction His time. The time and place fit well."5

***

Andrewes returns to his theme of *venerunt*; the coming of the magi; coming as they do to represent the Gentiles, and thus representing us who also may come. This coming of the Gentiles had long been promised and prophesized by many of the patriarchs, prophets and psalmists.

"And they who come, *magi*; . . . and they were Gentiles; and in this *Gentiles*, we. So come we in. *Then has God also to the Gentiles set open a door of faith*, at which door we enter, we with them and they with us, for they and we Gentiles both. The star is *stella Gentium*, and so ours; and we to direct our course by it. . . .

[What] was thus promised to, and by the Patriarchs, shadowed forth in the figures of the Law, the Temple, and the Tabernacle; [what] was foresaid by the prophets, and forsung of in psalms, that was this day fulfilled. *Venerunt*, here *they are come*, and *venimus*, *we* in them and with them, who not only in their own names, but in ours make sure their entry; came and sought after, and found and worshipped, their Saviour and ours, the Saviour of the whole world. . . .

The place He was born in, an inn, which is for all passengers of what country soever; the time He was born in of the tax, when *all the world came up to be taxed*; the very star which, as the nature of stars is, is common to all coasts and climates, peculiar to none; all show that from all coasts they may now come, that the Gentiles are now to be, *fellow-members, fellow partners, and fellow-heirs of one body*, co-partners and co-heirs of Christ and His birth. This for *stella Gentium*, so both theirs and ours."6

***

Magi, these Gentiles came from the East and not our West. For Andrewes this was quite significant as he believed that the Eastern Gentiles had been far more notorious sinners than their Western brethren, and therefore it was meet that in undertaking such a long and dangerous journey, they made amends for their forefathers' trangressions. Their coming too holds out much promise to us who are also sinners.

"For in that *they came from the East*, there lies further hope for us, . . . for [they are] not only Gentiles, *but sinners of the Gentiles*, sinners, and that chief sinners. For so were they of the East; greater, far greater sinners than the rest. For tell me, what sin was there that came not from thence? There was the tower set in hand, that should have confronted God; and of it came Babel, and from it confusion. Thence came all tryanny and oppression among men, from Nimrod who hunted and ranged over men as over beasts in a forest. Thence all idolatry and worship of false gods, both in earth from Belus' tomb first; and in heaven, from *the star of their God Rempham* which St. Stephen speaks of. Thence, *from the mountains of the East*, the prosperity of Balaam, false prophets who *love the wages of unrighteousness*, and from them all that naught is. And if in all these it did, it cannot be denied but that the whole world received their infection that way from the East.

And hence *appeared the grace of God which brings salvation to all men*, and to all sinners, as fair and clear as the star itself; that thence out of the mountains of the East God calls these to seek, and guided them to find Christ; that whence the poison first came, thence might come the [antidote]; and that as they were the first who went out, so they be the first who came in.

So the East sets us not farther back, but brings us nearer. . . . This for the star of the Gentiles first, and now the star of sinners, and chief sinners of the Gentiles, even oriental sinners."[7]

***

As *magi* were kings, their coming to the Christ-Child manifests that Christ is also for the grand and great on this earth. These Eastern kings did for Christ as His birth as Joseph of Arimathaea did at His death.

"*Stella magnatum, the star of princes and nobles also.* Yes, *stella regia,* the star royal; kings themselves have their hold and claim by it.

Christ is not only for russet cloaks, shepherds and such; . . . but even the grandees, great states such as these, *venerunt*, they *came* too; and when they came were welcome to Him. For they were sent for and invited by this star, their star properly.

These at His birth, at His welcome into the world; and others such as these at His death, at His going out of it. Then Joseph of Arimathea, an honourable counsellor, bestowed on Him a fair new tomb; and others came with *their hundred pound of sweet odours*. So that coming and going He was beholden to such."[8]

***

The wise men were not only rulers, but also *learned men*. Thus no degree of learning is a barrier to know the truth, rather it is an aid.

"For besides [being] . . . great [statesmen], they were also great learned men. . . .

This learning of theirs made them never the further from the Christ we see, it did them no hurt in their coming to Christ. . . .

This is their star, their guide; a guide apt and proper for them who knew the stars, for them who were learned. . . .

There is no star or beam of it; there is no truth at all in human learning or philosophy that thwarts any truth in Divinity, but sorts well with it and serves it, and all to honour Him Who says of Himself *Ego sum Veritas, I am the Truth.*"9

***

What of our coming? We should hither our steps with those of the magi. Unlike their tedious journey of many days, our coming requires only a short journey. Thus we have no excuse not to follow the star which will take us to Christ this day, not only in the cratch but to the altar. Our Bethlehem is also *the House of Bread.*

"It remains that what we may do we will do; that is, *come.* . . . We shall go in the company of wise men. . . .

It is an *ecce venerunt*, theirs indeed, if we weigh it well, whence they came and whither. . . . They came a long journey, no less than twelve days together. They came an uneasy journey, for their way lay through Arabia Petraea, and the craggy rock of it. And they came a dangerous journey, through Arabia Deserta too, and the black *tents of Kedar* there, then famous for their robberies. . . . And they came now, at the worst season of the year. And all but to do worship at Christ's birth. . . . So desirous were they to come . . . and to be there as soon as possibly they might; broke through all these difficulties. . . .

And we, what excuse shall we have if we come not? If so short and so easy a way we come not, as from our chambers hither, not to be called away indeed? Shall not our *non venerunt* have an *ecce*, *Behold, it was stepping but over the threshold, and yet they came not?*

And these were wise men, and never . . . the less wise for so coming; no never so truly wise in any thing they did, as in so coming. The Holy Spirit records them for wise, *in capite libri*, even in the beginning of the New Testament. . . .

And we, if we believe this, that this was their wisdom, if they and we be wise by one Spirit, by the same principles, we shall follow the same star, tread the same way, and so come at last whither they are happily gone before us. . . .

And how shall we that do? I know not any more proper way left us, than to come to [what] Himself by express order has left us, as the most special remembrance of Himself to be come to. When He came into the world, says the psalm, that is at His birth now, He said, *Ecce venio*. What then? *Sacrifice and burnt-offering You would not have, but a body have You ordained me.* . . . By the *offering*, breaking, and partaking of which *body, we are all sanctified*, so many as will come to it. *For given it is, for the taking away of our sins.* Nothing is more fit than at the time His body was ordained Him, and that is to-day, to come to the body so ordained.

And in the old Ritual of the Church we find that on the cover of the cannister, wherein was the Sacrament of His Body, there was a star engraven, to show us that now the star leads us thither, to His body there.

And what shall I say now, but according as St. John says, and the star, and the wise men say, *Come*. And He, Whose the star is, and to Whom the wise men came, says, *Come*. And let them who are disposed, *Come*. And . . . . take of the *Bread of Life, which came down from heaven* this day into Bethlehem, the house of bread. Of which Bread the Church is this day the house, the true Bethlehem, and all the Bethlehem we have now left to come to for the Bread of life — of that His heavenly life which we hope for in heaven. And this our nearest coming that here we can come, till we shall by another *venite* come, unto Him in His heavenly kingdom, to which He grant we may come.''[10]

References

[1] Andrewes, Vol. I, pp. 233–4.
[2] *ibid*., pp. 234–5.
[3] *ibid*., p. 236.
[4] *ibid*., pp. 237–8.
[5] *ibid*., p. 238.
[6] *ibid*., pp. 239, 241–2.
[7] *ibid*., pp. 242–3.
[8] *ibid*., p. 243.
[9] *ibid*., pp. 244–5.
[10] *ibid*., pp. 246–8.

NATIVITY SERMON No. 15
CHRISTMAS DAY 1622

Text: St. Matthew 2:1–2

Behold there came wise men from the East
to Jerusalem,
Saying, Where is He Who is born King of
the Jews? for we have seen His star in the
East, and are come to worship Him.

Ecce magi ab Oriente venerunt Jerosolymam,
Dicentes, Ubi est Qui natus est Rex Judaeorum?
Vidimus enim stellam Ejus in Oriente, et venimus
adorare Eum.

What is *proper and peculiar* to this day, but to worship the Christ-Child? The
purpose of the wise men's errand was in fact this; *to worship, to worship Him,*
their King, in His lowly habitation. Following in their footsteps, this too
should be the purpose of our errand upon this festival. Such was their desire
to worship the Christ that it became an act of faith and witness in order to
discover where they could do their obeisance. Undoubtedly the theme of the
sermon is worship.

"Their errand we may best learn from themselves out of their *dicentes* etc.
Which, in a word, is to worship Him. Their errand our errand, and the errand of
this day. . . .
They were no sooner come, but they tell it out; confess Him and His birth to be
the cause of their coming. . . . When they were come, their diligent enquiring Him
out by *ubi est?* For here is the place of it, asking after Him to find where He was.
And . . . [so] when they had found Him, the end of their seeing, coming, seeking;
and all for no other end but to worship Him . . . [by] their *falling down,* and their
offering to Him. Worship with Him with their bodies, worship Him with their
goods; their worship and ours the true worship of Christ."[1]

***

One of the key words in this text is *star.* This new star appeared in the heavens
to guide the kings. This star St. Paul described as proclaiming the salvation of
all, and is St. Peter's *daystar rising in our hearts,* while for St. John, Christ
Himself is the star.

"We have now got us a star on earth for that in heaven. The first in the
firmament; that appeared unto them, and in them to us — a figure of St. Paul's *the*
grace of God appearing, and bringing salvation to all men, Jews and Gentiles

alike. The second here on earth is St. Peter's, . . . The third in Christ Himself, St. John's star. *The generation and root of David, the bright morning star, Christ. . . .*

These three: The first that manifested Christ to them; the second that manifested them to Christ; The third Christ Himself, in Whom both these were as it were in conjunction. Christ *the bright morning star* of that day which will have no night; the *beatifica visio* of which day is the *consummatum est* of our hope and happiness for ever.

Of these three stars the first is gone, the third yet to come, the second only present."[2]

***

Andrewes draws out the aspect of faith as enshrined in the wise men's question of *where* rather than *whether*. He proceeds to outline what they believed of the Christ through this faith.

"They never ask *an sit,* but *ubi sit?* Not *whether* but *where He is born.* . . . Herein is faith, faith of Christ's being born, . . .

And what they believe they of Him? Out of their own words here; first that *natus,* that *born* He is and so Man He is, His human nature. And as His nature, so His office in *natus est Rex*. They believe that too. But *Judaeorum* may seem to be a bar; for then, what have they to do with *the King of the Jews*? They be Gentiles, none of His lieges, no relation to Him at all; what do they seeking or worshipping Him? But weigh it well, and it is no bar. For this they seem to believe: He is so *Rex Judaeorum, the King of the Jews* as He is *adorandus a Gentibus, the Gentiles to adore Him*. And though born in Jewry, yet Whose birth concerned them though Gentiles, though born far off in the *mountains of the east*. They to have some benefit by Him and His birth, and for that to do Him worship."[3]

***

Andrewes highlights the faith of *magi* which was evident as soon as they reached Judaea.

"They were no sooner come, but they spake of it so freely, to so many, as it came to Herod's ear and troubled him not a little that any King of the Jews should be worshipped beside himself. So then their faith is no bosom-faith, kept to themselves without saying anything of it to anybody. . . . The star in their hearts cast one beam out at their mouths. And though Herod who was but *Rex factus* could evil brook of *Rex natus*, must needs be offended at it, yet they were not afraid to say it. . . . So neither afraid of Herod, nor ashamed of Christ; but professed their errand, and cared not who knew it. This for their confessing Him boldly."[4]

***

The wise men by their example revealed the difference between *well-*

grounded faith and *lightness of belief*. In seeing the new star, assisted *by the light of their prophecy*, they immediately believed this star heralded some significant happening. The star was like the morning light drawing them, leading them and bringing them to the place where Jesus was born. We need to come for our morning light. Even though the star is long past, we have the holy writings to inspire us to a deep faith.

"[There is] the difference between *fidelis* and *credulus*. . . . Faith has ever as ground; *vidimus enim*, an *enim*, a reason for it, and is ready to render it. How came you to believe? . . . . *Vidimus enim, for we have seen a star* say the Magi, and this is a well-grounded faith. We came not of our own heads, we came not before we saw some reason for it — saw [what] set us on coming. . . .

But by this we see, when all is done, hither we must come for our morning light; to this book, to the word of prophecy. All our *vidimus stellam* is as good as nothing without it. The star is past and gone, long since. *Heaven and earth shall pass, but this word shall not pass.* Here on this, we to fix our eye and to ground our faith. Having this, though we neither hear angels nor see [the] star, we may by the grace of God do full well. . . . It is enough to ground our faith, and let the star go. . . .

There must be a light within the eye; else . . . nothing will be seen. And that must come from Him, and the enlightening of His Spirit. . . . He sending the light of His Spirit within into their minds, they then saw clearly, this the star, now the time, He the Child who this day was born. . . .

[Thus] the light of the star in their eyes, the *word of prophecy* in their ears, the beam of His Spirit in their hearts; these three made up a full *vidimus*."[5]

***

It was no use seeing and coming, without the doing. It is the last of these which is important. It was what the kings did when they travelled to and reached the Christ-Child. Faith was manifested in their efforts and works. The same must apply to us.

". . . now we shall come to *facientes*, see them do somewhat upon it. It is not saying nor seeing will serve [says] St. James; he will call, and be still calling for *ostende mihi, show me your faith by some work*. . . . You have seen His star, let Him now see your star another while. And so they do. Make your faith be seen; so it is, their faith in the steps of their faith. . . .

It is not commended to stand *gazing up to heaven* too long. . . . For they sat not still gazing on the star. Their *vidimus* begat *venimus*; their seeing made them come, come a great journey. *Venimus* is soon said, but a short word, but many a wide and weary step they made before they could come to say *venimus;* lo, here *we are come*. . . . [Their journey] was no summer progress. A cold coming they had of it at this time of the year, just the worst time of the year to take a journey, and specially a long journey. . . . The ways deep, the weather sharp, the days short, the sun farthest off, in *solsitio brumali, the very dead of winter. Venimus, we are come*, if that be one, *venimus, we are now come*, come at this time, that sure is another.

And these difficulties they overcame, of a wearisome, irksome, troublesome, dangerous, unseasonable journey; and for all this they came. And came it cheerfully and quickly. . . . It was but *vidimus, venimus,* with them; no sooner saw, but they set out presently. So as upon the first appearing of the star, . . . it called them away, they made ready straight to begin their journey this morning. A sign they were highly conceited of His birth, believed some great matter of it, that they took all these pains, made all this haste that they might be there to worship Him with all the possible speed they could. Sorry for nothing so much as that they could not be there soon enough, with the very first, to do it even this day, the day of His birth."[6]

***

What would we have done? Would we have made the same effort as the magi did? Andrewes thinks not. For one, we would not have undergone such an arduous trip in the depth of winter, and for another, such a hurried trip. Most of us would not make such an effort for Christ, ever hesitant, ever reluctant. Hence we are in danger of missing Christ altogether.

"And we, what should we have done? Sure these men of the East will rise in judgment against the men of the West, that is with us, and their faith against ours in this point. With them it was but *vidimus, venimus*; with us it would have been but *veniemus* at most. Our fashion is to see and see again before we stir a foot, specially if it be to the worship of Christ. Come such a journey at such a time? No; but fairly have put it off to the spring of the year, till the days longer, and the ways fairer, and the weather warmer, till better travelling to Christ. Our Epiphany would sure have fallen in Easter week at the soonest.

But then for the distance, desolateness, tediousness, and the rest, any of them were enough to mar our *venimus* quite. It must be no great way, first we must come; we love not that. . . .

Nor it must not be through no desert, . . . If rugged or uneven the way, if the weather ill-disposed, if any so little danger, it is enough to stay us. To Christ we cannot travel, but weather and way and all must be fair. . . .

But when we do it, we must be allowed leisure. Ever *veniemus*, never *venimus*; ever coming, never come. We love to make no great haste. To other things perhaps not *adorare*, the place of the worship of God. Why should we? . . . What talk you of twelve days? . . . What needs such haste? The truth is, we conceit Him and His birth but slenderly, and our haste is even thereafter. . . .

But what is *venimus* without *invenimus*? And when they come, they hit not on Him at first. No more must we think, as soon as ever we be come, to find Him straight. They are fain to come to their *ubi est*? . . .

We must learn . . . to ask where He is, which we full little set ourselves to do. If we stumble on Him, so it is; but for any asking we trouble not ourselves, but sit still as we say, and let nature work; and so let grace too, and so for us it will. . . . Regularly there is no promise of *invenietis* but to *quaerite*, of finding but to such as *seek*. It is not safe to presume to find Him otherwise. . . .

Christ has His *ubi*, His proper place where He is to be found; and if you miss of that, you miss of Him. And well may we miss, says Christ Himself.''[7]

***

If we do find *where* Christ is, what then? It should be to do Him homage as the magi did, and not the feigned worship of Herod. When we worship, it must be with our whole being — our body, our soul and our possessions.

''And now we have found *where*, what then? It is neither in seeking nor finding, *venimus* nor *invenimus*; the end of all, the cause of all is in the last words, *adorare Eum, to worship Him*. That is all in all, and without it all our seeing, coming, seeking and finding is to no purpose. . . .

Herod . . . would know where He were fain, and if they will bring him word where, he will come too and worship Him, that He will. None of that worship. . . .

We can worship God but three ways, . . . 1. The soul He has inspired; 2. the body He has ordained us; 3. and the worldly goods He has vouchsafed to bless us withal. . . . If He breathed into us our soul, but framed not our body, but some other did that, neither bow your knee nor uncover your head, but keep on your hats, and sit even as you do hardly. But if He has framed that body of yours and every member of it, let Him have the honour both of head and knee, and every member else. . . .

If all our worship be inward only, with our hearts and not our hats as some fondly imagine, we give Him but one of three; we put Him to His thirds, bid Him be content with that, He get no more but inward worship. That is out of the text quite. . . . And the text is a *vidimus*, and of a star; that is, of an outward visible worship to be seen of all. . . . There is a *vidimus* upon the worship of the body. . . . Let us see you fall down, so is there upon the worship with our worldly goods, that may be seen and felt *offerentes*. Let us see whether and what you offer. With both which, no less than with the soul God is to be worshipped.''[8]

***

As we come this day to give Him His worth, may we join in adoration with the angels, *magi* and all. Let us this day give Him homage, and fall down and worship Him.

''There now remains nothing but to include ourselves, and bear our part with them, and with the angels, and all who this day adored Him. . . .

We cannot say *vidimus stellam*; the star is gone long since, not now to be seen. Yet I hope for all that, that *venimus adorare, we be come thither to worship*. . . . If the same day-star be risen in our hearts that was in theirs, . . . it will bring us whither it brought them, to Christ, Who at His second appearing in glory will call forth these wise men, and all who have ensued the steps of their faith, and that upon the reason specified in the text; for I have seen their star shining and showing forth itself by the like beams; and as they came to worship Me, so am I come to do them worship. A *venite* then, for a *venimus* now. Their star I have seen, and give

89

them a place above among the stars. They fell down; I will lift them up and exalt them. And as they offered to Me, so I am come to bestow on them, and to reward them with endless joy and bliss on My heavenly kingdom.''[9]

References

[1] Andrewes, Vol. I, pp. 249–50.
[2] *ibid.*, p. 251.
[3] *ibid.*, p. 252.
[4] *ibid.*, p. 253.
[5] *ibid.*, 253, 255–6.
[6] *ibid.*, pp.256–7.
[7] *ibid.*, pp. 258–9.
[8] *ibid.*, pp. 260, 262–3.
[9] *ibid.*, pp. 263–4.

NATIVITY SERMON No. 16
CHRISTMAS DAY 1623

Text: Ephesians 1:10

That in the dispensations of the fullness
of times, He might gather together in one
all things in Christ, both which are in heaven
and which are on earth even in Him.

In dispensatione plenitudinis temporum, instaurare
omnia, in Christo, quae in caelis, et quae
in terra sunt, in Ipso.

The key words in this text are *gathering together in one*, and that gathering is into Christ. Everything has its season and hence this is the season for *gathering* into Christ, once we have found Him. This becomes the dominant theme of this sermon.

"There is for the most part in each text some one predominant word. That word in this is . . . . *gathering*, [more specifically] *gathering together into one again.* . . .

Christ is the 1. sum of our account, 2. the shutting up our discourse, 3. *the Head of the body* mystical whereto this gathering here is. We shall make no good audit without Him; no, nor good apology. Whatsoever be the premises, with Christ we must conclude. . . .

This season of the year [is] the gathering time with God and with us. So shall we dispense the season well.

Find the things, they will bring you to the season; find the fullness of things, you will find the fullness of seasons. Find the gathering, you will find the fullness; find Christ, and you will find the gathering, for the gathering is full and whole in Christ. . . . And this the first day we can find Him; for this day was He born, and so first to be found by us."[1]

***

Everything on earth has its time or season; the season of autumn is the time for *gathering*. Should not the same be applicable to the things of heaven? Should not there be a season for the soul as well as for the body? Andrewes argues that if we allow the seasonal sequence of events in the natural world, why not the supernatural too?

"Each [has] its several season to be gathered in. Now as *the things* have their autumn of maturity, so *tempora*, *the seasons*, have their fullness, and when the things are ripe and ready to be gathered, there is the season full. . . .

But are there seasons for the things on earth and their fullness, and are there not also seasons for the things in heaven, and for the filling of them? All for the relief of the bodily wants here below, none for the supply of spiritual necessities above? All for the body and never a season for the soul? If we allow them for the world, shall we not to the Church? . . . If it be sensible in the natural things, though not so easily discerned, yet it is as certain in the main revolution of *annus magnus, the great periodical year,* of the world's endurance.

It can never enter into any man to think that the great *Steward of this great household*, the world, should so far forget Himself, but if for all matters He *had appointed a season*, then for the greatest matter. If for every purpose under heaven, then for the highest purpose of all, that as we see concerns all the things in heaven and earth both. . . . Will not these have their seasons, and the seasons their fullness there, and that fullness the due dispensation of all other most worthy of God, the greatest work of the greatest Person?''[2]

***

Andrewes passes from the seasonal time of *gathering* to the *things* which are gathered, both in heaven and earth, proclaiming that those in heaven are always good. Indeed God, the chief Gatherer, loves gathering as this inevitably leads to unity.

"This sets us over the second part, from the seasons to the things; from the fullness of seasons to the gathering of things. And first . . . of what things? . . . *All*; and to show the extent of it, subdivided *into all in heaven, all in earth; . . .*

Of which gathering into one, I know not what the things in heaven have; the things in earth I am sure have good cause to be glad. In heaven is all good, and nothing but good. In earth to say the least, there is much evil. . . .

All these to be gathered, and well. Gathering God favours, for it ends in unity, to gather into one; and unity God loves. . . . God favours it sure, Himself is the gatherer. Scattering God favours not; that tends to division. . . . Gathering is good for us; unity preserves, division destroys.''[3]

***

Andrewes stresses that *gathering* is only part of what St. Paul is saying in his text; the whole meaning must be taken, that is *a gathering together again,* similar to St. Peter's *restoring*. This implies a previous desertion or departing or falling out from somebody or something. True, there was such a falling out when Adam disobeyed God, and such a scattering from Him, before the restoration. A *gathering* also implies a coming together as one. For Christians this uniting is in one person, Christ. So our *gathering* must always be striving towards this unity in Christ.

"It is not *a gathering*; but *a gathering together again* . . . It is not a collection, but a recollection. *Re* [shows] it is a new collection again, the second time. . . .

92

A returning to . . . implies a departing from. . . . One cannot be said to be gone from, that was never with; or to fall out, that was never in . . . So then together we were first, and in sunder we fell after. . . .

Together, our first original, which we had in Adam, while he stood with God together. . . . [There] came our misery, by Adam's not keeping his first estate, but scattering from God. But then comes *àvà* about, and makes all well again, by bringing us where we were at first. . . .

But when all is done *àvà* is it we must hold by. The first is gone, all perished by being scattered from. All must be recovered by being gathered to again. Our separation, our ruin, our reparation, our *àvà*, our *gathering again*, and not ours alone, but, *salus mundi* of *all in heaven, all in earth.* . . .

Everything that is gathered is . . . [into] one heap, . . . one flock, . . . one pile. . . . A headless gathering the Apostle cannot skill of. . . .

This gathering then, you see, is to the chief member, to the member who wears the crown. Thither, upward, the true gathering goes. . . . We may gather upwards . . . and make a head, and not the right head. . . .

And which is the right head ? . . . *Recapitulati in Christo* — it is Christ. . . .

And now we are arrived at Christ, we are where we should, our gathering is at the best. All in heaven, all in earth, gathered together, together again — again into one, one sum whereof Christ is the foot, one body whereof Christ is the Head. Gather then, and be gathered to Him; gather then, and be gathered with Him.''[4]

***

If we do not *gather* with Christ, then the opposite occurs, we scatter. Andrewes outlines the many *scatterings* which had happened before Christ's coming. Earth scattered from heaven, the Jews from the Gentiles and the Gentiles amongst themselves. Among such fragmentation, the law of the Levites, burnt offerings and sacrifices, and the work of the prophets could not bring a gathering; only the coming of Christ as a Child could achieve this.

''And so were all, all scattered without Christ, till He came . . . and got them again together. The seasons were all empty, the things all in heaps.

Things in heaven from things in earth, angels with *drawn swords at men.* Things on earth from things in heaven; men at but the sight of an angel ready to fall down dead. . . .

Scattered in point of religion. . . . Scattered in point of morality or moral philosophy. . . .

The Jews scattered from the Gentiles, and the Gentiles from the Jews, a main wall between.

The Gentiles scattered from themselves grossly; all in fractions, they. Nothing of a body, never a head; and yet many heads, but never a right one among them all. . . .

As the prophet Amos complains, and St. James alleges: . . . in a word, the whole world was then but a mass of errors, a chaos of confusion, *empty and void* of all saving grace or truth. Well likened to them who were scattered at the tower of Babel, where no man understood another; or to the people who were *scattered all over the land of Egypt to gather stubble, to pick up straws.* All then wandering hither and thither, and *seeking death in the error of their life. . . .*

But could not this gathering be *absque Christo,* in some other? It appears no. . . . A season of the Law written. Then the Priests and Levites but the gathering little the fuller for them.

Then came all the prophets, to no great purpose, thus neither . . .

It was time, more than time, when [what] was the only known way; . . . *Lo, I come. . . .*

By this *Ecce venio* of His a way was found, those who were thus distracted and scattered before, how to bring them together again. . . . The incorporating Christ, the ordaining Him a body, that is the *new and living way, through the veil, that is His flesh.* With that He comes this day, and gathers all again. . . .

All in heaven recapitulate into One, that is God; all in earth recapitulate into one, that is man. Gather these two now, and all are gathered, all the things in either. . . .

In man there was one-ward an abridgement of all the rest. Gather God and him into one, and so you have all. There is nothing, not anything, in heaven or earth left out. . . . All are in now; all reconciled, as it were, in one mass, all cast into one sum; recapitulated indeed truly and properly. . . .

For *God was in Christ reconciling the world. . . .* He did so *reconcile them in the body of His flesh. . . .* And there is good hope they who are one, will soon be at one; where unity is, union will be had with no great ado."5

***

At what season was this *Ecce venio, Behold I come,* fulfilled? *Diem Meum, My day,* Christmas. To commemorate this reconciliation, this gathering together again, Andrewes reiterates all the signs connected with His birth.

"When was this, at what season of the year? . . . When was *Ecce venio* fulfilled? We may know that by all the four Sundays in Advent now past, that to-day it is *Ecce venio,* . . . that though the Word was made flesh before, yet God was not *manifested in the flesh,* came not and *dwelt among us,* visibly to be seen till this day. . . . *In Christo nato,* then was this gathering of things in heaven and earth.

And in a sign it was then, look, there comes a choir of angels down, there comes a new star forth to represent the things in heaven, there comes together a sort of shepherds, and there is gathering to them a troop of great princes from the East to represent the things on earth, which consist, as these do, of high and low, noble and base, wise and simple; all to celebrate, and make show of this gathering, . . . And in their heavenly hymn there is mention of this gathering; *in excelsis,* and *in terris* set together, as if all in both were now in full and perfect harmony."6

***

There is a reason that God selects the season of winter for His coming. Usually in this season there is no *gathering* as nothing grows; it all has been done during autumn. So while there is nothing on earth to gather, God gives

94

us the greatest *gathering* possible, our restoration in Him. In a small way this is symbolized by our *gathering* of family and friends at Christmas.

"The text is of gathering, . . . and gives us great cause to admire the high wisdom of God in the dispensation of seasons; that now at this season, when we gather nothing, when nothing grows to be gathered, there should be a gathering yet and a great one; no, the greatest gathering that ever was or will be; and so by that means, the poorest and emptiest season in nature become the fullest and richest in grace.

Now we do ourselves in effect express as much as this. . . . For we also make it a season of gathering together, of neighbourly meetings and invitations. Wherein we come together, and both ourselves have, and we make each other partakers of, what we have gathered all the year before."[7]

***

This is the season for making our *gathering* as we follow God's example. What better place to start than with Christ at the altar.

"And even to begin now to imitate God in His time, when, and in His order how. His time. This is the time, God made His in; now we to take the same time to fall on gathering. . . . He began with heavenly things, we to keep the same order, follow His method, begin where He begins. . . . We shall the better dispense the season, if we gather to prayers, to God's word; if we begin with them, if with the dispensation of His holy mysteries gather to that specially.

For there we do not gather to Christ or of Christ, but we gather Christ Himself; and gathering Him we shall gather the tree and fruit and all upon it. For as there is a recapitulation of all in heaven and earth in Christ, so there is a recapitulation of all in Christ in the holy Sacrament. You may see it clearly: there is in Christ the Word eternal for things in Heaven; there is also flesh for things on earth. Semblably, the Sacrament consists of a heavenly and a terrene part, (it is Irenaeus' own words); the Heavenly — there the word too, abstract of the other; the earthly — the element."[8]

***

Even the elements in the Eucharist have their season for *gathering*.

"And in the elements, you may observe there is a fullness of the seasons of the natural year; of the corn-flour or harvest in the one, bread; of the wine-press or vintage in the other, wine. And in the heavenly, of the *wheat-corn* whereto He compares Himself — bread, even *the living Bread that came down from heaven* ; the true Manna, whereof we may gather each his gomer. And again, of Him, the true Vine as He calls Himself — the blood of the grapes of that Wine. Both these issuing out of this day's recapitulation, both in *corpus autem aptasi Mihi* of this day."[9]

***

95

One aspect of the Eucharist is a *gathering*, of which the priest is the dispenser of *the mysteries of God*, and thereby of its benefits. These are to be gathered and offered to Him in the highest heaven. It also gathers us to our fellow man, symbolized in the many grains in the bread, and the many grapes to make the wine.

"It is well known the Holy Eucharist itself is called, *Synaxis*, by no name more usual in all antiquity, that is *a collection or gathering*. For so it is in itself; for at the celebration of it, though we gather to prayer and preaching, yet that is the principal gathering the Church has, which is itself called a *collection* too by the same name from the chief; for *where the body is there the eagles will be gathered,* and so one *Synaxis* begets another.

And last, there is a *dispensation* . . . For it is our office, we are styled by the Apostle *dispensers of the mysteries of God*; and in and by them, of all the benefits that came to mankind by this dispensation in the fullness of season of all that are recapitulate in Christ.

Which benefits are too many to deal with. One will serve as the sum of all that the very end of the Sacrament is to gather again to God and His favour, if it happen, as often it does, we scatter and stray from Him. And to gather us as close and near as *alimentum alito*, that is as near as near may be.

And as to gather us to God, so likewise each to other mutually, expressed lively in the symbols of many grains into the one, and many grapes into the other. The Apostle is plain that we are all *one bread and one body, so many as are partakers of one bread,* so moulding us as it were into one loaf altogether. The gathering to God refers still to things in heaven, this other to men to the things in earth here. All under one head by the common faith; all into one body mystical by mutual charity. . . .

And even thus to be recollected at this feast by the Holy Communion into that blessed union, is the highest perfection we can in this life aspire unto. We then are at the highest pitch, at the very best we shall ever attain to on earth, what time we newly come from it; gathered to Christ, and by Christ to God; stated in all whatsoever He has gathered here laid up against His next coming. With which gathering here in this world we must content and stay ourselves, and wait for the consummation of all at His coming again. For there is an *ecce venio* yet to come."[10]

***

Our *gathering* here is but a prelude to that *gathering* which will come on that Last Day.

"This gathering thus here begun, it is to take end and to have the full accomplishment at the last and great gathering of all, which will be of the [living] and of the dead. When He will *send His angels, and they will gather His elect from all the corners of the earth,* will *gather the wheat into the barn, and the tares to the fire.* And then, and never till then, will be the fullness indeed, when God will be not,as

96

now He is, somewhat in every one, but *all in all*. *Et tempus non erit amplius, and there will be neither time*, nor season *anymore*. No fullness then but the fullness of eternity, and in it the fullness of all joy. To which, in the several seasons of our being *gathered to our fathers*, He vouchsafe to bring us; that as the year, so the fullness of our lives may end in a Christmas, a merry joyful feast, as that is!''[11]

References

[1] Andrewes, Vol. I, pp. 265–7.
[2] *ibid.*, pp. 267–8.
[3] *ibid.*, pp. 269–70.
[4] *ibid.*, pp. 270–2.
[5] *ibid.*, pp. 272–6.
[6] *ibid.*, pp. 276–7.
[7] *ibid.*, pp. 277–8.
[8] *ibid.*, pp. 280–1.
[9] *ibid.*, p. 281.
[10] *ibid.*, pp. 282–3.
[11] *ibid.*, p. 283.

NATIVITY SERMON No. 17

CHRISTMAS DAY 1624

Text: Psalm 2:7

I will declare the decree: the Lord has
said unto Me, You are My Son, this day
have I begotten You.

Praedicabo legem, de qua dixit ad Me Dominus:
Filius Meus Tu, hodie genui Te.

The psalmist announces what should be preached on this day, and introduces
the theme of preaching; what must be preached is that Christ's coming is
indeed a law. Christ Himself is both Preacher and the Lawgiver; as Preacher
let us hear clearly the message, *Filius Meus Tu, hodie genui Te, You are My
Son, this day have I begotten You.* Yet Christ had two begettings because of
His two natures — God and man, but on *hodie* it is the latter which is fulfilled,
preached and celebrated.

"What will He preach of? . . . *Filius Meus Tu, hodie genui Te.*
This text He preached on, as it might be at the bringing forth of a Son, . . . this
day the birth, this day the Sermon. . . .
Who preaches? . . . He to Whom it is said, *Filius Meus Tu,* is Christ. Christ then
preaches. And Christ is worth the hearing. . . .
And indeed so it was most meet that He should. He Who was the Lawgiver,
most meet to read upon His own law; He Who is the Son, most meet to preach
upon *Filius Meus Tu*; He Who was born, upon His own birth. . . .
This same *hodie* here is said *signanter*, that Christ was *begotten* to-day. For He
was *begotten* besides this, had more begettings than one. Two natures He had, . . .
One eternal, as the Son of God; the other temporal, as the Son of Man. . . .
But of the [two], more properly we apply it to this day's birth, His birth as the
Son of Man."[1]

***

The text deals with the decree or law. Andrewes asks how can *Filius Meus Tu*
in fact be a law? Yet it must be so, as Christ Himself has said so. He then
proceeds to show how it fits St. Paul's *lex fidei* and *lex factorum*. From now
onwards Christ, and therefore the Church, has a law to be preached and heard.

"*Filius Meus Tu,* how this should be a law, as here it is called. It looks not like
one. But said it must be, which Christ has said; a law He calls it, and a law we must
find it. Now be but two laws, as the Apostle tells us, *lex fidei* and *lex factorum*. . . .

Lex fidei. A law limiting what to believe of Him. Of Him, that is, of His Person, His Natures, and His Offices. . . .

Then *lex factorum.* Setting out first what He does for us; and then what we are to do for Him. What He does for us, *Filius Meus Tu,* to us He conveys all filial rights. What we do for Him, *Filius Meus Tu,* we to return to Him all filial duties. . . .

Praedicabo legem, says Christ. . . . We had well hoped, Christ would have preached no law, all Gospel He. . . . [But] a law He has to preach, and preach it He will.''[2]

***

Andrewes emphasizes one could not be a follower of Christ, unless one is prepared to accept His *laws* and those of His Church. Even the very Gospel has her laws.

''So if we will be His auditors, He tells us plainly we must receive a law from His mouth. If we love not to hear of a law, we must go to some other Church; for in Christ's Church there a law is preached. Christ began, we must follow. . . .

These very words *Filius Meus Tu,* etc. are as good Gospel as any in the New Testament; yet are here, as we see, delivered by Him under the terms of a law. . . . The words are plain, there is no avoiding them; a law He calls it, and a law it is.

. . . [Thus] they who are not for the law, are not for Christ. . . . Christ comes preaching the law, and they would live lawless; . . .

And then, that these words *Filius Meus Tu* are a law, and so as a law by Christ preached. So as in the very Gospel itself all is not Gospel, some law among it. The very Gospel has her laws. A law evangelical there is which Christ preached; and as He did, we to do the like.''[3]

***

As priests have a *commission* to preach the Gospel, it means that part of that, is teaching its law. Not to do so, disobeys Christ's command.

''Look but into the grand commission by which we all preach, which Christ gave at His going out of the world; *Go,* says He, *preach the Gospel to all nations teaching them* — what? *to observe the things that I have commanded you.* Lo, here is commanding, and here is observing. So the Gospel consists not only of certain articles to be believed, but of certain commandments also, and they to be observed. And what is that but *praedicabo legem!* . . .

Gospel it how we will, if the Gospel has not the *legalia* of it acknowledged, allowed and preserved to it; if once it lose the force and vigour of a law, it is a sign it declines, it grows weak and unprofitable, and that is a sign it will not long last. We must go look our salvation by some other way than by *Filius Meus Tu,* [if this] . . . be not preached, as Christ preached it; and Christ preached it as a law.''[4]

***

This law tells us particularly of *Filius*, the Son, the Son of God who is not adopted but begotten which means He is at one with the same nature which beget Him. Although the Son had two begettings, one eternal and the other *hodie genui*, it is the latter that is the important one for us, and must be preached. It is also the reason for celebrating Christmas.

"Of a Son. Whose Son? *Filius Meus*. And He who speaks it, who says *Meus*, is God; and so He to whom it is spoken, *the Son of God. . . .* and *the Son of God begotten*. For sons of God there be who are not begotten, they who come in another way, who come by adoption. To beget is an act of nature, and is ever determined in the identity of the same nature with him who did beget. And this [is] the difference. . . .

Begotten and *this day begotten*; *genui* and *hodie genui*; for begotten He had been before. Twice begotten He was. This day begotten and begotten *ante luciferum*, before there was any morning star. . . . We are to take notice of both these generations 1. of *Christus ante luciferum*, and of 2. *lucifer ante Christum*. . . . For that *ante luciferum* was not for us; His second begetting, His *hodie genui*, His this day's begetting is for us, is it we hold by. . . . *Hodie genitus* is the law, that we are to preach; that is, not His eternal, but his hodiernal generation. Not as God, of the substance of the Father, begotten before all worlds, but as Man, of the substance of His mother, born in the world; *when in the fullness of time God sent His Son, made of a woman*. And that was the *hodie genui* of this day."[5]

* * *

In discussing the manner of His begetting, Andrewes shows there is a strong resemblance between *genui, begetting* and *dixit, speaking*. He is the Word.

"There is a very near resemblance between *dixit* and *genui*, between begetting and speaking. To beget is to bring forth; so is to speak to bring forth also, to bring forth a word, and Christ you know is called the Word. . . .

When we think a word in our thought, and speak it there, within to ourselves, as it were in silence, and never utter it, this if you mark it well is a kind of conceiving or generation; the mind within of itself engendering a word, while yet it is but in notion, kept in and known to none but to ourselves. And such was the generation of the eternal Word, the Son of God, in the mind of His Father before all worlds; . . .

Now as the word yet within us in our thought, when time comes that we will utter it, does take to itself an airy body, our body, our breath by the vocal instruments being framed into a voice, and becomes audible to the outward sense; and this we call the second begetting or speaking: right so, the eternal Word of God, by *Dominus dixit*, by the very breath of God, the Holy Spirit, which has His name of *spiro, to breathe, (corpus autem aptasi Mihi,)* had a body framed Him, and with that body was brought forth, and came into the world. And so these words, *genui Te*, this very day, the second time, verified of Him. *Genui* and *dixit genui, said, and by saying, begot Him*; for how soon the angel's voice sounded in the blessed Virgin's ear, instantly was He incarnate in the womb of His mother.

Of both which words, *dixit* and *genui*, we can spare neither. There is good use of both. Of *genui*, to show the truth of the identity of His nature and substance with His Father who begat Him, and with His mother who bare Him. For to beget, is when one living thing brings forth another living thing, of the same nature and kind itself is. . . . That the manner of it was only as the word is purely and spiritually conceived in the mind. The one word, *genui*, noting the truth; the other word, *dixit*, the no way carnal, but pure and inconcrete manner of His generation."[6]

***

To verify that this *genui* is indeed a law, Andrewes takes St. Paul's division of it, into *lex fidei* dealing with Christ's person, nature and office, and *lex factorum*, what He does for us, which is the benefit of the law. Firstly *lex fidei*:

"Of His Person first. . . . Plain by the two Persons who are in the text, *Ego* and *Tu*, . . . the first and second persons of the Trinity. . . .

But of these Persons, . . . the first who is named, is *Filius Meus Tu*. He stands first in the verse before *genui Te*. We hear of *Filius* before ever we hear of *genui*; for that is the Person we hold by. By nature, *genui Te* should go before *Filius Meum*, but *quod nos, Filius Meus* is before *genui;* to show there is no coming to the Father but by Him, no interest in the Father but from and through Him. . . .

And in His Person we believe two natures, set down here in the two words, *hodie* and *genui*. . . . One is present, *hodie*, the other is perfectly past, *genui*. . . .

Genui, His eternal as perfect, and *hodie* as not yet perfect, His temporal; or vice versa, *hodie* represents eternity best, and *genui*, time, as being spent and gone; between them both, one way or other, they will show His begettings. You may weave *hodie* with *genui*, or *genui* with *hodie*, and between them both they will make up the two natures of Him Who was the *hodie genitus* of this day. Concerning whom we believe; as first, that He is one entire person and subsists by Himself, so second, that He consists of two distinct natures, eternal and temporal. The one as perfect God, the other as perfect Man.

Now for His offices . . . in the two words, *praedicabo* and *legem*. *Praedicabo*, . . . He does *preach*. And the word *legem* imports as much. . . .

So *Meus Filius* will prove a priest; . . . in Hebrews 5:4 the Apostle deduces His priesthood from these very words: *No, man*, says he, *takes unto him this honour*, that is, the honour of the Priesthood, *but he who was called of God, as was Aaron.* And then he adds, *No more did Christ, He took not this honour upon Him, to be our High-Priest; but that He said to Him, Filius Meus Tu, hodie genui Te, He gave it Him*. So that by virtues of these words, Christ was consecrate a Priest, as by virtue of the other, *posui Te Regem, He was set a King in Sion.*

And the place, Sion suits well with both. For Mount Sion had two tops. On the one was the Temple built, on the other was the King's palace situated. The one for *praedicabo*, the other for *legem*. In one, as King, he makes a law; in the other, as Priest, preaches it. First, *posui Regem*, and then *praedicabo legem*. . . .

We believe then for His offices, that He is both King and Priest. Has a Kingdom to rule, has a diocese to preach in. His kingdom, *the heathen, to the uttermost parts of the earth*; His diocese as large. His auditory all states, even the highest, kings and judges; for *praedicabo legem* concerns them all. And this for *lex fidei*, what it binds us to believe of Him.''[7]

***

Secondly, *the law of doing*. From what Christ has done, came the law of grace, by which we could become *the sons of God*.

''Now for *lex factorum*. First, what shall be done to them who live by and under the law? They speak of laws of grace: this is indeed a law of grace, no, it is the law of grace; not only as it is opposite to the law of nature, but even because it offers grace, the greatest grace that ever was. For what greater grace or favour can be done to any, than to have these words, *filius Meus tu*, said unto him? This law does it, *for to them who receive it, it gives power to be made sons of God*. . . .

He was *Filius Meus Tu*, needed no law to make Him [what] by nature He was. The law was for others which by this law were to be made [what] by nature they were not, that is, *the sons of God*. . . .

The Apostles says, *He was set and sent, that He might bring many sons unto God*, to whom God also might say, *filius Meus tu*. . . .

And who be those children? Those, whom He will regenerate, and beget anew by His *praedicabo legem*, the immortal seed; . . . for *of His own good will begat He us, by the word of truth, that we might be the first-fruits of His creatures*. . . . Of whom it will be said, *quod Filium filii*, that in and by this Son they will be His sons, all. And what was said to Christ, shall be said to them and every one of them, *filius Meus tu*.''[8]

***

The law also gives a *birthright*. Christ's birthright was manifested at His baptism and again at His transfiguration. Through our baptism we also receive our birthright.

''To this birth there belongs a birthright. . . . *Filius Meus Tu* . . . was said twice to Him. Once at His Baptism, *Hic est Filius Meus*. And so it is likewise at ours, to us, for therein we are made members of Christ, and the children of God. And again, *Hic est Filius Meus*, at His transfiguration in the mount. And we keeping the law of our Baptism, the same will be said to us likewise the second time; and when time comes, we shall also be *transfigured into the glorious image of the Son of God*. And this *lex factorum* on His part, this will be done for us by Him. This we called the gospel of the law.''[9]

***

The other part of the law of doing is our doing. What that is, is embodied in *praedicabo* and *legem*. Thus we must hear Him preach, and what is preached is law.

"And what will be done for us by Him? Which is the law of duty on our part required, and which we call the law of this gospel, implied in . . . *praedicabo* and *legem*. Either word has his condition. First, if he preach, that we bestow the hearing of Him. And then *legem*, that we know it is *a law* He preaches, and therefore so, and no otherwise than so, to hear it. . . .

His preaching is our law to live by; and law binds and leaves us not to live as we list. And if [what] is preached be law, it is to be heard as a law, kept as a law, to be made our *lex factorum,* as well as *lex fidei*. If we hear it otherwise, if we hear it not so, if we lose *legem*, we may let go *praedicabo* too and all."[10]

***

Andrewes concludes by revealing what the law of *filius Meus tu* gives — freedom. Thus it is a law of freedom as compared with the law of bondage under Sinai.

"Now if you ask what law it is here meant? No other but the law of these words, *filius Meus tu*; for *filius Meus tu,* in the body of it, carries the law that contains all filial duties, which is the perfect law when all is done.

For the law of a son of is more than all laws besides. For besides that it is *lex factorum*, that a son will do anything that is to be done, he will further do it out of filial love and affection, which is worth all. And this law, indeed, is worth the preaching. It is *the law that came from Sion.*

The *law of Sinai* that begins with *Ego sum Dominus*, . . . is a law of servitude, a law for the bond-woman and her brood. . . . That law is to give place, and in place thereof is to come the law of Sion, which we preach; the law of the free-woman, and *the children of promise*; the law of love, of filial love, proceeding not from *the spirit of bondage*, but from *the spirit of adoption*."[11]

***

Hodie is the time for us to make sure we do our part in *lex factorum* as it is the day when Christ fulfilled Scripture by being born. Therefore we must not put it off.

"We lack nothing now but the time. And as *legem* is the condition, so *hodie* is the time. . . . Not to defer, or to put it off, or make a morrow matter of it. . . . To look to this *hodie*, and not deceive ourselves, for no time but *hodie* has any promise. . . .

But *hodie genui* is more than *hodie*, for every day in the year while it lasts is *hodie*, but every day is not *hodie genui*. There is but one of them in the whole year, and that is this day. This day then to take, of all other *hodies*, not to let slip the *hodie* of this day. A day whereon this Scripture was fulfilled, whereon *dixit et*

103

factum est, whereon this Son was born and given us; a day whereon as it is most kindly preached. So it will be most kindly practised of all others. . . .

Praying to Him Who was the *hodie genitus* of this day, Him Who was begotten, and Him by Whom He was begotten. That we may have our parts, as on *praedicabo*, so likewise in *legem*; in both, *legem fidei*, to believe aright, and *legem factorum*, to live accordingly; that we performing the filial duties required, may obtain filial rights promised, and may be in the number of those to whom first and last *filius Meus tu* will be said, to our everlasting comfort.''[12]

References

[1] Andrewes, Vol. I, pp. 285–6.
[2] *ibid.*, p. 287.
[3] *ibid.*, pp. 287–8.
[4] *ibid.*, pp. 288–9.
[5] *ibid.*, pp. 291–2.
[6] *ibid.*, pp. 292–4.
[7] *ibid.*, pp. 294–297.
[8] *ibid.*, pp. 297–8.
[9] *ibid.*, p. 299.
[10] *ibid.*, pp. 299–300.
[11] *ibid.*, p. 300.
[12] *ibid.*, pp. 301–2.

AN INTRODUCTION
TO
THE LENTEN SERMONS

We are to "offer our bodies as well as our
souls, both a sacrifice to God"; as our soul by
devotion, so our body by mortification.

Vol. 1, p. 381.

Lent has always been a time for solemn preparation for the celebrating of our Lord's glorious Resurrection. Thus Andrewes' Lenten sermons with their message of fasting and penitence encourage us to prepare for Easter. The forty days is a time to take stock of our lives, and Andrewes warns us this may well be our last Lent and therefore the last opportunity to repent and return to God with renewed vigour and vision.

Fourteen of Andrewes' Lenten sermons have survived. Of these, eight or nine were preached on the first day of Lent, Ash Wednesday, while the remaining six or five at various times of the Forty Days.[1]

These sermons cover a much longer period than the Nativity ones, from 1589 to 1624, but the majority of them were delivered either in his younger days during the reign of Elizabeth or in his last years. As there are large gaps of time, these Lenten sermons do not achieve the unity of the Nativity ones. The six Lenten ones were all preached towards the end of the sixteenth century, before Elizabeth I, four at some of her country residences, and the other two at court. The first three Ash Wednesday sermons were delivered also before Elizabeth, two at Whitehall and the other at Greenwich. The remaining were preached at Whitehall in the presence of James I, except his 1624 one which was never delivered.

There is a great diversity of thought and theme amongst these sermons. Most of the Ash Wednesday sermons take as their starting point the set Epistle and Gospel for that day, with their message of repentance and fasting. For Andrewes repentance is absolutely necessary to live a healthy Christian life, and so he goes to great length to explain its meaning and purpose. Thus repentance is explained as being a "turning", which involves firstly to "look forward to God, and with our *whole heart* resolve to *turn* to Him", and secondly to "look backward to our sins wherein we have turned from God." In this "turning" there are two distinct parts:

One, conversion from sin; [and] the other contrition for sin. One resolving to amend [what] is to come, the other reflecting and sorrowing for [what] is past. One declining from evil to be done hereafter, the other sentencing itself for evil done heretofore.

Both of these, Andrewes warns, are needed for "a complete repentance".[2]

However he fears that like the "ceremony of giving ashes", which has gone, so has its "substance", repentance. Nevertheless "if that conversion into ashes be well thought on, it will help forward our turning."[3]

As we have seen in the Introduction Andrewes uses nature imagery to reinforce his teaching. So in Lent he uses the time of the season to help us repent of sins. Hence he urges us to take notice of what is going on all around us at this time of the year in order to stimulate us to a renewed life through repentance. When we look upon the fields we shall discover it is the time of planting. "There cannot be a fitter time than the Church has set . . . forth" for teaching repentance as "now is the time of the year to plant . . . [when] you will see nothing but men grafting and setting trees; it is the husbandry and the business of the month". Hence how "wonderfully fitly chosen therefore . . . that this [Lenten] tree may keep time with the rest." Cannot we follow suit and not defer our repentance "but take the time while it is [the] season . . . [so] that the mortifying of sin might end in the rising of Christ in us?"[4]

The fowls of the air also teach us that now, this Lenten time, is the time for repentance. The stork, turtle, crane and swallow all teach us by their habits that now is the "appointed time" to return to God through our fasting and repenting.[5]

Underlying his urgency for repentance is the need to remind us all that death is something that can happen to us in the twinkling of an eye. We must be prepared for it. Hence he reminds us that sin deadens us and is therefore destructive; it does nothing else but corrupts and corrupts:

O the damp and mist of our sin! so great that it darkens not only the light of religion which God teaches, but even the light of nature which her instinct teaches, even the reasonless creature itself.[6]

For Andrewes repentance was not just confessing sins, but also not continuing in them. This must be our intention too when we confess them.

Indeed Andrewes was rather sharp towards those who felt no need of repenting and wished to side-step it. Thus a shorter course is preferred by them "to pass the whole course of our life, and, in the whole course of our life, not to be able to set down, where, or when, or what we did, when we did [what] we call repenting; what fruits there came of it; what those fruits might be worth." It is only "a little before our death (and as little as may be), not till the world have given us over, then, lo, to come to our *quid faciemus*? to ask, *what should we do* ? when we are able to do nothing." Such an attitude towards repentance, Andrewes insists, is not the New Testament teaching. "This way, this fashion of repenting St. John knew it not; it is far from *fructus dignos*; St. Paul knew it not; it is far from his *opera digna*. And I can say little to it, but I pray God it deceive us not."[7]

Andrewes also presents repentance symbolically by describing it as a tree which must bear fruit, one of which was fasting. So Lent is also a time of fasting. Yet Andrewes laments it is often neglected for the "most part" by church-goers who are "so faintly persuaded of fasting as if it were no needful part of a Christian's duty." Thus he explains why the Church makes "this time of our return, a time of fast". It is not only to mortify the body, "that it may be a less mellow soil for the sins of the flesh," but also "as a chastisement for sin already past."

To the question, "And must we . . . fast?" Andrewes responds, "Indeed we must, or get us a new Epistle for the day, and a new Gospel too", as both command fasting. "Christ cannot say to us, *When you fast*, if we fast not at all." Therefore *When you fast*, should be, "now we fast, now we are at it this day".[8]

In so doing we simply follow the example of Christ Himself whose fasting is read as the Gospel for the First Sunday in Lent. "Christ's fasting . . . before His temptation was to show us it is good to fast against temptation" as this weakens the devil's "forces by keeping down *our fleshly lusts*, which, says St. Peter, *fight against the soul.*" This devout man makes it very clear that when we are serious about our fasting the devil does his utmost to persuade us either not to fast as this makes us hypocrites "like the Pharisees" or to fast for our own vain-glory. Yet if we persevere in following Christ's example we shall have His reward.[9] Other fruits of repentance are prayer, alms and good works.[10]

The first two Ash Wednesday sermons delivered to Elizabeth have a distinctly military tone. The 1599 one was preached as the Earl of Essex was setting out on his Irish campaign. Nevertheless because Andrewes believed that war was an act of justice "to punish sin", he gives it a distinctive Lenten tone. Thus for those going into combat, the need to repent of sin was never more applicable. "Sin is never so untimely as in the time of war, never so out of season as then; for that is the time of all times we should have least to do with it." It was therefore imperative that those who fought did not add sin upon sin. Hence in this sermon as indeed in all his Lenten ones, he insists that this time be one of remorse and repentance.[11]

The general Lenten sermons are quite different. They do not emphasize the disciplines of Lent as found in the Ash Wednesday sermons. Indeed most of them have *royal* and *stately* themes. They also reflect that the quality of government and the well-being of the State are a result of the care and wise ruling of the Prince. In all matters Elizabeth is commended. This commendation reaches its peak in the sermon on Lot's wife:

And blessed be God and the Father of our Lord Jesus Christ, that we stand in the presence of such a Prince, who has even accounted of perseverance, not only as of Regina virtutum, but as of virtus Reginarum. Who, like Zerubbabel, first by princely magnanimity laid the corner-stone in a troublesome time; and since, by heroical constancy, through many both alluring proffers and threatening dangers, has brought forth the Head-stone also with [Zechariah's] acclamation, Grace, grace, unto it. Grace, for so happy a beginning, and Grace for so thrice happy an ending. No terrors, no enticement, no care of her safety has removed her from her steadfastness; but with a fixed eye, with straight steps, with a resolute mind, has entered herself, and brought us into Zoar.[12]

Indeed, Andrewes held that true happiness for all people can only be achieved when both the Church and Crown work together as illustrated by the joint office of Aaron and Moses; "it is the rod of God that is in Moses and Aaron's hands."[13] Thus Church and Crown could never be separated in the preserving of good government.

These Lenten sermons reach their spiritual peak, in the two sermons on love. The first of these is Mary Magdalen's anointing of Christ. Despite its overtones of Elizabeth's alientation of Church revenue, it overflows with Mary Magdalene's selfless, spontaneous and lavish giving to our dear Lord as she poured her sweet but expensive ointment upon His head. Her "poor box of *nardus* will be matter of praise, and never die." Her loving act was highly commended by our Lord, and in turn Andrewes upholds her act to us so that in our generous giving our souls may also be "refreshed with the sweet joys of heaven."[14]

The second is the last of the general Lenten sermons in which Andrewes highlights St. Paul's Christ-like love "to those who are furtherest from love, and least deserve it." He wants us to learn from St. Paul's example of loving the "unlovable" brethren, as indeed many of the Corinthians seemed to be. He reminds us too that giving, even if we give all our goods to the poor, is nothing unless it is done lovingly.[15]

In this collection of Lenten sermons Andrewes presents many of the Christian virtues such as perseverance and constancy, frugality and temperance, good works and selfless giving; justice and faith, love and devotion, and sharing our possessions with the poor and needy. He also admonishes us against a false sense of security in our Christian living, and uses the example of Lot's wife who fell from grace at the last after having being faithful all her life. He also warns, through the parable of Dives and Lazarus, of the reality of hell-fire for those who do not share their earthly possessions with the poor and are oblivious of their needs. Overall these sermons remind us that we must be a *doing* Christian as well as a *praying* one. It is in loving our brethren that we can truly love God. This we can practise throughout Lent as well as our praying, repentance and fasting. Indeed they all should be intertwined. By practising all of these we are truly ready to meet our risen Lord on Easter morn.

Andrewes urges us to make good use of our Lenten time, as it is precious and may be the last opportunity to repent and do good works. Otherwise we shall have to face "the wrath to come", on Judgement day.

References

[1] Bliss suggests that the sermon delivered on Tuesday 5 March, 1595-96 was actually delivered on Ash Wednesday 5 March, 1594-95, in Lossky, p. 101.
[2] Andrewes, Vol. 1, p. 359.
[3] *ibid.*, p. 362.
[4] *ibid.*, p. 453.
[5] *ibid.*, pp. 351–2.
[6] *ibid.*, p. 349.
[7] *ibid.*, pp. 450–1.
[8] *ibid.*, pp. 367, 396–7.
[9] *ibid.*, pp. 388, 401, 410.
[10] *ibid.*, p. 443.
[11] *ibid.*, pp.329–31.
[12] *ibid.*, Vol. 2, p. 76.
[13] *ibid.*, p. 31.
[14] *ibid.*, pp. 59–60.
[15] *ibid.* pp. 101, 106.

ASH WEDNESDAY SERMON No. 1: 1598

Text: Psalm 78:34

When He slew them, then they sought Him;
and they returned and enquired early
after God.

*Cum occideret Eos, quaerebant Eum: et
revertebantur, et diluculo veniebant
ad Eum.*

The theme of this Lenten sermon is seeking God, and seeking Him in time to repent, and thus to turn away from sin and turn to God. The time for true repentance should be before *Cum occideret Eos, when He slew them,* and not afterwards as suggested in the text.

The implication of this text is that when the Israelites were spared, they never gave a thought to God, let alone sought Him. It was only in their adversity they turned to Him, not unlike most of us. We spend most of our time seeking other things rather than God and the things of God.

''And this verse a report how in the manner of repentance, expressed here under the terms of seeking and turning to God. Wherein this they did, this was their fashion: while He spared them, they sought Him not. . . .

Asaph expressly has set it down . . . that this and other errors of theirs are here upon the file, *that we would not be like our forefathers, a cross and crooked generation.* . . . Never to seek God but when He kills us.

In which foul indignity our age is certainly as deep as ever was that, and we need Asaph's instruction no less than they.

For as if there were no use of religion, but only *cum occideret,* so spend we all our whole time in the searching of other things. Not caring to ask, or seek, or confer about the state of our souls, even till *occideret* come.''[1]

***

If we put off repentance until the last moment we are in danger of losing our souls for ever. Now is not the time, we think; time for all that later. It is something that we seem to do over and over again. Yet what we should be doing is to seek Him before this *cum* by our repentance.

''Now sure, this course must . . . be prejudicial to our souls, and a number perish in it daily before our eyes. Yet we sit still, and suffer this custom to grow and gather beard. Neither delivering their souls, or at least our own, by telling them

seriously this is not the time, and then to seek is not the seeking God will allow.
. . .

Therefore, that we set ourselves to seek before this *cum* come; that is, in a word,
. . . seek God, as by repentance and the fruits, so by undelayed repentance and the
fruits, so by undelayed repentance, and the timely fruits of it; and be not like St.
Jude's, our seeking all summer withered and dry, and beginning to shoot out a
little about Michaelmas spring. Of which kind of shooting fruit can never come.''2

***

Andrewes emphasizes *our seeking* should always be before *His killing*. Yet
what we do is to put off this seeking while everything is going well for us.
When things are not going all right there is a different concern.

"For *cum occideret*, *His killing* stands before *our seeking*; whereas our seeking
should be first, and His killing come after. . . .

Our case before that time is lively expressed in: . . . *They spend their days in
vanity, and their years in turmoil in the world.* Our case then at that time in these
words, *cum occideret eos.* . . .

For in public, when in the days of safety, plenty and peace, we are in the sixth of
Amos, and are best at ease when *quaerebant* is furtherest from us; but if war,
famine, or contagion come, then we run to the second of Joel, *Sanctify a fast*, and
call for the Ark, and grow all godly on a sudden. What is this but *cum occideret*?
And in private, when while youth and strength and health do last, while the evil
day is far off, we are even at *cause the Holy One of Israel to cease from us;* but
when distress, danger or death comes, . . . then we cry, *Now is the day of tribulation and anguish;* . . . our seeking goes wholly by our killing — waxes and wanes,
is out and in, as that is near at hand or farther off.''3

***

Now to *quaerebant Eum*; seeking God is something most of us do sometime
in our life, but quite often it is put off until the end. While however we are
young and healthy, we do not give it a moment's thought. We would rather
spend our life in seeking vanity than true piety, or merely flattering God.
However the time of reckoning will come for each of us.

"All seek; . . . but *they* . . . *wasted all their days in vanity, and their years in
turmoiling in the world.* . . .

They, who in a verse after *flattered Him with their lips,* and gave Him all the
good words that might be, and meant no such things. The hypocrites, *they* sought.
. . .

And herein is [the] folly . . . that who greedily seek sin, at last would be glad to
be rid of it, and they who merrily scorn religion at last are glad to seek to it. . . .

[Yet while] age, sickness, death are afar off; youth, health and strength possess
them; there is no coming to them then. . . . *Cum occideret*, is not yet come; but

come that once as once it will to all, you will find *quaerebant* will have his place. . . . And even so we are fain to resolve.''4

***

Despite who we are or whatever way we choose to spend our time, most of us in the end want some kind of reckoning with our Maker. Irrespective of when we *seek*, we have to make the effort to do it; it will not suddenly drop into our laps. Most leave it until they think death is hovering over them, or when God seemingly strikes them with some affliction.

''First or last, all shall confess by seeking God is to be sought. Some before He kills, and happy are they; *when He kills*, all; hypocrites, heathens, atheists and all. . : . But seek it we must. For without seeking it will not be had. If it would they might sit still, and let it drop into their laps. . . .

We desire to die seeking, howsoever we live; all show certainly it is a *fiat, a thing to be done*, a good thing to seek God, even the enemies of it being judges of it. . . .

[Yet] seeking [is] so loosely, so slightly, so slenderly [done], as if what they sought were as good lost as found. . . . Never, as if it were about some matter of special moment. . . .

1. They turned them, says the text, as if before they sought without so much as turning them about.

2. They rose up, as though before they sat still and sought.

3. They did it early, and did not tarry till *cum occideret*, the sun were set, and light to seek by, but their *feet stumbled in the dark mountains*.

4. They *enquired*; so that before if you had ought to say to them you might, they had nothing to say to you.''5

***

This *death-bed* attitude in seeking reconciliation with our Maker is obviously unChristian. Our *seeking* God and repentance should be in response to what God is, and not to what we want from Him. Furthermore we want to be able to fix the time when we do our *seeking* when ideally it should be done all our life. Will any time be just right for such people, asks Andrewes?

''Another point . . . is the right seeking. Not seek Him for somewhat we would have of Him, but to seek Himself for Himself. It is one thing . . . to seek God for fruition; another to seek Him to make use of Him. One thing, says Christ to seek for the miracle, another for the loaves. . . . Such is our seeking for the most part; *cum occideret*, to have our turn served, to have our health restored, that we may seek Him no longer, but to our former riot again, *and to-morrow may be as yesterday and much more*. . . .

To find the time, we agree that as every weighty thing has, so the seeking of God is to be allowed a time too. What time is that? Verily, we should do it absolutely, all our life long; not when? but when not? without limitation, continually. . . .

111

God indeed is so to be sought, but we cannot so seek Him; other our affairs crave allowance out of our time. . . .

We cannot be brought to set down any certainty, but love to be left at large. Do it we shall, but indeed we cannot show when. . . . I demand, will any time serve."[6]

***

Christ made it clear that there was a definite time for repentance. It is not the time of *cum occideret*, but when He saves us. Unfortunately we so often believe we have more important matters each day than in seeking God, but the joy of the heart is in finding God.

"*Cum occideret*, it is not. Christ Himself expressly limited it before; said He, *I gave her a time to repent*. What time is that? Lest we might mistake it to be *cum occideret*, He adds, if we do it not in that time so by Him given, He will *cast us down on our beds*, the beds of affliction and sickness, and there *kill us with death*. So that the time He allows us to repent, is before we come thither. . . . Indeed our bed is not the place. . . .

Then if when He kills us is not it, when He saves us it is? It is indeed; and a cluster of it, an hour of *cum servaret* then is better than a vintage, a whole day of *cum occideret*. . . .

For sure as we seek God to save us, so He saves us to seek Him; if when we seek Him we are saved, when we are saved we should seek Him. . . .

[But] other great matters we have in hand, matters of more weight than seeking of God. As if His seeking were some petty business, slightly to be sought, and lightly to be found. Any time good enough for it. . . .

So evil are we affected to seek Him then, . . . we . . . seek . . . [the] miracle at the hour of death; that may give us days and elbow-room enough to seek other things, and to shrink up His seeking into a narrow time at our end, and tell us time enough then. For thus then we reckon; all the time we spend in it we lose the fruit of our life, and the joy of our hearts shall be taken from us, as if the fruit of life were not to find God, or as if any true hearts' joy God being not found. . . . Yes, *in the very tears of a penitent*, there is, says St. Augustine, more sound joy than *in all the games the theatre can afford*. But our taste is turned, and we relish not this seeking. By our flesh-pots we have lived, and by them we shall die, and so we do."[7]

***

And so our seeking repentance for most of us is left until we are almost senile and death calls us, and when our earthly seekings are all finished. Andrewes queries whether this will have the result we would like it to have. Thus he cannot commend this approach. In fact it is no seeking at all, but *a base ignoble creeping to*. Judgment is therefore upon us, not unlike that in the parable of the ten virgins. He concludes by insisting that true *seeking* is worth pursuing because it enables us to find God whom to know is full of more joy than any earthly pursuit.

112

"*Tandem* then, when we are come to the very last cast, our strength is gone, our spirit clean spent, our senses appalled, and the powers of our soul as numb as our senses, when a general prostration of all our powers, and the shadow of death upon our eyes, then something we would say or do which should stand for our seeking; but I doubt it will not serve. . . .

Would we then seek Him when we are not [able] to seek anything else? Would we turn to Him then when we are not able to turn ourselves in our bed? . . . Or *enquire after Him* when our breath fails us, and we are not able to speak three words together? . . . No time but when He takes time from us and us from it? . . . Shall I commend this seeking, turning . . . enquiring? No; . . . I commend it not. . . .

This time is the time when all hypocrites, atheists, tag and rag, come in and seek Him in a sort; and will not we be confounded to see ourselves in their number? No, to say what must be said for true it is, it is past the Devil's time. . . .

But in very deed it is no *seeking* at all. . . . For what is our *seeking* then? Is it not to lie still on our bed, and suffer a few words to be spoken in our ears? Have a little opiate divinity ministered to our souls, and so sent away? Sure this is rather to be sought than to *seek*. . . .

And justly they find Him not *ex lege talionis*. God Himself answers them; no, their own hearts answer themselves. Go: whom you have spent your life in seeking, seek to them now. Let them save you at this, whom you sought at all other times. . . .

[Nevertheless] His seeking is worth the while, and that it is not dispatched in a minute, but must have time. . . .

So seeking we shall safely seek; safely seek and surely find God, and with God whatsoever is worth the finding. But [what] we seek, we shall after *occideret* is past, find ourselves in His presence and at His right hand; in *Whose presence is the fullness of joy,* not as ours here, joys half empty. . . . [What] here we seek and cannot find with Him we shall, if we shall here indeed and in due time seek Him by the timely fruits of an undelayed repentance."[8]

References

[1] Andrewes, Vol. I, pp. 305–6.
[2] *ibid.*, pp. 306–7.
[3] *ibid.*, pp. 307–9.
[4] *ibid.*, pp. 309–11.
[5] *ibid.*, pp. 311–3.
[6] *ibid.*, pp. 313–4.
[7] *ibid.*, pp. 315–6.
[8] *ibid.*, pp. 317–320.

ASH WEDNESDAY SERMON No. 2: 1599

Text: Deuteronomy 23:9

When the host goes forth against your
enemies, then keep you from every
wicked thing.

*Quando egressus fueris adversus hostes
tuos in pugnam, custodies te ab omni re mala.*

As this sermon was preached as the Earl of Essex set out on his Irish campaign, the theme is war, but righteous war against the enemy. With this emphasis, it makes this Lenten sermon different from the others. Nevertheless Andrewes shows warring – or perhaps fighting – against our sins needs just as much successful campaigning as that against the foe. Indeed, before going off to combat which Andrewes believed was an act of justice to punish sin, it was imperative that the campaigners live a life guarding against sin. What was applicable to the soldier was also applicable to those who stayed at home. All need to live in a state of grace.

"This our host so going forth, our heart's desire and prayer unto God is, that they may happily go, and thrice happily come again, with joy and triumph to her sacred Majesty, honour to themselves, and general contentment to the whole land.
. . .

Moses does here out of his own experience bestow an advice upon us, . . . which advice is, that among our military points we would reckon the abatement of sin for one; that now this time of our going forth we would go forth against sin too, and keep from it as we would keep us from our enemy. If we could be but persuaded to reform our former custom of sin, it would certainly do the journey good. That therefore with other courses, some remembrance, some regard be had of this; that at this time sin do not so overflow among us, be not so very fruitful as before time it had. . . .

Moses [also tells] us, that *when our forces go forth against the enemy*, that we then, at that time, are in any wise *to keep us from wickedness*; by sorting these thus together does plainly intimate that when the time of war is, then is a fit time, a very good opportunity, to draw from sin and return to God. . . .

If they who go to war must keep themselves from sin, then is war no sin but lawful, and without sin to be undertaken. . . . We cannot better pattern it than by the Gospel of this day, *when you fast, be not like hypocrites* — by all Divines resolved thus. Fast you may sometimes; and then fasting, look you fall not into hypocrisy. And as in that, so in this: go you may sometimes; only when you go see you *refrain from sin* and then go and spare not. Out of which match of these two, fast and war, we may rise higher."[1]

***

What does leading an army have to do with the *forbearing of sin?*. A lot, suggests Andrewes; they are more like neighbours than strangers or even enemies, and so they stand together just as the prophet and the captain did in olden times.

"For what has the leading army to do with forbearing of sin? Yet God has thus sorted them as we see. Therefore policy of war whereto the former, and Divinity whereto the latter belongs, are not such strangers one to the other, as that one must avoid while the other is in place. But that as loving neighbours and good friends here they meet together [and] they stand together. . . . God Himself, in Whose imperial style so often proclaimed in the prophets they both meet. . . . And from God Himself no doubt was that happy and blessed combination which in most wars of happy success we find, of a captain and prophet sorted together; Joshua with Moses, . . . Baruk with Deborah, . . . Joash with Elisha; . . . the one leading against the enemy and annoying him, the other leading against sin and annoying it. . . .
These two then, *going forth with the host,* and *departing from sin*, being thus linked by God, our suit is, break not this link; God has joined them that we should join them. . . . For it is one of the diseases under the sun; in war all our thoughts run upon the host, looking to the host only and nothing but the host, and letting sin run thither it will without any keeper."[2]

***

Is there any need for a priest in time of war? Yes, says Andrewes, because those going off to fight need to be blessed and prayed for, just as Moses had prayed while Joshua fought.

"What good do these Churchmen? What use is there of them now at such a time as this? Yes, there is a use of them, and that in war we see. . . . Which God showed plainly in the first field that ever His people fought; . . . that Joshua's having the better or going to the worse depended not a little on the steadiness of Moses' hands, and that Moses staying behind and striking never a stroke did his part towards the attaining of the victory not much less than Joshua who went forth and fought manfully. Prayer then is of use."[3]

***

However for prayer to be effective, we must firstly rid ourselves of sin, as King Balak of Moab discovered. Thus in going off to war, it is imperative to keep oneself unspotted from sin.

"But what availeth prayer without keeping from sin? Therefore . . . we must . . . *arm ourselves with this mind of ceasing from sin*, that our prayers may be effectual. . . . The King of Moab, Balak, when he observed what prayer had wrought in the battle of Amalek, . . . sent for Balaam into his camp, to match prophet with prophet, and to oppose prayer unto prayer. But when all his altars and rams would do no good, Balaam [knew] well there is in sin a power to defeat any prayer. . . .

At this time in war, . . . *when you go . . . therefore keep yourself from sin.*"4

***

Yet it is not only during the time of war when we must forego sin, but also in times of peace. At all times we must resist sin.

"Sin certainly at all times is to be forborne. When it is war, and not only when it is war, but when it is peace too. *Take heed, lest at any time*, says Christ, *your hearts be overlaid with surfeiting, with drink*, etc. Not allowing us any time to be wicked in, . . . [But] at all times we be to refrain [from] sin."5

***

During times of war, however, there is the belief that this is a time to sin even more. How misconstrued is this thinking as it is sin in the first place which causes war.

". . . we see for the most part that even they who are the goers forth seem to persuade themselves that then they may do what they list; that at that time any sin is lawful, that war is rather a placard than an inhibition to sin. A thing so common that it made the heathen man hold that between *militia* and *malitia* there was as little difference in sense as in sound. . . .

[Truly] if we shall learn of God, if He will teach us, sin is never so untimely as in the time of war, never so out of season as then; for that is the time of all times we should have least to do with it. . . .

From the very nature of war first, which is an act of justice, and of justice corrective, whose office is to punish sin. Now then consider and judge even in reason, what a thing this is, how great, gross, and foul an incongruity it is to pour out ourselves into sin at the very time when we go forth to correct sin; to set forth to punish rebels, when we ourselves are in rebellion against God, His Word, and Spirit. . . . Therefore, since to go to war is to go to punish sin, certainly the time of punishing sin is not a time to sin in. . . .

If then our sins common unto us with other nations, . . . if war be the sickness and sin the surfeit, should we not at least-wise now while the shivering fit of our sins is upon us, diet ourselves a little and keep some order? . . . Shall we make our disease desperate, and hasten our ruin by not containing from sin that has cast us in it? . . . Is this a time of sin? Certainly, we cannot devise a worse. In the time of war it is high time to *keep us from sin*".6

116

***

Make no mistake: Satan and sin are God's enemies. If we wish to follow God, we must war against the devil and sin. We cannot expect God's blessing and protection otherwise.

"For if we shall hold of God, make Him sure, be certain of Him, we must break with sin. . . . Sin and Satan are His enemies, and no fellowship nor communion, no concord, no agreement, no part, no portion between them. If we shall draw Him into league, we must profess ourselves enemies unto His enemies, that He may do the like to ours. At one and the same time enter as an outward war with wicked rebels, so an inward hostility with our wicked rebellious lusts. . . . But if we shall needs hold on our league with hell, and continue our wonted intercourse with wickedness still, and go forth unto it when it beckons or calls, . . . and cherish it between our breasts; for not keeping from it He will keep from us, and withdraw His help from us, and put us clean out of His protection.

Therefore, without keeping from sin there is no keeping God, out of Whose keeping there is no safety."[7]

***

In order to keep away from sin, we should make a covenant with ourselves to help guard against sin. Andrewes lists ways to stay away from sin. These cover not only our actions but our words also, and apply to not only those going to battle, but to all at home.

". . . to make a covenant with himself, from henceforth more carefully to stand upon his guard, and not to go forth to sin or entertain it as a friend, but to repute it as an enemy and to keep him from it. . . .

And even so, there is a soil of sin that of itself vapours from our nature. . . . I say not, we should keep ourselves from this, but from provoking it by suffering our minds to wander in it; by not keeping our ears from such company, and our eyes from such occasions, as will procure it. . . . From that by the help of God we may keep ourselves well enough. From sins lighting upon our thoughts it is impossible, it cannot be; but from making there a nest or hatching ought, that we are willed to look to, and that by God's grace we may. . . . The heart not resolving or saying content, but keeping itself from going forth to any act; though wickedness be not kept from us because of the temptation, yet we are kept from it because of the repulse. . . .

Words, I say, as well as deeds. . . . And indeed, if in good words as in prayers there be force to help, I make no question but in wicked words, as blasphemies, irreligious sayings, there is force also to do mischief. Therefore keep from all . . . wicked words first, presumptuous terms of trust in our strength, . . . blasphemy; . . . and . . . from wicked works [of] sacrilege, . . . [and] to keep them from . . . profaning holy vessels or holy places with unholy usage. . . .

This advice is to take place . . . in us likewise who stay home; . . . by turning from sin to God, and that with a serious not shallow, and an inward not hollow repentance. Not confessing our sins to-day and committing them to-morrow, but everyone saying, *I have said, I shall henceforth more narrowly look to my ways.* . . . To conclude, if we shall, or when we shall be tempted to any of our former sins, to think upon God's counsel, *to remember the camp and not to do it*; to think upon them in the fields and their danger, and for their sakes and for their safeties to forbear it. . . .

Even so Lord, so let it be. Those whom you now carry forth by Your mercy, bring them back by Your might in this place of Your holy habitation."[8]

References

[1] Andrewes, Vol. I, pp. 321–3.
[2] *ibid.*, p. 326.
[3] *ibid.*, pp. 327–8
[4] *ibid.*, pp. 328–9.
[5] *ibid.*, p. 329.
[6] *ibid.*, pp. 329–31.
[7] *ibid.*, pp. 332–3.
[8] *ibid.*, pp. 333–6.

ASH WEDNESDAY SERMON No. 3: 1602

Text: Jeremiah 8: 4–7

Thus says the Lord: Shall they fall and
arise? Shall he turn away and not return?
Why then is this people of Jerusalem slidden
back by a perpetual backsliding? They hold
fast deceit, they refuse to return.
I hearkened and heard, but they speak not
aright: no man repented him of his wickedness,
saying, What have I done? Every one turned to
his course, as the horse rushes into the battle.
Yes, the stork in the heavens knows her appointed
times; and the turtle, and the crane, and the
swallow, observe the time of their coming; but My
people know not the judgment of the Lord.

Haec dicit Dominus: Numquid qui cadit, non
resurget? et qui aversus est, non revertetur?
Quare ergo aversus est populus iste in Jerusalem
aversione contentiosa? apprehenderunt mendacium,
et noluerunt reverti.
Attendi, et auscultavi: nemo quod bonum est
loquitor, nullus est qui agat poenitentiam
super peccato suo, dicens: Quid feci? Omnes
conversi sunt ad cursum suum, quasi equus, impetu
vadens ad praelium.
Milvus in Caelo cognovit tempus suum: turtur,
et hirundo, et ciconia custodierunt tempus adventus
sui: populus autem Meus non cognovit judicium
Domini.

The overall themes are sorrow for our hardness towards God, and our perpetual apathy towards sin. Yet even the hardest of sins can be melted. There is always a time for repentance, and Ash Wednesday reminds us that time is *now*. Just as the various birds know their appointed time, so we should know that Lent is the appointed time for repenting and mourning for our sins. Although none of us can attain perfection in this earthly pilgrimage, it is our constant committing of sins without any remorse that has not only grieved God, but given Him just cause for complaint against us.

"For true it is that not to fall nor err nor do amiss at all, is an higher perfection than our nature in state . . . can attain to. . . . Our estate . . . needs . . . more grace. . . .

If we have not been so happy as to stand and keep our way, let us not be so unhappy as not to rise and turn to it again. Best it were before we sin to say to ourselves, *What am I now about to do?* If we have not that, yet it will not be amiss after to say, *What have I done?* God will not be displeased to hear us so say. . . .

For seeing plain *poenitentiam agite* does but coldly affect us, it pleases God, *hac vice*, to take unto Him the terms, the style, the accents of passion. . . . And the passion He chooses is that of sorrow. . . . This sorrow He expresses by way of complaint. . . .

That He complains of is not that we fall and err, but that we rise not and return not; that is, still delay, still put off our repentance. And that, 1. contrary to our own course and custom in other things; we do it everywhere else, yet here we do it not; 2. Contrary to God's express pleasure. For glad . . . He would hear we do it, yet we do it not 3. Contrary to the very light of nature. For the fowls here fly before us, and show us the way to do it, yet we do it not for all that."[1]

***

How should we react to God's complaint? Of course we should yield to it, and like the fowls of the air return at the appointed time.

"And from the complaint, it is no hard matter to extract the redress. 1. To yield to but even as much for Him — for Him? No for ourselves — as everywhere else we use to do. 2. To speak [what] God so gladly would hear. 3. To learn [what] the poor fowls know, the season of our return, and to take it as they do. Three ways to give redress to the three former grievances."[2]

***

Whatever way we look at it, we cannot escape the fact that sin is a fall, an error, and indeed rebellion. Yet from a fall we may rise. There is no fall, no sin, from which we cannot rise above and receive God's grace. He is more than ready to receive us.

"Men rise, if they fall; and sin is a fall. We have taken up the term ourselves, calling Adam's sin Adam's fall. A fall indeed, for it fouls as a fall, for it bruises as a fall, it brings down as a fall; down from the state of Paradise, down to the dust of death, down to the bar of judgment, down to the pit of hell.

Again, men turn when they err, and sin is an error. . . . What can be greater than to go in the ways of wickedness they should not, and come to the end of misery they would not. It is then a fall and error. . . .

But what speak we of a fall and error? There is . . . [also] rebellion [which] makes it more grievous. . . .

There is sin, a fall: men fall against their wills, that is sin of infirmity. There is sin, an error: men err from the way of ignorance, that is sin of ignorance. . . . But rebellion, the third kind, that hateful sin of rebellion, can neither pretend ignorance nor plead infirmity. . . .

Taken all together. Sin, a fall, an error, a rebellion; we see *sin abounds*; will you see how *grace over-abounds?* Yet not such a fall but we may be raised, not such a departure but there is place left to return; no, nor such a rebellion, but if it sue for may hope for a pardon. For behold; He, even He, that God from Whom we thus fall, depart, revolt, reaches His hand to them who fall, turns not away from them who turn to Him, is ready to receive to grace them, even them who rebelled against Him. . . .

If you mark, He does not complain and challenge them for any of all those three, for falling, straying, or for rebelling; the point he presses is not our falling, but our lying still; not our departing, but our not returning; not our breaking off, but our holding out. It is not; Why fall, or stray, or revolt? But, Why rise you not? Return you not: Submit you not yourselves?''3

***

Andrewes warns of the danger of perpetual sin. It is not our original sin that God mourns over, but our constancy of adding sin: upon sin, the sin of Satan, rather than Adam's fall. Why do we want to pereptuate sin? There really is no valid reason for doing so, rather it is a case not of they *could not* but of *would not*, a matter of the heart rather than the mind.

''*Perpetual* is the word, and perpetual is the thing. Not why these, any of these, or all of these; but why these perpetual? To do thus, to do it and never leave doing it; to make no end of sin, but our own end; to make a perpetuity of sin, never to rise, return, repent — for repentance is opposite not to sin, but to the continuance of it — that is the point . . .

To speak of sin, that is the sin out of measure sinful; that is the offence that not only makes culpable, but leaves inexcusable. The fall is not Adam's but Lucifer's fall. . . .

This then to add sin to sin, to multiply sin by sin, to make it infinite, to eternize it as much as in us lies, that is it to which God cries, *O quare?* Why do you so? Why perpetual? . . .

Indeed why? For it would pose the best of us to find out the *quare?* a true cause or reason for so doing. . . . But they can show no reason why they will not. It were to be wished we would repent, or show good cause to the contrary.

But as before we violate our own custom, so here we abandon reason, we throw them both to the ground, order and reason, and stamp upon them both when we make perpetuities. . . . True cause or good reason there is none. Being called to show cause why, they tell not, . . . they stand mute, they cannot tell why; . . . [they] lie. . . . It is, says the Apostle, *the deceitfulness of sin that hardens* men in it, . . . There is some error sure.

But why is not that error removed? God answers that too. But the error has not taken hold of them, for then it might be cured, but they have taken hold of it fast hold, and will not let it go. That is, it is not in the weakness of their wits, but in the stubbornness of their will. For so is His conclusion. Not, *they could not*; but they *would not return. . . .* Their error is not in their heads but in their hearts, and if it be there, *forty years* teaching will do them no good. If they had a heart to understand, . . . they could not choose but return; but now return they will not, that is resolved; therefore they get them some lewd, irreligious, lying position, and with them close up their own eyes, even hood-wink themselves. Is it not thus? Yes sure; rather than return, to apprehend a lie. This is a woeful case. . . . Despair of pardon has made many a man desperate. Yes sure. And if that were it, if they would and God would not, they had some show of reason to abandon themselves to all looseness of life. But it is contrary; they would not return. For I for My part . . . says God, it is their *not* and not mine. . . . *I will not their death, I will their conversion*; this is my *volo.*"[4]

***

Is there hope? Yes, God's compassion asks, *Why will you not return?* God stretches out His hand towards us, and begs for our remorse. Surely knowing how much God yearns for our repenting should be sufficient to move us and admit, *This is what I have done.*

"And is there no hope? Will you not? O, why will you not? . . . If not why fall, or err, or revolt, yet only why *perpetual*? . . . He is willing enough. . . . He breaks out into a protestation, that if this be the lie we hold of, we may let it go when we will. . . . I stand wishing and waiting, and longing and listening to hear of it. . . . It is not all one, it is not neither here nor there with me whether you do it, it is a special thing I hearken after. . . .

Should not this move us? Now truly, if all other regards failed, and men for them should not return, yet for this and this only we ought to yield to it, that God should be listening so long for it and in the end be deluded.

God hearkens and listens, and after there is a kind of pause to see what will come of it. And lo, this comes of it, this unkind unnatural effect; after all this, not so much as a good honest confession. . . . He expects no great matter, no long process, but two words, but three syllables; . . . even softly said. . . .

Say it, *dic, dic*, says St. Augustine, *sed intus dic; say it, and say it from within*, say it as it should be said — not for form or with affectation, but in truth and with affection. Do but this onward and more will follow. . . . *What have I done?* . . . What a foul, deformed, base, ignominious act! which we shame to have known, which we chill upon, alone and nobody but ourselves. . . .

Sure to say it with the right touch, with the right accent, is worth the while."[5]

***

Our sins not only darken the light of religion but the light of nature which has her own instinctive teaching. From the cyclical life of God's creatures such as the swallow, crane, stork and turtle, which know instinctively that *they have a time to return . . . [and] observe*, we can also learn the true meaning of returning *at the appointed time* and repenting.

"O the damp and mist of our sin! so great that it darkens not only the light of religion which God teaches, but even the light of nature which her instinct teaches, even the reasonless creature itself. . . .

The lesson with these four, all of them, from the stork in the top of the fir tree to the swallow that builds under every pent-house, would take us forth, is [what] they themselves are so perfect in, that they may be professors of it. And it is of four sorts; 1. They have a time to return in. 2. That time is certain and certainly known. 3. They know it. 4. They observe it.

They have a time. The place, the climate, which the cold of the weather makes them to leave, they fail not but find a time to turn back thither again. This they teach us first who in this respect less careful and more senseless than they, find a time and times many, often and long, to take our flight from God; occasioned by no cold or evil weather for commonly we do it when times are best and fairest; but we can find no time, not so much as half a time, to make our return in. This must be learned. . . .

They have a certain time, when if you wait for them you shall be sure to see them come, and come at their appointed season; they will not miss. It will not be long, but you will see the swallow here again. This they teach us second; us who have sometimes some little persuasion *in modico, . . . we can never find a convenient set time for it.* Return we shall, that we will, but are still to seek for our season; and ever we will do, and never we do it. . . .

They have their certain time, and they know it. What time of the year the time of their return is, is commonly known; who knows not when swallows' time is? And our ignorance in not discerning this point does God justly upbraid us withal; and bids us, if we know not what time to take, to get us to these fowls, and to take their time, the time they return at; that is, now, even this time, this season of the year; to return with the swallows, and to take our flight back when they do theirs. Rather do thus than waste our lives as we do, and take none at all. . . . This is the the third they teach us.

The last lesson is, to observe it. Opportunity itself is a great favour, even to have it; but a second grace it is, to discern it when we have it; and a third better than both, when we discern it to observe and take it. And many are the errors of our life, but all the errors of our repentance come from one of these; either our ignorance that, while we have it, discern it not; or our negligence that, when we discern it, observe it not. . . .

By these four fowls, there is . . . taught . . . even the manner also how to perform our repentance. 1. That *vox turturis*, which is *gemebon*, a mournful note; 2. that the very name and nature of the stork, full of mercy and compassion; 3. that the swallow's nest, so *near the altar of God;* 4. that the painful watching, and abstinence of the crane, especially when they take flight, so credibly recorded in the natural histories; that these, emblem-wise, teach us 1. The mournful bewail our life past; 2. *The breaking off our former sins by works of mercy;* 3. The keeping near this place, the house and altar of God; 4. The abstinence and watching to be performed during this time of our return; that is, that all these are allied to the exercise of repentance, and are meet virtues to accompany and attend the practice of it."[6]

Not only can we learn the meaning of repentance from these birds, but also the meaning of judgment. If we do not heed the first natural warning, then we must the second. Be sure there is a Judgment day for all of us.

"This the turtle-dove mourns, the swallow chatters; this all of them sound as well as they can; this, if they serve not, as masters to teach us, they will serve as a quest to condemn us whom neither our own custom, reason, religion, before, nor now the light of nature, can bring to know so much as they. . . . This we should learn, but this we do not. . . .

The word judgment receives two constructions; for either by *judicium Domini* is meant that within us which is answerable to that secret instinct whereby the fowls are inclined to do this, which is the prick and *dictamen* of our conscience, the impression whereof is apparent in the most miscreant on earth; in whom nature itself shrinks and sighs when it has done amiss, and enjoys and lifts up itself when it has well done; and by which we are moved inwardly, as they by their instinct, to return, but that the motion with us passes, and with them not. . . .

Or else by *judicium Domini* is meant His visitation hanging over our heads, called therefore judgment, because it comes not casually, but judicially proceeds from God; that is, when God calls to judgment by invasion, by scarcity, by gentle, general diseases, and such like; and then the complaint is, that where we should imitate these fowls and return against the sweet spring and fair time of the year, that is, while the days of peace and prosperity last, we are so far behind them, as not against fair, no not against foul, against neither we can be brought to it; not in the days of adversity — no not against the winter of our life.

That they regard nature's inclination, so as every spring sure to come; we have lost our regard so even of judgment and all, as neither vernal nor hibernal repentance we bring forth. No, not the everlasting judgment of the Lord do we regard; to which sooner or later we must all come, and there receive the sentence under execution whereof we shall lie eternally. . . .

Regard judgment, when either it awakes from within, or when it threatens from without. And when any of these summons us before the great Judge, know for a certainty that the time of returning is come. . . .

And thus we be come to an anchor at this last word judgment. A word, which if with judgment we would but pause on, and roll it awhile up and down in our thoughts, duly weighing it and force of it, it would bring us about, and cause this whole Scripture to be fulfilled; make us fly as fast back as any fowl of them all. . . .

Did we hear this word, hear it and regard it aright, and *know the terror of it*, that God has fearful judgments in store; even here to meet with us; or howsover here we escape He has you a perpetual judgment behind, and that so straight as *the righteous shall scarce escape it*, so heavy as the mightiest shall not endure it, did we regard this one point we should find a withdrawing time for this so serious a work; we would say, and say that God should hear it, *What have I done?* We would rise, return, repent; and so His whole complaint should cease. O Judgment!"[7]

***

If we do not heed the signs given to us by God through His urging, through His creation, remember it is not God who loses through our unrepenting nature, but only ourselves. Shall we stay rebellious, or be the like the birds who return, and know their time for returning? Lent, Ash Wednesday is the proper day for our returning. It could be our *last swallow time.*

"He needs not our repentance, and our unrighteousness hurts Him not. It is I who shall win or lose by it, even the best thing I have to lose, my soul; He is in no danger, it is I, the hazard of whose eternal weal or woe lies upon it. And yet does God show Himself sorry for me, and shall not I be sorry for myself? . . . Shall my rebellions be *perpetual*? . . . Shall these swallows fly over me and put me in mind of my *return*, and shall not I heed them? . . . Shall I never once seriously set before me the judgments of the Lord? Ask these; ask them and answer them, and upon them come to a resolution, saying, I will rise and return. . . . I shall not see them fly but I shall think of the season of my returning; but above all I will not be without regard of God's judgment, than which nothing in this world is more to be regarded. . . . And that time is at this time now; now do these fowls return.

Who knows whether he lives to see them return anymore? It may be the last spring, the last swallow-time, the last Wednesday of this name or nature, we shall ever live, to hear this point preached. Why do we not covenant then with ourselves not to let this time slip? Surely lest no time should be taken the prophet points us at this, and ensuing the prophet's mind the Church has fixed her season at it. And nature itself seems to favour it, that at the rising of the year we should rise, and return when the zodiac returns to the first sign.

Let the prophet, let the Church, let nature, let something prevail with us."[8]

References

[1] Andrewes, Vol. I, pp. 339–40.
[2] *ibid.*, p. 341.
[3] *ibid.*, pp. 342–3.
[4] *ibid.*, pp. 343–5.
[5] *ibid.*, pp. 346–7.
[6] *ibid.*, pp. 349–52.
[7] *ibid.*, pp. 352–3.
[8] *ibid.*, pp. 354–5.

ASH WEDNESDAY SERMON No. 4: 1619

Text: Joel 2: 12–13

Therefore also now, says the Lord, Turn you
even to Me with all your heart, and with
fasting, and with weeping, and with mourning.
And rend your heart, and your garments, and
turn unto the Lord your God.

*Nunc ergo dicit Dominus: convertimini ad Me
in toto corde vestro, in jejunio, et in
fletu, et in planctu.
Et scindite corda vestra, et non vestimenta
vestra, et convertimini ad Dominum Deum
vestrum.*

Turning, and turning now, is the theme of this Lenten sermon. Everything in nature has its time for *turning*, and so does the Church. That time for the Church is Lent when we are bidden to turn to God in fasting and repentance.

"For this time has the Church made choice of this text. The time wherein, howsoever we have dispensed with it all the year beside, she should have us seriously to intend and make it our time of turning to the Lord. And that *now*, the first word of the text. . . .

It has seemed good to the Holy Spirit and to [the Church] to order there will be a solemn set return once in the year at least. . . . And that once is now at this time, for now at this time is the turning of the year. In heaven, the sun in his equinoctial line, the zodiac and all the constellations in it, do now turn about to the first point. The earth and all her plants, after a dead winter, return to the first and best season of the year. The creatures, the fowls of the air, the swallow and the turtle, and the crane and the stork, *know their seasons,* and make their just return at this time every year. Everything now turning that we also would make it our time to turn to God in.

Then because we are to turn *cum jejunio, with fasting*, and this day is known by the name of *caput jejunii, the first day of Lent*, it fits well as a welcome into this time — a time *lent* us as it were by God, set us by the Church, to make our turning."[1]

***

The text demands repentance with fasting, weeping and mourning, all of which we find unwelcoming. Yet it is a matter of weeping now or weeping later on Judgment day. Thus Andrewes urges us to do it now.

"There is in this text somewhat of *sal terrae*, something of the *grain of mustard-seed* in the Gospel; the points be such as we [want] not [to] hear of. Fasting is an *unwelcome point* to flesh and blood; but as for weeping and mourning, and rending the heart, *who can abide it?* . . . Abide what? These days? the abstinence in them? No, *but the great and fearful day of the Lord.* . . . Here is our choice, one of them we must take. And better thus turn unto God in some of these little days, than be turned off by Him in *that great day*, to another manner weeping than this of Joel — even to *weeping, and wailing, and gnashing of teeth. Knowing therefore this fear*, and that upon turning, the *hinges turns* of our well or evil doing for ever, to be content to come to it and to turn the heathen man's *non enam* into *enam tanti poenitere*. To this turning then."2

* * *

Repentance is like a circle, as we return to God after repentance from whom, by sin, we have turned away. Thus the *turning* is like a pivot. Unlike what is sometimes assumed, repentance involves far more than an amendment of life; true repentance carries with it a complete turning to God and away from sin in penitence and mourning.

"Repentance itself is nothing else but *a kind of circling* to return to Him by repentance from Whom by sin we have turned away. . . .

Which circle consists . . . of two turnings. . . . One, is to be done with the *whole heart;* . . . the other with it *broken and rent*. First, a *turn*, wherein we look forward to God, and with our *whole heart* resolve to *turn* to Him. Then a turn again wherein we look backward to our sins wherein we have turned from God, and with beholding them our very heart breaks. These two are . . . distinct, both in nature and names; one conversion from sin; the other contrition for sin. One resolving to amend [what] is to come, the other reflecting and sorrowing for [what] is past. One declining from evil to be done hereafter, the other sentencing itself for evil done heretofore. These two between them hereafter, the other sentencing itself for evil done heretofore. These two between them make up a complete repentance, or to keep the word of the text, a perfect revolution. . . .

There is a false imputation cast on us, that we should teach there goes nothing to repentance but amendment of life; that these of fasting and the rest we let run by, as the waste of repentance, no, that for fasting *we proclaim a fast from it*, and teach a penitence with no penal thing in it."3

* * *

Andrewes lingers on the meaning of repentance to show how Scripture presents it, and to illuminate the *turn*. To *turn* means to live with God every day of our journey, yet because of sin we make many *turns* away from the path. As our lives draw to a close there are other *turns* awaiting us.

"Diversely and in sundry terms does the Scripture set forth unto us the nature of repentance. Of renewing, as from a decay, of refining, as from a dross; of recovering, as from a malady; of cleansing, as from soil; of rising, as from a fall; in no one, either for sense more full, or for use more often than in this of turning. . . .

If then our life be a *way*, . . . the end of this way is to bring us to our end, to our sovereign good which we call happiness. . . .

From God then, as from the journey's end of our life, our way, we are never to turn our steps or our eyes, but with Enoch, . . . *still to walk with God* all our life long. Then should we never need to hear this *convertite*.

We are not so happy. There is one who maligns we should go this way, or come to this end; . . . which to pursue, we must step out of the way, and so do full many times, even *turn from God*, to serve our own turns.

And this is the way of sin, which is turning from God. When having in chase some trifling transitory, to follow it we even turn our backs upon God, and forsake the way of His commandments. . . .

For being entered into this way, yet we go too far in it; wisdom would have we staid and were advised whither this way will carry us, and where we shall find ourselves at our journey's end. And reason we have to doubt; for after we once left our first way which was *right*, there takes us sometimes . . . *a throbbing heart*; or as [St. Paul's says] certain *accusing thoughts* present themselves unto us which will not suffer us to go on quietly, our minds still misgiving us that we are wrong. . . .

We cannot with any comfort think on our journey's end, and hear as it were a voice crying behind us. . . . *This*, that you have lost, *is your way, walk in it*. Which voice if we hear not . . . go aside into some retired place, or in the still of the night hearken after it. . . .

A great blessing of God it is, for without it thousands would perish in the error of their life, and never return to their right way again. . . . And this is the first degree to help us a little forward to this turning.

Being thus turned to our hearts we turn again and behold . . . our turn will come that *our breath also must go forth, and we turn again to our dust*.

And when that is past, . . . Mercy that now sits in the throne, shall rise up and give place; Justice also shall have her turn. And then comes the last turn, *the sinners will be turned into hell, and all the people who forget* in time to turn unto God."[4]

***

Andrewes laments the discontinuing of the imposition of ashes upon this day because it was a yearly reminder of our *end*, that from dust we came, to dust we shall return. Ashes also remind us of our sins, and the need to mourn for them.

"There was . . . a ceremony of giving ashes this day, to put us in mind of this *converteris*. I fear with the ceremony the substance is gone too. If that conversion into ashes be well thought on, it will help forward our turning.

This returning to our heart, the sad and serious bethinking us there of nature's conversion into dust, of sins into ashes, for ashes ever presuppose fire; that the wheel turns apace, and if we turn not the rather, these turnings may overtake us; God's spirit assisting may so work with us as we shall think Joel's counsel good, that if we have not been so happy as to keep the way, yet we be not so unhappy as not to turn again from a way, the issues whereof surely will not be good."[5]

***

When we *turn,* it must be to God, and not from one sin to another, and it must be to God with all our hearts. Remember hypocrisy is a sin; the inward must not deceive the outward appearance.

"*Turn* and *turn to Me,* says . . . God. . . . Whither should we turn from sin but to God? . . . *If you return, return to Me, says the Lord*; which had been needless if we could turn to nothing else, were it not possible to find [many] turnings, leaving one by-way to take another, . . . and never to God at all. . . .

But the true turn is *ad Me*, so from sin to God. . . . [and] not this sin to that sin. . . . .

To Me, then, and *with the heart*; . . . heart and all must turn. . . . Hypocrisy is a sin; being to turn from sin we are to turn from it also, and not have our body in the right way, and our heart still wandering in the by-paths of sin. But if we forbear the act which the eye of man beholds, to make a conscience of the thoughts too, for unto them also the eye of God pierces. Thus it should be; else conversion it may be, but heart it has none. . . .

And as easily it is seen, when one goes to his turning with his whole heart. . . . Set him down what he should do, and he will do it. Not come near the place where sin dwells, refrain the wandering of his sense whereby sin is awakened, fullness and idleness whereof sin breeds, but chiefly corrupt company whither sin resorts. For conversion has no greater enemy than conversing with such of whom our heart tells us, there is neither faith nor fear of God in them."[6]

***

Once we have turned to God with all our heart, this is still not sufficient; it must be accompanied with fasting.

"All this will be done; *we will turn with the heart, with the whole heart.* Is this all? No, here is a *cum* we must take with us, *cum jejunio.* Take heed of turning *cum* into *sine,* to say with it or without it we may turn well enough; since it is God Himself who to our turning joins *jejunium,* we may not turn without it. . . . This is but the half-turn. Hitherto we have but looked forward; we must also turn back our eye and reflect upon our sins past, be sorry for them, before our turning be as it should. The hemisphere of our sins not to be under the horizon clean out of our sight must ascend up, and we set them before us. . . .

129

Flesh and blood reveals a far more easy way not encumbered with any of these. To *turn*, and yet not lose a meal all the year long; and not shed a tear, and not *rend* either *heart or garment*, . . . with this conceit they pass their lives, and with this they pass out of their lives, as it seems resolved to put their souls in a venture, and to come to heaven after their own fashion, or not come there at all. . . .

To take them as they stand. *Fasting;* which, were there nothing else but this, that the Church makes this time of our return a time of fast, it shows plainly in her opinion how near these two are allied, how well they sort together. Which fast the Church prescribes not only by way of regimen to keep the body low, that it may be a less mellow soil for the sins of the flesh, for this pertains to the former part so to prevent sin to come, but awards it as a chastisement for sin already past. . . .

And thus preach we fasting; neither as the physicians enjoin it, . . . nor as the philosophers in their morals, . . . nor as the States politic in their proclamations, . . . but as the holy prophets of God, as Joel straight after, we do *sanctificare jejunium*, prescribe it, and that to a religious end, even to chasten ourselves for sin by this forbearance. . . . For if in very sorrow we are to fast when *the Bridegroom is taken away*, much more when we ourselves by our sins committed have been the cause of His taking, no, of His very driving away from us.

And must we then fast? Indeed we must, or get us a new Epistle for the day, and a new Gospel too. For as God here in the Epistle commends it, so Christ in the Gospel presupposes it with His *cum jejunatis*, taking it as granted we shall fast. That sure fast we must, or else wipe out this *cum jejunio*, and that *cum jejunatis*, and tell God and Christ they are not well advised, we have found out a way beyond them to turn unto God without any fasting at all.

But how fast? . . . Two kinds of fasting we find in Scripture. 1. David's who fasted *tasting neither bread* nor ought else *till the sun was down*, no meat at all — that is too hard. 2. . . . Daniel's fast. . . . *He did eat and drink*, but *no meats of delight*, and namely ate no *flesh*. The Church . . . enjoins not for fast that of David, . . . she only requires of us that other of Daniel, to forbear *cibos desiderii*, and *flesh* is there expressly named, . . . content to sustain nature, and *not purvey for the flesh to satisfy the lusts thereof*. . . .

And He will not have His ordinance thus dallied with, fast or lose. . . . *Turn to God with fasting*, or be ready to show a good cause why, and to show it to God.''[7]

***

We must not only *fast* but *weep* for our sins, perhaps not as profusely as Mary Magdalene, nevertheless we need to shed some tears. If we cannot weep, we should at least be able to mourn for our sins.

''The next point . . . is weeping. Can we not be dispensed with that neither, but we must weep too? . . . Not as the saints of old. . . . Job's eyes *poured forth tears to God*; David's eye gushed out with water, . . . Mary Magdalene wept enough to make a bath. We urge not these. But if not pour out, not gush forth, says Jeremiah, *Will not our eyes afford a drop or [two]?*

130

Stay a little, turn and look back upon our sins past; it may be, if we could get ourselves to do it in kind, if set them before us and look sadly, and not glance over them apace; think of them not once, but . . . over and over; consider the motives, the base motives, and weigh the circumstances, the grievous circumstances, and tell over our many flittings, our often relapsing, our wretched continuing in them; it would set our sorrow in passion, it would bring down some — some would come; our hearts would turn, our repentings roll together, and lament we would the death of our soul as we do otherwise lament the death of a friend, and for the unkindness we have showed to God as for the unkindness we do that man shows us. . . .

This I wish we would try. But we seek no place, we allow no time for it. Other affairs take up so much as can spare little or none for this, which the time will come when we shall think it the weightiest affair of all.

And yet it may be, when all is done, none will come though, for who has tears at command? Who can weep when he lists? I know it well, they be the overflowings of sorrow, not of every sorrow, but of the sensual parts; and being an act of the interior parts, reason cannot command them at all times, they will not be had. . . .

If weep we cannot, mourn we can, and mourn we must. . . . Mourning they call the sorrow which reason itself can yield. . . . These and these sins I have committed, so many, so heinous, so often iterate, so long lain in; these deserve to bewailed even with tears of blood.

This we can . . . and pray we can, . . . though weep we cannot, yet wish for it and pray for it we can. . . . God help us! This mourn we can. . . .

And lastly, this we can; even humbly beseech our merciful God and Father, in default of ours to accept of the *strong crying and bitter tears which in the days of His flesh His blessed Son in great agony shed for us*. . . . These by the grace of God we may do in discharge of this point. Then let us do, and it will be accepted.''[8]

***

We must also rend our heart as it must suffer for our sins by feeling not only contrition, but also anger at our sinfulness.

''And so to the last, *Rend your hearts* — you see first and last, to the heart we come. For indeed a meal may be missed, a tear or two let fall, and the heart not affected for all that. . . . To the heart He comes again always, to verify that, . . . *if it be not done with the heart, if the heart do it not, nothing is done*. As in conversion the purpose of amendment must proceed from the heart, so in our contrition, the sorrow, the anger, for our turning way, must pierce to the heart; some passion to be, the heart must suffer.

And what must it suffer? Contrition. It should even be *ground to powder*. A *contrite heart,* it should be. If not that, *a broken heart,* broken in pieces, though not so small. If neither of these, yet with . . . some rent or cleft. . . .

Now this *rending*, if we mark it well, does not so properly pertain to the passion of sorrow, but rather to another, even to that of anger. *Their hearts rend for anger.* . . .

131

Sorrow, if it has no power to revenge, grows to be but a heavy dull passion; but if it has power, indignation and it go together. One cannot truly be said to be grieved with the thing done, but he must be angry with the doer and we, if we be sorry indeed for our sins, will be angry with the sinner. So was Job: *Therefore I abhor myself. Myself* says he, not so much the sin, which was done and past, and so incapable of anger, as myself for the sin. . . .

This . . . *indignation* is the essential passion, . . . or this *rending* here the principal and most proper act of a true turning unto God. . . .

Now if you ask how or which way we can come to make a rend in the heart, since no hand may touch it and we live? The meaning is not literal; but that the heart by reflecting on itself is able to make such an impression on it as the prophet may well call *a rent in the heart*. At first, even by good moral respects, wherewith the very heathen set themselves in passion against vice. That it is a brutish thing, so against the nobleness of reason; that a shameful, so against public honesty; that ignominious, so against our credit and good name; that pernicious, as shutting us out of heaven whither we would come, the greatest loss and *paena damni*, and pressing us down to hell which we . . . would fly, the great torment and *poena sensus*, for even the heathen believed the joys and pains of another world. And yet we for all this so evil advised as to commit it.

But these are . . . *drawn from man;* the Christian man . . . [has] his eye to God, Who with great indignation cannot but abhor himself for the manifold indignities offered to God thereby. To the law of His justice, to the awe of His Majesty, the reverend regard of His presence, the dread of His power, the long-suffering of His love, that being a creature of so vile and brittle consistence he has not sticked for some lying vanity, some trifling pleasure or pelting profit, to offend so many ways at once all odious in themselves and able to make a rent in any heart that will weigh them aright.

Sure if we take the impression right, so God may work with us, as these may work in us, a just indignation, which if once it be in fervour, what the hand can come to it will smite, and would the heart also, if it could reach it. And if it be in kind, it will award the body to fast, and the mind to spend some time in these meditations.''9

***

Andrewes concludes by insisting that we should endeavour to do what the Church has always taught us to do. At this time of the year, at the beginning of Lent, we are reminded it is the time to repent and mourn for our sins. *Now* is the time to do it, so that we can share in the joyful Resurrection.

''It remains that . . . we intend and endeavour to do as we have been taught.

And to do it now; . . . it is the time that all things turn, now is the only sure part of our time. [What] has passed is come and gone, [what] is to come may peradventure never come. . . .

The Church . . . has placed this *now* upon the time now begun, and commends it to us for the time of our turning to God. . . .

Perform it then, and when our turn is done God will begin His, *our repentance shall beget His*. If we turn from the evil we have done, He will turn from us the evil that should have been done to us. . . . Weigh the endless sorrow we shall escape by it; it admits no comparison. The contriteness is but *for an hour*, the consolation is *for ever*. . . .

It is so set by the Church, the time of it, that our Lent will end with an Easter, the highest and most solemn feast in the year, the memory of Christ's rising, and the pledge of our blessed and joyful resurrection."[10]

References

[1] Andrewes, Vol. I, pp. 356–7.
[2] *ibid.*, p. 358.
[3] *ibid.*, 358–9.
[4] *ibid.*, pp. 360–2.
[5] *ibid.*, p. 362.
[6] *ibid.*, pp. 363–5.
[7] *ibid.*, pp. 365–8.
[8] *ibid.*, pp. 369–71.
[9] *ibid.*, pp. 371–3.
[10] *ibid.*, pp. 373–4.

ASH WEDNESDAY SERMON No. 5: 1621

Text: St. Matthew 6:16

Moreover when you fast, be not, as the
hypocrites, of a sad countenance: for
they disfigure their faces, that they
may appear unto men to fast. Truly I
say unto you, They have their reward.

*Cum autem jejunatis, nolite fieri sicut
hypocritae tristes; exterminant enim
facies suas, ut appareant hominibus
jejunantes: Amen dico vobis, quia
receperunt mercedem suam.*

The theme for this sermon, from the Gospel appointed for Ash Wednesday, is
fasting. Christ takes it for granted that we do fast, so it is not a question of if
we *fast*, but how.

"The lessons . . . this day . . . all speak to us of fasting. . . . The Epistle, telling
us what we should do, *fast*; or, as the Gospel, taking it for granted that we shall
fast, and teaching us how to fast so as we may receive a reward for it at God's
hands. . . .
This being the Church's intent, this is her time, and this her text, what she
commends to us we commend to you, that you would take notice of it, and prepare
yourselves for it accordingly; that the Epistle be not sent, and the Gospel brought
you, and both in vain. . . .
Sure for fasting, how we practise it every one is to answer for himself; but that
we preach it, I take this day you all to witness. . . .
His purpose is . . . the lawful and laudable practice of alms, prayer and fasting,
all three. . . . Only, take this *caveat* from Me, *When you fast, beware of the sour
leaven of hypocrisy in your looks*, and of the love *to be seen of men* in your hearts,
and all is well; fast on and spare not. To God it is you fast, and *God your heavenly
Father will see it in secret, and will reward you for it openly.* . . .
[If] *to be seen of men,* . . . then follows the punishment; *you have received your
reward.* . . . but a punishment, and a grievous one, when we shall weigh how silly
a thing it is they receive — men's breath; and how great a one they lose by it —
God's reward."[1]

***

As fasting is not taken very seriously, Andrewes outlines how fasting has
been part of the Christian life ever since New Testament times, and how it has
been taught by the prophets, Our Lord, and the early Fathers.

134

"The first thing then we are to do, is to possess men's minds with a true conceit touching it. Men seem but faintly persuaded of it, as it were no needful part of a Christian man's duty. *When you fast;* yes, *when we fast* — what make you of this? . . . Take it right; here is *cum jejunio* in the Epistle, *cum jejunatis* in the Gospel. The precept is in Joel, *turn to Me with fasting,* and within a verse after, *sanctify Me a fast,* that is a precept, I am sure. . . . Here it stands thus; what Joel imposes, Christ supposes, implies the thing out of the prophet, and supplies the manner how from Himself. . . .

If we . . . go *to the Law itself* . . . he who fasted . . . not was to be cut off from the people of God. . . . One for both *integrale, an entire fast* from all upon the Kipparim day; and another for *portionale jejunium,* the Nazarites' fast. . . .

The prophets are for it too; under them and by their direction, to the standing fasts in the Law you have five more added. One in Esther, four in Zachariah. . . .

It went then as now it does. . . . In Zachariah they shrug at their fasts, What, and must we fast still? Yet more fasting? Have we not fasted enough, and have done it thus and thus long? A sign they would have been rid of their fasting. . . . But it would not be, they could not obtain it; the prophet held them to it and would not release them.

But this is of the Old Testament. When the New came what then? I had rather you heard St. Augustine than myself; *I going over in my mind the writings of the Evangelists and Apostles in the New Testament, see fasting is commanded, there is a precept for fasting. . . .*

Here you see *cum jejunatis,* a part of the Gospel, a head in Christ's first and most famous sermon, His sermon on the Mount. . . .

But laws and their precepts do often sleep and grow into disuse. How is *jejunatis* for practice? . . .

At Antioch, where *the disciples were first called Christians,* we find them at their fast. . . . Our Saviour said to them, *When He was gone they should fast.* So they did. St. Paul for one did it often. And for the rest they approved themselves for Christ's ministers, . . . *by their fasting.* And what themselves did, they advised others to do. . . . So that where the Church for this day, otherwise than her custom is on other days, have sorted us an Epistle out of the Old Testament and a Gospel out of the New; . . . she did it for this end, to show that fasting has the wings of both Cherubim to cover it; both Testaments, Old and New; Joel for the one, Christ for the other. So at all hands to commend it to us.

Sure in the prime of Christianity it cannot be denied it was in high esteem, *fasting,* in frequent practice, of admirable performance. Which of the Fathers have not homilies yet extant in the praise of it? . . . That either we must cancel all antiquity, or we must acknowledge the constant use and observation of it in the Church of Christ. That Christ said not here, *Cum jejunatis* for nothing. They who were under grace went far beyond them under the Law, in their *cum* and in their *jejunatis* both.[2]

***

Andrewes explains what is meant by fasting: temperance, abstinence, mortification, and acts of penitence, humility and sacrifice.

". . . when we fast we exercise the act of more virtues than one. First, an act of that branch of the virtue of temperance that consists, not in the moderate using, but in abstaining wholly. Abstinence is a virtue. . . . Secondly, an act or fruit of repentance; there is *poena in poenitentia*, in the very body of the word, something penal in penitence; and of that penal part is fasting; and so an act of justice corrective. . . . Thirdly, an act of humiliation, to humble the soul, which is both the first and most usual term for fasting in the Law and prophets. . . . Fourthly, T*hey who are Christ's*, says the Apostle, *have and do crucify the flesh with the lusts of it.* Fasting is one of the nails of the cross to which the flesh is fastened, that it rise not, lust not *against the spirit*, at least fasting we fulfil not the lusts of the flesh. Fifthly, . . . *by fasting and prayer*, not by prayer only, but by fasting and prayer. . . . Sixthly, and serve Him with the chief service of all, even sacrifice. . . . If *a troubled spirit be a sacrifice to God,* why not a troubled body likewise? And . . . *we are to offer our bodies as well as our souls, both a sacrifice to God*; as our soul by devotion, so our body by mortification. And these three, to offer to God 1. our soul by prayer, 2. our body by abstinence, 3. our goods by alms-deeds, has been ever counted the . . . *threefold Christian holocaust or whole burnt offering.* . . . Seventhly and lastly, the exercise of it by inuring ourselves to this part of true Christian discipline, serves to enable us to have *the mastery of our belly* against need be."[3]

***

Andrewes elaborates on *cum, when you fast.* As well as being our precept from the Gospel, we can also learn from the natural man who knows when to fast, especially in times of fear, sorrow, anger and desire.

"I say first, this very *when* shows Christ's liking of it, that there is a time allowed. Else would He allow it no *cum*, no *when*, no time at all. . . .

Again, when you fast; this when is a presupposing at least and *qui supponit ponit.* For can any man fancy that Christ would presuppose aught that were not required of us by God? . . .

No, His manner of the delivery, this breaking into it with a *cum autem*, but *when you fast*, as fast you will I make no doubt here, *but when* is plain positive. . . . This I say, is a precept, and more than a precept, more binding. . . .

And now to that *cum*, let us come. Allowing *jejunatis*, the thing, we cannot but allow it a time *when*. For there is a time *when* for *everything under the sun.* Only when that *when* shall be, we shall not so easily agree. We would . . . have our fast loose; be left to ourselves for the time — this *when* to be when ourselves please. And when will it be? Indeed the practice of the world would make one think this *when* to be without a *then*, . . . as if Christ had said, If ever you do, if at any time you feel yourself disposed, then to observe this caution. . . .

Nature itself will teach us *when*. Mark when nature will yield to it, when and in what case the natural man will fast, without eye to God or Christ, or religion at all. . . . The time of fear is a time of fasting with the natural man; . . . they in the ship with St. Paul when they looked every hour to be cast away, the tempest was such, there was, . . . *no spending of victuals* all that while. Will we naturally fast for fear of the wreck of our ships, and not be afraid as much of the wreck of our souls by sin, and fast for that? . . .

When the natural man is in any inward grief of heart, it will take away his stomach, he will fast. Says Tertullian, *fasting follows mourning, as feasting does mirth.* . . . Fasting and mourning, Joel joins them both. The afflicted soul in his prayer, *My heart was smitten with heaviness*; how then? *So that I forget to eat my bread.* . . . Upon sorrow for the death of a friend or a child can we fast then, *dictante natura*, and can we not do as much for our sins, the death of our souls? Does not nature teach us that? Nor for the death of Christ neither, which our sins were the cause of? There is another, a second *when*.

Thirdly, anger him thoroughly, the natural will to his fast. Ahab for cursed heart . . . to bed he goes and no meat would down with him. Could he out of his pure naturals for cursed heart leave his meat and fast, and cannot we do the like for just indignation at ourselves, for provoking God's anger with the cursed thoughts of our heart, and words of our mouth, and deeds of our whole body? . . .

Fourthly, the natural man when he is in the fervour of his desire, if it be an earnest desire, he will pursue that he desires so hard as he will forget his meat quite. Not a man so hardy as to *eat anything till sunset*, says Saul, when he had his enemies in chase; such was his desire of victory. . . .

Did we hunger and thirst for recovery of God's favour, as did Saul for his victory? . . . We would not think it much to fast as [he] did. . . .

These four, the proper passions all of repentance, and these four carry every one, as we say his fast on his back. Much more where they all meet, as in true earnest repentance they all should. . . .

For grief of heart, for worldly loss, for bodily fear of drowning, for bitter anger we can do it; why not for the grief of our grievous offences for fear of being drowned in perdition eternal? Why not for indignation of our many indignities offered God? Alas, it but shows our affections of sorrow, anger, fear, desire, are quick, have life, are very affections indeed in secular matters; but dead and dull, and indeed no affections at all but plain counterfeits in things pertaining to God, or that concern the estate and hazard of our souls.''4

***

Fasting also chastens the body, it strengthens our spiritual life of prayer and wards off various temptations assaulting the soul.

''Now if for the effect we fast, for the cause much more. Of these, of all other our miseries, the cause is within ourselves. Our sin, whereby God's anger is kindled, and these ever follow upon it. When therefore we would proceed against ourselves for sin, *humble ourselves* — the phrase of the Law; *chasten ourselves* — of the psalm; *punish ourselves* — of the prophets; *take revenge of ourselves* — the apostle's phrase. . . . Fasting is a punishment to the flesh; . . . and thereby to prevent His judgment by judging ourselves. . . .

Secondly, as it is a chastisement for sin when it is done, so has it always been held to have in it a medicinable force, a special good remedy to prevent sin, when it is not yet fallen on us or we into it; but grudges us only, as it were, and whereinto we are like to fall, for that we are not leading, even entering into temptation. . . . And this time we ground upon Christ's time of fasting; His fasting went immediately before His temptation.

No ways needful for Himself was Christ's fast. . . . It was not for Himself, it was for us, His fast; exemplary to teach us it will be a great advantage, if prepared by this exercise we shall encounter the evil spirit. . . . Christ's fasting then before His temptation is to show us, it is good fasting against temptation. At least, this way we shall weaken his forces, *by keeping down our fleshly lusts, which*, says, St. Peter, *fight against the soul.* . . .

But has fasting its use in evil things only, and repelling them? Has it not also in good things, and procuring them? Yes sure, . . . when there is use of earnest and hearty prayer, it will be the more earnest and hearty if *cum jejunatis* do also go with it. . . .

Even here presently before was Christ in a treaty of *prayer*; and here now immediately after it He . . . [speaks] of *fasting*. This was not for nothing; but as if He should give . . . an alliance between them to sanctify and support either the other. And namely, a special virtue in fasting, to awake up and quicken our devotion, thereby the better to elevate our minds unto God. We feel this or we feel nothing, that dull is our devotion and our prayers full of yawning, when the brain is thick with vapour and the heart pressed down with the charge of the stomach. . . . Our morning prayer that is the *incense*, says the psalm; our evening is but *the stretching out of our hands, in comparison of it, faint and heavy.*''[5]

***

The special time for *cum jejunatis* is Lent, appointed by the Church since the time of the apostles. Just as Mother Church has appointed times for prayer and the Sacrament, so she has done for fasting. Hence the forty days before Easter have always been a time of fasting and discipline.

''And so *cum jejunatis* is, when you fast by . . . the Church's *cum.* . . .

This I may say for this *cum*, it is no custom lately taken up. . . . It is a custom this of the Church's while it was *yet fresh and warm from Christ*; the Church which was the Mother of the Apostles themselves at all times kept, everywhere observed, there and ever since. . . . Lent was ever in the Church, . . . the fast so delivered, and by the Church ever and every where so kept, [while] the Council of Gangra . . . laid an anathema on them who keep it not. . . .

And sure in general, that this power should remain in the Church to prescribe us set times was most behoveful. . . . as in . . . prayer and the Sacrament, so in this holds us to our order of days and times established. . . .

But why this *cum* at this time now? Why forty days? Why before Easter? Why this fast? It is of all hands confessed, that ordained it was as a part of the discipline of repentance; and much was done in it about public penitents. Yet not for them only; but even with them out of the bowels of a mother the Church herself would become a penitent, and have all her children do the like. Herself become one; for the whole body of the Church has her faults beside the private offences of every

138

particular member. . . . For us to become penitents likewise; for who knows whether we be not as faulty in private as they, the open penitents in public? as great sinners as they, though not known for such? . . .

As to the number of days, . . . the time that God gave was forty days in the famous repentance of Nineveh; happy for the issue, recommended by Christ's own mouth and propounded to us as a pattern. . . .

For the season, . . . the Church has laid it most conveniently to end with the feast of Christ's rising, and so to go immediately before it; that against that time, as the Fathers in the first great Council of Nice wish it, all being restored, and all prepared by it, we may of all hands celebrate that high day and bring to *God a pure offering* — the very words of the Council. Then to end with that high feast, that the saying of Zachariah may be fulfilled, that our fast shall be to us *turned into high feasts*; as the highest and greatest of our religion, for which cause this fast is called *jejunium Paschale*, with reference to it; for Easter and Lent stand upon one base, both stand and fall together."[6]

***

Andrewes outlines the ways we can abstain.

"As to the manner of abstinence. It is sure the fast in kind, . . . *neither eat nor drink at all till night*. But *all are not capable of this saying*; yet he who can, let him. But for them who cannot, the Church, as a tender indulgent Mother unto all . . . is content to remit of the vigour of this . . . [and lays] no more on us than we can endure. . . .

[To] *no manner meat*, none at all, . . . what say you to not altogether none, but not such or such meat? — *no dainty alluring meats*, and namely, no flesh. . . .

[To] *not eat at all, not altogether any?* . . . . What say you to some, but *not so much?* . . . To cut off one meal, if both you cannot. . . .

[To] not *till night forbear;* . . . What say you to . . . not so soon as at other times? Put off the time of our repast; . . . if not *ad vesperam,* as near *vesperam* as we may. . . . These then or as many, or as much of these as we can, so to make some manner show, some countenance towards it; that if not keep pace with the ancient Church, yet not to give them over clean, not to fall behind them so far, till we lose sight of them quite, and so fall to abandon *cum jejunatis* altogether."[7]

***

Andrewes challenges us to examine our own consciences in relation to fasting, and to seek out if we do actually fast. If we have not, make this the Lent the beginning of our fasting, so that we can obey Our Lord's command, *cum jejunatis*.

"When fast we? Everyone to enter into his own heart and convent himself about the taking of these times, how often we have taken them. . . . .

But if as I doubt we have not taken them, then I ask, why have we not? Have we no sins to be censured? Are we in no fear of wrath to come? Our case sure is fearful, if we fear not.

Are our souls so very humble, our bodies so in subjection we need it not? I marvel it should be so; it should be needful for St. Paul, his body should need chastening, ours none. What is the Bridegroom always with us? . . . Do we never part? Does that time never come? Never, all our life long? . . . Whereof sure we should do well to bethink ourselves better, lest we be out of the Gospel quite. Christ cannot say to us, *When you fast.* if we fast not at all. . . .

Jejunatis, you know what tense it is. In the present tense He has put it, for at the present time He requires it. . . . He speaks as if He would have us fall in hand with it presently, and makes no future fast of it. The *cum* is already come, and we to do it now it is come; to make answer to Christ's *When you fast*, with now we fast, now we are at it this day, commonly called *caput jejunii, the head of it;* to which head I trust we shall allow a body, and so make a fast of it.

And even so then let us do. And He who says it will see it, and seeing it will see it will not go *without a reward* at His hands; see, that any hunger or thirst for Him and upon His word suffered will be satisfied at His heavenly table, at the great Easter Day, the day of the last Resurrection, where there will be no fasting any more, but a feast with all joy and jubilee for ever.''[8]

References

[1] Andrewes, Vol. I, pp. 375–7.
[2] *ibid.*, pp. 378–80.
[3] *ibid.*, pp. 380–1.
[4] *ibid.*, pp. 382–7.
[5] *ibid.*, pp. 388–90.
[6] *ibid.*, pp. 391–4.
[7] *ibid.*, pp. 394–5.
[8] *ibid.*, pp. 395–7.

ASH WEDNESDAY SERMON No. 6: 1622

Text: St. Matthew 6:16

Moreover when you fast, be not as hypocrites,
of a sad countenance, for they disfigure their
faces, that they may appear unto men to fast.
Truly I say unto you, They have their reward.

Cum autem jejunatis, nolite fieri sicut
hypoctriae tristes; exterminant enim
facies suas, ut appareant hominibus
jejunates: Amen dico vobis quia receperunt
mercedem suam.

The text is the same as the last year's Ash Wednesday's sermon, but whereas
that sermon focused on the opening verses, *when you fast*, this one focuses on
Be not like hypocrites, and the devil's cunningness in using this as a way to
lure us from fasting, or if we do fast to tempt us to do it for our pride and vain-
glory.

"Our last year's endeavours were out of the first two words, *Cum jejunatis*. . . .
Wherein if God has so blessed our endeavours that these two points be settled,
we may then go forward to the rest, that is *Be not like hypocrites*. If we resolve that
Christ's *when* will have a *then*, and then fast we will. The next point is a caveat,
what we are to take heed of when we fast; that we fast in secret, make no show of
it; our fast be to God and not to men, that we fast not for vain-glory as the
hypocrites do. . . .
[Be] *not sour like hypocrites* . . . Not like them . . . Not in their manner how.
Why, what do they? They are all for the countenance, and that they disfigure. In
making it their labour to have it appear in their countenance. And why do they so?
That so, *men may know them for fasters*. In making it their end *to be seen of men*.
. . .
What hurt will come of it? One would think none. . . . They make it their
reward, to be seen of men, . . . for though it seems no great harm to receive a
reward of praise, yet when we shall lay together how poor a thing it is they receive
— man's praise, and how great a one they lose by the means — God's reward, they
had been better without it. For when they have that, there is all, all that will come
of their fasting; *they have received their reward*, they have lost Mine.''[1]

***

When we have decided we shall fast, it is still no easy task, as the devil is there
waiting to lure us into all kinds of thoughts and ways of why we should not

141

fast, or if we do, to do it for the wrong motives. However, as Andrewes points out, what the devil actually does is to dupe us from committing one sin, only to sin in another, such as gluttony.

"When we have got past the first two words, when the thing is won and the time, and we resolved that fast we will, and when we will, and we set ourselves seriously to it; what, is all safe? Will the devil be gone away? . . . No indeed; but hovers about us still, as if there were yet somewhat for him to do. Our blessed Saviour, when the *Spirit led Him into the wilderness*, and He fell to His fast, it is said that *then the tempter came to Him;* so we must make reckoning he will to us. It is exceeding behoveful for us . . . to know the length of the devil's chain; that neither full nor fasting we are out of his reach, but he will be busy with us in them both. Attends our feasts, *to make our table a snare*; attends our fasts, *to turn them* as well as our prayers *into sin.* Eating, he is busy with us to make us eat like Esau. Fasting no less busy to make us fast like the pharisee. And look what in this in the rest; both alms and prayer too are subject to it. Therefore in and through all, whether we give alms, pray or fast, to have an eye to him in all. Praying, fasting, giving alms, he leaves us not, gives us not over till he has corrupted the manner, perverted the end; till one way or other he has sent them [amiss]. His first [attempt] is, *ne bonum, we do not [what] is good,* we fast not at all; his second is, *ne bonum bene, we do it not as we should,* by putting to it a wrong *sicut,* an undue manner; or a wrong *ut,* an undue end, that so we may do what God commands us for the devil's end. Sure it is not enough to be exercised in doing good, we must look to both the *sicut,* the manner how we do it, and to the *ut,* the end why we do it; or he [perhaps] go beyond us, and both spoil them and spoil us of our reward for them.
But then again take heed you be not caught here, and for doubt you may do it amiss be brought not to do it at all, but let all alone. That is another of his tricks; . . . *or policies of Satan.* For would any man think he would use this text, these very words of our Saviour, *Be not like hypocrites,* to draw men from fasting? He does. For finding here, fasting and hypocrites thus close together, and so that hypocrites use to fast, he persuades some, and such as ween themselves no fools, to think they cannot fast but they must *ipso facto* prove hypocrites. . . .
He prevails with them, not only to give over fasting themselves, but draws them further to grow jealous lest everyone who preaches for it be not justly to be suspected as that way given, as having in him some sparks of a pharisee. . . .
And will you see how compendious a way he devises to rid us clean of all hypocrisy? Thus: to keep no Lent, not to fast at all; and so he will warrant us we shall be sure to be clear from being any hypocrites. So to avoid hypocrisy he voids fasting quite. . . . What is this but . . . to cast out hypocrisy by gluttony? To cast out superstition with the *profaneness of Esau,* who rather than offend his belly cared not what became of his birthright?"[2]

***

Another superstition about fasting is that we are like Papists if we do.

142

"For no fear of hypocrisy now; *sicut hypocritae* is now gone. . . . As now in place of *be not like hypocrites*, is come a fear of *be not like Papists*; we shall be like Papists if we do. And not to fast is made a *supersedeas* to all Popery, as if that alone were enough to make us truly Reformed. This is all our fear now. . . . Fast not like them."[3]

***

Still another stratagem is adopted by the devil. Why not show off our fasting to all and sundry? Let others know we fast as well as pray and give alms.

"But if this way he succeed not to keep us from it but fast we will, then comes he about with a new strategem. And that by way of good wholesome counsel, that if we will needs fast, we would do it to some purpose; that is, do it so as we may be known to do it in any wise. For what purpose will it be to do it *in tenebris*? It is no work of darkness, or as good in a blind corner where no man can take notice of it, as if we were ashamed to be seen about so good a work. . . . And good reason, they be works of light, all three, alms, prayer and fasting, and so love to be brought to light, to be set on a candlestick, and to be seen. Therefore, as before in our alms he had devised we should call our alms-folk about us with a *trumpet*; and as in prayer, that we should do it in choice places where folk may come by and see us at it, and to be a good deal longer than ordinary, that so we may seem somewhat singular, and to have more in us than our fellows; so here now when it is fasting-day with us, to get us a fasting-day face at any hand. For that, except we be somewhat altered in countenance, no man will look at us or mark us, there will be not notice taken of it, and so as good not fast at all; but if it appear in our faces, we shall both get reputation to ourselves, and our profession shall receive credit besides. Thus does he meddle his chaff, mould in his sour leaven into Christ's *nova conspersio*, to make us do what God would have us for his own, to do God's work for the devil's end. *Sanctify me a fast*, as I told, shows there is sanctity in it, a holy duty it is, and he seeks to breed moths in it. For so the Fathers call hypocrisy *tineam sanctitatis*, *the moth that frets in sunder all that holy or good is*; and so by that means make it a mere moth-eaten fast.

Thus whithersoever we turn ourselves, he meets with us still. These are his designs. . . . First . . . he . . . offers us a licence not to keep Lent, to keep what diet we will; and if we refuse it threatens us he will get us presented for hypocrites. But if that moves us not, but we stand out resolute for all his scarecrow, then out he comes in a new style, falls to commend us as good orderly men, but withal to advise us friendly to do all so as may be for our best benefit, which is to have it seen in any wise."[4]

***

Andrewes diverts from his theme, in order to explain the true origin and meaning of *hypocrite*, a stage player, someone who acts out the character of another.

"The word hypocrite . . . is a known Greek word, and is in that tongue the ordinary and proper name for those whom the Latin term *histriones*, and we in English, *stage players*; such as in disguised attire and hair present themselves on a stage, and there often represent those whom, God knows, they are far from, but yet outwardly take upon them their persons as if they were.

And the ground of the word is, they are therefore called *hypocritae*, for that to give a true judgment of them, you must *judge them not by their player's coat above, but by what they are underneath in their own*, when their gorgeous and gay attire is off. . . .

The word in the tongue Christ spoke is . . . a *face-taker*, one who has got him a taken-on-face which is none of his own nor nothing like it, as in plays and shows the manner is. . . . The native sense of the word you see, and it is as if he had said in plain English, When you fast, be not like these same stage players. . . .

The heathen man long since observed . . . *the world was like a stage or theatre*, scarce a true face in it, all in a manner personate; and the actions in the world not much unlike to their acting of their parts in the acts and scenes of a stage-play; but our Saviour Christ goes further, He tells us here . . . [He] wants not [those] who make His Church a very stage, and play with religion, . . . so carrying themselves in things pertaining to God as if they had some play or pageant in hand. . . .

The hypocrite's whole labour is but his look. Blame him not, for he is nothing but look; nothing but face and case but a very outside only. As for any inward matter, he never looks after.

In which point, they suit well with players whose names they bear. . . . But gesture and gait, the carriage of his countenance, to say his part, to pronounce and to act it well, that is all that is cared for by him, or that is looked for at his hands. And even so it fares here; *contrition of spirit, a broken heart, unfeigned humility, truth in the inward parts* — these are most requisite in the true fast. It skills not a whit for any of these in the stage fast; so he can set his countenance well, have the clouds in his forehead, his eyes somewhat hollow, certain wrinkles in his cheek, carry his head like a bull-rush, and look like leaven, all is well. As for any inward accomplishment, he never takes thought for any."[5]

* * *

Andrewes suggests it is for the sin of vanity that we are hypocrites. Unlike the true Christian who only wishes God and the angels to see and know his deeds, the hypocrite must have other men to witness his.

"But why do they take all these pains to disfigure themselves? . . . *That they might be seen of men.* . . . Vain-glory, the ground of hypocrisy ever. . . . The hypocrite's end is as the player's end, both to be seen. You never see the play begin till the spectators be come, so many as they can get; nor no more will you see this fast acted, unless there be some to eye and to note it, . . . and it must be *of men*. Angel's eyes, God's eyes, will not serve the hypocrite's turn. . . .

O now I am seen! *O what a holy mortified man am I taken for!* . . . In all this is the point, this is the *ut* to be *seen of men*. Not that it is unlawful to be seen well-doing; you will easily put a difference between to be seen to do well, and to do well

144

to be seen. . . . It happens otherwise, many good people do well, and are seen so doing as it falls out, but beside their purpose quite. But none save this masked crew sacrifice themselves and their fasts to the eyes of men, and do what they do for no other end but that.''[6]

***

There will not be any problem in recognizing the hypocrite, suggests Andrewes. Unlike Christ he does not fast in a lonely or obscure place. The hypocrite lacks Christ's humility as he has assumed the devil's pride.

''You will easily discern them. You will not get one of them to do as Christ did, get him *aside out of the way into the wilderness*, fast there — no. Christ was not so well advised to do it there, in a desolate place where there nobody to meet Him or see Him at it. They be all for the eye, these; a perspective fast, or not at all. Nothing out of sight, never by their good-will where nobody to look on. The heathen man said well; *such a one would not be entreated to save a man's life in the dark, if he might*; not but by torch light. For all is lost, he is clean undone if nobody sees or looks upon him.

Well if it were the *Spirit of God [which] led Christ into the wilderness* to fast there like an hermit, you may well know what spirit it is that sets one up a stage there to fast like an hypocrite. . . .

And wherefore to be seen? . . . To be given out for such a one is a great faster. And why that? *That men seeing that good work of theirs might glorify God?* No indeed, but them; the earthly child, not the *heavenly Father*. And mark it when you will; there is no animal so ambitious, no chameleon so pants after air, as does the hypocrite after popular praise: . . . Saul [says]; *O grace me, for the love of God seem to honour me in the people's eyes*. . . .

Which very point makes the fast, . . . no fast at all; they extermine their countenances so long that they extermine fast and all. . . . For in the true fast it is as David says of his, *I sorrowed and my soul fasted*; it is an humbling of the soul. Else if it goes no further than the body, it is a fast without a soul. But these, though their stomach be empty, yet their souls do feed and feast all the while. . . . And even so, . . . one may eat and drink no more than the devil, and yet be as proud as the devil – why not? So as upon the matter, their fast is but even the devil's fast and no better.''[7]

***

Humility should be the foundation for fasting, following our Lord's example. The devil, ever willing to ensnare us, suggests it should be an act of pride, and so the praise of men is coveted. In such coveting we have won our reward, a fleeting one compared to the eternal reward which comes from all our action, including fasting, being for God's praise.

''Fasting then being an act of humility, if the devil can make it matter of pride, *he has what he would*. . . . The pharisees, whom Christ would have us *non sicut*,

145

they were in their own conceits the *non sicuts* of the world. They tell it God, *non sicut alii, not like other men*. Others did but fast once a week, if that; they twice, and never missed. . . . So pride will grow of fasting. Being then ordained to take down the soul, if he can bring it to puff it up, and so turn our fast into sin, that is even a fast of the devil's own choosing. . . . If we fast for our own praise, we fast for ourselves not for God neither. . . . Now what God should reward should be done for God. And with God a righteous thing it is to put men over to receive their rewards at their hands for whom they fasted, that they pay them their wages that set them on work; for at His hands they are likely to receive none, seeing for Him they did it not. . . .

It is a poor thing they receive, . . . this goodly reward of popular praise which they so itch after. . . .

But is this, be it passion or what it will, of any endurance? will it hold? No indeed! . . . No better witness of this than our Saviour Himself, Who heard, *Hosanna in the highest,* and *not Him but Barabbas . . .* within the space of a seven night. . . .

But now comes the hurt; for when it will come to this that we are so to receive it as in full payment; . . . as it will be our last pay, our final and full recompense and satisfaction for all that ever we have done — then it goes hard.

And that is it Christ means, and that is it every good mind fears; that here will be all, a few good works, a little warm breath, a blast of vain praise, of a sort of vain men. And when we have this, we have no more for ever to receive or look for besides this. . . . That the receiving of this cuts us off from another infinitely above and more worth than this. The reward we receive, nothing less to be regarded; the reward we lose, the damage we incur, nothing more to be feared. Lay these together, we shall find it a punishment, such a punishment as no man would ever wish his very enemy more. . . .

They have received their reward, you will read in St. Gregory, that never did any saying so sound in his ears, so run in his head, reign in his heart, work upon his conscience, as he deeply protests as did these. This he took for one of the most fearful sayings in the whole Bible; that what he did here receive, were it praise or preferment or what other earthly thing, it should be his last receipt, his final reward, his portion for ever, his Amen.''[8]

***

Andrewes urges us to judge for ourselves which reward is the more worth seeking after, the earthly or the eternal. Surely it must be for the eternal. With that in mind he presses us to observe Christ's command to fast, now during this Lent for God, and certainly not for the eyes of men.

''And now judge whether this receiving be not a loss invaluable, this reward a punishment unsufferable, this Amen to be prayed against of all. . . .

For do but ask; why do they this wrong to their faces? To seem to men to fast. And what then ? Then they will be *commended of men*. And what then? No, there is all, . . . because you make this your reward, it will be your reward; . . . no more fearful punishment in the world.

146

Knowing then this fear, we persuade, exhort, entreat men, and no otherwise than Christ here does, to fast. And the *cum* is now come; now then to do it. Not to do it as these, yet in anywise to do it. To fast to God, not to the world; to our hearts, not to other men's eyes; to conscience, not to form. Not to set us up a stage to do it, but with Christ to do it apart *in secret.* . . . Fast then, do it to be seen of Him; and being done not for men but for Him, Him will you be sure of to cast His eyes to look on it to like it, to regard it and reward it both. . . .

Our secret fast will have His open reward. It may be, even here upon earth He will *make our light break forth as the morning.* If here He do not, there He will. The less earth answers, the more heaven reserves. In that day is another manner praise, if praise be it; another manner reward than earth has any. Both together, *Merces magna nimis,* Abraham's reward, *an exceeding great reward,* it exceeds the heart of man to think how exceeding great."9

References

1 Andrewes, Vol. I, pp. 398–400.
2 *ibid.,* pp. 400–2.
3 *ibid.,* p. 403.
4 *ibid.,* pp. 404–5.
5 *ibid.,* pp. 406–7, 409.
6 *ibid.,* pp. 409–10.
7 *ibid.,* pp. 410–2.
8 *ibid.,* pp. 412–5
9 *ibid.,* pp. 415–6.

ASH WEDNESDAY SERMON No. 7: 1623

Text: St. Matthew 3:7–8

O generation of vipers, who has warned
you to flee from the wrath to come?
Bring forth therefore fruits meet for
repentance.

Progenies viperarum, quis demonstravit
vobis fugere a ventura ira?
Facite ergo fructum dignum poenitentiae
(vel, proferte igitur fructus dignos poenitentia.)

Our repentance must lead to action, that is bearing forth fruits in our lives, and there is no more appropriate time for this than during Lent. Repentance is represented as a tree bearing fruit, one of which is *fasting*, and another is its recuperative power to counter *the fruit of the forbidden tree.*

"To speak of repentance at the time of fasting, or of fasting at the time of repentance, is no way out of season; as tree and fruit they stand. Of these fruits, fasting is one. And this we now begin, a worthy fruit, even from year to year religiously brought forth in the Church of Christ. That we go not from one when we fall upon the other. The time of repentance will fall out to be a *cum jejunatis.*
Repentance is here brought in, and presented to us as a tree with fruit upon it. The tree of God's planting, the fruit medicinable, of the nature of a counter-poison against our bane taken by the fruit of another tree. The fruit of the forbidden tree had envenomed our nature, the fruit of this tree to expel it, to recover and cure us of it.
Now this metaphor of trees and fruit puts us in mind that the manner of fruit-trees is, once a year they bear fruit. All do so, once at least; and if all, this tree likewise within the same compass, to bring forth hers.
And though at no time repentance comes amiss — good all year long, it may be taken every day, for repentance would be as familiar to us as sin itself, and as the one so the other daily; yes at some time more than other, and at this time most proper, for then we have special use of it. That the body and the soul may keep time; and when we take physic for the body, we may do it likewise for the other.
. . .
This medicine is to be taken fasting, as the rules of physic are, and as medicines use to be. Men come neither eating nor drinking to take physic; when we will take that, we take nothing else. Thus fasting is a friend to physic both of soul and body. When we repent, no man will advise us to do it upon a full stomach, but *cum jejunatis.*

148

Of this tree and fruit God knowing the great need we have, has a special care we be not without it; that it be planted and growing still in our gardens, and that it bear us fruit whereof we have so continual use. As that paradise was termed the forbidden fruit, so may this as truly the fruit bidden, it is so enjoined, so called for of us.''[1]

***

One of the first fruits from the tree of repentance is *returning to God*, as preached by both St. John the Baptist, and Christ, and then His Apostles as commissioned by their Lord. For them repentance became like the corner stone of the building. Andrewes laments that this is often not the case with us as we choose to adopt a *fruitless*, superficial repentance.

"St. John [Baptist] is at it at first. It is his very first word, *repent*. . . . So begins he, and so begins Christ; takes it up after him, word for word the same; *Repent, for the Kingdom of heaven is at hand*. . . . It is the *first-fruit of their lips*, both.

And as our Saviour Christ began with it Himself, so gives He it in charge to His Apostles, . . . and . . . at His Ascension, He renewed and enlarged their commission and sent them *to all nations*. That repentance first, . . . and then *remission of sins* after, should be preached in His name. . . .

Ever they stood on it as the ground-work, the fundamental point of all the rest. So it is expressly termed, *the foundation of repentance from dead works*. On which foundation, would God more cost were bestowed! that while we are busy aloft on the scaffolds in our high points, the groundsills of religion decay not for want of looking to. To lay them surely; which St. John does here . . . when he saw in the throng of auditory [many] scribes and pharisees, hypocrites, he knew where they would be straight; — we should have an *agite*, a repentance with a penitential face and all acted. Repent? Yes in any wise that they would, and could do it full well and never trouble themselves with any such matter as fruit. This made Him lay it anew, to his *agite* to put a *facite*, to *agite poenitentiam*, a *facile fructus*. Else he disclaims fruitless repentance. It is none of his; it will do them no good, it will never quit them of the *wrath to come*. . . .

Tell them directly there is no other way, but that they do but beguile themselves, while they vainly imagine to slip through God's wrath with their fruitless, formal, slight kind of repentance.''[2]

***

The *wrath* of God, that *wrath* to come, must be taken seriously by the impenitent. It cannot be escaped, except by a true repentance, bringing forth good fruit. Yet so many of us are reluctant to bear fruit.

"The *wrath to come*. . . . There is no falling into it when it comes, nor no abiding it till it comes. Fly from it we must, and fly from it we may. . . . There is no flying God's wrath but by a true repentance. There is no true repentance without fruits, and those worthy and well becoming it. *Bring forth fruits*, therefore. . . .

It is the only true way; let no man teach you any other way to fly it. . . . And if repentance bears fruit then it is a tree. . . .

Bring forth. . . . All in carrying in, little in bringing forth. For to take our age at the best, . . . and this is our virtue, we carry well in, we are still carrying in; but nothing or as good as nothing comes from us, bring we forth. . . . All our time is spent in hearing, in carrying in repentance seeds, and other good seeds many. All in hearing in a manner, none in doing what we hear; none in bringing forth repentance, or any other good fruit. . . .

As there is a time . . . in the parable wherein the sower goes forth and carries with him good seed and casts it in, so there is a time too, says the psalm, that the *reaper comes back and brings his sheaves with him*, the sheaves which the seed he carried in *brought forth*. But with us it is otherwise. . . .

Now that ground, says the Apostle, that receives such a quantity of seed and returns no more for it, is near a curse. . . .

Well, there has been old carrying in, and little else; let us have some bringing forth another while. Be not always lading in, *bring forth* somewhat; else we stumble at the very threshold of the text and are not come to the first word of it, *proferto, bring forth.*

Bring forth fruit. With much ado at last somewhat there comes. Forth they bring, but what is it? It is well known trees bring forth somewhat else before fruit. And somewhat brought forth there is, but it is but leaves. Fruit it should be, leaves it is; there is all our product. . . . We plant not for leaves. . . . We count that no bringing forth; . . . fruit it is we are willed to *bring forth*. . . . Not the fruits of your lips, they be but leaves; but *fructus operis*, that fruit."[3]

***

If we find it hard to bring forth worthy fruits of repentance, then it behoves us to ponder on *the wrath to come*. The apostles in their various writings focus on this. Yet it is only when we are threatened by the eternity of hell, that we are stirred to repentance. Quite often this is not sufficient incentive for *ventura*, to ponder on the things to come such as judgment and hell fire, because our present existence is too comfortable.

"We must then cast our eye back to this *flying from the wrath to come*. . . .
Many are the therefores why we should repent, and of [many] natures. *The goodness of God*, says [St. Paul], *does even lead us to repentance*; and well is he who will be led. But these here would not be led. St. John had used that before. Do it, *repent*, and the *kingdom of heaven is at hand* — hard by you. One would think this would have done it, have even led them to it. It stirred them not; he is [willing] to lay heaven by, and the life, joy, glory to come, and to take him to hell, to the anguish tribulation, torments there, for all these are in the *wrath to come*. . . .
Strange, but such is our *indoles; the kingdom of heaven* works not with us as does *wrath to come*, so does sin bewitch us. For the loss of heaven, . . . we would never abstain from it. . . . Repent or you lose heaven; . . . repent or you must to hell, the place of *wrath to come* — that bites soon, that makes an *igitur*, that will move us; and fly from it to make us fly to repentance.

St. John takes the course to show us somewhat to come; he chooses *ventura*, for the things present carry us and keep us from repentance. Present good cheer, present sport and mirth, present good company, present twenty things else, they make us no firm soil for these fruits to grow in. . . . For in all our jolity, before we venture too far it will not be amiss to look to those *ventura*, and what will come of it. . . .

Moses does wish but this, *O si*, O that men would look . . . to the hindmost days, to the latter end! . . . The prophets do the like: . . . it is Jeremiah [who says], *My people this sin they like, and that sin they love, but what will be the end of this?* . . . Yes, our blessed Saviour Himself, and He should move us, most earnestly with tears in His eyes, *O that you had known in this your day!* and could not speak out the rest for weeping. His meaning was, the *ventura*, what was to come upon them. So much does it import us some time to open a window that way. The clapping it to, and the putting them from us out of our sight makes us we care not, never look after the tree or the fruit. *Ventura* would much help forward this *proferte fructus igitur*.

These *ventura*, three of them, . . . the axe first; for sure our days be numbered; there is a line stretched upon every one of our lives, and it no long line neither; . . . death will come with his axe and down we go, . . . and then we are past fruit-bearing for ever. . . .

After the axe comes the fan, to show whether our bringing forth be corn or chaff, which is our doom after death. So long ago told of by old Enoch in his Maranatha, that *the Lord will come,* come to *judgment; and we shall stand* before His judgment-seat and the fan go over us; and there by these fruits here, and by these fruits only all will go, for none is in heaven but by it. Sinners both they in heaven and they in hell; only this difference, they in heaven had these fruits, they in hell had them not. . . .

After the fan comes the fire. The fan divides the corn and the chaff, sends each to his own place, the corn to the garner, the chaff to the fire, and *every tree that brings not forth good fruit, thither too.* . . . How will you *escape the damnation of hell,* says Christ? . . .

Now I shall but ask the prophet Isaiah's question, *Who of us can dwell in consuming fire?* That is our fire which, as it consumes, so will it be consumed itself; but then he comes over again, but *who is able to abide in everlasting burnings?* That can none do? . . . This, lo, is the wrath, the very dregs of the wrath to come. But *who regards the power of this wrath?* They I fear me least that will feel it most.''[4]

***

The old ceremony of placing ashes upon the forehead reminded the receiver of such hell-fire. Although the ceremony of ashes has gone, Andrewes hopes *the memory of them* has not.

''. . . upon this day they were wont, by the ceremony of giving ashes, to put men in mind of this fire. For ashes were not given to put men in mind of their mortality; dust had been more proper to have done that. . . . But ashes, they come not without

151

fire; where they are, fire must have been first. And so they most meet to represent fire and make us think of it. The ashes, they be blown away, but not the memory of them, I hope. . . . Sure these ashes laid well to the root of the tree, it has been thought will make it bear the sooner. The present fear of future wrath for sins past will put some force into this *igitur*; if this will not, nothing will; this or nothing making the sap to ascend; this or nothing bring them forth.[5]

***

Yet there is hope. Take comfort in that this wrath is *to come*. Therefore we have time to do something about averting it. From Christ, we have learnt there is only one way to escape it, and that is to repent. It is *repent* or *perish*.

". . . you have seen the terror; shall I open you a *door of hope in the valley of Achor?* All is not terror in *ventura*; there is some comfort, that it is but *to come* — this wrath it is yet *to come*. So while it is yet to come, there is time given us to take order for it before it comes; that the fruit may come before the wrath, and not the wrath before the fruit; for then we are gone for ever. . . .

Fly from it, I say, for there is no meeting it, no abiding of it when it comes; no standing it out, but fly from it we must, says the text; and fly from it we may. . . .

But if there be a flight there is no flying it, not with the wings of an eagle, not with the six wings of a seraph; only the wings of repentance will fly from it. . . . You need not fly, you need not stir no more than a tree, but keep your standing, and bear your fruit, and it will not come near you but fly over you, as did the destroying angel their houses in Egypt. *To come* it is, this wrath; fly from it we may, this way to do it. . . . Is there no way but this?

Christ Himself [says], *Unless you repent* . . . there is no iron, no adamant [that] binds so hard. . . . If any but Christ had said it, we might have sought some evasion. Now when it is He who tells us, there are but two ways, repent, or perish, choose you whether; repent here for a time, or perish there under God's wrath for ever; not to repent and not to perish, is not possible.

Which dilemma of Christ's no way to be avoided makes of the [two] to choose this fruit of repentance, rather than to fall into t*he wrath to come*; to fly to the one, to fly from the other, which otherwise we are of ourselves but coldly affected to. For though it be somewhat bitter, this fruit, yet sure we are if it were ten times more, the bitter pains of *ira ventura* are far beyond it. . . .

Will we conclude then with the psalmist, *What man is he who would deliver his soul from the wrath to come?* And they all began at once to say, That would I; yes even they who shall not escape it will yet say, That would I; Why, by the bringing or not bringing forth of this fruit all goes, depends the coming, or not coming of this wrath; — coming if you do not, not coming if you do bring them forth."[6]

***

We may agree there is no other way; but somehow we are reluctant to start now, and we put it off. In fact Andrewes indicates that the Greek tense used, the *aorist*, suggests something already done. Thus instead of *bringing forth*, it is rather *have done bringing forth.* Bearing forth fruit, however, does not happen overnight; it takes time. Thus the longer we leave the *now*, the less chance we have of our tree bearing blossom, let alone fruit.

"But often it falls out, when we are agreed of the thing, we are not so for the time. Will we at all bring them forth? If we shall, we shall take some time to do it in. . . . At what time then? . . . What tense is *proferte*? the present; do it then in the present. It requires an act instantly to be done, bring them forth out of hand. This is a small note; but it is no small matter to get this small note born well away, to get our repentance into the present tense. . . .

To tell you the truth . . . the word is not *bring forth* at this time, . . . but . . . in the aorist . . . tense . . . *having done bringing forth* . . . And I would to God we had even done so, had done bringing them forth, for then all fear were past! . . .

But well, to take no advantage of that tense, we will be content with the present. . . . No not now; this is not a time, we have appointed other business which we cannot put off. . . . If not now, when? . . . It be as near now as may be, for fear *ventura* come not too soon, and take tree and all. This is sure, the sooner the better because the more likely; the latter the worse, because the less certain. . . .

Fruit requires a time to bring them forth; who ever heard of fruit brought forth on a sudden? . . . I take it to be an error and that of dangerous consequence, teaching repentance, to think it a matter of no more moment than to be dispatched in a moment, commonly our repentance is too soon done."[7]

***

The most convenient time to begin our repentance, is the *now*, now during Lent, that special time reserved not only for fasting but also for repenting. If the teaching from Holy Scripture and of the Church is not sufficent to arouse us of *ventura*, perhaps the season itself, bringing forth her fruit and ushering in the return of the birds, might be an incentive.

"But if we mean as we say, would do it at *a convenient time*, we cannot find so convenient a time as this. Take it first as the time of the fast, that time may seem to claim a property in it. They go always together; in the Law their solemn repentance was ever at the time of their general fast. In the prophets, Joel tells, the *best turning to God,* that is repentance, is *cum jejunio*. . . . In the Gospel John Baptist, the preacher, *came neither eating nor drinking.* And our Saviour, though He did both, yet this fast He kept, though not for any need He had of it Himself, but . . . *to give us an example* and to point us who had need what time to do it in. Which has ever since from year to year been religiously observed, both as a time of public penance, and as a time of general abstinence in the Church of Christ, convenient for the time of fast.

And convenient [it is] for the time of the year. For if it will be the tree in the first psalm, to *bring forth fruit in due season,* . . . that season is at this season. . . . You can never *bring forth* at a better time. The season is now come . . . when the trees will fall in travail, and they and the earth both make proffer toward, and give pledges in their buds and blossom of fruit that is coming, and will follow in due time. . . .

If we shall keep time with the heavens, now the heavens return to their first degree; it is turning time in heaven. If with the fowls of heaven, and them Christ bids us look to, they know their times just, and just at this time make their return, the poor swallows and all; and so let us that the prophet Jeremiah upbraid us not with them. So whether we shall go by heaven and the fowls of heaven, or by earth and the fruits of the earth, they all invite us to the dispensation of this season. . . . It has so fallen out, that repentance, fasting and the very season of the year for the most part hit together. That of Nineveh the most famous; by the springing up of Jonah's gourd we may guess what time it was, we know what time it is when gourds spring. . . .

And take this beside, that in that first month, the trumpet's first blast of all was to assemble them to their Kipher, their great repentance day, that was their first work of all. . . . Nisan is also called Abib of the first bringing forth of fruits in it. Now in Nissan was the time when their Paschal Lamb was slain and eaten. The same is also the time of the killing of ours, of St. John Baptist's Lamb, *the Lamb of God*, when *Christ our Passover* was offered, offered for us in sacrifice, offered to us in Sacrament. . . .

And we now at this time to set those sour herbs and see them come up wherewith the Passover is to be eaten, which are nothing else but these *fruits of repentance*. Now to set them, that then we may gather them to serve us for sauce to the Paschal Lamb. Thus every way we may say with the Apostle, *Behold this is the due season*, Behold now is the convenient time. Now then, *Bring them forth.*"[8]

***

Andrewes pleads with us not to let this Lent slip by without repentance. If we but understood the implication of *ira ventura* we would not rest until we *brought forth fruit*. Then we can be assured that the *wrath to come* will not be upon us and we shall have everlasting life.

"If we did but truly apprehend the words *ira ventura*, our eyes would not sleep, nor our eyelids slumber, nor the temples of our heads take any rest, till we had taken straight order with ourselves. For the *when*, when it should be, at what time we should not fail but to do it, and nothing should let us but perform it once to purpose, and seal to ourselves this fruit; that yet once we may assure ourselves we are in good earnest, and that done it is, and such and such were the fruits we had of it.

A time, whensoever it will happen, which will be to us no less memorable than the day of our birth, . . . and as much joy and comfort shall we take in the remembrance of it as of any of them. The rest and repose our spirits will find upon the accomplishment of it, will be worth our pains and abundantly recompense our going through with it.

And when you come back again to St. John Baptist, and to bring him word you have *brought forth this fruit*, he will then show you *Agnus Dei.* . . . And that sight will be worth all. . . .

We shall be sure to fly the *wrath to come*, . . . and instead of it the *kingdom of heaven* will come near to us and we to it. For *repent* and *it is at hand*, say St. John and Christ both. It is our daily prayer it may come, and this is the way to make it come. . . . We shall sanctify thereby this time of fast, and as it has ever been counted, make it a holy time; and we in it shall have *our fruit in holiness, and the end everlasting life.*''9

References

1 Andrewes, Vol. I, pp. 417–8.
2 *ibid.*, pp. 418–9.
3 *ibid.*, pp. 419–23.
4 *ibid.*, pp. 424–7.
5 *ibid.*, p. 427.
6 *ibid.*, pp. 427–9.
7 *ibid.*, pp. 430–1.
8 *ibid.*, pp. 431–3.
9 *ibid.*, p. 434.

ASH WEDNESDAY SERMON No. 8: 1624

Text: St. Matthew 3:8

Bring forth therefore fruits meet
for repentance.

*Proferte fructus igitur dignos
poenitentiae.*

Again *repentance* is treated metaphorically, and described as a tree showing
forth her fruits, such as prayer, fasting and almsgiving. This tree is seen as
replacing the tree of innocency which withered and died under our disobedience, and hence its fruits are *worthy* and medicinal to counter the *unworthy*
and poisonous fruits of the other. It is these worthy fruits we are asked to
consider during Lent, and if not already part of our lives to ponder very
seriously about including them. Otherwise we shall have to face the wrath of
God.

"Bring forth fruits, therefore. What fruits? Fruits of repentance, fruits growing on a tree called repentance; for the fruits ever carry us to the tree that carries them.
If we be to have fruit, it must be brought forth; if brought forth it must be, there
must be a tree to bring it forth. That tree is repentance. . . .

St. John [Baptist's] . . . metaphor of tree and fruits, and axe and root . . . seems
to refer us . . . to . . . the forbidden tree. That tree had fruit; this tree to have so too.
Tree for tree, fruit for fruit. The worthy fruits of repentance for the unworthy fruits
of disobedience. The fruit of that tree was our bane, the fruit of this to be our
medicine. The fruit of that made *ira ventura* to come, the fruit of this will turn it
away.

It is true the fruits of this tree of repentance . . . were not *principally intended.*
There was another, a more excellent plant called the tree of innocence, the fruit
whereof was, *ne peccetis, not to sin at all.* . . . The forbidden fruit was no sooner
taken, but that tree withered and died, could never be got to grow in our nature
since. . . .

That tree failing, it pleased God of His great goodness to graft upon a new stock
this second plant, the plant of repentance, to the end it might serve for a counter-
poison, the fruit of it against the venom of the forbidden fruit. To the end also that
it might serve to supply that other of innocency. . . . That if we cannot present God
with the fruit of innocency at the seat of His justice, yet with the fruit of repentance
we may at the throne of His grace.

And this tree will grow in our soil, our soil will bear it, and with good tending
bring forth fruits, worthy fruits, which we may offer unto God and He will take it

in good worth. And this is the tree we must trust to now, and blessed be God that so we may.''[1]

***

Repentance is described by Andrewes as a tree with liveliness, and it is those heart-felt passions such as anger which inject real feeling into our repentance. So often our emotions are alas lifeless and dull which is reflected in the kind of repentance we make.

''We are to treat of repentance as a tree first. To speak properly, repentance is a virtue, a moral virtue, a branch of justice, . . . and so should be delivered in moral terms. . . . It is not though, . . . but most-what set out in the terms of some one passion of the mind or other. And why so? For no other cause, but that we are so dead and dull when we are about it, this business, as if repentance were a very log and no quick or live tree. Which cannot be, repentance being from *dead works*, and therefore cannot be a dead thing itself, but have a life in it. Mark it when you will, the Holy Spirit as it were of purpose still chooses to express it under some term of passion, as sorrow, fear, anger and the like, rather than the other way. . . . For passions be quick, there is life in them. . . . He would have us affectionate when we are about this work, and not . . . cold and . . . calm, . . . [then] there is hope of some fruit. . . .

Now if affections give life, the quicker the affection the more life it gives. And there is none quicker than that of anger, . . . because most life and spirit appears in that; fear and sorrow and the rest are but dull and heavy in comparison of it. . . .

The passion of anger . . . strikes upon *ira ventura* in the text, . . . [and] leads us by the hand unto it. One anger to another, God's anger to ours, God's to come to ours for the present. For by our anger for the present we turn away His to come. Our anger is a *supersedeas* to His. Or if you will have it in terms of justice, judging ourselves we shall not be judged of the Lord.

But our anger and generally all our affections are . . . used . . . most where they should be least, and again least where they should be most. For take . . . a worldly man, and let him but overreach himself in some good bargain, in matter of profit, you will see him so angry, so out of patience with himself as often it casts him into some disease. There lo, is repentance in kind; there is [what] makes it a tree, the spirit of life. Ours for the most part towards God is dull and blockish, neither life nor soul in it.''[2]

***

A healthy, lively tree bears much fruit, unlike the barrenness of an unlively tree. Our repentance should be like the lively tree, always bringing forth fruit, and therefore clearly visible. Yet how often our repentance is such that it does not inspire us to witness for Christ at all.

157

"But we may not stand thus about the tree, we are called on for *proferte*, to bring somewhat forth; else how shall we know it is a tree and no log? . . . It is the bringing forth that makes the difference.

Bringing forth is opposite to keeping in, we must have no kept-in repentance. Forth it must come, forth it must be brought. From whence? from within. Carrying in before, keeping in now; all within are against, utterly against *proferte*.

St. John [Baptist] saw well which way the world would go. Men would have their repentance . . . *a matter to be sped, dispatched, shuffled up within, between their conscience and them*. . . . There within they have it, . . . where nobody can see what they have. Under the bushel much, but nothing on the candlestick that any man can see. So instead of *proferte*, we should have *praeferte*, nothing but pretending, . . . says St. John, no bosom repentance; bring it out, show it. For upon St. John's *proferte* is grounded St. James' *show me your faith*; and it holds in repentance too, . . . *not only a pretence or fair show to be made of our conscience within, but some outward thing to be done and executed upon it;* somewhat to be brought forth. Take heed of this error, as if repentance were a matter merely mental or intentional. It is not good notions in the brain, nor good motions in the mind will serve, these are but the sap within; look to the branches, what see you there? Look to *proferte*, what is brought forth."[3]

***

What must be brought forth is fruit, not buds or blossoms or leaves but fruit. The kind of fruits produced by the tree of repentance are the works of prayer, fasting and almsgiving to counter the sins of the spirit, flesh and world respectively.

"Many things does a tree bring forth, and [many] of them as forerunners to the fruit, as boughs and leaves, and buds and blossoms. St. John mentions none of them, passes by them all; stays at none till he comes to the fruits. That is [what] the tree was planted for. Not to make materials, not to give shadow, not for the green boughs nor the gay blossoms, nor for anything but for the fruit. . . . Fruit is [what] it was first set, and for which it is let grow; and when there is no longer hope of bringing forth fruit, *down with it,* says the Lord of the soil, *why troubles it the ground any longer?* And then comes *ira ventura* with his axe, lays it to the root and down it goes, and into the fire it is cast; and seeing it will not serve for fruit, makes it serve for fuel — the end of all unfruitful trees. Mark it well this. It is the fruit of repentance; not repentance itself, but the fruit it is sought for. That is all in all. So not only a bearing, but a fruit-bearing repentance.

And good reason. For if the one tree, sin, if that have brought forth fruit, so must repentance, the other tree, do likewise. It is true in sin the sense, and so the soul, is first in fault. In at that gate it first comes, and out at that it must first go. But sin has her fruit in the body, so is repentance to have hers too. Repentance is to be incorporate and bring forth her fruits in the body. The soul alone not to be put to penance, all laid upon it; the body to share, as in the pleasure so in the pain.

Perhaps in their sin that lies smothering in the thought within, never comes *in actum*, there may be be some question whether repentance alone may not serve.

But if it has brought forth the forbidden fruit, the body, the body must have her fruit in repentance also. To both said it is, said it must be, *proferte igitur fructus.*

And what be these fruits? . . . St. Paul . . . preached, *Men should turn to God and do works worthy of repentance. . . .* St. Paul's *works* are St. John's *fruits*; fruits and works are all one. *Every good work is a good fruit.* To do a work then of repentance is to bring forth the fruits of repentance. . . . Otherwise, . . . *we do but dally, all is but counterfeit*, [says St. Augustine]. No serious repentance if somewhat be not done. . . .

To grow to more particulars we [seek] the works of repentance as they may best answer and suit with the works of sin. Now all sin grows out of these three heads, and may be reduced to one of them, the spirit, the flesh and the world. . . . Now it is contrary much against each of these to be deprived of that it loves and delights in.

The spirit loves to be at liberty to range and scatter itself in many manner thoughts; or if it fix, to do it upon some pleasing object. Confine the spirit, make it undertake some task of devotion, set it to pray, to read, to meditate, which is a dry object and nothing pleasing to it; fix it so, and you punish it. For nothing is more irksome. It is *vexatio spiritus.*

The flesh that loves to fare well — put it to fast; loves to sleep and take her ease — put it to watch, or lie hard; loves *vesitiri mollibus*, gird it with sackcloth; loves mirth and good company — make it retire and sit pensive: abridge it of these all or any, and you punish it more or less I warrant you.

The world and the worldling, they love to part with as little as they can. Charge them with anything that will be to them chargeable, it punishes them shrewdly, and is to them a punishment.

Thus then these three may be met with, each of them if they have made a fault. For neglect of serving of God, with some task of devotion more than ordinary. For fullness of bread with that truly *sacra fames*, the exercising of fasting. For looseness of life, with works tending to the taking down of the flesh, and making it less fleshly. For taking [what] was others, to depart with [what] was our own. For want of bowels with works of mercy. In a word, with suffering what we would not, for doing what we should not. So punishing our evil concupiscence in that it is so bent to, and making it leave that for which it left God. So the triplicity stands thus: For spiritual sins, prayer and works of devotions; for fleshly, works pertaining to *castigo corpus meum;* for wordly, alms, and works of charity and compassion. . . .

A fruit, which if we would frame ourselves to bring forth in kind, there would come with it both the other fruits besides. For if we could so fast as we should, it would abate lusts certainly, which otherwise, keep the body high, you will hardly bring low; — that fruit. And if we could so fast it would mend our devotion much, our prayers would not be so full of yawning as we find them; — that fruit. And if we could so fast, there would be the more left to enable us to be so much the more plentiful in alms than we be — that fruit. So as a good increase or yield would come of this third fruit well brought forth. . . .

These three in special are chosen out, but in general any as well as these. . . . There is not a virtue of them all but you may make the work of it a fruit of repentance."[4]

***

159

The fruits of repentance have both an outward and inward effect. With the former they become an offering to God, and with the latter they heal our former stained souls and corrupt bodies.

"Of fruits . . . to be offered as a present, . . . we have in all but three things to offer unto God, to present Him with: the spirit or soul, the body, and our worldly goods. The offering of the soul is the pouring it out in prayers and other works of that kind. Of the body, the chastening it by exercises that way tending. Of our goods, by distributing and doing good with them in alms and offerings. . . .
They are [also] medicinable. . . . Repentance is the physic of the soul and body both, . . . as a corrective of what is past, so preservative . . . of what is to come. When the sinner is corrected, has correction given him for the former, he corrects his ways, amends his life for ever after. *Castigo corpus* serves for what has been done; in *servitutum redigo* serves , that he do it no more. Both to wreak ourselves for so often offering so foul indignities to heaven and the God of heaven in our former bad course of life, and to keep under the flesh, and hold the concupiscence in awe, that it run not again into the former riot. This latter, we call *amendment of life*."5

***

How worthy is our fruit of repentance? The quality depends very much on the depth of our repentance. If it is superficial, then the fruit is worthless. Yet even the most worthy fruit can never balance the *unworthiness of our sins*. Nevertheless we are to strive to attain the same degree of worthy fruit *as the saints and servants of God* of old possessed. Do we? So often we seem content to offer God the *wind-falls*.

"In our repenting, commonly we make such haste, as we take away before the fruits come. . . . Our tears, if any, dry straight; our prayers, if any, quickly tedious; our alms, indeed pitiful; our fasts, fast or loose upon any least occasion; and so our repentance, if any, *a repentance needing another, . . . to repent us of it. . . .* So that if any fruit, fruit of no worth. And if the fruit be of no worth, no more is the tree.
. . .
How worthy? . . . Shall we put them into the balance to weigh the worthiness of our fruits with the unworthiness of our sins, and the consequent of our sins? . . . At this beam, no fruit of ours will hold weight; none so found worthy; no, not if we could, I say not shed or pour out, but even melt into tears, and every tear a drop of blood. . . . The infinite incomparable high worth of Him Who in our sin is wronged, the foul contempt that is therein offered, are far above the worth of any of our fruits. . . .
How worthy then? . . . As worthy as the possibility of our nature will reach to, . . . as the saints and servants of God are reported to have brought forth in former ages; . . . that indeed were somewhat worth, if it might be had. . . . Their *knees have grown weak through fasting*, they have *all wet their pillows with their tears*; they have *restored bribes, and that fourfold*, given in alms at once, *half of all that*

ever they had. This were indeed somewhat worth; but of this, I doubt our worthiness will be found short. . . .

And yet were there in us any portion of that heroical free spirit, of that Christian magnaminity that was in the fathers of our faith, . . . so poor fruit would not content us. But we, neither to our power nor a great deal short of it, endeavour ourselves, any never so slight and slender will serve us well enough. . . .

Do we think to post God off with any, it skills not what fruit? with wind-falls, with worm-eaten stuff? Isaiah's *sour grapes*? Jeremiah's *rotten figs*? Nothing comes amiss. Hold we Him in so vile account as any is good enough for Him, it is well with Him if He get any?''[6]

***

Andrewes insists there is no other way. Our manifold sins have assured us of that. If we wish to escape the *wrath to come*, true repentance, producing its fruit, is needed. This is the only way set out by the Law, John the Baptist and St. Paul.

''Is there any other way to take our *dignos* by? . . . Not so. . . . Only *fruits worthy of repentance*; that is, such as may well beseem persons as be truly penitent. . . . Laying by sin, as it is an aversion from an infinite good, for so it is infinite, admits no measure or degree; but considering it as it is a conversion to the creature and that more or less; so it falls within compass of more or less worthy. . . .

It has been held no way safe for us to make our own assessment, and as safe a way as could be would ever be taken for the soul. Better some other body do it; and who will that other body be?

In the Law, everyman was not left to Himself. The *offering for sin*, which was to them a fruit of repentance, it was rated ever, ever taxed by the priest. . . . And here now in St. John's time, which was the interval . . . between the Law and the Gospel, at the *baptism of John, they knew not what to do.* . . . To St. John they come, with their *quid faciemus?* And *what shall we do?* All three one after another, the publicans, the soldiers, the common sort, and they had all their answers severally. . . . And under the Gospel, there we see for the Corinthian St. Paul said, *Thus much is enough*, this will serve; his conscience may be quiet, I restore him to the Church's peace. And the Canons penitential which were made in the times under the persecution, the very best times of the Church, lay forth plainly what is to be followed and observed in this kind. . . .

We have learned, I know not where, a new, a shorter course, which flesh and blood better likes of; to pass the whole course of our life, and in the whole course of our life not to be able to set down where or when or what we did, when we did [what] we call repenting; what fruits there came of it, what those fruits might be worth. And but even a little before our death — and as little as may be — not till the world has given us over, then, lo, to come to our *quid faciemus?* To ask *what we should do* when we are able to do nothing. . . .

This way, this fashion of repenting, St. John knew it not; it is far from his *fructus dignos*; St. Paul knew it not, it is far from his *opera digna*. . . . It is not good trying conclusions about our souls. *Here is the plain way*, this is the straight path laid out before us by him who was *sent to prepare the ways of the Lord, and to make his paths straight*; and go we which way we will, we shall hear the voice behind us, crying to *Haec est via, ambulate in ea*. Set your tree, bring forth your fruits, see to them; altogether unworthy they would not be, somewhat worth, raised to some degree of worthiness.''7

***

As God is always merciful, He responds to the smallest effort made, just as He did to the poor widow's two mites. For our part we must do what we can. In order to do that we must use this Lent, and the example of the seasonal occupation as a time of examination, and ask ourselves the nature of our repentance. Is it suffcient to ward off the *wrath to come*?

''We doing our endeavours to raise them to what degree we can, He for His part will not be behind, but relieve and help us out. *God even waits that He may have mercy on us*. And therefore laying away His rigour, will not go exactly to work, but be ready to relieve and repute that worthy that is not all out so. . . .

Yet let us never think, be so base as to conceive, He will hold for such any at all, let them be what they will, it skills not how worthless, how far from all degrees towards it. No; but such as wherein He sees some conscience made, some care taken, some zealous desire, some earnest endeavour appear. Some proffers, at least, towards those seven degrees in 2 Cor.7, which may serve to assure ourselves and to show the world, we dally not with repentance but make a serious matter of it and go to it in good earnest; in witness whereof, this and this fruit we have brought forth. Somewhat like yet, somewhat beseeming persons truly penitent, whereto He would say, *My grace is sufficient for you*. And in that we may rest.

It remains we examine ourselves touching these points; 1. Our repentance, is it like a live tree, and not a dull heavy mood, neither life nor soul in it? 2. Have we set it on growing, brings it forth at all? 3. Is it fruit it brings forth? . . . . 4. The fruit it brings, is it aught worth for the quantity, the quality, the well lasting of it? God grant it be so, and thanks be to God if it be so!

But this *proferte* will ask some time. . . . It is altogether an error to think repentance is a matter of no more than to be dispatched in a moment.

There be two words, words of weight; one is St. Peter's, and that is *to withdraw, go aside, to retire and be private, to sequester ourselves to our repentance;* the other is St. Paul's, *to take us a time, no, to make us a time, a vacant time, a time of leisure to intend fasting and prayer*, two fruits of repentance. I ask then, did we never *withdraw ourselves* to that end? What was the place where we so did? Did we at any time *take any such vacant time*? What was the time and when, when we so did? I doubt ours had been rather a flash, a qualm, a brunt, than otherwise, rather a gourd of repentance than any growing tree. A time there must needs be for this *proferte*.

Now the time St. John gives is but . . . *ira, ventura*, vita ventura, . . . two words: in that it is *wrath* and *God's wrath*, there is just matter of fear; in that it is *ventura*,

162

to come, but to come, and not yet come, there is hope yet some good may be done before *that come that is to come.*

If these fruits come, the wrath when it comes will not come upon us but pass by us, and not touch any fruit-bearing tree. . . .

Now there cannot be a fitter time than that the Church has set us forth, that is now, at this time of the year. For now is the time of the year to plant in. In the picture of the months, in this next month, you will see nothing but men grafting and setting trees: it is the husbandry and the business of the month, wonderfully fitly chosen therefore that this tree may keep time with the rest. And now is the time that the sap goes up; so as there could not be a fitter time for St. John to call upon us. Look abroad, they begin now to *bring forth*; now best speaking for *proferte*. To which *proferte, differte* is clean contrary. Defer it not then but take the time while it is in season.

And with high wisdom is this time so set that the time of our repentance, the forty days of it, end in the Passover, in the passing of *ira ventura* over us, as did the destroying angels over the houses in Egypt. That the mortifying of sin might end in the rising of Christ in us. The use of fruit is fruition; and this is the fruition in this life, even the fruits of the Spirit, fear and love and joy in the Holy Spirit. And in the life to come, the fruit of the tree of life in the midst of Paradise; instead of *ira ventura, vita ventura, gaudia ventura, the glory and joy eternal of the life to come.* To which life, glory, and joy, bring us Almighty God.''[8]

References

[1] Andrewes, Vol. I, pp. 435–6.
[2] *ibid.*, pp. 437 -8
[3] *ibid.*, pp. 438–9.
[4] *ibid.*, pp. 439–442, 444.
[5] *ibid.*, pp. 445–6.
[6] *ibid.*, 446–8.
[7] *ibid.*, pp. 449–51.
[8] *ibid.*, pp. 451–4.

LENTEN SERMON No. 1
11th March 1589

Text: Psalm 75:3

The earth and all the inhabitants thereof
are dissolved: I bear up the pillars of it.

*Liquefacta est terra, et omnes qui habitant
in ea: Ego confirmavi columnas ejus.*

David, through his music, teaches us at this Lenten time the significance of being in tune, and therefore preserving harmony between God and ourselves. Such melodic music always has vitality to enthuse the listener. When David composed this particular psalm he was very conscious of the need for such harmony because of the dissension existing between himself and Saul. This text by its very nature also uses architectural imagery to convey strength, but strength in contrast with weakness, such as the strength of Israel under David as compared with its weakness under Saul. As its setting is in the early kingdom period, where king was both ruler and judge, Andrewes has weaved throughout this sermon how the alliance between Church and State is still observed in his own time under the rule of the Prince. Thus religion and justice continue to be the two essential pillars of the State.

"In which holy and heavenly use of his harp, [David] does by his tunes of music, teach men how to set themselves in tune. How not only to tune themselves, but how to tune their households. And not only there, but here in this psalm, how to preserve harmony. . . .

For the time of setting this song, by general consent of all expositors, being the latter end of the long dissension between the houses of David and Saul, evident it is, the estate of the land was very near to a *perdas*, and needed *ne perdas* to be sung unto it. . . .

[David] found the land a weak land, by means the strengths and pillars of it were all out of course by the misgovernment of Saul. . . .

The style whereof runs in the term of architecture, very aptly resembling the government to a frame of building; the same set upon and borne up by certain bases and pillars, the strength whereof assures, or the weakness endangers the whole; and David himself to a skilful builder, surveying the pillars, and searching into the decays; repairing their ruins, and setting them into course again. . . .

For sure, in such lands where this their song, *the earth is weak,* their music is all out of tune. . . .

This music is heavy, and therefore David saw the song must be new set. And so he does set it anew, changing it into a more pleasant note, *But I will strengthen it.*

And when the note is so changed, *in that day will this song be sung in the land of Judah, We have a strong city; salvation has God set for the walls and bulwarks of it.*

This music has life in it, and heartens the inhabitant afresh; quails the enemy and resolves the neighbour to say, *Yours are we, O David, and on your side, you son of Jesse"*[1]

***

Each Jewish temple had two main pillars supporting the archway, one representing God and His worship, and the other Justice and its execution through the Spirit. This Spirit was also a source of strength, evident in Israel's government under Moses. When St. Paul spoke of rulers, he advised that the base or the pillar for their government was prayer.

"For such was the manner of the Jewish building — arch wise, upon two main pillars to set it. We may see it by Samson's desire so to be placed as the two supporters of the temple might be in his two hands. . . . [David] tells us what they be, . . . 1. *Celebrabimus Te Jehova* . . . and 2. *Justitias judicabo* . . . .. God and Right, the pillars; the worship of God, and the execution of justice or right. . . .

God is a pillar; so is His most common name in the Hebrew — Adonai, *My pillar.* And His Son, a Rock; not only Peter's Rock, but David's Rock too; the Rock both of the Church and Kingdom. And His Spirit, a Spirit not of holiness only and truth, but a *Spirit of judgment* to them who sit on the throne; and a *Spirit of strength* for them who keep the battle from the gate. . . .

Even the strength and establishing of *Si credideritis stabiliemini*, by which not only the devil's *darts* are repelled in the spiritual, but *the armies of the aliens are put to flight in earthly warfare.* Therefore Moses made such reckoning of *Celebrabimus*, . . . [as] he opposes . . . them all, . . . and [matched] them all, in the posterity of the sons of God, the invocation of His name, begun and set on foot, first by Enoch, as the main pillar of strength which the people of God trust to. And St. Paul is bold . . . where, laying as it were, the chamber-beams and stories of each Christian government . . . as the base or pillar of all, and that which bears up, and gives strength to all, sets prayer; prayer to be made, that so princes preserved; that so peace maintained; that so knowledge intended; that so godly and honest life practised; that so salvation attained. Reckoning invocation as a special pillar of each estate; and as a prerogative royal, prayer for all men, but above all men for princes."[2]

***

One pillar would have been sufficient if everyone trusted in God. But as some have no faith at all, the second pillar of justice is needed to resolve the outcome of men's sins. Yet for both pillars to remain upright, they must be supported by a prince who rules righteously.

"Now if all men had faith . . . this one pillar have been enough; but because all men have not religion, but there be in the *world evil and absurd men*, therefore needed the second, therefore needed *Justitias judicabo*. . . .

Which kind of men are of two sorts; Therefore it is *justitias* 1. The enemy or Egyptian smiting Israel from without; 2. The injurious Israelite wronging his brother, from within. Why then, *Sit nobis Rex*, says the people, which is a perfect comprehension of this pillar of justice to do them right, and to defend them by war, when need is, against the foreign enemy; by justice, when cause is, against the domestic oppressor. Against the one Jehoshaphat places *garrisons*, that is against outward hostility; against the other he ordains *judges*, that is, inward injury. . . .

Thus have we the two pillars of the earth, each strengthening the other: Religion rooting Justice within; Justice fencing Religion without, and they both making an arch of government irremovable.

Yet, these two pillars, as strong and as steady as they are, except they be looked to and upheld, except they have an upholder and that a good one, Religion will cleave, and Justice bend, and they both sink, and the whole frame with them. Therefore mention is made here of a person put in trust with the bearing them up. . . .

Which person is . . . . the chief person in any government. He it is upon whom both these lean; he is the head, who guides these two arms; he the breath of life in both . . . yes, of all the body. . . .

Familiar it is, . . . but very full or forcible, the simile of Isaiah; wherein he compares the prince to *a nail driven into a wall*, whereon are hanged all, both the vessels of service and the instruments of music; that is, he bears them up all. And great cause to desire God, fast may it stick and never stir, this nail; for if it should, all our cups would batter with the fall, and all the music of our choir be marred; that is, both Church and country be put in danger. . . .

And, where such support has wanted, both have lain on the ground. For, both of Micah's idolatry, that is corrupt religion, and of the villany offered at Gibeah, and of the outrage committed by them of Dan, both in rifling houses, and sacking whole towns, that is, of open injustice, God renders no cause, but this, *non erat Rex*; the pillars went down, *ego* wanted. Without . . . an established government, we should have no commonwealth."[3]

***

Unless sincere religion is maintained by the ruler, justice will decline, just as it did in the time of Saul. David had to restore true worship after he succeeded Saul. Once that was restored and honoured, justice also returned.

"Joyful indeed every way, but joyful especially if this *ego* be not Saul, but David. David, who gives strength unto the pillars, and not Saul, an impairer or weakener of them. It is David's complaint; . . . he found the land weak when he came to it. So Saul had left it. It is his promise that as Saul by his slackness had brought the estate low, so he by his vigilance would raise it up again.

King David, in his oration to the states of his realm . . . [stated that] *the ark was not sought to in the days of Saul*; that pillar was not looked to. Sought to it, was after a sort, religion; but nothing so as it should. . . .

So God saw this mind in Saul to His ark and was wrath; withdrew from him His religious and good spirit, and sent upon him a profane and furious spirit, which carried him on first to a sinful life, and never left him till it had brought him to a shameful death. . . .

Now where Religion thrives not, the other of Justice will not hold long; when one staff is broken, the other holds not whole long after. . . .

Whereas, in kindly justice, the rigour of *frangam cornua* comes not at first, but clemency gives gracious warning, with *Dicam imprudentibus*. So without regard thereof, as upon any displeasure, without any word at all, [Saul's] javelin went straight to nail men to the wall, they knew not wherefore. Thus did justice decay after religion, and one pillar fall upon another, whereof ensued his overthrow, and the land dangerously sick of the palsy. Whereof David complains, and prays, *Heal the sores thereof, for it shakes*. . . .

And first, of the first that is, the stone which Saul and his builders cast aside. For coming to the kingdom, . . . consecrates all his laws with his act *de Arcâ reducendâ*. . . .

And, when [the ark] was brought back, set such an order for the service of it by the Levites, for maintenance so bountiful, so reverend for regard, so decent for order, so every way sufficient, as the care of the Temple might seem to reign in his heart. As indeed it did, and as he professes, *he could not sleep* till he had set a full order for God's matters, and brought this pillar to perfection. Which his care was *secundum cor Dei*, and God would signify so much by the ceremony in the coronation of the kings of Judah. Wherein, putting not only the diadem imperial, but the Book of the Law also, upon the king's head, it was intended that Book should be as dear to them as their crown, and they equally study to advance it. And in putting the sceptre of justice in their hands, and in laying the key of the House of David on their shoulders, what else was required, but as they executed the one with their hand, so they should put to the other, arm and shoulder and all? That is, as David here expresses it, two *celebrabimuses* to one *judicabo.*"[4]

***

In the course of justice, David pursued peace, not in a military sense, but in a civil manner for his people. Under David the land became strong, as he lived favourably in the eyes of both God and man. Andrewes concludes that these two pillars can always stand fast for our time too.

"I speak not of his military justice, . . . but . . . peace; *he executed judgment and justice to all his people. The king's power*, says he, *loves judgment*, — not power in injury, but power in judgment . . . that is, to build up, not to decay the building. . . . He professes after in this psalm, the wind should blow no man to preferment, out of what quarter soever it came, but God by His graces should point them to it. And sure, the diligent description the Holy Spirit uses of his worthies and men of place, shows him to have been most exact in this point. . . .

167

And for depressing the wicked, it was his morning work, as he testifies . . . in a most heavenly order, with *dicam* first, as being set over men, and therefore willing to *lead them with the cords of men*, that is fair and gentle, yet effectual persuasions. And never did the dew of heaven more sweetly refresh the grass, than does a favourable saying pierce the inferior from a mouth of a prince. . . . He even sweetly sang their several duties to them. To his court, his Church, his Judges, his commons, all in one. I will add this, that if David offended in ought, . . . that he used *dicam* too much and *frangam* not often enough. . . . and when David was to leave this world, it lay on his conscience, his clemency used in Joab's and Shimei's case. *A dear and precious thing is the meanest blood in the eyes of David* — so he says. And that made his people more afraid *for* him than *of* him, and to value his life at *ten thousand* of their own; and that, so many subjects, so many of his guard; not, so many subjects, so many conspirators, as Saul complained.

Yet because clemency is both one foot of the throne, and severity at some other time for time must be kept in this music does no less support it; therefore, where saying will not serve, nor singing, *frangam* must sometimes be used; where the rod condemned, let the sword be drawn. It is God's own course. . . .

Thus did David repair Saul's ruins; . . . [and] did . . . show himself . . . a skilful upholder of these two main pillars, which bear us and give strength to every land. And by this means he changed both the nature and the name of his country, finding it *Jebus*, that is, *conculcata*, and so indeed it was, a city condemned and trodden down with every foot; and leaving it a new name, Jerusalem, and so it was, *Salem Jeru*, a city to be feared and envied of all round about it. So the land grew strong, and the pillars fast, and David, for his fastening, in favour with God and man. God, Whom he praised, graciously assisting him; and men, whom he preserved, willingly serving him.

The Lord Who has sent forth the like strength for our land, establish the good things which He has wrought in us! The Lord so fasten the pillars of our earth, that they never be shaken! The Lord mightily uphold the upholder of them long, and many years; that we may go forth rejoicing in His strength, and make our boast of His praise, all our life long.''[5]

References

[1] Andrewes, Vol. 2, pp. 4–5.
[2] *ibid.*, pp. 6–8.
[3] *ibid.*, pp. 9–11.
[4] *ibid.*, pp. 11–4.
[5] *ibid.*, pp. 14–5.

LENTEN SERMON No. 2
24th February 1590
St. Matthias Day.

Text: Psalm 77:20

You did lead Your people like sheep,
by the hand of Moses.

Deduxisti sicut oves populum Tuum, in
manu Moysis et Aaron.

The theme running through this sermon is of God's leadership for His people.
This was often through His chosen vessels such as Moses and Aaron. The text
illustrates how God protects the Israelites through their turbulent experiences
as evidenced in the verses preceding this verse of psalm seventy-seven. He
led them to a haven where there were many blessings, once Moses and Aaron
had defeated their enemies.

"Some, either present or imminent danger, and that no small one, had more
than usually distressed the [psalmist] at the writing of this psalm; wherewith his
spirit, for awhile, being tossed to and fro in great anguish, as may appear by those
three great billows in the seventh, eighth, and ninth verses, yet at last he comes to
an anchor in the tenth verse, *upon the remembrance of the right hand of the Most*
High. Which right hand, in one even tenor throughout all ages, not only to that of
David's, but even to this of ours, has ever showed itself a right hand of pre-
eminence and power, . . . in the final confusion of his enemies, . . . [and] the final
deliverance of His people. . . . The last verse . . . of the deluge was the rainbow; of
the Egyptian bondage was the Feast of the Passover; . . . and . . . in this verse
ensue a calm to God's people. This is the blessed period that shuts up [this]
psalm."[1]

***

Andrewes summarizes this text as follows: God Himself, His hand, His
people, and the blessings which come from God.

"To begin with God, Who begins this verse, by Whom and to Whom we lead,
and are led, and in Whom all right leading both begins and ends. . . .
Whose names soever we hear, whose hands soever we feel, whose countenance
soever we behold, we must yet look up higher, and see God in every government.
To Him we must make our apostrophe, and say, *You lead.* . . . For He it is [who]
leads properly; and in strict propriety of speech Moses and Aaron lead not, but

God by the hands of Moses and Aaron. And that thus it is, that God is the Person who leads, and all other but hands under Him and unto Him. . . .

Your people. . . . For this people are, in the fifteenth verse before said to be *the sons of Jacob and Joseph.* . . . But . . . God's leading has no marches. This people and all people are His; and He by special prerogative is *Rex universae terrae, King* not of one people, or of one country or climate, but *of all the people of the whole earth.* . . .

By the hands. For as He guides the people by the hands, so He guides the hands themselves, by whom He guides; rules by them, and rules them; rules by their hands, and rules in their hearts; is both *the Shepherd of Israel,* leading them like sheep, and farther leads Joseph also, their leader, *like a sheep.* That is, they be *reges gentium, kings of the nations,* but He is *Rex regum, King over kings themselves.* Moses and they with him be *guides,* as St. Paul calls them; but Jesus Christ is *the Arch-guide.* Aaron and his family be *shepherds* as St. Peter terms them; but Jesus Christ is *the high and sovereign Shepherd over all.*"[2]

***

From God's leadership there are two contrasting consequences, *comfort* and *fear.*

"Of comfort, . . . from God's ruling, [a] matter of joy. For if we will be ruled by Him, He will appoint over us a ruler *according to His own heart*; He will *[direct] her with the blessings of goodness*; He will deliver the power of Sisera into her hands; *He will clothe her enemies with shame, and make her crown flourish on her head, and set the days of her life as the days of Heaven.*

Secondly, matter of fear too. *The Lord is Ruler, let the people tremble.* For if they fall to be unruly, He can . . . send them a Rehoboam without wisdom, or a Jeroboam without religion, or Ashur a stranger to be their King; or, which is worst of all, as disordered anarchy, *quia non timuimus Jehovam.* Therefore in *joy and trembling* let us acknowledge God and His supreme leading. . . . *The Lord does lead us, let the land rejoice.*"[3]

***

In every good ruler, God is clearly seen.

"Wherefore when we see that careful mind in a prince, I will uses Moses' own words, to carry a people in her arms, as if she had conceived them in her womb, as no nurse, nor mother more tender; and again, when we see this tumultuous and tempestuous body, this same sea of popularity kept in a quiet calm, and infinite millions ebbing and flowing as it were, that is, stirring and standing still, arming and disarming themselves, killing and being killed, and all at the monosyllables of one person, *Go and they go, Come and they come, Do and they do it*; let us see God sensibly in it, and the power of God, yes the miraculous power of God; and say with the prophet, You are the God Who does wonders, *You lead Your people like sheep by the hands of Moses and Aaron.*"[4]

All leadership should have a singular purpose, to lead His people into His truth and *the way of His commandments*. Under such leadership four features emerge: order, correctness, gentleness and certainty of direction.

". . . the chief of all [leadership] . . . is the leading [of] us in His heavenly truth, and in the way of His commandments, to the land of the living. . . .

And in this leading there be these four points. For that it be a leading, it must be orderly without straying, skilfully without erring, gently without forcing, and certainly without missing our journey's end. . . . It must be *sicut oves* whom the good Shepherd, in the twenty-third psalm, leads to a place, and to a place meet for them, *where there is a green pasture by the waters of comfort*. So was it in this people here. They were led out of Egypt to sacrifice to God, and to learn His law in the mount of God, Sinai; and from thence also to Sion itself, His own rest, and holy habitation. And even so our people are led from the wanderings of this world unto the folds of God's Church, where, as the prophet says in the seventy-third psalm, first God will a while guide them with His counsel, and after will receive them into His glory. And this is the end of all leading."[5]

***

God will surely lead all His people; however at the moment He can only lead them as far as to *the borders of His sanctuary*.

"But in this life here, we come no farther than *the borders of His sanctuary*, as . . . in the next psalm, in the way whereof if God lead us *constantly*, not after our wanton manner, out and in when we list, all the other inferior leadings shall accompany this one. For this leading leads them all. He shall lead our counsellors that they will advise the counsels of His own heart; He will lead our judges, that they will pronounce the judgments of His own mouth; He will lead our forces into Edom, the strong cities and holds of the enemy; He will lead our navy in the sea by unknown paths to the place it would go. . . . Through all the dread dangers of the world, through the perils of the Red Sea, through the perils of the desert, through the malice of all our enemies, He will safely lead us, and surely bring us to His promised Kingdom, where we shall see the *goodness of the Lord in the land of the living*. . . .

That all this good is for the people, worthy not so much as the least part of it."[6]

***

The Israelites were God's people whom he created and redeemed. As His people were precious to Him, God raised up leaders to protect them.

"For there is in *Tuus*, not only they be men, . . . but that they be God's own people and flock. . . . His people, *because He made them*; and so, the lot of His inheritance. His people again, because *He redeemed them* from Egypt with His mighty arm; and so His peculiar people. His people the third time, because He redeemed their souls by His sufferings; and so, a people purchased most dearly, purchased even with the invaluable high price of His most precious blood. This is that, that sets the price on them. For over such a flock, so highly prized, so dearly beloved, and so dearly bought, it may well beseem any to be a guide. Moses, with all his learning; Aaron, with all his eloquence; yes, even *kings to be their foster-fathers, and queens to be their nurses.* No leading too good for them. I conclude with St. Augustine upon these words; . . . *and trust me, it is no poor praise to protect this poor flock, but a high service it is, and will be highly rewarded.* Christ will take and reward it, as done to Himself in person.''[7]

***

Thus there is a difference between being *Your people* and simply *the people.* Unlike the latter who are driven forcibly, the former are led like sheep, that is, gently. When we submit to the Shepherd it is possible to become tame and gentle like a lamb, even though by our earthy nature we are wild and un-tamed. However those who remain wild are liable to the censure of the Church.

"First, as a note of difference between . . . . Your people, and the people. . . . Every people is not *sicut oves,* nor everyone among the people. There is a people, as the psalmist speaks, *sicut equus et mulus, like the untamed horse or mule, in whom is no understanding;* and among the people there be too many such. Surely, by nature we are all so, wild and unbroken as the ass-colt, says Job. Which wildness of nature when they are untaught, and taught to submit themselves to government; to become gentle and easy to be led *sicut oves*: led to feeding, led to shearing, to feed those that feed them; tractable of nature, and profitable of yield; it is a good degree and a great work is performed on them. For by it, . . . they become God's people. For His people are *populus sicut oves,* and they who are not His, are *populus sicut hirci, a people like he-goats,* in nature intractable, in use unserviceable.

Now, being His people, they come to have an interest in *duxisti,* the benefit. For *populus sicut oves* must be led gently; but *populus sicut hirci* must be driven forcibly. *Duxisti* is not for both; it is a privilege. And if there be any who retain their wild nature, or degenerate from sheep into goats, as [many] do daily; for them Aaron has a rod to sever them from the fold by censure of the Church. And if that will not serve, Moses has another which he can turn into a serpent and sting them; yes, if need so require, sting them to death by the power secular. For *nachah* is leading, and the sound remaining, *nacah* is smiting; and a necessary use of both. The one for Your people like sheep who will be led; the other for the strange children like goats, who will not stir a foot farther than they be forced.''[8]

***

There are times however when *His people* act just like sheep, wandering anywhere, and therefore they are in need of a shepherd. Being part of a flock has the advantage of always having the protection of a shepherd, and a sense of belonging and unity.

"But now again, when they be brought thus far to be like sheep, they are but like sheep though; that is a weak and unwise cattle, far unable to guide themselves. Which shows their need of good government, and though they be the people of God, yet that Moses and Aaron be not superfluous. For, a feeble poor beast we all know a sheep is; of little or no strength for resistance in the world, and therefore in danger to be preyed on by every wolf. And as of little strength, so little reach. None so easily strays of itself, none is so easily led awry by others. . . .

These two defects do mainly enforce the necessity of a leader. For they want sight, as blind men, and they want strength, as little children, stir not without great peril, except they have one to lead them. And both these wants are in sheep, and in the people too.

If then they *like sheep*, what is both their wisdom? Sure to be in the unity of a flock. And what is their strength? Truly to be under the conduct of a shepherd; in these two is their safety. For if either they single themselves and stray from the fold; or if they be a fold and yet want a shepherd, none more miserable than they. And indeed in the Holy Spirit's phrase it is the ordinary note of a private man's misery, to be *tanquam ovis erratica, as a stray sheep from the flock*; and of the misery of every estate politic, to be *tanquam grex absque pastore, as a flock without a shepherd*. Therefore, guiding they need — both the staff of unity, *bands* to reduce them from straying, and the staff of order; *beauty,* to lead them so reduced. And would God they would see their own feebleness and shallowness, and learn to acknowledge the absolute necessity of this benefit; in all duty receiving it, in all humility praying for the continuance of it, that God break not the fold, and smite not the shepherd for the flock's unfaithfulness!"[9]

***

Although God is the true Guide, He nevertheless chose leaders, such as Moses and Aaron, to assist in this leading of *His people*. Sometimes through them, He bestowed good things, sometimes evil things, depending what was needed for the *good* of *His people*.

"This estate of guiding being wholly invested in Him, there being but one God and one Guide, He would not keep it unto Himself alone as He might, but it pleased Him to send *Moses His servant, and Aaron whom He had chosen*, to associate them to Himself in the commission of leading. . . .

God's hands they be; for that by them He reaches unto us *duxisti*, and in it religion and counsel and justice and victory, and whatsoever else is good. *He sends His word to Moses first, and by him*, as it were through his hand, *His statutes and ordinances unto all Israel*.

And not good things only, but if they so deserve, sometimes evil also. For as, if they be virtuous, such as Moses and Aaron, they be the *good hand* of God for our benefit, such as was upon Ezra; so if they be evil, such as Balak and Balaam, they be the *heavy hand* of God for our chastisement, such as was upon Job. But the hand of God they be both. . . .

Out of which term, of *the hands of God*, the people first are taught their duty, so to esteem of them, as of God's own hands; that as God rules them by *the hands of Moses and Aaron*, that is, by their ministry, so Moses and Aaron rule them by the hands of God, that is, by His authority. It is His name they wear, it is His seat they sit in, it is the rod of God that is in Moses and Aaron's hands. If we fall down before them, it is He who is honoured; if we rise up against them, it is He who is injured; and that *peccavi in Caelum et in te*, must be our confession, *against heaven and them*, but first against heaven and God Himself, when we commit any contempt against Moses or Aaron.''[10]

***

The hands of both Moses and Aaron were necessary as they led their people in the wilderness: one for ecclesiastical and the other for civil government.

''These two, as two arms, did God appoint in the wilderness, to lead His people by. Afterwards . . . did He yet set another, even the power and authority regal, in the place of the head, as Himself terms it; and to it, as supreme, united the regiment of both. The consideration of which power I meddle not with, as being not within the compass of this verse, but only with the hands of regiments ecclesiastical and civil, which, as the two cherubim did the ark, overspread and preserve every estate. One, says Jehoshaphat, dispensing *res Jehovae, the Lord's business*, the other dealing in *negotio regis, the affairs of state*. One, says David, intending *the worship of the tribes*, the other, *the thrones for justice*. One, says St. Paul, being for us in *things pertaining to God;* the other in *matters of this present life*. . . .

Both [hands] are absolutely necessary, and a maimed and lame state it is, where either is wanting. The state of Israel, in the seventeenth of the Judges, without a civil governor proved a very mass of confusion. . . . Miserable first, if they lack Joshua, and be as *sheep wanting that shepherd*. And miserable again, if they lack Jesus, and be as *sheep wanting that Shepherd*. Moses is needful, in the want of water, to strike the rock for us, and to procure us supply of bodily relief. Aaron is no less. For he in like manner reaches to every one food of other kind, which we may worse be without, even *the Bread of life* and water out of *the spiritual Rock*, which is Christ Jesus. Moses we need, to see our force led against Amalek, for safeguard of that little we hold here in this life; and Aaron no less, to preserve our free hold in everlasting life: for . . . the legions of our sins, the very forces of the prince of darkness are overthrown by the spiritual weapons of Aaron's warfare. Moses may not be spared from sitting and deciding the causes which are brought before him. No more may Aaron, whose *urim* gives answer in doubts no less important; and who not only with his *urim* and *thummim* gives counsel, but by his incense and sacrifice obtain good success for all our counsels. In a word, if Moses' rod be requisite to sting and devour the wicked, Aaron's is also to receive the good

and to make them to fructify. . . . Moses and Aaron [made] a complete government. . . .

They be hands, and they need each other. Moses needs Aaron, for Moses' hands
are heavy and need a stay; and Aaron it is who keeps them steady, by continual
putting the people in remembrance that they be subject to principalities. . . . And
so many ways does Aaron support, and make both more easy and more steady, the
hands of Moses.

And Moses, for his part, is not behind, but a most jealous preserver of Aaron's
honour and right everywhere. Everywhere mild save in Aaron's quarrel, and with
those only who murmured against Aaron, and said he took too much upon him.
. . .

It is good therefore they be respective each to other; Aaron help Moses in his lot;
and Moses, Aaron in his; that they stand in the gap one for another; that so their
unity be hand in hand as the unity of brethren, strong and hard to break as the bars
of a palace.''[11]

***

Andrewes concludes his sermon on the leading of God's people with the
prayer that His appointed leaders will guide them to the *celestial kingdom*.

"The Lord, by Whose Almighty power all governments do stand, those especially wherein the people are led in the way of His sanctuary; as He has graciously
begun to lead us in that way, so leave us not till we have finished our course with
joy! Knit the hearts of Moses and Aaron, that they may join lovingly; teach their
hands, and fingers of their hands, that they lead skilfully; touch the hearts of the
people, that they may be led willingly; that by means of this happy conduct, surely
without error, and safely without danger, we may lead and be led forward, till we
come to the fruition of His promise, the expectation of our blessed hope, even the
eternal joys of His celestial kingdom, through Jesus Christ our Lord!''[12]

References

1 Andrewes, Vol. 2, pp. 16–7.
2 *ibid.*, pp. 18–9.
3 *ibid.*, pp. 19–20.
4 *ibid.*, pp. 21–2.
5 *ibid.*, pp. 22, 24.
6 *ibid.*, pp. 24–25.
7 *ibid.*, p. 27.
8 *ibid.*, p. 28.
9 *ibid.*, pp. 28–9.
10 *ibid.*, pp. 30–1.
11 *ibid.*, pp. 32–6.
12 *ibid.*, p. 36.

LENTEN SERMON No. 3
13th March 1593

Text: St. Mark 14: 4–6

And there were some who had indignation
within themselves, and said, Why was this
waste of the ointment made?
For it might have been sold for more than
three hundred pence, and have been given
to the poor. And they murmured against her.
And Jesus said, Let her alone, why trouble
you her? She has wrought a good work on Me.

Erant autem quidam indigne ferentes
intra semetipsos, et dicentes, Ut quid
perditio ista unguenti facta est?
Poterat enim unguentum istud vaenumdari
plus quam trecentis denariis, et dari
pauperibus. Et fremebant in eam.
Jesus autem dixit, Sinite eam, quid illi
molesti estis? Bonum opus operata est in Me.

This sermon centres around the selfless and extravagant giving of the penitent and loving Mary Magdalene for our dear Lord. Andrewes compares the
generosity of Mary, and its acceptance by Christ with the cries of *waste* and
denouncing by Judas and his counterparts ever since.

"This action of waste, which by some is brought, and by Christ traversed, was
against a woman, says St. Mark, . . . which woman, as St. John has it, was Mary
Magdalene, now a glorious saint in heaven, some time a grievous sinner upon
earth.

St. Augustine notes; of all those who sought to Christ, she was the only sinner
that for sin only, and for no bodily grief or malady at all, sued and sought to Him.
Of whom being received to grace, and obtaining a *quietus est* for her many sins, a
benefit inestimable, *et quod nemo scit nisi acceperit, which they only know and
none but they who have received it*, as much was forgiven her, so much she loved.
And seeking by all means to express, her *multam dilectionem propter multam
remissionem*, as Christ says, *her sins, which are many are forgiven*, nothing she
had was too dear. And having a precious confection or ointment of *nardus*, the
chief of all ointments, . . . and in it too not of the leaf, but of the very choice part
thereof, of the spike or flower, both for making true, and for the value costly, that
did she bestow. And that frankly, for she did not drop but pour; not a dram or two,
but a whole pound; not reserving any, but breaking box and all; and that not now
alone, but three several times, one after another.

This she did; and, as it may seem, the coherence fell out not amiss. This outward ointment and sweet odour she bestowed on Christ for the *oil of gladness,* for the *spiritual anointing* (as St. John) and the *comfortable savour of His knowledge* (as St. Paul calls it), He bestowed on her.

This, as it was well done, so was it well taken of Christ; and so should have been of all present but for Judas, says St. John. Who, liking better *odorem lucri ex re qualibet,* than any scent in the apothecary's shop, seeing that spent on Christ's head that he wished should come into his own purse, repined at it. But that so cunningly, in so good words, with so colourable a motion. 1. that it was a needless expense, indeed *a waste*; 2. that it might have been bestowed much better to the relief of many poor people; as that he drew the disciples, some of them, to favour the motion, and to dislike of Mary Magdalene and her doing. So that both they and he joined in one bill; but he of a wretched covetous mind, they of a simple plain intent and purpose, thinking all that was spoken had been well meant.''[1]

***

In condemning Mary Magdalene, they were in fact condemning our Lord who defends her loving action, and commends it as an example for others.

''Which action of theirs, for that it was brought not only against her who bestowed it, but even against Christ also who admitted it, though not so directly; as it were against her with *ut quid perditio?* against Him with *ut quid permissio?* for that also it might be a dangerous precedent in ages to come, if nothing were said to it, and shut all boxes and bar all ointments for ever; our Saviour Himself takes on Him to plead her cause. Not only excusing it in *sinite illam,* as no *waste,* but also commending it in *bonum opus,* as *a good work*; that the ointment was not so pleasant to His sense, as her thankfulness acceptable to His Spirit; that the ointment, which then filled the house with the scent, should fill the whole world with the report of it; and as far and wide as the Gospel was preached, so far and wide should this act be remembered, as well for her commendation who did it, as for our imitation that should hear of it.''[2]

***

Andrewes contrasts the reaction of Judas and Christ to Mary's devotional, although extragavant act. While Judas saw it as *waste*, Our Lord accepted it as an act of good works.

''We see both the occasion and sum of these words read, which may aptly be said to contain in them disputation or plea about Mary Magdalene's act, whether it were well done or no. Whereof there are two principal parts; Judas with some *ad appositum, against it,* to have Mary Magdalene reformed, and her box converted to better uses; Christ for it, and against them; *sinite,* that He would have it stand, yes that He would have it acknowledged, for that it was *bonum opus.*''[3]

***

177

Mary's act raises the issue of how we should use everything given to us in life, whether it be our time or possessions. *Perditio,* idle waste, of any kind is contrary to the Christian gospel.

"We begin with . . . *Ut quid perditio* etc. . . . Religion and reason, both teach us, in all things, to regard both *quid* and *ut quid*; no less to what end we do, than what we do, and both of them censure not only what is done to an evil end wickedly, but what is done to no end vainly. *Quem fructum, What fruit,* says St. Paul, a good question; and if it have none, *ut quid terram occupat, why troubles it the ground?* says Christ. So that religion allows not waste, censures idleness, and in all things calls us to our *ut quid haec?*

And this as in all things, in waste of time, waste words, addle questions, so yet chiefly in [what] we call *bonum utile*. The very goodness of which things is in their use, and they no longer good than they have a use, which if they lose they cease to be good. So that in them not only those things that are misspent upon wicked uses, but even those also that idly spent to no use, they are lost, lavished, and no good comes of them. And therefore in them, *ut quid perditio* indeed? is well said. This they learned of Christ Himself, Who, in the gathering of the broken meat, gave charge, *ut ne quid perdatur, that no waste should be made.* Indeed, *ut quid perditio ulla, whereto either this or any waste at all?* So that religion is an enemy to riot, and good husbandry is good divinity.

It is God's will, that of our goods *justitia condus sit, justice should be [the] purveyor,* and they rightly gotten; *temperantia promus, temperance the steward,* and they not wastefully spent. Consequently neither waste in buying . . . [nor] in spending . . . [nor] in giving. . . . The reason whereof is well set down; that, if we waste it in needless expenses, we shall not have enough for necessary charges; if we lavish out in wasting, we shall leave but little for well-doing. . . . But this riotous misspending, where no need is, has eaten up our Christian bestowing where need is. Less waste we must have, if we will have more good works. It is truly called *perditio*; it is the loss and destruction of all our good deeds, and I pray God it be not also of our reward for them."[4]

***

If Judas' intention had been honourable, there would have been great merit in wanting to give to the poor because this is the endearing gift of all charity.

"Now follows Judas' plot, the use he wishes it put to . . . [is] sale to be made, the money to be divided, and the poor to be relieved. This is his supplication, and this second is better than the former. . . . In that he speaks not to have it spared, but to have it converted to better uses. And this is a blessed conjunction, when honest sparing and charitable relieving, when frugality and liberality go together. Such is this motion, whereto no man can take exception. Naturally our [hearts] yearn, and we have an inward compassion at the misery of our brethren; and God's law wills not to hide ourselves from our own flesh, but when we have served our need, to give to the poor.

The motion then is both frugal and charitable; and besides, if we look more narrowly into it, there appears great zeal in it. All waste things he wishes the poor had. Yes, it seems he reckons it waste that the poor is not the better for; that to be misspent that might be better spent, and is not. And very exactly drives to this point; that our goods may go, not to some end, not to some good end, but to the very best end of all, the relief of the poor. Sure, when I consider the sobriety, bounty, zeal of the speech, I think many wise heads could not in so few words have contrived a better or more pithy motion; than that which is otherwise lavished upon one may be employed to the benefit of many; that these so many hundreds may be bestowed rather in nourishment, than in ointment; rather on necessary relief, than upon needless delight; rather on a continual good, than on a transistory smell; rather that many hungry bellies filled, than that one head anointed. Sure, howsoever it was meant or applied, the speech, in itself considered, is to very good purpose; even Judas' speech, without Judas' application."5

***

Andrewes relates Judas' attitude towards Mary Magdalene with those who complain about money spent on Christ's body, the Church.

"Judas, it was well known what he was. . . . The case is like, when they who have wasted many pounds complain of that penny waste which is done on Christ's body, the Church; or, when they who in all their whole dealings, all the world sees, are unreformed, seriously consult how to reform the Church. When they who do no good with their own, devise what good may be done with Mary Magdalene's; they who have spent and sold and consumed themselves, and never in their whole lives showed any regard of the poor; when they talk of charitable uses. *O dolor!* says Augustine; . . . *Ut quid perditio*? does but evil fit their mouths. God help us, when Judas must reform Mary Magdalene!"6

***

Judas' disenchantment was echoed by some of Christ's other disciples. Similarly John's disciples questioned the feasting and drinking of Christ's followers, just as some today question the Church's authority.

". . . [many] well-disposed and of the better sort of Christ's disciples join with him, and take part against Mary Magdalene. [They] rather carried with the speech than heeding the speaker, were drawn into the society of the same repining. And this sure is *scandalum magnum*, when evil counsel meets with easy relief, and subtilty finds credulity. When the pharisees can persuade John's disciples to muster with them and say, *Why do we and John's disciples fast?* . . . When Judas can say, Why do I, and Christ's own disciples reprove this? So it is with us; not to see *homines perditos queri de perditione, them speak of waste who have wasted themselves.* . . . Pretences; [what] was able to deceive Christ's disciples, deceives them too. And this is the difference; that the disciples in a good meaning went with him, because they saw he said well; but Judas, upon a greedy covetous mind, to

179

have his own turn served. For, *cui bono*? if it had come to the poor, who should have had the distribution? It was his office; so that it may be he spoke for himself, which did plainly appear by the issue. For upon better information given by Christ, the disciples were answered and remained content. But Judas grew enraged and fell from evil to worse, from covetous to malice, from sacrilege to treason; even to this dangerous resolution, *vendere naredum*, or, if not, *vendere Christum*, and to subvert Him Whom he might not spoil. For all the world, as some in our time who sought help of authority, while they had hope that way to prevail; but when that came not, since begin to hold they will and may do it without stay for authority, and seek subvert the state they cannot form to their fancy. My hope is and so is my prayer, that those who have hitherto been carried with their plots and pretences, now they be informed and see what the truth is, may do as the disciples, leave Judas in his murmuring, and let Mary Magdalene be quiet.''[7]

***

From the disciples' example we should learn to be wary of *oiled speeches* and any kind of pretence like that of Judas, and to learn from them.

''From the disciples' too easy belief we learn *credit omni verbo,* not to trust phrases and oiled speeches too fast; never by the list to conclude of the cloth. . . . But if we hear much ado about *ut quid perditio*, to stay and think. May not this be Judas who speaks now as once it was? And if it be, to suspect when he speaks well. Of this assuring ourselves, what St. Paul tells us of sadly, that not only Mary Magdalene will be reformed, and her ointment maligned, and the poor opposed, but even Christ Himself preached, *obtentu, under pretence*. Therefore it stands us in hand to look to the disposition as well as the position; and not to run headlong to say straight *ut quid* as fast as they. . . .

And indeed all we learn . . . is *novisse et odisse,* to *know and avoid*. To know such there be as cover sacrilege with zeal, and with good uses cover no good intents. To know them and avoid them. And the better to do that, to make the end of him who here used it, and see what became of him; how from this sin, by God's just judgment, he fell to *perditio*; and from it, after to make away himself. To whom in that case truly might have been said, *ut quid perditio* indeed.''[8]

***

Our Lord's response to Judas' questioning of Mary's anointing was full of tenderness and appreciation. *Let her alone*; what she is doing is a *good work*; she is doing it for Me, says Jesus. However as Andrewes indicates, Mary has never been left alone, as even to-day her very act of love and giving is criticized. Yet it is her selfless and complete giving that we must imitate rather than the greed of Judas or that of Ananias in the early Church.

''Wherein He [i.e. Christ] keeps this order; . . . she not to be troubled for it; . . . it was a good work; and therefore she not only to be excused, but to be commended for it; . . . [and] the reason and warrant of both, *in Me* for that it was done upon

180

Him, on whom nothing that is bestowed can be said to be lost, but must and ought to be said to be well bestowed. . . .

Such acts as this was, are to be let alone, and they who so disposed, not to be troubled. Sure He foresaw many would be meddling, many *ut quids* would be framed, and many *potuits* devised, and much business be made, about Mary Magdalene's ointment, and about works of that nature; that every otherwhile, some motions, petitions, plots would be framed about altering of it. To this day they will not let her alone, but disquiet her still. He has therefore left in His gospel these words, as a fit answer, to stay their hands, and stop their mouths, for ever. *Sinite illam, Let them be, suffer them to remain.* . . .

And this request, to my poor conceit, is very reasonable: . . . It is not *imitamini illam,* or *adjuvate illam; do you the like contribute to her charge,* further and help her what you may; which yet He would have us. . . . Yet hinder her not, trouble her not. That she has spent, of her ability she has done it; she has not had of you one penny toward her three hundred, nor she asks you none. Seeing you are at no cost, why should it grieve you? If you like not to follow her, yet let her alone. . . .

You must let it alone, says Christ, it is *bonum opus.* . . . This He pleads is not any [waste], unless, which God forbid, good works be waste with us. And therefore joins issue upon the word *haec*; that is, that is done upon Him is no waste at all, as Judas termed it; but, as He christens it by a new name, *bonum opus.* . . .

Indeed, if Judas sometime before had said it to Mary Magdalene, in the days of her former vanity, when she wasted thus much, and peradventure many a penny more, on her riot and wantonness; then indeed, *ut quid perditio haec?* had hit right. But now it was not on herself, but on Christ's head, it is out of season. . . .

Thus, you see, Judas is answered, and the work quit from the name of *perditio.* So far from *perditio,* that it is *bonum opus.* A *good work,* indeed; as proceeding from a good mind, posessed with the virtue of virtue, thankfulness. For mercy bestowed on Him, Who only is good and goodness itself; Who here allows it for good, causes it to be registered in His Gospels for good, in the day of judgment will pronounce it good; rewards it for good in this world, with a good name; in that to come, with all the good of His kingdom, where no good is wanting.

The third remains, *upon Me* wherein properly is meant His natural body of flesh, which should not always be with us. But they of whom we have learned to interpret the Scriptures, in a manner all extend it to His mystical Body too; and, as they think, by good consequence. That seeing He gave His natural Body to be bought and sold, rent and torn, crucified and slain for His Body mystical; His Body mystical is certainly dearer to Him, and better He loved it. And then, if He will accept that is done to the less, and make it *bonum opus;* He will much more [what] is done to the more beloved; and it will never go for less, never did I am sure. The Scriptures record, as a good work, [what] was laid down at the *Apostles' feet,* no less than this that was laid upon Christ's own head; and in them, Ananias, a Church robber, and Judas a Christ robber, . . . [an] evil end came to both; and both are good remembrances for them who seek and say as they did."9

***

Although giving to the poor is highly commended, it does not take priority over giving to Christ first. (Andrewes does not seem to stress that by giving to the poor, we also give to Christ.) Our duty is to follow His commendation, rather than Judas' request. After all, every gift we give Him comes from Him, and we are simply returning what is His to Him. How can we not give when He has given so much, even His precious blood?

"*Pauperibus* is not the only good work; . . . He certainly to be served first. To which work, not only those of wealth, Mary Magdalene with her three hundred pence; but even poor and all, the poor widow with her mites is bound, . . . even to add something to the offerings of God; and if not *nardus*, yet with oil to anoint His head, as Himself requires. . . .

Secondly, by *in Me* it plainly appears, how Christ stands affected to works of this kind. For permitting them, standing for them, defending and commending them, He shows plainly, He will be content with such as it is. . . . He [is] the very pattern of true frugality, and an enemy to all excess, yet this service, chargeable as it was, He well allows of. . . .

It is Christ Jesus, Who has not spared to anoint us with His own blood, and our souls with all the comforts and graces of His Holy Spirit. If towards us neither blood nor life were too dear on His part, shall on ours any *nardus* be too dear, or any cost too much, that is on Him bestowed? . . .

It is Christ who created for us nard and all other delights whatsoever, either for use and necessity we have; or for fruition and pleasure we enjoy. It is He who has enriched us that we be able to bestow it, by this long prosperity, plenty and peace, as no other kingdom under heaven."[10]

***

Andrewes pleads that we follow the example of Mary Magdalene even though, like Mary experienced, we may be misunderstood, ridiculed and even maligned for our good works. It is Mary and not Judas who, wherever the Gospel is preached, will be well spoken of, and will be *refreshed with the sweet joys of heaven*. Providing we are not dismayed, and do as Mary did, this will be our joy too.

"But I trust we shall stand to Christ's judgment, and rather take part with Him for Mary Magdalene, than with Judas against her; that we may be with Mary Magdalene, that are of her mind, which at the hour of death we all shall desire. . . .

From this unhappy conjunction of Mary's good work and Judas' evil speech, this first consideration offers itself, nothing pleasant, but wholesome and requisite to be called to mind of all that mean to do well. That things well done will be evil taken, and often good affections have no good constructions, and that received with the left hand that is reached with the right.

For this her act that was well done, if Christ knew what it was to do well, yet we see it is disdained, grudged at, and she molested for it. . . . Be a thing done to never so good purpose, yet some Judas will mutter and malign, and come forth with his *ut quid?* Some Judas will cast his dead fly into Mary Magdalene's box of ointment.

No one creature had so good experience of this as this poor woman had. Three special virtues of hers the Gospel records, and in every one of the three she was repined at. 1. When, in the bitterness of her soul she showed her repentance with tears, Simon the Pharisee did what he could to disgrace her. 2. When, in a hungry desire to receive comfort by the word of grace, she showed her devotion in sitting at Christ's feet, Martha, her own sister, made complaint of her. 3. And now here again the third time; when, in an honest regard of her duty she shows her thankfulness for comfort received, Christ's own disciples both grudge and speak against her. So that, if she washes His feet with tears, it contents not; if she anoint His head with balm, it is matter of mislike; if she sit still and say nothing, it is all one; still Mary is found fault with, ever her doings stand awry.

This is the lot and portion of all those who will follow their steps. . . . Whereby many times [what] is commended in heaven is condemned in earth, and Judas' bag carries away even from Christ's. Whereby many times all good is said of them by whom little good is done. . . . Such is the deceitfulness of the sons of men. . . . It serves us, I say, to see and to sorrow at, . . . and to prepare ourselves to it, and resolve that though we do well, yet we shall be evil spoken of. . . .

Though we be evil spoken of, yet not to be dismayed or troubled with this hard measure, but to go one and do as Mary Magdalene did: not once, or twice, but three . . . times, one after another; neither to hold our hand or shut our box, nor spare our ointment, if things well done be evil taken. To look not to Judas on earth, who disliked, but to Christ in heaven who approves it, and in all three cases made an answer for Mary Magdalene, against Martha, Simon and Judas, and all her accusers. To know that [what] in Judas' divinity is *perditio*, in Christ's divinity is *bonum opus*. In regard therefore of our own duty, to be resolute with the apostle [Paul], *Quod facio hoc et faciam, What I do, that I will do*. . . . Assuring ourselves, that it is well done; and will be commended on earth and rewarded in heaven. On earth; for posterity will better like of the shedding, than of the sale of this ointment. In heaven; for the day will come, *qui male judicata rejudicabit, when all perverse judgments will have judgment against them;* and Mary Magdalene will look cheerfully on Him on Whom she bestowed it, and Judas ruefully behold Him from Whom he sold it.

This is Mary Magdalene's part, as Christ tells; that howsoever Mary Magdalene be, in Simon's house, or in a corner, found fault with, amends will be made her; and as wide as the world is, and as far as the Gospel will sound, *she will be well spoken of*. Yes, when the great and glorious acts of many monarchs will be buried in silence, this poor box of *nardus* will be matter of praise, and never die. And contrary, howsoever Judas' motion may find favour and applause in the present, yet posterity will dislike and discommend it; and he be no less infamous and hateful, than Mary famous and well spoken of, in all ages to the end of the world.

This is her portion from Christ; her soul refreshed with the sweet joys of heaven, and her name as *nardus* throughout all generations. This is [Judas'] lot from the Lord; a name odious and loathsome to all who hear it, and his *portion with hypocrites*, in the lake of fire and brimstone.''[11]

References

[1] Andrewes, Vol. 2, pp. 37–8.
[2] *ibid.*, pp. 38–9.
[3] *ibid.*, p. 39.
[4] *ibid.*, pp. 40–1.
[5] *ibid.*, pp. 41–2
[6] *ibid.*, p. 43.
[7] *ibid.*, p. 44.
[8] *ibid.*, pp. 45, 47–8.
[9] *ibid.*, pp. 48–52.
[10] *ibid.*, pp. 53–5.
[11] *ibid.*, pp. 57–60.

LENTEN SERMON No. 4
6th March 1594

Text: St. Luke 17:32

Remember Lot's wife.

Memores estote uxoris Lot.

Lot's wife is the example of a *relapsing righteous person*, and an example to us of the necessity for perseverance unto the end. Our Lord used her looking back to show that it was possible for those who have received grace to fall from it, even in the last hours of their life. We must keep our hand to the plough and not look back ever.

"The sentence is our Saviour's. . . . Before in verse 18, He had said that *the days of the Son of Man should be as the days of Lot*, in two respects: . . . of the suddenness of the destruction that should come; [and] . . . of the security of the people on whom it should come. . . .
There are in Lot's story two very notable monuments of God's judgment. The lake of Sodom and Lot's wife's pillar. The one, for punishment of resolute sin; the other of faint virtue. For the Sodomites are an example of impenitent wilful sinners; and Lot's wife of imperseverant and relapsing righteous persons. . . .
To the first in state of sin, Moses propounds *the vine of Sodom and grapes of Gomorrah, quae contacta cinerescunt, that if you but touch them turn to ashes*. To the other in state of grace, Christ here, Lot's wife's pillar. . . . So that, . . . Lot's wife be our example, and we that sprinkle ourselves with the salt of her pillar, *ne putrescamus*, that we turn not again to folly, or fall away from our steadfastness."[1]

***

Not to persevere is nothing new as there are many examples of it from both the Old and New Testaments. Perseverance is essential to reach heaven.

"Needful then for religion, to call on this virtue; and as for religion to call on, so for our nature to be called on. Wherein there is *tenellum quid, a tender part* not able to endure the cross, for which we need the virtue of patience; so is there also *a flitting humour*, not able to endure the tediousness of anything long; for which we no less need the virtue of perseverance. The psalmist, in the seventy-eighth psalm, says, our nature is as a bow, which, when it is bent to his full, except it be followed hard till it be sure and fast, starts back again, and is as far off as ever it was. [St. Paul] compares it to flesh, as it is, which will *sine sale putrescere*, and if it be not corned, of itself brings forth corruption. And to help this our evil inclination forward, there be in all ages dangerous examples to draw us on. The Israelites, after they had passed the Red Sea and all the perils of the desert, and were now come even to the borders of Canaan, even there say, *Bene nobis erat in Aegypto, We were better in Egypt*; *let us make a captain and return thither*. The Romans, in the New, as the first so glorious professors that St. Paul says, *All the world spoke of their faith*, after, when trouble arose, and St. Paul was called *coram*, of the same Romans he says, *Nemo mihi adfuit, sed omnes deseruerunt, None stood by me, all shrunk away*.

. . . The wavering and amaze of others who stand in the plain with Lot's wife, looking about, and cannot tell whether to go forward to little Zoar or back again to the ease of Sodom; show plainly that Lot's wife is forgotten, and this is a needful *memento, Remember Lot's wife.''* [2]

***

Lot's wife's sin resulted from her looking *back*, and her punishment was being turned into a salt pillar. Her sins of disobedience as well as those of inconstancy and clinging to her earthly possessions are sober reminders to us on our earthly pilgrimage.

''. . . concerning this unfortunate woman we find . . . in the nineteenth verse of Genesis, what she did; *that she drew back, or looked back*; this was her sin. The effect, that she was turned into a salt stone; this was her punishment. And these two are the two memoranda concerning her to be remembered. First of her fault.

The angel had given charge to Lot and his company, in the seventeenth of that chapter, *Escape for your life, stay not in the plain, look not once behind you lest you perish. Escape with your life*. She trifled for all that as if no peril were. *Stay not on the plain*, yet stayed she behind. *Look not back less you die*. She would and did look back, to die for it. So that she did all that she was forbidden, and regarded none of the angel's words, but despised the counsel of God against her own soul. This was her sin, the sin of disobedience, but consists of sundry degrees by which she fell, needful all to be remembered.

1. The first was that she did not *severe custodire mandatum Dei, strictly keep her to the angel's charge*, but dallied with it and regarded it by halves; that is, say what he would, she might use the matter as she would; go, or stay and look about as she list. Such light regard is like enough to have grown of a wandering distrust; lest happly, she had left Sodom in vain, and the angel feared them with [what] should never be. The sun rose so clear and it was so goodly a morning, she repented she came away. Reckoning her sons-in-law more wise in staying still, than Lot and herself in so unwisely departing. Which is the sin of unbelief, the bane both of constancy and perseverance. Constancy in the purpose of our mind, and perseverance in the tenor of our life.

2. From this grew the second. That she began to tire and draw behind, and kept not pace with Lot and the angels. An evil sign. For ever fainting is next step to forsaking. . . .

3. This tiring, had it grown of weakness or weariness or want of breath, might have been borne with; but it came of another cause, which is the third degree. It was, says the text, at least to look back, and to cast her eye to the place her soul

longed after. Which shows, that the love of Sodom sticked in her still; that though her feet were come from thence, her heart stayed there behind; and that in look and thought she returned thither, whither in body she might not. . . .

4. Looking back might proceed of [many] causes, so might this of hers, but that Christ's application directs us. The verse before says, *Somewhat in the house*; something left behind affected her, of which He gives us warning. She grew weary of trouble, and of shifting so often. From Ur to Haran; thence, to Canaan; thence to Egypt; thence to Canaan again; then to Sodom, and now to Zoar; and that, in her old days, when she would [willingly] have been at rest. Therefore, in this wearisome conceit of new trouble now to begin, and withal remembering the convenient seat she had in Sodom, she even desired to die by her flesh-pots, and to be buried in the *graves of lusts*; wished them at Zoar that would, and herself at Sodom again, desiring rather to end her life with ease in that stately city, than to remove, and be safe perhaps, and perhaps not in the desolate mountains. And this was the sin of restlessness of soul, which affected her eyes and knees, and was the cause of all the former. When men weary of a good cause which long they have holden, for a little ease or wealth, or . . . what other secular respect, fall away in the end; so losing the praise and fruit of their former perseverance, and relapsing into the danger and destruction from which they had so near escaped.''[3]

***

Lot's wife's perishing is a clear reminder that we can never be secure that we shall not fall from grace. We may be a Christian for what seems all our lives, and at the last fail in our faithfulness. That was the sad thing about Lot's wife as for over thirty years she had been faithful. Yet she chose to turn her back on God's mercy at the last — a sober reminder indeed.

''. . . this woman had continued now thirty years, for so they reckon from Abraham's going out of Ur to the destruction of Sodom. This, this is the grief, that she should persist all this time, and after all this time fall away. The rather, if we consider yet further, that not only she continued many years, but sustained many things in her continuance, as being companion of Abraham and Lot in their exile, their travel, and all their affliction. This is the grief, that after all these storms in the broad sea well passed, she should in this pitiful manner be wrecked in the haven. And when she had been in Egypt, and not poisoned with the superstitions of Egypt; when lived in Sodom, and not defiled with the sins of Sodom; not fallen away for the famine of Canaan, nor taken harm by the fullness of the city of the plain; after all this, she would lose the fruit of all this, and do and suffer so many things all in vain ; this is the first. Remember it.

The second is no [less] inferior; that at that instant she woefully perished, when God's special favour was proffered to preserve her; and that when of all other times she had means and cause to stand, then of all other times she fell away. Many were the mercies she found and felt at God's hands by this very title, that she was Lot's wife. For by it she was incorporated into the house and family, and made partaker of the blessings of the faithful Abraham. It was a mercy to be delivered from the errors of Ur; a mercy, to be kept safe in Egypt; a mercy, to be preserved

187

from the sin of Sodom; a mercy, to be delivered from the captivity of the five kings; and this the last and greatest mercy, that she was sought to be delivered from the perishing of the five cities. This no doubt does mightily aggravate the offence, that so many ways before remembered by God in trouble, she so coldly remembered Him; and that now presently, being offered grace, she knows not the day of her visitation; but being brought out of Sodom, and warned of the danger that might ensue, having the angels to go before her, Lot to bear her company, her daughters to attend her, and being now at the entrance of Zoar, the haven of her rest; this very time, place, and presence, she makes choice of to perish in, and to cast away [what] God would have saved; in respect of herself, desperately; of the angels, contemptuously; of her husband and daughters, scandalously; of God and His favours, unthankfully; forsaking her own mercy, and perishing in the sin of wilful defection. . . .

This relapse in this manner, that the world might know it to be a sin highly displeasing His majesty, God has not only marked it for a sin, but salted it too, that it might never be forgotten.''[4]

**

The salt of pillar was erected to remind us of God's punishment for sin, yet its very saltiness should have a savoury effect upon us, so that we do not fall as this poor woman did. Its main savour is perseverance, and not succumbing to a false sense of security.

"Now this pillar was erected, and this verdure given it, for our sakes. For, among the ways that the wisdom of God uses to dispose of the sin of man, and out of evil to draw good, this is one and a chief one, that He suffers not their evil examples to vanish as a shadow, but makes them to stand as pillars for ages to come, with the heathen man's inscription, *Look on me, and learn by me* to serve God better.

And an high benefit it is for us, that He not only embalms the memory of the just for our imitation, but also powders and makes brine of the evil for our admonition; that as a scent from Mary Magdalene's ointment, so a relish from Lot's wife's pillar, should remain to all posterity. . . .

This woman, in her inconstancy, could He have sunk into the earth, or blown up as saltpetre, that no remembrance should have remained of her. He does not, but for us and for our sakes He erects a pillar: and not a pillar only to point and gaze at, but a *pillar or rock of salt*, whence we may and must fetch wherewith to season whatsoever is unsavoury in our lives. . . . For sure, though Lot's wife was evil, her salt is good. Let us see then how to make her evil our good; see if we can draw any savoury thing from this example.

1. [What] we should draw out, is perseverance, . . . as Gregory calls it, *the preserver of virtues,* without which, as summer fruits, they will perish and putrify; the salt of the covenant, without which the flesh of our sacrifice will take wind and corrupt. . . .

2. Now perseverance we shall attain, if we can possess our souls with due care, and rid them of security. Of Lot's wife's security, as of water, was this salt here

made. And if security, as water, do but touch it, it melts away presently. But care will make us fix our eye, and gather up our feet, and forgetting [what] is behind, *tendere in anteriora, to follow hard towards the prize of our high calling.*

3. And to avoid security, and to breed in us due care, St. Bernard says, Fear will do it. *Vis in timore securus esse? securitatem time; the only way to be secure in fear, is to fear security.*"[5]

***

The only hope for eternal bliss for the just is to persevere right to the end. Andrewes lists ways of doing this so we can avoid Lot's wife's sin, and learn from her example.

"... what her case was these four ways, and what ours may be who are no better than she was, will search us like salt, and teach us, that as, if we remember what we have been, we may, says St. Bernard, *erubescere*; so, if we remember what we may be, we may *contremiscere;* that we see our beginnings, but see not our ending; we see our *stadium,* not our *dolichum.* And that, as we have great need to pray with the psalmist, *You have taught me from my youth up until now — forsake me not in my old age, now when I am grey-headed;* so we had need stir up our care of continuing, seeing we see it is nothing to begin except we continue; nor to continue, except we do it to the end.

Remember, we make not light account of the angel's *serva animam tuam*; blessing ourselves in our hearts, and saying, *non fiet tibi hoc*; we shall come safe, go we never so soft, Zoar will not run away.

Remember, we be not weary to go whither God would have us — not to Zoar, though a little one, if our soul may there live; and never buy the ease of our body, with the hazard of our soul, or a few days of vanity with the loss of eternity.

Remember, we slack not our pace, nor stand still on the plain. For if we stand still, by still standing we are meet to be made a pillar, even to stand still, and never to remove.

Remember, we look not back, either with her on the vain delights of Sodom left; or with St. Peter or St. John behind us, to say, *Domine, Quid iste?* both will make us forget our calling. . . .

But specially remember we leave not our heart behind us, but that we take that with us, when we go out of Sodom; for if that stay, it will stay the feet, and writhe the eye, and neither the one or the other will do their duty. Remember, that our heart wander not, that our heart long not. This care, if it be fervent, will bring us perseverance."[6]

***

Her punishment should act as a deterrent for us and to encourage us even more to the eternal cost of hesitating.

"Now, that we may the better learn somewhat out of her punishment too; let us also, that as to her, so to us, God may send some unusual visitation, and take us suddenly away, and in the act of sin too.

Remember the danger and damage; it is no less matter we are about, than *perdet animam*. Which if we do, we frustrate and forfeit all the fruit of our former well-continued course; all we have done is vain. Yes, all that Christ has done for us is in vain; Whose pains and sufferings we ought specially to tender, knowing that *supra omnem laborem labor irritus, no labour to lost labour*; and Christ then has lost His labour for us.

Remember the folly; that *beginning in the Spirit* we *end in the flesh*; turning our backs to Zoar, we turn our face to Sodom. . . .

Remember the disgrace; that we shall lose our credit and account while we live, and shall hear that of Christ, *Hic homo*, and that other, *Quid existis in desertum videre? A reed shaken with the wind*.

Remember the scandal; that, falling ourselves, we shall be a block for to make others full; a sin no lighter, no less, nor lighter than a mill-stone.

Remember the infamy; that we shall leave our memory remaining in stories, among Lot's wife, and Job's wife, Demas and Ecebolius, and the number of relapsed, there to stand to be pointed at, no less than this heap of salt.

Remember the judgment that is upon them after their relapse, though they live that they do even with her here *obrigescere, wax hard and numb*, and serve others for a *caveat*, wholly unprofitable for themselves.

Remember the difficulty of reclaiming to good; *seven evil spirits* entering instead of one, that their *last state is worse than the first*.

And lastly, remember that we shall justify Sodom by so doing, and her frozen sin shall condemn our melting virtue. For they in the wilfulness of their wickedness persisted till fire from heaven consumed them; and they being thus obdurate in sin ought not she, and we much more, to be constant in virtue? . . .

Each of these by itself, all these put together will make a full *memento*, which if she had remembered, she had been a pillar of light in heaven, not of salt on earth. It is too late for her; we in due time yet may remember it."[7]

***

As we remember the ways to avoid making the same mistake of Lot's wife, so we must also remember Christ's teaching and follow Him who makes our eternal bliss possible.

"And when we have remembered these, remember Christ too that gave the *memento*; that He calls Himself *Alpha and Omega*, not only *Alpha* for His happy beginning, but *Omega* for His thrice happy ending. For that He left us not, nor gave over the work of our redemption, till He brought it to *consummatum est*. And that on our part, *summa religionis est imitari Quem colis, the highest act of religion, is for the Christian to conform himself, not to Lot's wife, but to Christ, Whose name he wears*. And though *versus amor non sumit vires de spe, true love indeed receives no manner strength from hope,* but, though it hope for nothing, loves nevertheless; yet to quicken our love, which often is but faint, and for a full

190

memento, remember the reward. Remember how Christ will remember us for it; . . . eternity itself, never to expire, end, or determine, but to last and endure for ever and ever. . . .

Yet it is not needless, but right requisite, that we who are the Lord's re-membrancers put you in mind, that as perseverance is the queen of virtues, *quia ea sola coronatur*; so is it also, *quia Satanas ei soli insidiatur, for that all Satan's malice, and all his practices are against it.* The more careful need we to be, to carry in our eye this example, which God grant we may, and that our hearts may seriously regard, and our memories carefully keep it, *Ut haec columna fulciat nos, et hic sal conduit nos, that this pillar may prop our weakness, and this salt season our sacrifice*, that it may remembered, and accepted, and rewarded in the day of the Lord!'"[8]

References

[1] Andrewes, Vol. 2, *ibid.*, pp. 61–2.
[2] *ibid.*, pp. 63–4.
[3] *ibid.*, pp. 66–8.
[4] *ibid.*, pp. 68–70.
[5] *ibid.*, pp. 71–2.
[6] *ibid.*, pp. 73–4.
[7] *ibid.*, pp. 74–5.
[8] *ibid.*, pp. 75–7.

LENTEN SERMON No. 5
5th March 1596

Text: St. Luke 16:25

Son, remember that you in your life-time
received your good things, and likewise
Lazarus evil things; but now he is comforted,
and you are tormented.

*Fili, recordare quia recepisti bona in vita
tua, et Lazarus similiter mala: nunc autem
hic consolatur, tu vero cruciaris.*

The key words in the text are the opening ones, *Son, remember*. Abraham's message is a very sobering one because it warns us, who have been given much, that we must remember we have a duty by it, and share our goods with the poor and less affluent. If not, we also shall face everlasting torment.

"Thus Scripture has the name given it in the very first words; *Recordare fili, Son, remember*; it is a remembrance.

There be many sermons of remembrance here on earth; this is one from heaven, from the mouth of Abraham. . . .

That it is such a remembrance, that it touches our estate in everlasting life; that is, the well or evil hearing of this *recordare* is as much as our eternal life is worth. For we find both in it. That our comfort or torment eternal — comfort in Abraham's bosom, torment in the fire of hell — depends upon it; and therefore as much as we regard them, we are to regard it. . . .

To Abraham's sons then, and every one. But specially such of his sons as presently are in the state that this son here sometimes was, of whom it is said, *He had received good things in his life*. By virtue whereof, I find, this *recordare* little, I will not say how little, but sure too little for that we have received. . . .

For we all have received, yet not all our case alike, but of some more than other. For, some have received in far more plentiful manner than other some, and they therefore more deeply interested in it. And look, who among us have received most, then it most concerns; and they of all other most need to look to it.

If you ask, why they more than others? For that, besides the duty, to whom a great *recepisti* is given, of them a great *recordare* will be required. The danger also helps them forward. For so it often happens unhappily; that whereas *recepisti* is made, and so may well be, a motive for us to remember; so cross is our nature, none is so great an enemy to *recordare* as it. Our great receiving is often occasion of our little remembering. And as a full diet in the vessels of our body, so a plenteous receipt breeds stoppings in the mind and memory, and the vital parts of our soul."[1]

***

We should take heed and be thankful that our Lord has revealed to us the fate of the rich man after his maltreatment and neglect of Lazarus. Thus Christ with Abraham, Dives himself, all forewarn us about the torments of hell.

"Our Saviour Christ unlocks hell-gates to let us see it. In discoverings what sighs and what sufferings are in the other world, He shows us one lying in them, to whom Abraham objects, that this frank receiving had marred his memory. And as he shows us his fault, so . . . what came to him for it, in that strange and fearful consequent; *Now therefore you are tormented.* . . .

It is His intent in reporting of it, that our remembering of it should keep us from it. *Non vult mortem, et minatur mortem ne mittat in mortem,* says Chrysostom. *He would not have us in that place, yet He tells us of that place, to the end we never come in that place.*

Yes, it is Abraham's desire too we should not be overtaken, but think of in time; and prevent it before it prevents us. And therefore he lifts up his voice, and cries out of Heaven, *Recordare fili.*

And not only Abraham, but he who was in the place itself, and best knew the terror because he felt it — felt that in it as he heartily wishes and instantly sues that they whom he loves or any wishes well to, may some way take warning. *Ne et ipsi veniant, That they also come not into that place of torment.*

This use Christ on earth, Abraham from heaven, and he out of hell, wish we may have of it. And we, I trust, will wish ourselves no worse than they; and therefore look to our *recordare,* carry it in mind, and (in *recordare* there is *cor* too) take it to heart, and by both in time take order, *Ne et ipsi veniamus.*"[2]

***

Andrewes suggests that the two sections of the verse, meeting *at the middle word, now therefore,* form a cross with all its implication. Such a cross should be an effectual reminder to us of our duty to share our possessions with the less fortunate.

"The verse itself, if we mark it well, is in figure and proportion an exact cross. For as a cross it consists of two bars or beams so situated, as the one does quarter the other. *You received good things, and Lazarus received evil.* The two lie clean contrary, but meet both at the middle word, *Now therefore*; and there, by a new antithesis, cross each other. . . . And to make it a perfect cross, it has a title or inscription to set over it; and this it is, *Recordare fili.* And sure next to the cross of Christ, and the memory thereof, this cross of Abraham's invention and exaltation is of all others most effectual. And I verily persuade myself, it we often would fix it before our eyes, and well mark the inscription, it would be a special preparation to our passover, meaning by our passover our end, whereby pass we must [before] long into another state, either of misery or bliss; but whether of misery or bliss, it will lie much in the use of this word *recordare.* . . .

193

To quarter out this cross. Two parts it stands of, which two parts are two estates. One past, the other present; the one in memory, the other in experience. Now both memory and experience — memory of things past, and experience of things present — are both handmaids to providence, and serve to provide for things to come. And of all points of providence, for that which is the highest point of all, that our memory of it keep us from experience of this place, this conclusion.''3

***

We all have to face death, and it is in death that the rich man and Lazarus meet at the cross. While the poor man is unscathed by the cross, the rich man feels all its torture and anguish, a torture that extends for all eternity. There is no escaping, no relief and no comfort whatsoever. A very sobering thought for us who so often *shun* the poor while we keep on going about our daily routine.

''But *nemo dives semper dives;* and again, *nemo pauper semper pauper. They who be rich in it will not ever be rich, nor they who are poor, poor always. It came to pass,* says the Scripture, that the beggar died. *Mortuus est etiam et dives, and the rich man,* for all his riches, died also. . . .

But that is no final end. . . . Death . . . has two . . . passages; and through it, as through one and the same city gate, the honest subject walks abroad for his recreation, and [the] lewd malefactor is carried out to his execution.

Two states then there be after death, . . . one of comfort, and the other of torment.

And that both these take place *presently.* For immediately after his death, and while all his *five brethren* yet lived, and [before] any of them were dead, he was in his torments, and did not expect the general judgment, nor was not deferred to the end of the world.

And to make it a complete cross, for so it is, as the poor and the rich meet here, . . . and go two contrary ways, every one to *his own place.* Lazarus to his bosom, the rich man to his gulf; and one's misery ends in rest, the other's *purple and fine linen* in a flame of fire. . . .

One would think this wood would make no cross, nor these premises such a *now therefore.* But to him who was thus and had thus, all this plenty, all this pleasure, *post tantas divitas, post tantas delicias,* to him is this spoken, but *now you are tormented.* Which first estate, as it was rich, so it was short; therefore I make short with it to come to *cruciaris.* . . .

Cruciaris is but one word, but much weight lies in it; therefore it is not slightly to be passed over, as being the special object of our *recordare,* and the principal part of the cross indeed. Two ways our Saviour expresses it: one . . . is *torture,* another . . . is *anguish of the spirit*; referring this to the inward pain, and that to the outward passion, the soul being there subjected by God's justice, to sensual pain, for subjecting itself willingly to brutish sensuality in this life, it being a more noble and celestial substance.

Of which pain St. Chrysostom notes, that because many of us can skill what torment the tongue has in extremity of a burning ague, and what pain our hands feel when from the hearth some spark lights on it; Christ chose to express them in these two. Not but they may be incomparably greater than these, yes far above all we can speak or think; but that flesh and blood conceives but what it feels, and must be spoken to it as it may understand. And it is a ground, . . . torments are uttered far beyond all conceit, which, labouring to avoid, we may, but labouring to express, we shall never do it. . . .

[This] torment [is] comfortless, wherein no manner [of] hope of any kind of comfort. . . . *Relief* is denied, even to *a drop of water*; neither of the comfort of delivery at last. . . . Their case is such, *ut non possint*, that they cannot presently, or for ever, look for any passage from thence, but must there tarry in torments everlastingly, so neither comfort of relief, or of delivery; nor the poor comfort, which in all miseries here does not leave us. An end will come; no end will never come, which *never* is never deeply enough imprinted nor seriously enough considered. That this *now* will be still *now,* and never have an end; and this *cruciaris* be *cruciaris* for ever, and never declined into a preterite tense, as *recepisti* was. This is an exaltation of this cross, above all else; none will ever come down from it, none will ever beg our body to lay it in our sepulchre. . . .

His remembering will do him no good; but though he remember it in sorrow and in the bitterness of his soul, yes though his sorrow be above measure sorrowful, it will profit him nothing. . . .

This then is his cross. We long, I know, to have it taken down; our ears are dainty, and the matter melancholic, and we little love to hear it stood on so long. But Chrysostom says well, of that fire: *Nunquid, si tacuimus, extinximus? If we speak not of it, will it go out?* No, no: *sive loquamur, sive taceamus, ardet ille; speak we, or keep we silence, it burns still, still it burns.* Therefore let us speak and think of it, and let it stand in the name of God. . . . If to hear of it be painful, to feel it will be more."[4]

***

Many of the early Fathers such as St. Gregory and St. Augustine were troubled by this *Now therefore*. If they were, so should we be.

"St. Gregory confessed by himself, that never any sentence entered so deep into his soul as this. And . . . St. Augustine . . . could not get it out of his mind. For he, sitting in the See of Rome, when it was grown rich and of great receipt, was as he says still in doubt of *recepisti*; whether his exalting into that Chair might not be his recompense at God's hands, and all that ever he should receive from Him for all his service. And ever he doubted this *recepisti*, which we so easily pass over, and whether his case might not be like. Thus did the good Father, and, as I think, not unwisely; and would God, his example herein might make due impression, and work like fear, in so many as have in the eyes of all men *received the good things in this life*! For this may daily be seen everywhere, that [many] who received them if ever any did, and that in a measure heaped up and running over, carry themselves so without remembrance or regard of this point, as if no such simile were in the Scripture as that of the needle's eye; no such example as of this rich man, no such *recordare* as this of Abraham which we have in hand. . . .

We must then join issue upon the main point, we cannot avoid it; to enquire how this *Now therefore* comes in; and how far and to whom this consequent holds."[5]

Andrewes makes it clear the rich man was not banished to hell because of his riches and having good things, but because he never thought of the poor; he was oblivious of their plight, and thus never shared his plenteousness with them.

"Was he therefore *tormented* because he *received good things*? Is this the case of all them who wear purple and fare well in this life? Shall everyone, to whom God reaches such *good things* as these, be quit for ever from Abraham's bosom? By no means. . . .

It was not therefore because he was rich; for then must Abraham himself have been subject to the same sentence. No, one may be so rich, and so use his riches together, . . . and no ways hinder, but help forward his account, and bring him a second *recipies* of the *good things* of that eternal life. . . .

Neither was it because he came by them unduly, by such ways and means as the soul of God abhors. . . .

Neither was it because he received them and wrapped them up. For as his receipts are in this verse, so his expenses in the nineteenth. So much in purple and linen, so much in feasting.

Neither was it, because receiving plenty, he took his portion of that he received in apparel or diet. . . . Or that he feasted, . . . *in all sumptuous manner.* . . . None of these it was. . . .

What was it then that brought him thither, or, as St. Bernard calls it, what was his *scala inferni, the ladder by which he went down to hell?* that we may know, what is the difference between Abraham's receipt and his; and when *recepisti* will conclude with *cruciaris*.

St. Chrysostom does lay the weight on the word *recepisti*, in his natural or proper sense. For it is one thing, says he, . . . *to receive or take*; another . . . to *receive it as it were in full discharge and final satisfaction.* And the same distinction does Christ Himself observe in the sixth chapter of St. Matthew. Both have, and both receive; but they who do *receive them* as a pledge of God's further favour; but they who do *receive them as a full and complete reward,* and have no more to receive, but must thereupon release and quit claim all demands in whatsover else. . . .

Then all is in the choice where we shall lay our *recepisti*; whether here or there, in this or that life; in purple and silk, and the delights of the world, or in the rest and comfort of Abraham's bosom. Whether we will say; Lord, if I may so receive, that I may be received; if I may receive so the good of this life, that I be not barred the other to come, *tanquam arrham, as the earnest of a better inheritance, Ecce me.* But if my receiving here shall be my last receipt, if I shall receive them *tanquam mercedem, as my portion for ever*, I renounce them; put me out of this receipt, and reserve my part in store for the land of the living. And of evil. If it must come here or there, with St. Augustine, *Domine, hic ure, hic seca, ibi parce; Let my searing and smart be here; there let me be spared;* and from *cruciaris*, the *torment* to come, *libera me Domine*.

To very good purpose said the ancient Father; *Quisque dives, quisque pauper; Nemo dives, nemo pauper; animus omnia facit. It is somewhat to be rich or poor, it is nothing to rich or poor; it is as the mind is; the mind makes all.* Now, says, St. Chrystosom, what mind he carried is gathered out of Abraham's doubling and trebling. *Tu, tua, and tua: recepisti tu, bona tua, in vitâ tuâ;* which words are working words, as he takes them, and contain in them great emphasis. Understanding by *tua*, not so much that he had in possession, as that he made special reckoning of, for that is most properly termed ours; *Animus omnia facit.*"[6]

***

The rich man's mistake was to think that there was no other life but what was now. He ignored the eternal values in living and the life of grace, and therefore he had no concept of sharing his riches with Lazarus.

"This life is called *his life*; not because he lived in it, but because he so lived in it as if there had been no other life but it. And in his account there was no other; *give him this life, let this day be his day, take to-morrow who will.* This did not Abraham; for *he saw a day,* and that after this life, that rejoiced him more than all the days of his life. . . .

Abraham willing him to remember he had received such things, implies, in effect, that he had clean forgotten that any such things he had ever received. . . .

Now, not remembering he had received them, no marvel if he forgot why he received them, or with what condition; fogetting God in heaven, no marvel if he remembered not Lazarus on earth. Verily, neither he nor any man receive them as proprietaries, but as stewards and as accountants, as Christ tells us above in this chapter. Not for ourselves only, or for our own use, but for others too; and among others, for Lazarus by name. If Lazarus receive not, it was his fault, and not God's, Who gave him enough to supply his own uses and Lazarus' wants too. . . . But he it seems, receives them . . . for himself alone, and nobody else; that Abraham says truly *Recepisti tu — tu et nemo alius; You and yours and nobody besides.* For his *recepisti* ended in himself, and he made himself *summam omnium receptorum.* For if you call him to account by the writ of *redde rationem*, this must be his audit. In purple and linen so much, and in belly-cheer so much; so much on his back, and so much on his board, and in them ends the total of his receipt; except you will put in his hounds too, which received of him more than Lazarus might. This is indeed *recepisti tu solus.*"[7]

***

We must learn from the rich man that we do not create the *gulf* which existed between him and Lazarus by the way we live, but should live modestly without waste and by meeting the needs of our brethren.

"While he lived, he was as a gulf swallowing all; *now therefore* the gulf has swallowed him. Remember this for a special point. For if our purple and fine linen swallow up our alms; if our too much lashing on, to do good to ourselves, make us in state to do good to none but ourselves; if our riotous wasting on expenses of vanity, be a gulf and devour our Christian employing in works of charity; there is danger in *recepisti*, even the danger of *now therefore*; *gurges eras et in gurgitem projicieris, a gulf you were, and into the gulf you will go.*"8

***

In being so occupied with bodily needs and pleasures, the rich man over-looked he also had a soul with various needs and functions.

"For whereas he consists of two parts, a body, and a soul, he remembered the one so much as he quite left the other out of his *memento*. For his *recepisti tu* was his body, and nothing else. Now reason would, the body should not take up the whole receipt, but that the poor soul should be thought upon too. Purple and silk, and *Ede, bibe,* they are but the body's part but alms and works of mercy, they be the souls's. May not our souls be admitted suitor that we would remember them, that is, remember Lazarus? for that is the soul's portion; for the other part, he and we all remember fast enough."9

***

Andrewes pleads that we should remember that there does exist the four last things, taught as far back by Moses, which the rich man and his brethren chose to ignore until it was too late.

"*Would God says Moses, men would remember the four novissima*; 1. That there is a death; 2. there is a judgment; 3. there is a heaven; 4. there is a hell. But of all four, *novissima inferni, . . . the nethermost, the place of torments.* The prophets said as much; Jeremiah [says], Ever think that an end there will be, *Et quid fiet in novissimo, what will become of us in that end? Who among us,*says Isaiah, *can endure devouring fire?* who can dwell with *ardores sempiterni, everlasting burn-ings?* These he had, and if he had heard these, it is plainly affirmed, *audiant ipsos* would have done it; they would have kept him for ever coming in that place. But these also, living, he strove to forget, and as ingenderers of melancholy, to remove them far away. And that he might the more easily do it, it was thought not amiss to call their authority into question, whether they were worth the hearing or not. It is in effect confessed by him, that *his five brethren* and he were of opinion, that the hearing of Moses and the prophets was a motive far unworthy to carry such men as they. It was for nothing he complains of his *tongue; illa lingua, with that tongue,* he had scorned the holy oracles; peradventure that place wherein he now lay, with that tongue which in that place now lay, with that tongue which in that place feels the greatest torment, and from that place the smallest comfort; both which it had before profanely derided. . . .
    Fili recordare—*optime dictum sed sero, excellently well said, but too late,* says St. Bernard. For alas! comes Abraham in now with *recordare*. . . . It is too late. . . . While it was time, and when it might have done him good, then he would not

endure it; now he is [willing] when it is out of time, to know what in time might have done him good; and may do others, if in time they look to it. Indeed, to him now it is of no use in the world, but only to let him see by what justice he is where he is, and what he suffers he suffers deservedly. The best is Abraham has more sons than this son, and they may take good by it, and have use of that whereof he had none. With this son it is too late, with some others it is not. Not with us we are yet upon the stage, our *jam vero* is not yet come. And for us is this inscription set up, and for our sakes both Christ reported, and St. Luke recorded this *recordare*.
. . .

This is the right use of this title; God forbid we should have no use of it, till we come where he is! But it is therefore set over his head in that life, that we may read it in this; read it and remember it; remember it, and never have title set over ours.

It will be good then sometimes to keep some day holy to the exaltation of this cross, and to set this title before our eyes; to approach it and read it over; yes not once, but often to record this *recordare*."[10]

***

How we spend this life determines how we spend eternity. One important matter is how we have served Christ through His needy and poor. Thus Andrewes concludes with various warnings if we do not remember the less fortunate. The only effectual way to *remember* is by praying constantly that we do alleviate the plight of the poor.

"That this life, short though it be, and in a manner a moment, yet *hoc est momentum unde pendet aeternitas, on it no less matter depends than our eternity;* or bliss or bane, comfort or torment. . . . It stands us then in hand to take perfect impression of this *recordare*; and, as St. Augustine says, *oblivisci quid simus, attendre quid futuri simus, to forget what we now be, to consider what we shall be* without all question [before] long, but we know how soon. . . .

Three things then I wish for conclusion; 1. that we may remember; 2. remember in time; 3. remember effectually. That we may remember the fire, the thirst, and the torments; and know what they mean by memory rather than by sense. . . .

That we do it in time, that we be not in his case, never *lift up our eyes* till we be *in hell*, nor remember that may do us good till it be too late.

That we do it effectually from the heart; for there is a heart in *recordare*, and that this being our greatest business, we make it not our least care.

Our remembering will be effectual, if we pray to God daily we may so receive as we may be received. And our remembering will be effectual, if it have the effect, that is, make us remember Lazarus. *Quotidie Lazarus*, you may find Lazarus if you seek him, everyday; no, you will find him, though you seek him not. Our present estate, by present occasion of the dearth now upon us, makes the memory more fresh than at other times it would be. Remember then, our being remembered there lies on this their remembrance here, and upon their receiving our *recipies* or rather *recipieris*.

And remember that day, wherein what we have received will be forgotten, and what He has received of us, will be remembered, and nothing else will be remembered, but *quod uni ex minimis*.''[11]

References

[1] Andrewes, Vol. 2, pp.78–9.
[2] *ibid.*, pp. 79–80.
[3] *ibid.*, pp. 80–1.
[4] *ibid.*, pp. 82–6.
[5] *ibid.*, pp. 87–8.
[6] *ibid.*, pp. 88–91.
[7] *ibid.*, pp. 91–2.
[8] *ibid.*, p. 92.
[9] *ibid.*, p. 93.
[10] *ibid.*, pp. 93–5.
[11] *ibid.*, pp. 96–7.

LENTEN SERMON No. 6
4th April 1596

Text: 2 Corinthians 12:15

And I will very gladly spend and be spent
for you; though the more abundantly I love
you, the less I be loved.

*Ego autem libentissime impendam, et
superimpendar ipse pro animabus vestris,
licet plus vos diligens, minus diligar.*

As evident from his text Andrewes dwells on the Christ-like love that St. Paul
had for the Corinthians who manifested very little love and kindness in their
lives, let alone reciprocated the love showered upon them by Paul.

"The words be St. Paul's, and to the Corinthians. . . . It is love that speaks, and
unkindness that is spoken to. . . . This must needs be love; and that unkindness,
that requits such love with such an *etsi; etsi minus diligar, though the more I love,
the less I be loved.*
Many ways it may be manifest, that St. Paul loved the Church of Corinth, more
than many others loved them, for he laboured more for them. By the time he spent
with them, a year and half full — scarce with any so much. . . . By two of his
largest epistles sent to them — not to any the like. And in one of them we see here,
how frank and how kind a profession he makes, *in qua omne verbum charitatis
igne vaporatur, wherein every word carries a sweet scent of love's perfume,*
[says] . . . St. Gregory. . . . All these together may prove his *magis diligam*, the
abundance of his love to Corinth.
Now there should be in love the virtue of the load-stone, the virtue attractive, to
draw like love to it again. There should be, but was not. For their little love
appeared by their many unloving exceptions which they took to him. To his office;
. . . to his person; . . . to his preaching; that he was . . . *not so eloquent by much*, as
[many] of them were; or his sermons of the *Corinthian fashion*. Indeed, I know not
how, but he could not hit on their vein.
This cold infusion of so faint regard on their parts might have quenched his
love. It did Apollo's, . . . but him it did not. *Charitas qua aedificabat,* was like
lime, slacked not but rather kindled, with water. For not withstanding all these,
such was his zeal, and he *tantus zelator animarum*, that we see his affection, and
we hear his resolution what it is. Unkind they might be, but no unkindness of
theirs, or verdict never so hard, or censure so sharp; no *minus diligar* should move
him, or make him love their souls . . . less."[1]

***

Andrewes compares the magnamity of Paul's love, especially for the indifferent or hostile, with the coldness of ours in similar situations. The essential difference is that St. Paul loved souls for Christ's sake, and His love reached out to those who were hardest to love, even the insensitive Corinthians.

". . . I cannot choose but marvel at his love, which truly is admirable; and more at their *minus*, than his *magis*. But at his heroical spirit most of all, whom such and so great unkindness could not overcome. The rather, when I . . . compare it with ours in these times; in which, a kind of love we have, such as it is, but such as it will not endure St. Paul's [test], or if in some degrees it do, if it be not respected straight, not as it deserves, . . . if it be crossed with any unkindness, it grows abrupt. Every *minus diligar*, makes it abate; and far we are from this Christian magnamimity, to resolve with him in the eleventh chapter, *Quod facio, hoc et faciam, what I do, that I will do still*. Or here, love I will still, *though the more I love the less I be loved*.

The thing loved, is the Corinthians' souls. And as Corinth itself was situated in a narrow land between two seas, so are they in the verse; having on the one side, the sea of self-love, in the former part; and on the other, the gulf of unkindness, in the latter. Through either of which St. Paul makes a first and second navigation, if happily he may so *adire Corinthum*, gain their souls to Christ, more precious to him than Corinth itself and all the wealth in it. . . .

[His] love . . . [stretched] itself to those who are fatherest from love, and least deserve it; . . . [and] to spend and be spent most willingly."[2]

***

So that we do not confuse spiritual love with the physical one of lust, Andrewes illustrates the difference between them.

"But then, lest we mistake our term of love, as easily we may, and confound it with lust, we must look to . . . *pro animabus, soul-love*, he means all the while. *Love*, the fruit of the Spirit; not lust, the weed of the flesh. Not of this flesh, sister to worms, and daughter to rottenness; but of the spirit allied to the angels, and *partaker in hope of the Divine nature* itself. And not of one only, but *animabus, of souls* — more than love of one soul; many souls, many thousands of souls, of a whole state or country. Them to love, and to them thus to prove our love, is it which St. Paul would teach, and it which we need to learn."[3]

***

The most precious bestowing we can give to another is love, given unconditionally. Such love St. Paul was willing to bestow upon the Corinthians, unlike our attempts in loving.

"Yes, *I will bestow*. Now alas, what can Paul bestow? Especially upon wealthy citizens? . . . Indeed, if silver and gold be all, and nothing else worth the bestowing, nothing will come under *impendam*, but it; his bestowing is stalled. But by the grace of God there is something else. There be talents, . . . and there be *treasures of wisdom and knowledge, in Christo Jesu*, says St. Paul. . . . [But] the truth is, men have no sense of their souls till they be ready to part with them; and then is St. Paul's *impendam* called for, and never seriously before, when their case is such as they can little feel what the bestowing is worth. . . .

This . . . Corinth needs; and the more wealthy it is, the more [it needs] . . . But be it little, or be it much, he who gives all leaves nothing ungiven, and therefore his *impendam* is at the highest. . . .

Majorem hoc nemo, says Christ, *greater love has no man than this, to bestow his life*. . . . [Yet] we see many . . . for self-love cries to us, Spare our living; but in any wise . . . spare our life. [There] is nothing but *impendere ne impendamur; to spend all we have, to spare ourselves*. But St. Paul . . . without any reservation at all of himself; to do or suffer, *to spend or be spent*. . . .

With men . . . when a displeasure is done [to] us, say we not, we weigh not so much the injury itself, as the malicious mind of him who did offer it? . . . And will you see the mind wherewith St. Paul will do both these? . . . Bestow he will, . . . most gladly, in the very highest of all, in the superlative degree. To spend, and spending to make no more reckoning of it than of chaff: no, it is more, to be glad of our loss, more glad than others would be of their gain. To be spent, and in being spent not to hold our life precious; nor so, but to rejoice in it, and as if death were advantage; *in hoc est charitas*, certainly. Death of itself is bitter, and loss is not sweet. Then, so to alter their natures as to find sweetness in loss whereat all repine, and gladness in death which makes all to mourn, verily herein is love. . . . One may part with all his goods to feed the poor, and yet have no love; and then though he do *impendere, bestow* all he has; . . . *he is nothing* if he [lacks] this affection, which is love indeed, the very soul of love.''[4]

***

St. Paul's love for the Corinthians was all the more remarkable when they were such an unkind and heartless people.

"We marvel at the love: we shall more marvel when we see what manner of men on whom it was bestowed. . . .

This is St. Paul's case, to meet with unkindness. . . . And as he to be pitied, so they to be blamed. . . . St. Augustine says well, *No more kindly attractive of love, than in love to [direct]; for exceeding stony is that heart, which, though it like not to love first, will not love again neither;* either first, or second. Yet so hard were theirs that neither one way nor other, *recte* nor *reflecte*, would either begin or follow. No, not provoked by all those so many forcible means, that St. Chrysostom makes a wonder at it, *Quomodo non converterentur in amorem, that they were not melted and resolved into love itself.* . . .

But all this while he lived still under hope, hope of winning their love for whose sakes he had trod under the foot the love of himself; hope that it had been but *impendam* all the while, he should have had returned his own again at least. . . . For this is as much to say as all is to little purpose; for to his grief he must take notice, they care for none of them, nor for him ever a whit the more; yes, rather the less by a great deal. So that all . . . be in vain. . . . For that is not *impendam*, but *perdam;* not spent, but cast away. . . . To have them an *esti* in our love; . . . this *though in vain*, though our *impendam* prove a *perdam*; that is it. To be able to turn the sentence and say, *though the more I love the less I be loved, yet will I bestow, yes, be bestowed*, and that *most gladly*, for all that. It is hard, I confess; but *solus amor erubescit nomen difficultatis, love endures not the name of difficulty*, but shames to confess anything too hard or too dangerous for it. For verily, unkindness is a mighty enemy, and the wounds of it deep. . . .

But neither can this appal the apostle, or dislodge his love, . . . and shows he will hold his resolution, [in spite of] all unkindness. *Minus diligar* will not do it; unkindness must yield, love will not."[5]

***

The greatest love of all is to give one's life to one's enemies as taught by our Saviour and exemplified in His own life, and lived out by St. Paul.

"And now we are come to the highest, and never till now, but now we are; that farther we cannot go. The very highest pitch of well-doing the heathen man saw in part; for he could say, *beneficium dare et perdere, to bestow love and lose it*, is well done; but that is not it. This is it: *beneficium perdere, et dare, to lose the first and yet bestow the second*. . . .

Yes, the love of loves, Christ's own love, what was it? *Majorem hac charitatem nemo habet, quam ut vitam quis ponat pro amicis.* Whereto St. Bernard rejoins well, *Tu majorem habuisti Domine, quia Tu vitam posuisti etiam pro inimicis: greater love than this has no man, to bestow his life for his friends.* Yet Lord, says St. Bernard; *You had greater, for You bestowed Your life for Your very enemies.* And to this love it is that St. Paul aspires, and near it he comes; that in some sort we may likewise say to him, *Tu majorem habuisti Paule, Yes, your love Paul was greater*, for you are ready to do the like; not for your enemies, but for your unkind friends, the next degree to professed enemies."[6]

***

The object of St. Paul's love was simple, to save souls for Christ's sake. In Corinth he certainly had a challenge with its vain and fleshly pleasure seekers of its inhabitants. Yet he persevered, always seeking to find Christ in them. What St. Paul found amongst the Corinthians is not very different from the way people live today, always lavishing more on the body than on the soul.

". . . what this object may be, so amiable, whereon St. Paul has set his affection so, that for it he will do and suffer all this; and that, so willingly without any exception, so constantly without any giving over. All this is nothing but the zeal of souls, . . . it is for their souls, all this. For their souls; and let their bodies go.

Which first draws the diameter that makes the partition between the two loves; the love which St. Paul found, and the love which St. Paul left at Corinth. For he found [what] is *scelus corporam, the body's unruly affection*, and infection too otherwhile; if ever in any place, there it abounded, but he left *zelus animarum*, the soul's perfection. Indeed it falls out sometimes, that in carnal love, or rather lust than love, we may pattern all the former; and find, as the Wise Man speaks, some one destitute of understanding, wasting his whole substance, hazarding his life, and that more willingly than wisely, perhaps to gain nothing but a scorn for his labour, and yet persisting in his folly still; and all this, in the passion of concupiscence to a vain creature; pleasing his fancy to the displeasing of God, and to the piercing of his soul one day with deep remorse for it; and except it do, to the utter ruin both of body and soul. We have here at Corinth, a strange example of it. . . . But what need we to sail to Corinth? Even in our own age we have . . . found examples of it; of love set awry and sorted amiss, diverted from the soul where it should be bestowed, and lavished on the body, where a great deal less would serve. It is St. Augustine's wish, O that we would in this kind stir up others, and ourselves with them be stirred up, but even to bestow such love on the immortal soul, as we see daily cast away on the corruptible body! What, but so much, and no more? Till it might be more, would God it were but as much in the mean time! Yet more and more it should be. St. Jerome's complaint [is], *But the people of God, unhappy in this point, have not the courage or constancy in the love of the Spirit, that the wicked world has in the lust of the flesh.* That courage? No, nothing like. *Ad erubescebtiam nostram dico, to our shame it must be spoken.* Look but to the first point, *impendam*; does not the body take it wholly up? And, if we fail in the lower, what will become of the rest? Well, St. Paul's love is, and ours must be if be right, *pro animabus, soul-love*, which may serve for the first point of the sequestration."[7]

***

St. Paul labours to save the soul because it is eternal, and therefore very precious. Yet it was because he loves Christ who loves every soul that Paul persevered so arduously and generously to imitate His Master. We must learn to follow Paul's example. How we spend eternity depends essentially on how much we have allowed Christ's love to penetrate our being and thus dictate our every thought and action.

"But why *pro animabus*, what is there in the soul so lovely that all this should be said or done for it? Why for souls? Why? 1. Why, take the soul out of the body which so much we dote on, but even half an hour, and the body will grow so out of love, so deformed, so ugly, so every way loathsome, as they who now admire it will then abhor it; and they who now cannot behold it enough, will not then endure once to come near it, nor within the sight of it. This a natural man would answer: The soul is to be regarded of the body, for it makes the body to be regarded. 2. But a Christian man will say more for it. That the love of Christ must be the rule of the love of Christians, and ours suitable to His. And Christ has valued the soul above the world itself, in direct affirming that he, that to win the world hazards his soul, makes but an unwise bargain; which bargain were wise enough, if the world were more worth. Says Chrysostom, *If you would prize your souls better, you would bestow more on them.* This is nothing. Christ has valued your souls; valued and

205

loved them above Himself; Himself, more worth than many worlds, yes, if they were ten thousand. I come now to the point. Is Christ to be loved? Why, all that St. Paul hitherto has professed, all and every part of it, it was but to the souls at second-hand. His eye was upon Christ, all the time of his profession. But because Christ has by deed enrolled set over His love to men's souls, and willed us towards them to show whatsoever to Him we profess; therefore, and for no other cause, it is, that he stands thus affected. For that those souls Christ so loved, that he loved not Himself to love them. . . . *Dying for my soul, Lord, You showed that my soul was dearer to You, than Your own self.* In love then to Christ, we are to love them who Christ loved, not *sicut Seipsum, as Himself,* but *plusquam Seipsum, more than himself*; and therefore has changed the *sicut* of the *Law, sicut teipsum, as yourself* into a new *sicut, sicut Ego vos, as I have loved you.* And how did He love us? . . . A degree higher than Paul; not, when we loved Him little, as faint friends, but hated Him greatly as sworn enemies. For He is it was who professed this art first.The words are indeed Christ's own; the primitive and most proper uttering them belongs to Him. None ever so fully or so fitly spoken or can speak them, as the Son of God on the cross, from the chair of his profession. And of Him, there St. Paul learnt *hoc carmen amoris.* Himself confessed as much in the fifth chapter of this epistle, that it was love; not his own love, but Christ's love, *charitas Christi extorsit,* that brought these words from him. His they be not, but *ore tenus*; the tongue his, but Christ the speaker. His they were; His they are, out of whose mouth, or from whose pen, soever they come.''8

***

Love in its perfect state is seen only in the life of Christ.

''We are come then now, where we may read love in the very original; yes, in the most complete perfection that ever it was. *Profitente Christo, Christ Himself, the professor,* says, 1. *Impendam* . . . bestow He will. . . . Even whatsoever Himself is worth, He will bestow; His kingdom, and the fullness of joy and glory in it for ever.

2. *Impendar* That? why *consummatum est,* it is done already; all hands and feet, head and heart, opened wide; and all, even to the last drop of blood bestowed for us on His cross, where the love of souls triumphed over the love of His own life.

3. *Libentissime, most gladly.* Witness that speech, *A baptism, I have to be baptised* with and *quomodo coarctor, how I am pained till I be at it!* And that too that to him who moved Him not to bestow, but favour Himself, He used no other terms than to the devil himself, *Avoid Satan.* Proof, enough, say I, how willingly He went, and how unwillingly He would be kept from it.

4. And for his *esti,* would God it were not too plain! Both at His cross, where the louder their *crucifige,* with the more strong crying and tears He prayed *Pater ignosce*; and ever since, *usque hodie, till now,* when all may see our regard is as little as His love great, and He respected as if He had done nothing for us. Every part of His love, and the profession of His love, but specially the *etsi* of His love passes all. For Christ by deed enrolled has set over His love to them. Which is that

that sets such a price upon them, and makes them so amiable, if not in their own kindness and loveliness, yet in the love of Christ Himself."9

***

What use is St. Paul's experience in Corinth for us? It is very valuable, suggests Andrewes, as it teaches us what is meant by Love, that is, being Christ-like to all.

"It serves first to possess our souls of that excellent virtue, *major horum, the greatest of the three*; no, the virtue without which the rest be but ciphers; the virtue that shines brightest in Christ's example, and stands highest in His commendation, love.

But love, the action of virtue, not the passion of vice. Love, not of the body, the *vile body* — so the Holy Spirit terms it — but of the soul, *the precious soul* of man. Love of souls; the more, the more acceptable. If of a city, well; if of a country, better; if of a county or kingdom, best of all.

And for them, and for their love, to be ready to prove it by St. Paul's trial; to open our *impendam*, to vow our *impendar*, and as near as may be to aspire to the same degree of *libentissime*. Verily, they who either, as the Apostle, for the winning of souls; or for the defence and safety of souls, many thousands of souls, the souls of a whole estate, in high and heroical courage have already passed their *impendam*; and are ready to offer themselves every day to *impendar*, and with that resolute forwardness which we all see, for it is a case presently in all our eyes; they who do thus, no good can be spoken of their love answerable to the desert of it. Heavenly it is, and in heaven to receive the reward.

But when all is done, we must take notice of the world's nature. For, as St. Paul left it, so we shall find it, that is, we shall not perhaps meet with that regard we promise ourselves. St. Paul's *magis diligum* met with a *minus diligar*.

Therefore above all remember his *etsi*. For to be kind, and that to be unkind; to know, such we shall meet with; yes, to meet with them, and yet hold our *etsi*, and love nevertheless; this certainly is that love, *majorem qua nemo*; and there is on earth no greater sign of a soul thoroughly settled in the love of Christ, than to stand thus minded. Come what will come, *magis* or *minus, si* or *etsi*, frown or favour, respect or neglect; *Quod facio, hoc et faciam, What I do, I will do*, with eye to Christ, with hope of regard from Him, let the world be as it is, and as it ever has been."10

***

In so many ways we are like the Corinthians, the enemy of Truth and Love until Christ intervenes and touches us.

"When we were deep in our *minus diligar*, and smally regarded Christ; no, *cum iminici essemus*, to take as we should, when *we were His enemies*, of His over-abundant kindness it pleased Him to call us from the blindness of error to the knowledge of His truth; and from a deep consumption of our souls by sin, to the

207

state of health and grace. And if St. Paul were loved when he raged and breathed blasphemy against Christ and His Name, is it much if for Christ's sake he swallow some unkindness at the Corinthians' hands? Is it much if we let fall a duty upon them, upon whom God the Father drops His rain, and God the Son drops, yes sheds His blood, upon *evil and unthankful men?* . . .

The more we love, the less they; of Christ it never can, nor ever will be said. For St. Paul, for the little love at their hands, found the greater at His. Though the more he loved, the less they loved him; yet the less they loved, the more Christ loved him. Of Whom to be loved, even in the least degree, is worth all the love of Corinth, and all Achaia too. . . . And indeed, all other loves of the flesh, or world, or whatsoever else, will perish and come to nothing; and of this, and this only, we may say *impendam* truly.''[11]

***

We too must love; this we can do if we always keep our eyes on Christ. Love can, and will transform our lives.

"So that, to make an end, though it be that St. Bernard says, *Perfectus amor vires non sumit de spe, Perfect love receives no manner strength from hope*; yet for that our love is not without his imperfections, all under one view we may with one eye behold Christ's *magis diligam*, when we were scarce in our *minus*, no scarce loved Him at all; and with the other look upon *impendam*, that what we do herein, though at men's hands we find no return, at Christ's we shall, and it will be the best bestowed service that ever we bestowed, that we bestow in this kind.

Now would God, the same Spirit which here wrote this verse would write it in our hearts, that those things are thus; that such a *rependum* there will be, and we well assured of it, *ut et nos converteremur in amorem, that we might be transformed into this love!*''[12]

References

[1] Andrewes, Vol. 2, pp. 98–9.
[2] *ibid.*, pp. 100–1.
[3] *ibid.*, p.101.
[4] *ibid.*,pp. 102–6.
[5] *ibid.*, pp. 107–9.
[6] *ibid.*, p. 109.
[7] *ibid.*, pp. 110–11.
[8] *ibid.*, pp. 111–2.
[9] *ibid.*, pp. 112–3.
[10] *ibid.*, pp. 114–5,
[11] *ibid.*, pp. 115–6.
[12] *ibid.*, p. 116.

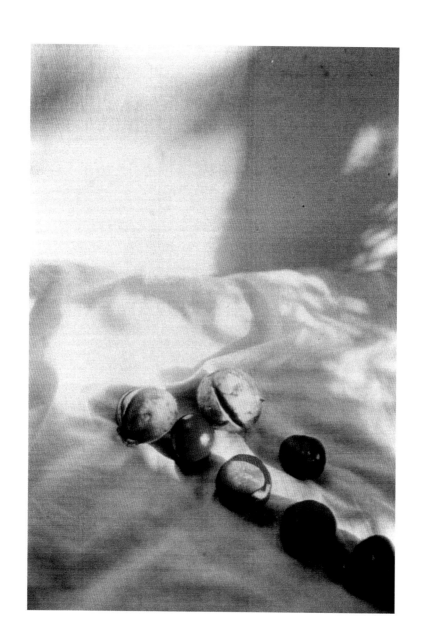

INTRODUCTION
TO
PASSION SERMONS

It is well known that Christ and His cross were
were never parted, but that all His life long
was a continual cross.

Vol. 2, p. 166.

Gethesemane — Gabbatha — Golgotha — all are so realistically and painfully painted by Andrewes that we almost feel the agonized sufferings born of our dear Saviour piercing our own body and soul:

In Gabbatha they did not whip Him, . . . they ploughed His back, and made not stripes, but long furrows upon it. They did not put on His wreath of thorns, and press it down with their hands, but beat it on with bats, to make it enter through skin, flesh, skull and all. They did not in Golgotha pierce His hands and feet, but made wide holes like that of a spade, as if they had been digging in some ditch.[1]

Who would doubt then that for Andrewes the centre of Christian contemplation is the Crucifixion? Although in his collection of sermons,there are only three Passion sermons, preached on Good Friday in 1597, 1604 and 1605 respectively before the reigning monarch, spiritually, they are the most intense. When they are read they should be seen as forming the first chapter of the Paschal sermons. For Andrewes, although meditatively the cross is more prominent, he holds Christ's death and resurrection as being inseparable. "Christ's dying and His rising are so linked together, and their audits so entangled one with another, as it is very hard to sever them."[2]

This unity is expressed superbly in his 1623 Paschal sermon. Taking as his text "Who is this Who comes from Edom, with red garments from Bozrah?", Andrewes unfolds how Christ's garment became "red". This is he does in his winepress imagery — a double wine press where Christ is both pressed and the presser. From the trampling of grapes flows red wine, symbolic of the Christ's blood which gushed out at His trampling upon at Gabbatha and Golgotha. This blood in turn symbolized "the cup of salvation". On Easter day, now clothed in white, He is the wine presser. Andrewes questions why Christ could not have only been the wine presser? In other words, why did the purity of Christ have to be stained? The answer: It was for our sins, and as our sins have so polluted us, our Saviour had to bear "sin's colour". "Coming then to save us, off went His white, on went our red; laid by His own righteousness to be clothed with our sin. He to wear our colours, that we His; He in our red, that we in His white."[3]

In these three Good Friday sermons Andrewes conveys the tremendous love and joy which flow from the cross, but simultaneously manifesting its immense cost with the torturing afflictions our dear Saviour suffered as He hung upon it. It was not only the physical pain He had to bear, but the racking of His soul with all its "unknown sorrows", far worse to bear than physical torments, especially when He had been forsaken by "His Father from heaven". Yet the main reason that "His skin and flesh [were] rent with the whips and scourges, His hands and feet wounded with the nails, His head with the thorns, His very heart with the spear-point" was because of our wretched sinfulness. We cannot blame Pilate nor Caiphas nor even God's justice for His Passion and Death; "we who for our sins, our many great and grievous sins" were His executioner.[4]

With such galling grief for our sins, our Lord from the cross beckons us to stop as we "pass by". "Is it nothing to you" my sorrow? Andrewes pleads that we "consider" this suffering and "then the inestimable benefit that grows unto you from this incomparable love." As we behold the side which was pierced by the soldiers, let our hearts be pierced by the same "spear point", and acknowledge that "it was the sin of our polluted hands that pierced His hands, the swiftness of our feet to do evil that nailed His feet, the wicked devices of our heads that gored His head, and the wretched desires of our hearts that pierced His heart" which really were the nails and the spear.[5]

Despite the love which was outpoured upon the cross, and the outstretched arms which yearn to reach everyone, there are still so many of us who keep on walking by, never pausing, and never looking up to see our Saviour. To such people Andrewes warns, that if we do not "willingly" look upon Him, at least on Good Friday, then we shall "do it by force" on Judgment Day. "One way or other, look upon it we must."[6]

Andrewes assures those who do "regard", do "consider", and are "pierced" will feel their hearts warm from "His heart of compassion and tender love, whereby He would and was content to suffer all this for our sakes." In turn their hearts will begin to love Him Who "was content . . . to deform Himself into the shape of a servant, a felon . . . [and] to lay down His crown of glory . . . [for] a crown of thorns . . . [for] joy of saving us."[7]

On the cross, our Lord is the "Author" of our faith, but He is also the "Finisher" of it, not in His broken Body but in His glorified One sitting on the throne. "There He is the prize" to all the faithful who in this life run "the race of our faith" with Him.[8] It is as our "Finisher" that gives us "hope" when we contemplate the Cross.

There is also the joy of the Cross which anticipates the joy of Easter. Even on this "day of heaviness", this most "evil day", it is also a "good day, a day of joy and jubilee" because the Paschal Lamb, both "Priest and Sacrifice" has "restored . . . [us] from our exile." "By the purchase of His blood we are entitled to . . . the kingdom of heaven."[9]

The works of darkness have done its worst by crucifying our Saviour, but He has triumphed over all evil.

As we meditate upon these Passion sermons, Andrewes bids us to let *the suffering Servant* move us; stand at the foot of the cross and be bathed in the water and blood which flows from His wounded side, assured that by the water we are cleansed from sin, and incorporated in Him and His sufferings at our Baptism, and by the blood we are partakers of "*the cup of salvation*" in the Holy Sacrament.[10]

But remember, if we do not stand in the shadow of His cross on Good Friday we cannot enjoy the light of day breaking over the Easter garden.

References

1 Andrewes, Vol. 2, p. 170.
2 *ibid.*, p. 195.
3 *ibid.*, Vol. 3, p. 75.
4 *ibid.*, Vol. 2, pp. 143–4; 150–1.
5 *ibid.*, pp. 126, 142, 153.
6 *ibid.*, p. 135.
7 *ibid.*, pp. 175–6.
8 *ibid.*, pp. 129, 164.
9 *ibid.*, p. 153.
10 *ibid.*, p. 134.

PASSION SERMON No. 1
GOOD FRIDAY 1597

Text: Zechariah 12:10

And they will look upon Me Whom they
have pierced.

Respicient in Me, Quem transfixerunt.

The theme of this Passion sermon is *piercing.* Zechariah's prophecy is fulfilled in St. John's description of the Passion with the piercing of His side by the Roman soldiers. Yet the piercing our Lord felt went deeper than the actual wound; He was hounded all his life like a hart by Herod, while His very soul had been pierced by the sharpness of our sins. Andrewes urges us to look upon our Saviour's piercing, and in gazing upon it, to have our souls pierced by His tremendous love.

". . . the Holy Spirit is our warrant, Who in St. John's Gospel reporting the Passion, and the last act of the Passion — this opening of the side, and piercing of the heart — our Saviour Christ says plainly, that in the piercing the very words of the prophecy were fulfilled, *Respicient in Me Quem transfixerunt.*

Which term of piercing we shall the more clearly conceive, if with the ancient writers, we sort it with the beginning of Psalm 22, the Psalm of the Passion. For, in the very front or inscription of this Psalm, our Saviour Christ is compared *cervo matutino, to the morning hart*; that is, a hart roused early in the morning, as from His very birth. He was by Herod, hunted and chased all His life long, and this day brought to His end, and, as the poor deer, stricken and pierced through side, heart, and all; which is it we are here to behold.

There is no part of the whole course of our Saviour Christ's life or death but it is well worthy our looking on, and from each part in it there goes virtue to do us good; but of all other parts, and above them all, this last part of His piercing is here commended unto our view. Indeed, how could the prophet commend it more, than in avowing it to be an act of grace, as in the [first] part of this verse he does? *Effundam super eos Spiritum Gratiae, et respicient,* etc., as if he should say, If there be any grace in us, we will think it worth the looking on.

Neither does the prophet only, but the apostle also, calls us unto it, and wills us what to *look unto,* and regard, *Jesus the Author and Finisher of our faith.* Then specially, and in that act, when for *the joy of our salvation set before Him He endured the cross, and despised the shame*; that is, in this spectacle, when He was pierced."[1]

***

Our gazing upon the Cross should be something we do all our life, but on Good Friday it is imperative that we fix our eyes on Him, to share His suffering as He hangs on the Cross because it is our sins which nailed Him there.

"To *look unto* . . . surely is continual, all our life long, to be done by us, and at all times some time to be spared unto it; but . . . most requisite at this time, this very day which we hold to the memory of His Passion, and the piercing of His precious side. That, though on other days we employ our eyes otherwise, this day at least we fix them on this object, *respecientes in Eum.* This day, I say, which is dedicated to no other end, but even to lift up the Son of Man, as Moses did the serpent in the wilderness, that we may look upon Him and live; when every Scripture that is read sounds nothing but this unto us, when by the office of preaching Jesus Christ is lively described in our sight, and as the apostle speaks, is *visibly crucified among us;* when in the memorial of the Holy Sacrament, *His death is showed forth until He come,* and the mystery of this His piercing so many ways, so effectually represented before us."[2]

***

It is the sight of Christ's piercing, His side being pierced which makes His crucifixion different from any other. It is also different because it was on behalf of others.

'First . . . Isaiah had said, *Morietur, Die He will, and lay down His soul an offering for sin.* . . . Daniel tells us, *Occidetur, He will die, not a natural, but a violent death.* . . . The Psalmist, the more particularly to set it down, describes it thus: *They pierced My hands and feet;* which is only proper to the death of the Cross. Die, and be slain, and be crucified. But sundry else were crucified; and therefore the Prophet here, to make up all, adds, that He should not only be *crucifixus,* but *transfixus;* not only have His hands and His feet, but even His heart pierced too. [This] very note severs Him from all the rest, with as great par-ticularity as may be; for that, though many besides at other times, and some at the same time with Him were crucified, yet the side and the heart of none was opened, but His, and His only.

Secondly, as to specify Christ Himself, and in His person, to sever from the rest of His doings and sufferings, what that is that chiefly concerns us, and we espe-cially are to look to; and that is this day's work — Christ pierced."[3]

***

Andrewes focuses on the spear-point which pierced the side and heart, and indeed the very soul of our blessed Saviour.

"In the Passion, we first consider the degree; for *transfixerunt* is a word of gradation, more than *fixerunt,* or *suffixerunt,* or *confixerunt* either. Expressing unto us the piercing, not with whips and scourges; nor of the nails and thorns, but of the spear-point. Not the whips and scourges, wherewith His skin and flesh were pierced; nor the nails and thorns wherewith His feet, hands and head were pierced; but the spear-point which pierced, and went through, His very heart itself; for of that wound, of the wound in His heart, is this spoken. . . .

Of the body's piercing there can be no question, since no part of it was left unpierced. . . .

Of the soul's too, it is certain, and there can be no doubt of it neither; that we truly may affirm, Christ, not in part, but wholly, was pierced."4

***

Andrewes queries whether a soul can be pierced? The answer is "yes", as shown so clearly in His Mother. As predicted by Simeon, Mary's soul was pierced as she stood by the cross. Yet Her piercing was nothing like the anguish suffered by our dear Lord when His soul was pierced.

"And may a soul then be pierced? Can any spear-point go through it? Truly Simeon says to the blessed Virgin by way of prophecy, that *the sword should go through her soul* at the time of His Passion. . . . And if through hers which was but *animo compatientis,* through His much more, which was *anima patientis;* since compassion is but passion at rebound. However, it is not a sword of steel, or a spear-head of iron, that enters the soul, but a metal of another temper; the dint whereof no less gores and wounds the soul in proportion, than those do the body. So that we extend this piercing of Christ further than to the visible gash in His side, even to a piercing of another nature, whereby not His heart only was stabbed, but His very spirits wounded too."5

***

Our Lord's sufferings were full of anguish, and intense pain, not only from the physical cruelties he suffered but from the jeering, reviling and scorning which were hurled at Him from his executioners and onlookers at Golgotha. If these were not enough, He also has to bear our indifference to Him, our *incessant sinning* and lack of penitence as He hangs on the cross.

"Jesus began to be distressed and in great anguish. . . . Yes, that His strange and never else heard of sweat — drops of blood plenteously issuing from Him all over His body, what time no manner of violence was offered to His body, no man then touching Him, none being near Him; that blood came certainly from some great sorrow wherewith His soul was pierced. And that His most dreadful cry, which at once moved all the powers of heaven and earth, *My God, My God, etc.* was the voice of some mighty anguish, wherewith His soul was smitten; and that in other sort, than with any material spear. For *derelinqui a Deo* — the body cannot feel it, or tell what it means. It is the soul's complaint, and therefore without any doubt His soul within Him was pierced and suffered. . . .

To this edge of sorrow, . . . it will strike deep into any heart; especially being wounded with so many sorrows before. But the more noble the heart, the deeper; who bears any grief more easily than this grief, the grief of a contumelious reproach. *To persecute a poor distressed soul, and seek to vex Him that is already wounded at the heart,* why, it is the very pitch of all wickedness; the very extremity that malice can do, or affliction can suffer. And to this pitch were they come, when after all their wretched villanies and spittings, and all their savage indignities in reviling Him most opprobiously, He being in the depth of all His distress, and for very anguish of soul crying, *Eli, Eli, etc,* they stayed those who would have relieved Him; and void of all humanity then scorned, saying, *Stay, let alone, let us see if Elijah will now come and take Him down.* This barbarous and brutish inhumanity of theirs, must . . . pierce deeper into His soul, than ever did the iron into His side.

To all of which if we add, not only that horrible ingratitude of theirs, there by Him seen, but ours also no less than theirs by Him forseen at the same time; who make so slender reckoning of these His piercings, and, as they were a matter not worth the looking on, [condescend] not so much as to spend an hour in the due regard and meditation of them; no, not that only, but further by incessant sinning and that without remorse, do most unkindly requite those His bitter pains, and as much as in us lies, *even crucify afresh the Son of God, making a mock of Him and His piercings.* These I say, for these all and every of them in that instant were before His eyes, must of force enter into, and go through and through His soul and spirit; that what with those former sorrows, and what with these after indignities, the prophet might truly say of Him, and He of Himself, *upon Me*; not whose body or whose soul, but whom entirely and wholly, both in body and soul, alive and dead, they have pierced and passioned this day on the cross.''[6]

***

If Christ had not incorporated our sins into His body, then we would be still excluded from the eternal joys of heaven. Hence in a very real sense it was we as well as His executioners who drove the nails into His hands and feet, and pierced His very side and heart.

''*He laid upon Him the trangressions of us all;* who should, even for those our many, great and grievous transgressions, have eternally been pierced, in body and soul, with torment and sorrows of a never-dying death, had not He stepped between us and the blow, and received it in His own body; even the dint of the wrath of God to come upon us. So that it was the sin of our polluted hands that pierced His hands, the swiftness of our feet to do evil that nailed His feet, the wicked devices of our heads that gored His head, and the wretched desires of our hearts that pierced His heart. We who *look upon,* it is we who *pierced Him*; and it is we who *pierced Him,* who are willed to *look upon Him.* Which brings it home to us, to me myself who speak, and you yourselves who hear; and apply it most effectually to every one of us, who evidently seeing that we were the cause of this His piercing, if our hearts be not too hard, ought to have remorse to be pierced with it. . . .

We are the cause thereof, as verily we are, even the principals in this murder; and the Jews and others, on whom we seek to derive it, but only accessories and instrumental causes thereof. Which point we ought as continually, so seriously to think of; and that no less than the former. The former, to stir up compassion in ourselves, over Him who was thus pierced; the latter, to work deep remorse in our hearts, for being authors of it. That He was pierced, will make our hearts melt with compassion over Christ. That He was pierced by us who look on Him, if our hearts be not *flint* as Job says, or as *the nether mill-stone* will breed remorse over ourselves, wretched sinners as we are.''7

***

Our dear Lord invites us to His sufferings, knowing that only those who contemplate with faith upon the cross, will profit from His Passion and Death. Andrewes warns us if we do not care to look upon Him now, we cannot expect Christ to look upon us on Judgment Day.

''Yes Christ Himself, pierced as He is, invites us to it. . . .

Our own profit, which is wont to persuade well, invites us; for that as from the brazen serpent no virtue issued to heal but unto them who steadily beheld it, so neither does there from Christ but upon those who with the eye of faith have their contemplation on this object; who thereby draw life from Him, and without it may and do perish, for all Christ and His Passion.

And if nothing else move us, this last may, even our danger. For the time will come when we ourselves will desire, that God looking with an angry countenance upon our sins, would turn His face from them and us, and look upon the face of His Christ, that is, *respicere in Eum*, which will be justly denied us, if we ourselves could never be gotten to do this duty, *respicere in Eum*, when it was called for of us. God will not look upon Him at ours, Whom we would not look upon at His request.''8

***

When we take time to *look into Him*, we shall begin to visualize Christ's sufferings, and gradually be pierced by our sins as the cause of them.

''In the act itself are enjoined three things: 1. That we do it with attention; for it is not . . . only *upon Him*, but *into Him*. 2. That we do it often, again and again, with iteration, for *respicient* is *re-aspicient*. Not a single act, but an act iterated. 3. That we cause our nature to do it, as it were, by virtue of an injunction. . . .

First then, not slightly, superficially or perfunctorily, but steadfastly, and with due attention, *to look upon Him*. And not to look upon the outside alone, but to look into the very entrails; and with our eye to pierce Him Who was thus pierced. *In Eum* bears both.

Upon Him if we *look*, we shall see so much as Pilate showed of Him; — *ecce Homo*, that He is a Man. . . . And He was innocent. . . . His enemies themselves being His judges.

216

Among those who be innocent, the more noble the person, the greater the grief, and the more heavy ever is the spectacle. Now if we consider the verse of this text, we shall see it is God Himself and no man who here speaks, for to God only it belongs to ''pour out the Spirit of grace'', it passes man's reach to do it; so that, if we look better upon Him, we shall see as much as the centurion saw, that this party thus pierced *is the Son of God.* The Son of God slain! Surely he who has done this deed is *the child of death,* would every one of us; *Et tu es homo, you are the man.* You are they, for whose sins the Son of God has His very heart-blood shed forth. Which must needs strike into us remorse of a deeper degree than before; that not only it is we who have pierced the part thus found slain, but that this party, whom we have thus pierced, is not a principal person among the children of men, but even the only-begotten Son of the Most High God. Which will make us cry out with St. Augustine, *Now sure, deadly was the bitterness of our sins, that might not be cured, but by the bitter death and blood-shedding Passion of the Son of God.* And this may we see looking upon Him.''9

***

We must continue our looking *into Him* so as to penetrate into His very soul where we shall discover that tender and great love He had for us — in giving His life for us.

''But now then, if we look *in Eum, into Him,* we shall see yet a greater thing, which may raise us in comfort, as far as the other cast us down. Even the heart of compassion and tender love, whereby He would and was content to suffer all this for our sakes. For that, whereas *no man had power to take His life from Him,* for He had power to have commanded twelve legions of angels in His just defence; and without any angel at all, power enough of Himself with his *Ego sum,* to strike them all to the ground; He was content notwithstanding all this, to lay down His life for us sinners. The greatness of which love passes the greatest love that man has; *for greater love than this has no man, but to bestow his life for his friends,* whereas He [condescended] to lay it down for His enemies. Even for them who sought His death, to lay down His life, and to have His blood shed for them who did shed it; to be pierced for His piercers. Look how the former *in Eum* works grief, considering the great injuries offered to so great a Personage; so, to temper the grief of it, this latter *in Eum* gives some comfort, that so great a Person should so greatly love us, as for our sakes to endure all those so many injuries, even to the piercing of His very heart.''10

***

Our looking *into Him* should be something we do quite often, and at some length. If we do, we shall discover, our hearts being pierced too, and in turn, telling us that our sins were the cause of His wounds. By acknowledging our sins through our repentance we can at least prevent His wound from widening.

"*Respicient* that is *re-aspicient*, not once or twice, but oftentimes to look upon it; that is, as the prophet says here, *iteratis vicibus,* to look again and again; as the apostle says, *recogitare, to think upon it over and over and over again*, as it were to dwell in it for a time. . . . Surely, the more steadily and more often we shall fix our eye upon it, the more we shall be inured; and being inured, the more desire to do it. For at every looking some new sight will offer itself, which will offer unto us occasion, either of godly sorrow, true repentance, sound comfort, or some other reflection, issuing from the beams of this heavenly mirror. . . .

Look and lament, or mourn, which is indeed the most kindly and natural effect of such a spectacle. *Look upon Him Who is pierced*, and with looking upon Him be pierced yourself. A good effect of our first look, if we could bring it forth. At [least], if we cannot *look and be pierced*, yet *that it might be, that with looking on Him we might be pricked in our hearts*, and have it enter past the skin, though it go not clean through. . . .

Now, as the first is *respice et transfigere, look upon Him and be pierced*, so the second may be, and that fitly, *respice et transfige, look upon Him and pierce*; and pierce that in you that was the cause of Christ's piercing, that is, sin and the lusts thereof. For as men who are pierced indeed with the grief of an indignity offered, withal are pricked to take revenge on him who offers it, such a like affection ought our second looking so kindle in us, even to take a wreak or revenge upon sin, *quia fecit hoc, because it has been the cause of all this.* I mean, as the Holy Spirit terms it, a mortifying or crucifying; a thrusting through our wicked passions and concupiscences, in some kind of repaying those manifold villanies, which the Son of God suffered by means of them. At leastwise, as before, if it kindle not our zeal so far against sin, yet that it may slaken our zeal and affection to sin, . . . that we have less mind, less liking, less acquaintance with sin, for the Passion-sake. For that by this means we do in some sort spare Christ, and at least make His wounds no wider; whereas by affecting sin anew we do what in us lies to crucify Him afresh, and both increase the number, and enlarge the wideness of His wounds."[11]

***

It was our Lord's love which enabled Him to bear our sins. Thus it was not only grief but love that pierced His tender but tormented heart. As we look *into Him* let our looking be pierced with love for Him Who died for us.

"Now, as it was sin that gave Him these wounds, so it was love to us that made Him receive them, being otherwise able enough to have avoided them all. So that He was pierced with love no less than with grief, and it was that wound of love [that] made Him so constantly to endure all the other. Which love we may read in the palms of His hands, as the Fathers express it out of Isaiah 49:16, for *in the palms of His hands He has graven us,* that He might not forget us. And the print of the nails in them, are as capital letters to record His love towards us. For Christ pierced on the cross is *liber charitatis, the very book of love* laid open before us. And again, this love of His we may read in the cleft of His heart. Says St. Bernard, *the point of the spear serves us instead of a key, letting us through His wounds see*

218

His very heart, the heart of tender love and most kind compassion, that would for us endure to be so entreated. . . .

Which sight ought to pierce us with love too, no less than before it did with sorrow. With one or both, for both have power to pierce; but especially love, which except it had entered first and pierced Him, no nail or spear could ever have entered. . . . *Look and be pierced with love of Him* who so loved you, that He gave Himself in this sort to be pierced for you.''[12]

***

As we look *upon Him* and *into Him,* let us believe and trust in Him. Such belief will in turn enable us to hope in Him for the promise of everlasting joy and felicity.

"*Respice et crede.* And well may we believe and trust Him, Whom looking a little before we have seen so constantly loving us. For the sight of that love makes credible unto us, whatsoever in the whole Scripture is affirmed unto us of Christ, or promised in His name; so that we believe it, and believe all. Neither is there any time wherein with such cheerfulness or fullness of faith we cry unto Him, *My Lord and My God,* as when our eye is fixed upon *the print of the nails, and on the whole in the side* of Him who was pierced for us. . . .

And believing this of Him, what is there the eye of our hope will not look for from Him? What would not He do for us, Who for us would suffer all this? It is St. Paul's argument, *If God gave His Son for us, how will He deny us anything with Him?* That is, *respice et spera. Look upon Him, and His heart opened, and from that gate of hope promise yourself, and look for all manner of things that good are.* Which our expectation is reduced to these two: The deliverance from evil of our present misery; and the restoring to the good of our primitive felicity. By the death of this undefiled Lamb, as by the yearly Passover, look for and hope for a passage out of Egypt, which spiritually is our redemption from the servitude of the power of darkness. And as by the death of the Sacrifice we look to be freed from whatsoever evil, so by the death of the High Priest look we for and hope for restitution to all that is good; even to our forfeited estate in the land of the Promise which is heaven itself, where is all joy and happiness for evermore. *Respice et spera, look and look for;* by the Lamb who is pierced to be freed from all misery, by the High Priest who is pierce fruition of all felicity.''[13]

***

Respice et recipe, look and receive. Daily we receive grace from Him, but especially we have received the waters of Baptism, and His most precious Blood in the Holy Sacrament. With so much lavished upon us, let us return His goodness, by our giving to Him, lavishly.

"Now, inasmuch as His heart is pierced, and His side opened, . . . there issued out *water and blood.* . . . Mark it running out, and suffer it not to run waste, but receive it. Of the former, the water, the prophet speaks in the first words of the next

219

chapter, that out of His pierced side God *opened a fountain of water to the House of Israel for sin and for uncleanness;* of the fullness whereof we all have received in the sacrament of Baptism. Of the latter, the blood, which the prophet . . . calls, *the blood of the New Testament,* we may receive this day; for it will run in the high and holy mysteries of the Body and Blood of Christ. There may we be partakers of the flesh of the Morning Hart, as upon this day killed. There may we be partakers of *the cup of salvation, the precious blood, which was shed for the remission of sins. . . .*

And shall we always receive grace, even streams of grace issuing from Him Who is pierced, and shall there not from us issue something back again, that He may look for and receive from us that from Him have, and do daily, receive so many good things? No doubt there will, if love which pierced Him have pierced us aright. . . . Or if we have nothing to render, yet ourselves to return with the Samaritan, and falling down at His feet, with a loud voice, to glorify His goodness, Who finding in us the estate that other Samaritan found the forlorn and wounded man, healed us by being wounded Himself, and by His own death restored us to life. For all which His kindness and thankful acknowledgement, we are certainly worthy He should restrain the fountain of His benefits, which hitherto has flowed most plenteously, and neither let us see nor feel Him any more.

But I hope for better things — that love, and so great love, will pierce us, and cause both other fruits, and especially thoughts of thankfulness to issue from us.''[14]

***

There may be some who are reluctant to *look upon Him.* However this is one thing we cannot escape. At one time or another we shall be forced to *look upon Him.* Therefore it is better to do it now voluntarily, than later by force. One way or the other look upon Him we must.

''For the Holy Spirit did easily foresee, we would not readily be brought to the sight, or to use our eyes to so good an end. . . . And neither willingly they begin to look upon it, and having begun are never well till they have done and look off it again. . . .

[Truly] it falls out often, that of Christ's; . . . nature is not inclined, and where it is not inclined, force must be offered. . . . Therefore *do it willingly, or do it by force.* Do it, I say, for done it must be. Set it before you and look on it; . . . though it be not with your ease, *respice, look back upon it* with some pain; for one way or other lool upon it we must.

The necessity whereof, that we may better apprehend it . . . [is] by Christ to himself at His second coming, sitting as our Judge upon His throne, in the end of the world. *Behold He comes in the clouds, and every eye will see Him, yes, even they who pierced Him.* . . . The meaning whereof is, Look upon Him here if you will; enjoin yourselves if you think good, either here or somewhere else; either now or then, look Him you will. And they who put this spectacle far from them here, and cannot endure *to look upon Him Whom they have pierced, and be grieved for Him,* while it is time; a place and time will be, when they will be enforced to look upon Him, whether they will or no, and *be grieved for themselves, that they had no grace to do it sooner.* Better compose themselves to a little mourning here, with some benefit to be made by their beholding, than to be drawn to it there when it is too late, and when all their looking and grieving will not avail a [bit]. For there *His look will be amiable to them who have respected His piercing here, and dreadful on the other side to them who have neglected it.* And they who have inured themselves this looking on here, will in that day *look up and lift up their heads with joy, the day of their redemption being at hand;* so they who cannot bring themselves to look upon Him there, will not dare to do it the second time, but cry to the mountains, *Fall upon us, and to the hills, Hide us from the face of Him Who sits upon the throne.*"[15]

***

Ideally our eyes should be constantly fixed upon the cross and our hearts given completely to our Saviour. If we cannot do this, we must be prepared to look upon Him when He chooses to look upon us again, as he did with Peter, and to respond as Peter did — to weep hot bitter tears for our denying Him.

"How long we shall continue so doing, and when must we give over? Let this be the answer: *Donec totus fixus in corde, Qui totus fixus in cruce.* Or if that be too much or too hard, at the least, *Look upon Him till He look upon you again.* For so He will. He did upon Peter, and with His look melted him into tears. He who once and twice before denied Him and never wept, because Christ looked not on him, then denied and Christ looked on him, *and he went out and wept bitterly.* And if to Peter . . . how much more will He not deny us like favour, if by looking on Him first we provoke Him in a sort to a second looking on us again, with the prophet saying, *I have set You, O Lord, before me; and again, O Look You upon me, and be merciful unto me, as You use to do to those who love Your Name. That love Your name* which is *Jesus, a Saviour;* and who love that sight wherein most properly Your Name appears, and wherein You chiefly show Yourself to be *Jesus a Saviour.*"[16]

***

If we persevere in our looking *upon Him* and *into Him,* focused on His grief and love, we shall feel the comfort of His grace swelling within our hearts. The experience should be similar to that of the two travellers on the road to Emmaus on that first Easter day when they met and conversed with Christ, but above all they felt their hearts burn.

"And to conclude, if we ask, How shall we know when Christ does thus respect us? Then truly, when fixing both the eyes of our meditation *upon Him Who was pierced,* — as it were one eye upon the grief, the other the love wherewith He was pierced, we find by both, or one of these, some motion of grace arise in our hearts; the consideration of His grief piercing our hearts with mutual love again. . . . *Did*

221

we not feel our hearts warm within us? That, from shame and pain He suffered for us; this, from the comforts and benefits thereby procured for us.

These have been felt at this looking on, and these will be felt. It may be at the first, imperfectly, but after with deeper impression; and that of some, with such *none knows*, but He who has felt them. Which that we may endeavour to feel, and endeavouring may feel, and so grow into delight of this looking.''[17]

References

[1] Andrewes, Vol. 2, pp. 119–120.
[2] *ibid.*, pp. 120–1.
[3] *ibid.*, pp. 121–2.
[4] *ibid.*, pp. 122–3.
[5] *ibid.*, p. 123.
[6] *ibid.*, pp. 123–5.
[7] *ibid.*, pp. 126–7.
[8] *ibid.*, pp. 127–8.
[9] *ibid.*, pp. 128–9
[10] *ibid.*, pp. 129–130.
[11] *ibid.*, pp. 130–2.
[12] *ibid.*, p. 132.
[13] *ibid.*, p. 133.
[14] *ibid.*, pp. 133–5.
[15] *ibid.*, pp. 135–6.
[16] *ibid.*, pp. 136–7.
[17] *ibid.*, p. 137.

PASSION SERMON No. 2

GOOD FRIDAY 1604

Text: Lamentations 1:12

Is it nothing to you, all you who pass by?
Behold, and see if there be any sorrow like
unto My sorrow, which is done unto Me, wherewith
the Lord has afflicted Me in the day of
His fierce anger.

*O vos omnes, qui transitis per viam, attendite
et videte si est dolor sicut dolor Meus: quoniam vindemiavit
Me ut locutis est Dominus in die irae furoris
Sui.*

The theme is affliction, *the pain of the body*, and grief, *sorrow of the soul*. Although written by Jeremiah to express the misery facing his own people at the hand of the Chaldeans, the text is nevertheless most appropriate to our Saviour in His Passion and Death.

"To be afflicted and so afflicted as none ever was, is very much. In that affliction, to find none to respect him or care for him what can be more? . . .
I demand then, *of whom speaks the prophet this? Of himself or some other?* This I find; there is not any of the ancient writers but do apply, yes in a manner appropriate, this speech to our Saviour Christ. And that this very day, the day of His Passion, truly termed here the day of God's wrath, and wheresoever they treat of the Passion, ever this verse comes in. . . . None can say, neither Jeremiah nor any other, *si fuerit dolor Meus,* as Christ can; no day of wrath like to His day, no sorrow to be compared to His, all are short of it, nor His to any, it exceeds them all.
And yet, according to the letter, it cannot be denied but they be set down by Jeremiah in the person of his own people, being then come to great misery; and of the holy city, then laid waste and desolate by the Chaldeans. . . .
Be it then to us . . . as most properly it is, the speech of the Son of God, as this day hanging on the cross, to a sort of careless people, that go up and down without any manner of regard of these His sorrows and sufferings, so worthy of all regard. Have you no regard? Of all you who pass by the way, consider and behold, if there were sorrow like to my sorrow, which was done unto me, wherewith the Lord afflicted me in the day of the fierceness of His wrath."[1]

***

From the cross Our Lord bids us *who pass by* to regard His sufferings and then to consider the pain of such suffering.

"Have you no regard etc.? To ease this complaint, and to grant this request, we are to regard; and that we may regard, we are to consider the pains of His Passion. Which, that we may reckon no easy common matter of light moment, to do or not to do as we list; first, a general stay is made of all passengers, this day. For, as it were from His cross, does our Saviour address this His speech to them that go to and fro, the day of His Passion, without so much as entertaining a thought, or [condescending] a look that way. *O vos qui transitis, O you who pass by the way,* stay and consider. To them frames He His speech, who pass by; to them, and to them all, *O vos omnes, qui transitis,* O all you who pass by the way, stay and consider.''[2]

***

Although some who *pass by* may have urgent business, if they knew Whom they were passing, nothing would be as urgent as stopping and giving recognition to Him Who hangs upon the cross.

''[What] know we their haste? Their occasions may be such, and so urgent, as they cannot stay. Well, what haste, what business soever, pass not by, stay though. As much to say as, be they never so great, your occasions; they are not, they cannot be so great as this. How urgent soever, this is more, and more to be intended. The regard of this is worthy the staying of the journey. It is worth the considering of those, that have never so great affairs in hand. . . . Thither then let us come.''[3]

***

Andrewes asks us to consider His sorrow, an emotion we all feel at times, but our Lord's grief is greater than any human sorrow or grief.

''What we are called to behold and consider, is His sorrow. And sorrow is a thing which of itself nature inclines us to behold, *as being ourselves in the body,* which may one day in the like sorrowful case. Therefore will every good eye turn itself; and look upon them who lie in distress. Those two in the Gospel who passed by the wounded man, before they passed by him, though they helped not as the Samaritan did, yet they looked upon him as he lay. But, this party here lies not, He is lifted up as the serpent in the wilderness, that unless we turn our eyes away purposely, we can neither will nor choose but behold Him. . . .

Now then, because as the quality of the sorrow is, accordingly it would be considered — for if it be but a common sorrow the less will serve, but if it be some special, some heavy case, the more would be allowed it; for proportionally with the suffering, the consideration is to arise; to raise our consideration to the full, and to elevate it to the highest point, there is upon His sorrow set a *si fuerit sicut,* a note of highest eminency; for *si fuerit sicut,* are words that have life in them, and are able to quicken our consideration, if it be not quite dead; for them we are provoked, as it were, to *consider,* and considering to whether ever any *sicut* may be found to set by it, whether ever any like it.''[4]

***

Once we have paused at the cross, the first things we must consider are *the pains of His body, His wounds and His stripes.*

"Our very eye will soon tell us no place was left in His body, where He might be smitten and was not. His skin and flesh rent with the whips and scourges, His hands and feet wounded with the nails, His head with the thorns, His very heart with spear-point; all His senses, all His parts laden with whatsoever wit or malice could invent. His blessed body given as an anvil to beaten upon with the violent hands of those barbarous miscreants, till they brought Him into this case of *si fuerit sicut.* For Pilate's *Ecce Homo!* his showing Him with an *Ecce,* as if He should say, Behold, look if ever you saw the like rueful spectacle; this very showing of his shows plainly, He was then come into woeful plight, so woeful as Pilate very believed His very sight so pitiful, as it would have moved the hardest heart of all to have relented and said, This is enough, we desire no more."[5]

***

Next we must consider *the sorrow of the soul* where pain is felt to the utmost. For our dear Saviour this began in the garden of Gethesemane as He prayed most fervently to His Father that His will be done, continued with the crowds calling for His crucifixion and ended with the jeerings as He hung upon the cross. However His most intense grief and agony came from His Father's abandonment of Him. He was indeed all alone.

"Give me any grief, save the grief of the mind, . . . says Solomon, *The spirit of a man will sustain all his other infirmities, but a wounded spirit, who can bear?* And of this, this of His soul, I dare make a case, *Si fuerit sicut.*

He began to be troubled in soul, says St. John; *to be in agony,* says St. Luke; *to be in anguish of mind and deep distress*, says St. Mark. To have His soul round about on every side environed with sorrow, and that sorrow to the death. Here is trouble, anguish, agony, sorrow, and deadly sorrow; but it must be such, as never the like, so it was too.

The estimate whereof we may take from the second word of melting, that is, from His sweat in the garden; strange, and the like whereof was never heard or seen.

No manner violence offered Him in body, no man touching Him or being near Him; in a cold night, for they were [reluctant] to have a fire within doors, lying abroad in the air and upon the cold earth, to be all of a sweat, and that sweat to be blood; and not as they call it *diaphoreticus, a thin faint sweat,* but *grumosus, of great drops*; and those so many, so plenteous, as they went through His apparel and all; and through all streamed to the ground, and that in great abundance; read, enquire, and consider, *if ever there were sweat like this sweat of His.* Never the like sweat certainly, and therefore never the like sorrow. . . . That hour what His feelings were, it is dangerous to define; we know them not, we may be too bold to determine of them. To very good purpose it was, that the ancient Fathers of the

Greek Church in their Liturgy, after they have recounted all the particular pains, as they are set down in His Passion, and by all, and by every one of them, called for mercy, do after all shut up all with this; *By Your unknown sorrows and sufferings, felt by you, but not distinctly known by us, Have mercy upon us, and save us!*

Now, though this suffice not, nothing near, yet let it suffice, the time being short, for His pains of body and soul. For those of the body, it may be some may have endured the like, but the sorrows of His soul are unknown sorrows, and for them none ever has, . . . or ever will suffer the like, . . . or near the like in any degree. . . .

His own, they among whom He had gone about all His life long, healing them, teaching them, feeding them, doing them all the good He could, it is they who cry, *Not Him, no, but Barabbas rather; away with Him, His blood be upon us and our children.* It is they who in the midst of His sorrows shake their head at Him, and cry, *Ah, you wretch;* they who in His most disconsolate estate cry *Eli, Eli,* in most barbarous manner, deride Him and say, *Stay, and you will see Elijah come presently and take Him down. . . .*

His most sorrowful complaint of all others; not that His friends upon earth, but that His Father from heaven had forsaken Him; that neither heaven nor earth yielded Him any regard, but that between the passioned powers of His soul, and whatsoever might any ways refresh Him, there was a traverse drawn, and He left in the state of a weather-beaten tree, all desolate and forlorn. Evident, too evident, by that His most dreadful cry, which at once moved all the powers in heaven and earth, *My God, My God, why have You forsaken Me?* Weigh well that cry, consider it well, and tell me, *if ever there were cry like that of His;* never the like cry, and therefore never the like sorrow.''[6]

***

His soul was so agonized that it was parched and barren, absolutely devoid of any *divine comfort.*

''His soul was even as a scorched heath-ground, without so much as any drop of dew of divine comfort; as a naked tree, no fruit to refresh Him within, no leaf to give Him shadow without; the power of darkness let loose to afflict Him, the influence of comfort restrained to relieve Him. . . .

Add to this Person those wounds, that sweat and cry, and put all together, and I make no manner question the like was not, will not, cannot ever be. It is far above all that ever was or can be. Men may drowsily hear it and coldly affect it, but principalities and powers stand abashed at it. And for the quality both of the Passion and the Person, that never the like, thus much.''[7]

***

Who was responsible for such a sacrifice and Christ's agonized soul? Not Pilate, not Caiphas, not the soldiers but God's justice; hence His wrath was poured out upon His Son.

226

"It was God Who did it. An hour of that day was the *hour of the power of darkness*; but the whole day itself . . . was the day of the wrath of God. God was a doer in it; *wherewith God has afflicted Me. . . .*

This was in the very fierceness of His wrath. His sufferings, His sweat, and cry, show as much; they could not come but from a wrath *si fuerit sicut*, for we are not past *non sicut*, no not here. . . .

What caused this wrath? God is not wrath but with sin, nor grievously wrath but with grievous sin. And in Christ there was no grievous sin, no sin at all. God did it, the text is plain. And in His fierce wrath He did it. For what cause? For, God forbid, God should do as did Annas the high-priest, cause Him to be smitten without cause! God forbid, says Abraham, *the Judge of the world should do wrong* to any! To any, but specially to His own Son, that His Son, of Whom with thundering voice from heaven He testifies, all His joy and delight we in Him, *in Him only He was well-pleased.* And how then could His wrath wax hot to do all thus unto Him?

There is no way to preserve God's justice, and Christ's innocency both, but to say as the angel said of Him to the prophet Daniel, The Messiah *will be slain, will be slain but not for Himself. Not for Himself.* For whom then? For some others. He took upon Him the person of others, and so doing, justice may have her course and proceed.

Pity it is to see a man pay that he never took; but if he will become a surety, if he will take on him the person of the debtor, so he must. Pity to see a silly poor lamb lie bleeding to death; but if it must be a sacrifice, such is the nature of sacrifice, so it must. And so Christ, though without sin in Himself, yet as a surety, as a sacrifice, may justly suffer for others, if He will take upon Him their persons; and so God may justly give way to His wrath against Him.''[8]

***

Was anyone else responsible for His sufferings? Definitely! – us. Our sins, our most grievous sins. We were indeed the principal cause of His Passion.

"He took upon Him our infirmities, and bare our maladies. He was wounded for our iniquities, and bare our maladies. He was wounded for our iniquities, and broken for our transgressions; the chastisement of our peace was upon Him, and with His stripes were we healed. All we as sheep were gone astray, and turned every man to his own way; and the Lord has laid upon Him the iniquity of us all. All, all, even those who pass to and fro, and for all this regard neither Him nor His Passion. . . .

It was we who for our sins, our many great and grievous sins, *si fuerit sicut*, the like whereof never were, should have sweated this sweat and have cried this cry; should have smitten with these sorrows by the fierce wrath of God, had not He stepped between the blow and us, and latched it in His own body and soul, even the dint of the fierceness of the wrath of God. O the *non sicut* of our sins, that could not otherwise be answered! . . .

It is we — we wretched sinners that we are, who are to be found the principals in this act, and those on whom we seek to shift it, to drive it from ourselves, Pilate and Caiphas and the rest, but instrumental causes only. And it is not the executioner who kills the man properly, that is, they; no, nor the judge, who is God in this case; only sin, *solum peccatum homicida est, sin only is the murderer,* to say the truth, and our sins the murderers of the Son of God; and the *non sicut* of them the true cause of the *non sicut* both of God's wrath, and of His sorrowful sufferings.''9

***

Why then did our blessed Saviour endure such agonized suffering for us, miserable sinners, and *take upon Him our debt and danger*? The reason: Love — pure, unconditional love for us.

"He . . . needed not for any necessity of justice, for no lamb was ever more innocent; or for any necessity of constraint, for twelve legions of angels were ready at His command, but because He would.

And why would He? No reason can be given but because He regarded us. Mark the reason. And what we were? Verily, utterly unworthy even His least regard, not worth the taking up, not worth the looking after. . . . For when He saw us a sort of forlorn sinners, *damned as fast as born,* as being by *nature children of wrath,* and yet still *heaping up wrath against the day of wrath,* by the errors of our life, till the time of our passing hence; and then the *fierce wrath of God* ready to overwhelm us and to make us endure the terror and torments of a never dying death, another *non sicut* yet, when, I say, He was in this case, He was moved with compassion over us and undertook all this for us. Even then in His love He regarded us, and so regarded us that He regarded not Himself, to regard us.

Bernard says most truly, *In suffering all this for us You show, Lord, that we were more dear to You, that You regard us more than Your ownself,* and will this regard find no regard at our hands?

It was sin then, and the heinousness of sin in us, that provoked wrath and the fierceness of His wrath in God; it was love, and the greatness of His love in Christ that caused Him to suffer the sorrows and the grievousness of these sorrows, and all for our sakes. . . .

[What] set the high price on this sacrifice, is this; that He who offers it unto God, is God. But if little had been suffered, little would the love have been thought that suffered so little, and as little regard would have been had of it.''10

***

Such love as shown by Christ in His Passion and Death has brought us many benefits: healing, refreshment, grace, salvation, reconciliation and inheritance. Though for Him a day of much suffering, for us a day of joy.

"Consider then the inestimable benefit that grows unto you from this incomparable love. . . . *By His stripes we are healed,* by His sweat we are refreshed, by His forsaking we receive grace. That this day, to Him the day of the fierceness of God's wrath, is to us the day of the fullness of God's favour, as [Paul] calls it, *a day of salvation.* In respect of that He suffered, I deny not, an evil day, a day of heaviness; but in respect of that which He by it has obtained for us, it is as we truly call it a good day, a day of joy and jubilee. For it does not only rid us of that wrath which pertains to us for our sins; but further, it makes that pertain to us whereto we had no manner of right at all.

For not only His death as by the death of our sacrifice, by the blood of His cross as by the blood of the Paschal lamb, the destroyer passes over us, and we shall not perish; but also by His death, as by the death of our High Priest, for He is Priest and Sacrifice both, we are restored from our exile, even to our former forfeited estate in the land of Promise. . . . Our sins . . . deprived us of Paradise, a place on earth; but by the purchase of His blood we are entitled to a far higher, even the Kingdom of Heaven; and His blood, not only the blood of *remission*, to acquit us of our sins, but *the blood of the Testament too*, to bequeath us and give us estate in that heavenly inheritance. . . .

Is this not worth the regard? Sure if anything be worthy the regard, this is most worthy of our very worthiest and best regard."[11]

***

There are still many who continue to pass by, and so the cry continues, *Is it nothing to you?* If you would just ponder on the worth of such sufferings for your own sakes, you would stop and look upon your Saviour.

"*Have you no regard?* . . . None? . . . and it touches you so near, . . . even as near as your soul touches you, and will you not yet regard it? . . . What will move you? Will pity? Here is distress never the like. Will duty? Here is a Person never the like. Will fear? Here is wrath never the like. Will remorse? Here are sins never the like. Will kindness? Here is love never the like. Will bounty? Here are benefits never the like. Will all these? Here they be all, all above any *sicut*, all in the highest degree."[12]

***

Our lack of regard for Him, made His Passion even more bitter.

"Truly the complaint is just, it may move us; it wants no reason, it may more; and it wants no affection in the delivery of it to us, on His part to move us. Sure it moved Him exceeding much; for among all the deadly sorrows of His most bitter Passion, this, even this, seems to be His greatest of all, and [what] did most affect Him, even the grief of the slender reckoning most men have it in; as little respecting Him, as if He had done or suffered nothing at all for them. For lo, of all the sharp pains He endures He complains not, but of this He complains, of no regard; [what] grieves Him most, [what] most He moans is this. It is strange He should be in pain, such pain as never any was, and not complain Himself of them, but of want of regard only. Strange, He should not make request, O deliver Me, or relieve Me! But only, O consider and regard Me! In effect as if He said, None, no deliverance, no relief do I seek; regard I seek. And all that I suffer, I am content with it, I regard it not, I suffer most willingly, if I may find at your hands, regard."[13]

If we did not hear His complaint and commiserate with it, nature certainly did.

"Truly, this so passionate a complaint may move us, it moved all but us; for most strange of all it is, that all the creatures in heaven and earth seemed to hear this, His mournful complaint, and in their kind to show their regard of it. The sun in heaven shrinking in his light, the earth trembling under it, the very stones cleaving in sunder, as they had sense and sympathy of it, and sinful men only not moved with it. And yet it was not for the creatures this was done to Him, to them it pertains not; but for us it was, and to us it does. And shall we not yet regard it? Shall the creatures, and not we? Shall we not?"[14]

***

If we do not regard Christ on this day, on another day we shall be forced to. Hence it is wiser to grant Christ His request *now* and *look upon Him*, before facing Him on Judgment Day.

"It will quickly be here, a day of like *fierce wrath* against us, for not regarding Him. . . . In that day, there is not the most careless of us all but will cry as they did in the Gospels, *Pertains it not to You, care You not that we perish*. Then would we be glad to pertain to Him and His Passion. Pertain it to us then, and pertains it not now? Sure now it must, if then it will.

Then to give end to this complaint, let us grant Him His request, and regard His Passion. Let the rareness of it, the nearness to us, let pity or duty, fear or remorse, love or bounty; any of them or all of them; let the justness of His complaint, let His affectionate manner of complaining of this and only this, let the shame of the creatures' regard, let our profit or our peril, let something prevail with us to have it in some regard."[15]

***

Andrewes concludes by petitioning God to have mercy upon us, for even when we do regard Him it is often done so listlessly. However if we do make the effort to consider Him, we shall feel our heart warm towards Him.

"But God help us poor sinners, and be merciful unto us! Our regard is a *non sicut* indeed, but it is backward, and in a contrary sense; that is, no where so shallow, so short, or so soon done. It should be otherwise, it should have our deepest consideration this, and our highest regard.

But if that cannot be had, our nature is so heavy, and flesh and blood so dull of apprehension in spiritual things, yet at leastwise some regard. Some I say; the more better, but in any wise some, and not as here no regard, none at all. Some ways to show we make account of it, to withdraw ourselves, to avoid our minds of other matters, to set this before us, to think upon it, to thank Him for it, to regard Him, and stay and see whether He will regard us or no. Sure He will, and we shall feel our *hearts pricked* with sorrow by consideration of the cause in us — our sin; and again, *warm within us*, by consideration of the cause in Him — His love; till by some motion of grace He answers us, and shows that our regard is accepted of Him.''[16]

***

Good Friday is that very special day of the year when we should not indeed pass Him by. On this day we should linger awhile, contemplating what *the Son of God did and suffered for us.*

''And this, as at all other times, for no day is amiss but at all times some time to be taken for this duty, so specially on this day; this day, which we hold holy to the memory of His Passion, this day to do it; to make this day, the day of God's wrath and Christ's suffering, a day to us of serious consideration and regard of them both.

It is kindly to consider *opus diei in die suo, the work of the day in the day it was wrought*; and this day it was wrought. This day therefore, whatsoever business be, to lay them aside a little; whatsoever our haste, yet to stay a little, and to spend a few thoughts in calling to mind and taking to regard what this day the Son of God did and suffered for us; and all for this end, that what He was then we might not be, and what He is now we might be for ever.

Which Almighty God grant we may do, more or less, even every one of us, according to the several measures of His grace in us!''[17]

References

1 Andrewes, Vol. 2, pp. 138–140.
2 *ibid.*, p. 141.
3 *ibid.*, pp. 141–2.
4 *ibid.*, p. 142.
5 *ibid.*, pp. 143–4.
6 *ibid.*, pp. 144–6.
7 *ibid.*, pp. 147, 149.
8 *ibid.*, pp. 149–150.
9 *ibid.*, pp. 150–1.
10 *ibid.*, pp. 151–2.
11 *ibid.*, pp. 153–4.
12 *ibid.*, p. 154.
13 *ibid.*, p. 155.
14 *ibid.*
15 *ibid.*, pp. 155–6.
16 *ibid.*, p. 156.
17 *ibid.*, pp. 156–7.

PASSION SERMON No. 3
GOOD FRIDAY 1605

Text: Hebrews 12:2

Looking unto Jesus the Author and Finisher
of our faith; Who, for the joy that was set
before Him, endured the cross, despising the
shame, and is set down at the right hand of
throne of God.

*Aspicientes in Authorem fidei, et Consummatorem
Jesum; Qui proposito Sibi gaudio, sustinuit
crucem, confusione contempta; atque in dexterâ
sedis Dei sedet.*

In this Passion sermon, Andrewes unveils the crucifixion as the very centre of our belief and spiritual life. Our meditations should constantly focus on the cross, but on this day, Good Friday, it should absorb all our attention. And so to help us to concentrate on His crucifixion, Andrewes paints in penetrating details the very pains Our Saviour's body had inflicted upon it; the agony of His soul; and the intense shame He endured from the despicable, disdainful and degrading treatment dealt out to Him by the soldiers and spectators. All these He endured in order to release us from the yoke of sin, and to pay the ransom for them. It is these sufferings and shames which dominate in this sermon.

"Of our blessed Saviour's whole life or death, there is no part but is *a theory* of itself, well worthy our looking on; for from each part thereof there goes virtue to do us good. From each part, but of all, from the last part, or act of His Passion. Therefore has the Holy Spirit honoured this last part only with this name, and none but this. This is the *theory* ever most commended to our view. To be looked on He is at all times and in all acts; but then, and in that act, especially, *when for the joy set before Him, He endures the cross, and depised the shame.* . . .

The view whereof, though it be not restrained to any one time, but all the year long, ought to be frequent with us; and blessed are the hours that are so spent! Yet if at any one time more than other, certainly this time, this day may most justly challenge it. For this day was this Scripture fulfilled, and this day are our ears filled full with Scriptures about it. So that though on other days we employ our eyes otherwise, yet this day at least we would, as exceeding fitly the apostle wishes us, *cast our eyes from other sights*, and fix them on this object, it being the day dedicated to the lifting up of the Son of Man on high, that He may draw every eye unto Him."[1]

***

Living out the Christian life is likened by the writer to the Hebrews to a race. If run well there is a prize at the end of it. For us Jesus as Lord and *the Finisher of our faith* is our prize. However some of us move very slowly. When we feel we cannot complete the race, we should remember we have the saints in heaven to assist us, and Christ as the end.

"This our profession he expresses in the former verse in the terms of a race or game, borrowing his similitude from the games of Olympus. For from those games, famous then over all the world, and by terms from them taken, it was common to all writers of that age, both holy and human, to set forth, as in the running the laborious course, so in the prize of it, the glorious reward of a virtuous life.

Which race, truly Olympic, because they and we, the most of us, either stand still, or if we remove do it but slowly, and are ready to faint upon every occasion; that we may run the sooner, and attain the better, two sights he sets before us to comfort us and keep us from fainting. One, a cloud of witnesses, . . . that is the Saints in heaven, witnesses as able to depose this race may be run, and this prize may be won, for they have run the one, and won the other long ago. These look on us now, how well we carry ourselves, and we look to them, that we may carry ourselves well in the course we have undertaken. . . .

"He wills us *to turn our eyes from them,* and to turn hither, and to fasten them here on Jesus Christ, *the Author and Finisher of our faith. . . .* The saints, though they be guides to us, yet are they but followers to Him. He the *Arch-guide*, the Leader of them and us all. Look on Him. They but well willers to our faith, but neither authors nor finishers of it. He, both. Both Author to call us to it, and set us in it; and Finisher to help us through it, and reward us for it. Look to Him. . . .

Of our faith, and of the whole race of it He is the *Author,* casting up His glove at the first setting forth. He is the *Finisher*, holding out the prize at the goal end. By His authority . . . our course is begun; we run not without warrant. By His bounty it will be finished and crowned in the end; we run not in vain, or without hope of reward." 2

***

Christ is not only *the Author* of our faith but also *the Finisher* of it.

"He wills them to have an eye to Him and His example, Who first and last, *from the cratch to the cross,* from St. Luke's time that *He began to do and teach,* to St. John's time that He cried *consummatum est,* gave them not over *sed in finem usque dilexit eos,* but *to the end loved them.* And so must they Him, if they do Him right. Both set out with Him, as *Author* by a good beginning; and hold out with Him, as *Finisher,* to a far better end; and follow Him in both Who is both. Were He the *Author* only, it would serve to step forth well at the first. But He is the *Finisher* too; therefore we must hold out to the last. And not rend one of them from the other, seeing He requires both, not either, but both; and Jesus, a Saviour of none but those, who follow Him as *Finisher* too, and are therefore marked in the forehead with Tau the last letter of the Hebrew, as He Himself is Omega, the last of the Greek Alphabet. . . . *Jesus, the Author and Finisher of our faith*. For these two to look upon Him, and in these two to be like unto Him. . . .

[In] His Passion . . . by the *cross*, He is *Author;* by the *throne*, He is *Finisher of our faith*. As Man on the *cross, Author;* as God on the *throne, Finisher*."³

***

The main ingredients needed to run the race well, and thence to win the prize are love and hope.

"What moves the mother to all the travail and toil she takes with her child? She hopes for nothing, she is in years, suppose; she will not live to receive any benefit by it. It is love and love only. Love first.

And then hope. What moves the merchant, and so the husbandman, and so the military man, and so all the rest? All the sharp showers and storms they endure, they love them not. It is hope, and hope only, of a rich return.

If either of these will serve us, will prevail to move us, here it is. Here is love, love in the cross; *Who loved us, and gave Himself for us, a sacrifice* on the cross. Here is hope, hope in the throne. *To him who overcomes will I give to sit with Me in My throne*. If our eye be a mother's eye, here is love worth the looking on. If our eye be a merchant's eye, here is hope worth the looking after."⁴

***

Our Saviour's love was manifested in *the cross He endured* and *the shame He despised*. Andrewes pleads for us to return such love.

"Two things are to us most precious, our life and our reputation. . . . Life is sweet, the cross cost Him His life. Honour is dear, shame bereft Him His honour. In the race which, before us and for us, our blessed Saviour ran, these two great blocks, death and disgrace were in His way. Neither stayed Him. To testify His love, over both He passed. Put His shoulders under the cross and endured it, to the loss of His life. Set His foot upon shame and despised it, to the loss of His honour. Neither one nor other, life or honour, held He dear, to do us good. O, if we should hazard but one of these, for any creature living, how much ado would we make of it, and reckon the party eternally obliged to us! Or if any should venture them for us, we should be the better every time we saw him. O that it might be so here! O that we would meet this love with the like measure! Certainly in His Passion, the love of us triumphed over the love of His life and honour both."⁵

***

It was sin which brought Him to such degradation, despising and desolation. The chief of our sin, disobedience, is rooted in the sinning of Adam and Eve through their desire for pleasure and pride. However these are vanquished on the cross by the opposing virtues emanating from our Saviour.

234

"Now [what] moved them to disobey, was partly pleasure, and partly pride. Pleasure — O the fruit was delightful to see and to taste. Pride — it promised an estate equal to the highest. Behold then in His Passion, for our pleasure His pain, and for our pride, His shame and reproach. Behold Him in His patience, enduring pain for our wicked lust; in His humility, having shame poured on Him for our wretched pride. *The Lord of life,* suffering death; *the Lord of glory,* vile and ignominious disgrace. . . . So, by His enduring pains and painful death, expiating our unlawful pleasure; and by His sustaining shame, satisfying for our shameful pride."6

***

The cross and shame can never be separated as they are *folded and twisted together.* Christ endured shame through patience and embraced it by humility.

"The cross, the heathen termed *cruciabile lignum, a tree of torture*; but they called it also, *arborem infoelicem, et stipitem infamem, a wretched infamous tree.* So it was in His crown; the thorns pricked Him, there was pain; the crown itself was a mere mockery, and matter of scorn. So in His robe; His purple body underneath in great pain certainly, His purple robe over it, a garment of shame and disgrace. All along the Passion, thus they meet still together. In a word, the prints of His Passion, [St. Paul] well calls *stigmata Christi.* Both are in that word; not only wounds, and so grievous, but base and servile marks, and so shameful, for so are *stigmata.* Thus shame and cross, and cross and shame run interchangeably. . . .

Enduring is the act of patience, and patience has pain for her object. Despising shame is the property of humility, even of the highest humility."7

***

Our blessed Saviour's endurance of the cross began at His birth and continued all through His life, culminating with His crucifixion.

"It is well known that Christ and His cross were never parted, but that all His life long was a continual cross. At the very cratch, His cross began. Then Herod sought to do [what] Pilate did, even to end His life before it began. All His life after . . . was nothing but a perpetual *gainsaying of sinners* which we call crossing; and profess we cannot abide in any of our speeches or purposes to be crossed. He was in the psalm of the Passion ... *a morning hart,* that is, a hart roused early in the morning; as from His birth He was by Herod, and hunted and chased all His life long, and this day brought to an end, and as the poor deer, stricken and wounded to the heart. This was His last, last and worst; and this we properly call His cross, even this day's suffering. To keep up then to our day, and the cross of the day. *He endured the cross. . . .*

The cross is but a little word, but of great contents: . . . *heavy to be named, more heavy to be endured.*"8

235

***

His dying on the cross was *bloody and barbarous, torturous* and gory.

"Sanguis Jesu, the blood of Jesus. And Who was He? Sure, by virtue of the union personal, God; and so this blood, blood of God's own bleeding, every drop whereof was precious, more precious than that whereof it was the price, the world itself. . . . Yet was this blood wastefully spilt as water upon the ground. . . .

For the blood of the Cross was not only the blood of Golgotha, but the blood of Gabbatha too. For all deaths, this was peculiar to this death, the death of the Cross; that they who were to be crucified, were not be crucified alone, which is the blood of Golgotha, but they must be whipped too before they were crucified, which is the blood of Gabbatha; a second death, yes worse than death itself. . . . They rent His body with the whips; they gored His head with the thorns; both these in Gabbatha. And again twice in Golgotha, when they nailed His hands and His feet; when He was thrust to the heart with the spear. This is *sanguis crucis* . . .

Now this bloody whipping and nailing of His . . . was not blood alone, as in the opening of a vein, but it was blood and pain both. The tearing and mangling of His flesh with the whips, thorns, and nails, could not choose but be exceeding painful to Him. . . . All rigour, all cruelty was showed to Him, to make His pains the more painful. In Gabbatha they did not whip Him, . . . [but] *they ploughed His back, and made* not stripes, but *long furrows upon it.* They did not put on His wreath of thorns, and press it down with their hands, but beat it on with bats, to make it enter through the skin, flesh, skull, and all. They did not in Golgotha pierce His hands and feet, but made wide holes like that of a spade, as if they had been digging in some ditch. . . .

And the cross is a rack, whereon He was stretched, till, says the psalm, all His bones were out of joint. But even to stand, as He hung, three long hours together, holding up the arms at length, I have heard it avowed of some that have felt it to be a pain scarce credible. But the hands and feet being so cruelly nailed, parts of all other most sensible by reason of the texture of sinews, there in them most, it could not but make His pain out of measure painful. It was not for nothing . . . *that the most sharp and bitter pains of all other have their name from hence, and are called cruciatus, pain like those of the cross,* says the heathen man. It had a meaning that they gave Him, that He had for His welcome to the cross, a cup mixed with gall or myrrh, and for His farewell, a sponge of vinegar; to show by the one the bitterness, by the other the sharpness of the pains of this painful death.

Now, in pain we know the only comfort of *gravis* is *brevis;* if we in it, to be quickly out of it. This the cross has not, but is *mors prolixa, a death of dimensions, a death long in dying.* And it was therefore purposely chosen by them. Blasphemy they condemned Him of; then was He to be stoned; that death would have despatched Him too soon. They indicted Him anew of sedition, not as of a worse fault, but only because crucifying belonged to it; for then He must be whipped first, and that liked them well, and then He must die by inch-meal, not swallow His death at once but *taste* it, . . . and take it down by little and little. And then He must have His legs and arms broken, and so was their meaning His should have been.

Else, I would gladly know to what purpose provided they to have a vessel of vinegar ready in the place, but only that He might not faint with loss of blood, but be kept alive till they might hear His bones crash under the breaking, and so feed their eyes with that spectacle also. The providence of God indeed prevented this last act of cruelty; their will was good though. All these pains are in the cross, but to this last specially . . . that He might feel Himself die, and endure the pains of an enduring death.''9

***

His endurance of pain was not only physical, this was but one half; the other, His spiritual agony, was of far greater intensity.

''Was His soul free the while? No; but suffered as much. As much? no more, infinitely much more on the spiritual, than His body did on the material cross. For a spiritual cross there was too; all grant a cross beside [what] Simon of Cyrene did help Him to bear. Great were those pains, and this time too little to show how great; but so great that in all former He never shrank, nor once complained, but was as if He scarce felt them. But when these came, they made Him complain and cry aloud, *a strong crying*. In all those no blood came, but where passages were made for it to come out by, but in this it strained out all over, even at all places at once. This was the pain of *the press*, so the prophet [Isaiah] calls it, *torcular*, wherewith as if He had been in the wine-press, all His garments were stained and gored with blood. Certainly the blood of Gethesemane was another manner of blood than that of Gabbatha, or that of Golgotha either; and that was the blood of His internal Cross. Of the three Passions that was the hardest to endure, yet that did He endure too.''10

***

Besides the physical and spiritual pain He endured, there was also the shame of the cross to bear; the indignities He suffered from all the insults and jeerings. And if this were not enough, there was also the curse of God to shoulder.

''But now there is a further matter yet to be added, and that is shame. It is hard to say of these two, which is the harder to bear; which is the greater cross, the cross or shame. Or rather it is not hard. There is no mean part in misery, but if He be insulted on, His being insulted on more grieves Him than does the misery itself. But to the noble generous nature, to whom *the value of his honour is above all value*; to Him the cross is not the cross, shame is the cross. And any high and heroical spirit bears any grief more easily, than the grief of contemptuous and contumelious usage. . . . Now in His death, it is not easy to define, whether pain or shame had the upper hand; whether greater, *cruciatus* or *scandalum crucis*.

Was it not a foul disgrace and scandal to offer Him the shame of that servile base punishment of the whip, not to be offered to any but slaves and bondmen? . . .

Then was it not yet a more foul disgrace and scandal indeed to appoint Him for His death that dishonest, that foul death, the death of malefactors, and of the worst sort of them? . . . To take Him as a thief, to hang Him between two thieves; no, to count Him worse than the worst thief in the gaol; to say and to cry, *Save Barabbas and hang Christ!* Yet this shame He despised too, of being *in forma malefici.*

If base, if dishonest, let these two serve; use Him not disgracefully, make Him not a *ridiculum Caput*, pour not contempt upon Him. That did they too, and a shame it is to see the shameful carriage of themselves all along the whole tragedy of His Passion. Was it a tragedy, or a Passion [i.e. sport]? A Passion it was, yet by their behaviour it might seem a May-game. Their shouting and outcries, their harrying of Him about from Annas to Caiaphas, from him to Pilate, from Pilate to Herod, and from him to Pilate again; one while in purple, Pilate's suit; another while in white, Herod's livery; nipping Him by the cheeks, and pulling off His hair; blindfolding Him and buffeting Him; bowing to Him in derision, and then spitting in His face; was as if they had not the Lord of glory, but some idiot or [blockhead] in hand. . . .

Is there any worse yet? There is. For though contempt be had, yet [malice] is beyond it, as far as earnest is beyond sport. . . . [Malice] I call it, when in the midst of His misery, in the very depth of all His distress, they [gave] Him not the least compassion; but as if He had been the most odious wretched [despicable person] and abject of men, the very outcast of heaven and earth, stood staring and gaping upon Him, wagging their heads, writhing their mouths, yes, blearing out their tongues; railing on Him and reviling Him, scoffing at Him and scorning Him; yes, in the very time of His prayers deriding Him, even in His most mournful complaint and cry for the very anguish of His Spirit. These vile indignities, these shameful villanies, so void of all humanity, so full of all [malice], I make no question entered into His soul deeper than either nail or spear did into His body. . . . Men hid their faces at this, not to see this sight, the sun was darkened, drew back his light, the earth trembled, . . . the powers of heaven were moved.

Is this all? No, all this but *scandalum,* there is a greater yet remaining than *scandalum,* and that is *maledictum crucis;* that the death He died was not only servile, scandalous, opprobrious, odious, but even execrable and accursed, of men held so. For as if He had been a very reprobate, in His extreme drought they denied Him a drop of water, never denied to any but to the damned in hell, and instead of it offered Him vinegar in a sponge; and that in the very pangs of death, as for one for whom nothing was evil enough.

All this is but man, and man is but man, his glory is shame oftentimes, and his shame glory; but what God curses, that is cursed indeed. And this death was cursed by God Himself, His own mouth, as [St. Paul] deduces. When all is said we can say, . . . this is the hardest point of His shame, and the highest point of His love in bearing it. . . . The shame of a cursed death, cursed by God, is a shame beyond all shames, and he who can despise it, may well say *consummatum est,* there is no greater left for him to despise. O what contempt was poured upon Him! O how was He in all these despised! Yet He despised them all, and despised to be despised in them all.''[11]

***

There was one even greater suffering than all of the above; this was *quo animo*, Christ's suffering of the soul. Yet He counted all this joy to be our Saviour. With joy He had left His heavenly abode, and was content to submit to all torture and tribulation.

"These, all these, and yet there remains a greater than all these, even *quo animo, with what mind*, what having in His mind, or setting before His eyes, He did and suffered all this. . . .

To endure all this is very much, howsoever it were. So to endure it as to make no reckoning of it, to despise it is more strange than all the rest. Sure the shame was great; how could He make so small account of it? and the cross heavy; how could He set it so light? They could not choose but pinch Him, and that extremely; and how then could He endure, and so endure that He despised them? It is the third point, . . . the marrow of the Sacrifice; even the good heart, the free forward mind, the cheerful affection, wherewith He did all this. . . .

Says St. Chrysostom, *for He was in the joys of Heaven; there He was, and there He might have held Him,* Nothing did or could force Him to come thence, and to come hither thus to be entreated. . . . Yet He was content, *being in the form of God, instead of it*; thus to transform, yes, to deform Himself into the shape of a servant, a felon. . . . Content to lay down His crown of glory, and instead of it to wear a crown of thorns. Content, what we shun by all means, that to endure loss of life; and what we make so great a matter of, that to despise, loss of honour. All this, with the loss of that joy and that honour He enjoyed in heaven. . . .

But the other sense is more praised, in comparison. For indeed, the joy He left in heaven was rather joy wherein He did already sit, than *joy set before Him.* . . . For that is, in comparison of a certain joy, which He comparing with the cross and shame and all, chose rather to go through them all than to go without it. And can there be any joy compared with those He did forego? Or can any joy countervail those barbarous usages He willingly went through? It seems, there can. What joy might that be? Sure none other, but the joy He had to save us, the joy of our salvation. For what was His glory, or joy, or crown or rejoicing, was it not we? Yes truly, we were His crown and His joy. In comparison of this joy He exchanged those joys, and endured these pains; this was the honey that sweetened His gall. And no joy at all in it but this, to be Jesus, *the Saviour* of a sort of poor sinner. None but this, and therefore pity He should lose it. . . .

A Saviour in propriety of speech be rather a title, an outward honour, rather than an inward joy; and so should have been *prae honore*, rather than *prae gaudio*; yet He expresses it in the term of joy rather than that of honour, to show it joyed Him at the heart to save us; and so as a special joy, He accounted it.

Sure, some such thing there was that made Him so cheerfully say to His Father in the psalm, *Ecce venio, Lo I come.* And to His disciples in heart, This, this is the Passover that *desiderio desideravi*, as it were embracing and even welcoming His death. . . . which joy if ever He showed, in this He did, that He went to His Passion with psalms, and with such triumph and solemnity, as He never admitted all His life before. And that this His lowest estate, one would think it, He calls His exaltation, *cum exaltatus fuero*. And when any would think He was most imperfect, He esteems and so terms it, His highest perfection. . . . *In hoc est charitas, here is love*. If not here, where? But here it is, and that in his highest elevation. That the joys of heaven set on the one side, and this poor joy of saving us on the other, He quit them to choose this. That those pains and shames set before Him, and with them this joy, He chose them rather than forego this.

Those joys He forsook, and this He took up; and to take it, took upon Him so many, so strange indignities of both sorts; took them and bare them with such a mind, as He not only endured but despised; nor that neither, but even joyed in the bearing of them, and all to do us good. So to alter the nature of things as to find joy in death whereat all do mourn, and joy in shame which all do abhor, is a wonder like that of the bush.

This is the very life and soul of the Passion, and all besides *the anatomy*, the carcass without it. So have we now the whole object, both what, and with what mind.''12

***

All that is left now, is for us on this Good Friday to respond dutifully to all His sufferings. Although we may not see Him physically, yet through our faith we may truly behold Him.

''We are enjoined to look upon Him. How can we, seeing He is now higher than the heavens, far out of our sight, or from the [teaching] of any mortal eye? Yes, we may for all that. . . . Moses is said to have seen *Him Who is invisible*; not with the eyes of flesh, so neither he did, or we can; but, as there it is, *by faith*. So He did, and we may. And what is more kindly to behold *the Author* of faith, than faith? or more kindly for faith to behold, than her *Author* here at first, and her *Finisher* there at last? Him to behold first and last, and never to be satisfied with looking on Him, Who was content to buy us and our eye at so dear a rate.

Our eye then is the eye of our mind, which is faith; . . . and our looking to Him here, is our thinking on Him there; on Him and His Passion over and over again, *till He be as fast fixed in our hearts as ever He was to His cross*, and some impression made in us of Him, as there was in Him for us.''13

***

In our *looking* upon Jesus, all kinds of distractions enter our minds, so that we do not behold Him for long. More pleasant wordly sights attract us and lure us away from the Cross. So often our *looking* involves sin — sin the reason for the Cross. Therefore there is even more reason why we should stand at the foot of the Cross and gaze upon that broken Body.

''In this our looking then, two acts be rising from the two prepositions; the one before, *looking from*; the other after, *looking upon or into*.

There is *from* abstracting our eye from other objects to look hither sometime. The preposition is not idle, nor the note, but very needful. For naturally we put this spectacle far from us, and endure not either often or long to behold it. Other things there be, please our eyes better, and which we look on with greater delight. And we must *look off of them*, or we shall never *look upon* this aright. We must . . . work force to our nature, and . . . inhibit our eyes, and even wean them from other more pleasing spectacles that better like them, or we shall do no good here, never make a true *theory* of it. I mean, though our prospect into the world be good, and we have both occasion and inclination to look thither often, yet ever and anon to have an eye this way; to look from them to Him, Who, when all these will come to an end, must be He who will finish and consummate our faith and us, and make perfect both. . . . But chiefly, from the baits of sin, the concupiscence of our eyes, the shadows and shows of vanity round about, by which death enters at our windows; which unless we can be got back from, this sight will do us no good, we cannot look on both together. . . .

Therefore look from it, that look to Him; or as the word gives it rather *into Him*, than to Him. . . . Which proves plainly, that the Passion is a piece of perspective, and that we must set ourselves to see it if we will see it well, and not look superficially on it; not on the outside alone but *pierce into it*, and enter even into the inward workmanship of it, even of His internal Cross which He suffered, and of His entire affection wherewith He suffered it.

And we may well look into Him; *His body is full of stripes*, and they as lattices; His wounds they are as windows, through which we may well see all that is within Him, says St. Bernard, *The nails and spear-head serve as keys to let us in.* We may look into the palms of His hands, wherein says [Isaiah], He has graven us, that He might never forget us. We may look into His side, St. John uses the word *opened.* . . . We may through the opening look into his very [heart], the [heart] of kindness and compassion that would endure to be so entreated. Yes, that very heart of His, wherein we may behold the love of our salvation to be the very heart's joy of our Saviour.''[14]

***

When we give time to look *from,* and *into* we shall see so many virtues emanating from His bloody and bruised body: faith, patience, humility, perseverance and love.

''All virtues are there visible, all, if time would serve: now I name only those five, which are directly in the text.

1. Faith is named there; it is, it was most conspicious there to be seen, when being forsaken of God, yet He clasps as it were His arms fast about Him, with *Eli, Eli, My God, My God,* for all that.

2. Patience in *enduring the cross.*

3. Humility in *despising the shame.*

4. Perseverance, in that it was nothing for Him to be *Author,* unless He were *Finisher* too. . . .

5. *Ratio idealis* of all, the band and perfection of all, love, in the signature of love, in the joy which He found in all this. . . . For sure, if ever aught were truly said of our Saviour, this was: that being spread and laid wide open on the cross, He

241

is *Liber charitatis*, wherein he who runs by may read, *Sic dilexit*, and *Propter nimiam charitatem*, and *Ecce quantam charitatem*; love all over, from one end to the other. Every stripe as a letter, every nail as a capital letter. His *livores* as black letters, His bleeding wounds as so many rubrics, to show upon record His love towards us.''15

***

Another reason for learning to look *into* Him is that we shall also see what sin is and what it does. Therefore we shall not be so eager to pursue it any more. Perhaps it may even move us to weep for our sins which drove those nails into His hands and feet.

''Sure this spectacle, if it be well looked into, will make sin . . . not look so well-favoured in our eyes as it did; it will make us while we live have a less liking to look towards it, as being the only procurer and cause of this cross and this shame. No, not only *to turn our eye from it*, but *to turn our feet from it* too; and to run from, yes, to fly from it, *as from the face of a serpent*.

At leastwise, if not to run from it, not to run to it as we have; to nail down our feet from running to sin, and our hands from committing sin, and in a word have St. Peter's practice of the Passion, *to cease from sin*. This abstractive force we shall find and feel; it will draw us from the delights of sin. And not only draw us from that, but draw from us too something, make some tears to run from us, or, we be dry-eyed that not them, yet make some sighs of devotion, some thoughts of grace, some kind of thankful acknowledgements to issue from our souls. Either by way of compassion as feeling that He then felt, or by way of compunction as finding ourselves in the number of the parties for whom He felt them. It is a proper effect of our view of the Passion, this, as St. Luke sets it down at the very place . . . that they returned from it *smiting their breasts* as having seen a doleful spectacle, themselves the cause of it.''16

***

If we deliberate long enough at the foot of the Cross we shall find our hearts moving towards Him, and responding to Love looking down on us; we in turn will be able to manifest in our own lives those virtues which radiate from our dear Saviour during His passion: faith, patience, humility, perseverance and love.

''For first, who is there who can look unto those hands and feet, that head and that heart of His that endured all this, but must *at first sight* see and say, *Ecce quomodo dilexi nos?* If the Jews who stood by said truly of Him, at Lazarus' grave, *Ecce quomodo dilexit eum!* When He shed but a few tears . . . how much more truly may it be said of us, *Ecce quomodo dilexit eos!* for whom He has *shed both water and blood*, yes even from His heart, and that in such plenty? And He loving us so, if our hearts be not iron, yes, if they be iron, they cannot choose but feel the magnetical force of this loadstone. For to a loadstone does He resemble Himself,

242

when He says of Himself, *Were I once lift up, omnia traham ad Me.* This virtue attractive is on this sight to draw our love to it.

With which, as it were the needle, our faith being but touched, will stir straight. We cannot but turn to Him and trust in Him, that so many ways has showed Himself so true to us. Says St. Ambrose, *Prove to us of any that he loves us indeed, and we shall trust him straight without any more ado,* we shall believe any good affirmed of him. And what is there, tell me, anywhere affirmed of Christ to usward, but this love of His, being believed will make it credible.

Now our faith is made perfect by *works* or *well-doing,* says St. James; it will therefore set us in a course of them, of which, every virtue is a *stadium,* and every act a step toward the end of our race. Beginning at humility, the virtue of the first setting out; *let the same mind be in you, that was in Christ Jesus, Who humbled Himself,* and so proceeding from virtue to virtue, till we come to patience and perseverance, that keep the goal end. . . .

And as the rest move us if we stand still to run, so if we run already, these two, patience and perseverance; patience will make us . . . *not to be weary,* not in our minds, though in our bodies we be; and perseverance will make us *not to faint or tire,* though the time seem long and never so tedious. . . . But hold on our course till we finish it, even till we come to Him, Who was not only *Author,* but *Finisher;* Who held out till He came to *consummatum est.* And so must we finish, . . . not like those, of whom it was said, *you did well for a start,* but like our [Writer to the Hebrews] who said, and said truly, of himself, *I have finished my course, I have held out the very end."* [17]

***

We shall love more easily if we can exercise that other virtue — hope. That will enable us to look forward to seeing Him as the *Finisher* on His throne in heaven where He bids us to join Him.

"But our love without hope is but faint; that then with better heart we may thus do and bestir ourselves, it will not be amiss once more to lift up our eyes, and the second time to look on Him.

We have not yet seen the end, the cross is not the end; there is a better end than so, *and is set down in the throne.* . . . Here is a new sight; . . . *Ecce homo!* Pilate's sight we have seen. *Ecce Dominus et Deus meus!* St. Thomas' sight we now shall [have]. The former in His hanging on the cross, the beginning of our faith. This latter sitting on the throne, the consummation of it. . . . He sits now at ease Who before hanged in pain. . . . All changed; His cross into ease, His shame into glory." [18]

***

Two feelings we shall not experience this side of the grave are *glory and rest.* We shall only know these in heaven, provided while here on earth we have not lived a life of ease, and have been prepared to suffer and be despised for

Christ. However if we run the race to its end we shall obtain our prize — Christ on His throne in heaven.

"Glory and rest, rest and glory, are two things that meet not in this world. . . . He who will have glory must make account to be despised often and broken of his rest; and he loves his ease better, must be content with a mean condition far short of glory. Here then these meet not; there our hope is they will, even both meet together, and glory and rest kiss each the other.

And the right hand adds yet a degree further, . . . so that if there be any rest more easy, or any glory more glorious than other, there it is on that hand, on that side; and He placed in it in the best, in the chiefest, the fullness of them both. At God's right hand is not only power, power while we be here to protect us with His might outward, and to support us with His grace inward; but at *His right hand also is the fullness of joy for ever*, and the fullness of it for evermore. . . .

The love of His cross is to us a pledge of the hope of His throne, or whatsoever else He has or is worth. For if God has given us Christ, and Christ thus given Himself, what has God or Christ They will deny us?

To put it out of all doubt, hear we His own promise Who never breaks His word. *To him who overcomes will I give to sit with Me in My throne*. Where to sit is the fullness of our desire, the end of our race, *omnia in omnibus*; and further we cannot go."[19]

***

Andrewes concludes with his prayer that the crucifixion scene will inspire us to love our blest Redeemer, and that in turn will encourage us to hope to witness the final triumphant scene in heaven.

"Let us now turn to Him and beseech Him, by the sight of this day, by Himself first, and by His cross and throne both — both which He had set before us, the one to awaken our love, the other to quicken our hope — that we may this day and ever lift up our eyes and heads, that we may this day and ever carry them in our eyes and hearts, look up to them both; so look that we may love the one, and wait and hope for the other; so love and so hope that by them both we may move and that swiftly, even run to Him; and running not faint, but so constantly run, that we fail not finally to attain the happy fruition of Himself, and of the joy and glory of His blessed throne; that so we may find and feel Him as this day here, the *Author*; so in that day there, the *Finisher of our faith*, by the same our Lord Jesus Christ! Amen."[20]

References

[1] Andrewes, Vol. 2, pp. 158–159.
[2] *ibid.*, pp. 159–160, 162.
[3] *ibid.*, p. 163.
[4] *ibid.*, p. 164.
[5] *ibid.*, p. 165.
[6] *ibid.*, pp. 165–6.
[7] *ibid.*, p. 166.
[8] *ibid.*, pp. 166–7.
[9] *ibid.*, pp. 169–171.
[10] *ibid.*, p. 171.
[11] *ibid.*, pp. 172–4.
[12] *ibid.*, pp. 174–7.
[13] *ibid.*, p. 177.
[14] *ibid.*, pp. 177–9.
[15] *ibid.*, pp. 179–180.
[16] *ibid.*, p. 181.
[17] *ibid.*, pp. 181–3.
[18] *ibid.*, p. 183.
[19] *ibid.*, pp. 183–4.
[20] *ibid.*, p. 184.

BIBLIOGRAPHY

Andrewes, L. *The Works of Lancelot Andrewes*, eds. J. Bliss & J. P. Wilson, 11 vols. (The Library of Anglo–Catholic Theology, J. H. Parker, Oxford, 1841–54).

Andrewes, L. *The Moral Law Expounded* (London, 1642).

Andrewes, L. *The Private Devotions of Lancelot Andrewes, (Preces Privatae)*, translated with an introduction and notes by F. E. Brightman, and including "Lancelot Andrewes" (1926) by T. S. Eliot, (Gloucester, Mass., 1978).

Drake, R. Ed. *A Manual of the Private Devotions and Meditations of . . . Lancelot Andrewes* (London, 1648).

Eliot, T. S. *For Lancelot Andrewes: Essays on Style and Order* (London, 1928).

Hacket, J. *Scrinia Reserata*, (London, 1693).

Lossky, N. *Lancelot Andrewes the Preacher (1555–1626)*, trans. by A. Louth (Oxford, 1991).

Wellesby, P. A. *Lancelot Andrewes* (London, 1958).

Wren, C. *Parentalia* (London, 1750).